T0330342

The Handbook of Hybrid Securities

For other titles in the Wiley Finance series
please see www.wiley.com/finance

The Handbook of Hybrid Securities

Convertible Bonds, CoCo Bonds, and Bail-In

Jan De Spiegeleer
Wim Schoutens
Cynthia Van Hulle

This edition first published 2014
© 2014 Jan De Spiegeleer, Wim Schoutens and Cynthia Van Hulle

Registered office
John Wiley & Sons Ltd, The Atrium, Southern Gate, Chichester, West Sussex, PO19 8SQ, United Kingdom

For details of our global editorial offices, for customer services and for information about how to apply for permission to reuse the copyright material in this book please see our website at www.wiley.com.

Wiley publishes in a variety of print and electronic formats and by print-on-demand. Some material included with standard print versions of this book may not be included in e-books or in print-on-demand. If this book refers to media such as a CD or DVD that is not included in the version you purchased, you may download this material at http://booksupport.wiley.com. For more information about Wiley products, visit www.wiley.com.

Designations used by companies to distinguish their products are often claimed as trademarks. All brand names and product names used in this book are trade names, service marks, trademarks or registered trademarks of their respective owners. The publisher is not associated with any product or vendor mentioned in this book.

Limit of Liability/Disclaimer of Warranty: While the publisher and author have used their best efforts in preparing this book, they make no representations or warranties with the respect to the accuracy or completeness of the contents of this book and specifically disclaim any implied warranties of merchantability or fitness for a particular purpose. It is sold on the understanding that the publisher is not engaged in rendering professional services and neither the publisher nor the author shall be liable for damages arising herefrom. If professional advice or other expert assistance is required, the services of a competent professional should be sought.

Library of Congress Cataloging-in-Publication Data

Spiegeleer, Jan de.
  The handbook of hybrid securities : convertible bonds, coco bonds, and bail-in / Jan De Spiegeleer,
Wim Schoutens, Cynthia Van Hulle.
      pages cm—(The Wiley finance series)
  Includes bibliographical references and index.
  ISBN 978-1-118-44999-8 (hardback)
  1. Convertible securities—Handbooks, manuals, etc.   2. Convertible bonds—Handbooks, manuals, etc.
I. Schoutens, Wim.   II. Van Hulle, Cynthia,   III. Title.
  HG4652.S67 2014
  332.63′2044—dc23
                                                                    2013046701

A catalogue record for this book is available from the British Library.

ISBN 978-1-118-44999-8 (hardback)   ISBN 978-1-118-45000-0 (ebk)
ISBN 978-1-118-45002-4 (ebk)   ISBN 978-1-118-86265-0 (obk)

Cover image: Shutterstock.com

Set in 10/12pt Times by Aptara, Inc., New Delhi, India
Printed in Great Britain by CPI Group (UK) Ltd, Croydon, CR0 4YY

To Klaartje, Charlotte, Pieter-Jan and Willem
Jan

To Ethel, Jente and Maitzanne
Wim

To my mother
Cynthia

Contents

Reading this Book

The target audience for this work on hybrid securities is very broad. The absolute beginner will find in it a sufficient course to become familiar with this asset class. More advanced users working in areas such as trading, portfolio, or risk management will be introduced in detail to the latest advances in numerical techniques to value and hedge these instruments. Hybrid financial instruments combine properties of both shares and corporate bonds into one, but mastering their price dynamics is far from a walk in the park. Blending the properties of two easy-to-understand asset classes such as equity and bonds into a hybrid does not leave us with an instrument having straightforward properties. Hybrids are therefore often misunderstood and mis-sold: what for some looks like an equity instrument with bond-like risk could turn out to deliver a bond-like return with equity volatility. The reality is hence very different from the perceived risk and results in an asset that can have multiple sources of risk: market risk, default risk, different levels of equity and interest rate convexity, etc. In the case of contingent convertibles, the newest category in hybrid debt, there are phenomena such as the "death spiral" that deserve our attention. These are situations where a forced conversion of a bond into shares would trigger a wave of sell orders on the underlying share. This book devotes different chapters to CoCo bonds, including the newly developed pricing models, taking into account different features of these special instruments.

Preferreds or preference shares are on first sight the easiest member of the hybrid family to be understood and fully mastered. The reality is far different, and many investors dealing with this instrument that looks like a bond were confronted with equity-like volatility. This became very clear in the spring of 2008, when US banks chose to strengthen their balance sheet massively through the issuance of preferreds. Traders, portfolio managers, and even retail investors loaded up on these instruments and had to deal with a complete implosion of their portfolio in the heat of the credit crunch. This destructive process was speeded up by the default of Lehman Brothers.

Mastering hybrids is not constrained to financial calculus only. Proposals and regulations such as, for example, Basel III and the Dodd–Frank Act dramatically changed the financial landscape from 2010 onwards. Some hybrid securities are not going to be allowed anymore as regulatory capital. National regulators are now putting the emphasis on instruments that in principle have the capacity to be really loss absorbing through their design. This is where contingent convertibles started to play an important role in 2010. Regulation has clearly been driving innovation and regulators became financial engineers! This is not a book on financial regulation, but it nevertheless covers the big overhauls that reshaped the financial landscape.

A handbook can never be of any value to a practitioner if there is no mention at all of what the regulatory implications of each of the different instruments are.

The quantitative part of this book is very pragmatic. The first steps into the landscape of hybrid instruments will take place in a perfect Black–Scholes world. Later on, when using, for example, constant elasticity of variance, the stochastic processes simulating the share price movements become more look-alikes of the real world. Subsequently, we link the default probability of an issuer of hybrid debt to its share price level. In a final step, hybrids are priced as derivative instruments with multiple sources of risk: equity, interest rate, and credit. This multi-factor approach deals with the exact nature of hybrid instruments, where several state variables are at work. The valuation model turns into a blend of debt and equity. The more advanced quantitative audience, consisting of arbitrageurs, portfolio managers, or quantitative analysts, will be introduced to methods such as the American Monte Carlo simulation. All of these techniques are mainstream methods in exotic equity derivative pricing but have not made their landing on the hybrid desks yet. As many numerical examples as possible have been added to enrich this book.

www.allonhybrids.com

On our webpage, www.allonhybrids.com, the interested reader can find more examples and reading material as a supplement to this book. The characteristics of most contingent convertible bonds are provided as well. For each of the CoCo bonds the pricing model is embedded in a spreadsheet that is available for download.

Acknowledgments

This book is the work of its authors but without the support of our colleagues, people we met on seminars, and the referees of the papers we published, all of this would not have been possible. We would like to thank explicitly Professor Luc Keuleneer (KPMG), Professor Stefan Poedts (KU Leuven), Professor Theo Vermaelen (INSEAD), Professor Jan Dhaene (KU Leuven), Professor Dilip Madan (University of Maryland), and Professor Jose Manuel Corcuera (Universitat de Barcelona) for their support. Our gratitude goes to Philippe Jabre, Julien-Dumas Pilhou, Romain Cosandey, James Cleary, Jan-Hinnerk Richter, Henry Hale, Philipe Riachi, and Mark Cecil from Jabre Capital Partners (Geneva) for their guidance and advice. Many thanks to Francesca Campolongo, Jessica Cariboni, Francesca Di Girolamo, and Henrik Jonsson from the Joint Research Centre (European Commission), Wim Allegaert (KBC) and Stan Maes (DG Internal Market and Financial Services at the European Commission). We thank David Cox and the staff at London Financial Studies. From Assenagon Asset Management we remember our productive cooperation with Vassilios Pappas, Michael Hunseler, Robert Edwin Van Kleeck, and Stephan Hoecht. Our gratitude and respect also go to Marc Colman, Carole Bernard, and Andrea Mosconi from Bloomberg for the enthusiasm and professionalism with which they embrace the asset class of convertible bonds.

1

Hybrid Assets

1.1 INTRODUCTION

This chapter provides a general introduction to the different categories of hybrid debt and delivers the basic knowledge needed to move deeper into hybrid territory. Hybrid instruments are often misunderstood and hence mismanaged. They are not equity instruments with bond-like risk. Neither are they instruments with bond returns flavored with equity risk. Further, it is also difficult to come up with a standardization when it comes to categorizing hybrid debt. In this introductory chapter we cover the obvious and well-known instruments, such as preferreds and convertible bonds. These are the cornerstones of corporate hybrid debt. The chapter also contains a primer on bail-in capital, contingent convertibles, and financial hybrid debt such as Tier 1 and Tier 2 bonds.

1.2 HYBRID CAPITAL

Hybrid securities are located at the crossroads between debt and equity. This asset class combines properties of common equity and corporate debt. The most outspoken subcategories of hybrid securities are convertible bonds and preference shares (preferreds). Further, in the capital structure of banks and corporates, one can also find quite often hybrid instruments belonging to the category of subordinated debt. These are hybrid bonds and have an equity-like character because of their long (sometimes perpetual) maturity, deep subordination, loss absorption, and the possibility of a coupon deferral. These securities illustrate that the split between debt and equity is a continuum and far from crystal clear. Moody's, Standard & Poor's (S&P), and Fitch have each developed their own proprietary methodologies to determine the equity character to be attributed to a hybrid bond. Needless to say, the outcomes sometimes differ very much between these three rating agencies for one and the same bond.

Hybrids have never received the same amount of attention from investors, the financial press, or researchers as the two main stream asset classes – bonds and equity. Investment banks have typically structured their trading operations in fixed-income and equity departments. The first desk covers corporate debt and senior debt, while the second desk takes care of equity trading. Bond and equity trading also has a much larger scope than hybrids. Equity trading is indeed much broader than just buying or selling shares. The equity derivatives market for listed or exotic options is enormous, and has in turn been given a boost with the rise of the structured product market. The same holds for the fixed-income desks, where trading corporate bonds has received support from the advent of the credit default swap (CDS) market. Credit derivatives offer the owners of corporate debt the possibility to buy protection on these securities. According to ISDA,[1] the gross notional amount of all CDS contracts outstanding was \$25.9 tn on December 31, 2011. The size of this CDS market is a multiple of the GDP of

---

[1] International Swaps and Derivatives Association.

Table 1.1   ALCOA: Structure of the liabilities on the balance sheet (Q4, 2011). The equity component consists of share capital, retained earnings, and minority interests

Liabilities (mn USD)	
Current	6 013
Loans	3 750
Bonds	12 587
Convertible Bonds	575
Preferred	55
Equity	17 140
TOTAL	**40 120**

Source: Bloomberg.

the United States, which was by contrast $15.6 tn. Hybrids do not have a similar firm link with a vast underlying derivatives market. From this perspective, the hybrid market stands more or less on its own feet.

Companies use a wide spectrum of instruments to finance their balance sheet. Here also, equity and standard corporate debt dwarfed the hybrid bonds. Hybrids remain, without doubt, the smallest component on the average corporate balance sheet. ALCOA, an aluminum producer in the United States, has, for example, a $40 bn balance sheet financed through $17 bn of equity, a $3.7 bn loan, and $12.6 bn in bonds. The hybrid component of the liabilities is rather limited and consists of a $55 mn preferred and a $575 mn convertible bond (Table 1.1).

In Figure 1.1, we show an example of a capital structure including a new kid on the block, namely, the contingent convertible or CoCo. This newcomer in the hybrid family is typically issued by a financial institution and contributes to the loss absorbency of the balance sheet. Indeed, in case the regulatory capital of a financial institution fails to meet a predetermined level, these contingent convertibles convert into shares or suffer a write-down. One can consider them as automated measures to swap debt into equity or write down the face value of debt, without causing default.

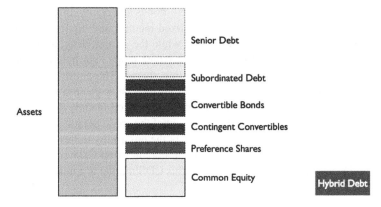

Figure 1.1   Sample balance sheet of a financial institution.

1.3 PREFERREDS

Preferreds are a straightforward mixture between debt and equity. These look at first sight like a combination between equity and bonds. Preferreds offer regular income payments, have no voting rights, and are senior to common stock since they have priority over common equity in dividends payouts. Are preferreds equity investments with bond-like characteristics or should we consider them as bonds with an equity-like behavior? We use the preferred share of ALCOA as a concrete example to develop a possible answer to this question. The ALCOA preferred pays a coupon of 3.75% on a face value of $100. This corresponds to a quarterly payment of $0.9375 every 3 months (January, April, July, and November). A summary of the instrument-specific features of the ALCOA preferred is given in the Table below.

ALCOA 3.75% Preferred			
ISIN	US0138172004	SEDOL	2021786
ISSUE DATE	January 20, 1947	CALL PRICE	100.00
ISSUE SIZE	55 M	FACE VALUE	100
STOCK	ALCOA INC	MATURITY	PERPETUAL
COUPON	3.75%	FREQUENCY	QUARTERLY

The closing price of the ALCOA preferred on April 20, 2012 was $83.56. We apply a yield measure such as a current yield on the ALCOA bond to compare this preferred security against the bonds of the same issuer. The current yield (CY) is given by:

$$\text{Current Yield } (CY) = \frac{\text{Coupon}}{\text{Bond Price}} = \frac{0.0375}{83.56} = 4.49\% \tag{1.1}$$

The current yield indicates the annual income one earns on an investment in this preferred security if everything else remains unchanged. Under this assumption, the price of the preferred itself does not change. Through the current yield one looks at a preferred as a pure income instrument such as a bond. The theoretical price P of an instrument paying a perpetual cash flow C given an interest rate r is given by:

$$P = \lim_{n \to \infty} \frac{C}{(1+r)} + \frac{C}{(1+r)^2} + \frac{C}{(1+r)^3} + \cdots + \frac{C}{(1+r)^n}$$
$$= C \sum_{i=1}^{\infty} \frac{1}{(1+r)^i} = C \sum_{i=1}^{\infty} x^i$$

Using the convergence of series $\sum_{i=0}^{\infty} x^i$ to $\frac{1}{1-x}$ we obtain:

$$P = \frac{C}{r}$$

Given a 30-year US government bond rate of 3.12% on April 20, 2012, the theoretical price of the ALCOA preferred would hence be equal to $120.19 = ($3.75/0.0312)$. This value is considerably higher than the actual closing price of the preferred on that day. The difference is explained by the financial risk of the preferred. The income stream generated by a preferred is indeed not risk free. The dividend or coupon payments can be canceled by the issuer without triggering an immediate default event as would be the case for a bond. For preferreds, a failure to pay the dividend does not invoke a default on the issuing company. As a result, investors demand a higher yield. The ALCOA preferred is yielding 137 bps more than a risk-free security such as a US government bond of a similar maturity. This yield difference is the compensation for the dividend-suspension risk of the ALCOA preferred.

Further, there is a cumulative dividend right attached to the ALCOA preferred. This implies that the unpaid accumulated preferred stock dividends must be paid before any dividends are paid out to the common stock holders. Hence, if there was a suspension in the dividend stream of the preferred security, the share holders would rank after the preferred bond holders. In such a situation, ALCOA would only be allowed to start paying out dividends to the share holders after the holders of this preferred stock had received all the dividends canceled earlier.

It is tempting to categorize an instrument such as a preferred, that distributes on a timely basis a fixed cash flow, as a bond. The fact that this instrument ranks just above common equity on the balance sheet, however, signals a different message. From that perspective one could indeed imagine that preferreds are shares in disguise and carry the same volatility as equity. In Figure 1.2, the historical 30-day volatility of the ALCOA preferred is plotted against the price volatility of the shares and a corporate bond issued by ALCOA. This graph illustrates how early 2011, the preferred demonstrated a volatility close to bond volatility, whereas in the final months of 2011, the opposite is true. The preferred then became as volatile as the listed shares of the same issuer. The graph in Figure 1.2 compares the volatility of preferreds, bonds, and equity using the annualized realized volatility over a 1-month period. This 1-month period is a rolling window for which a realized volatility number is calculated. A similar graph can be constructed for a different rolling window (3-month, 6-month, etc.). Doing this for a lot of different time periods allows us to construct a volatility cone as explained in [46]. To

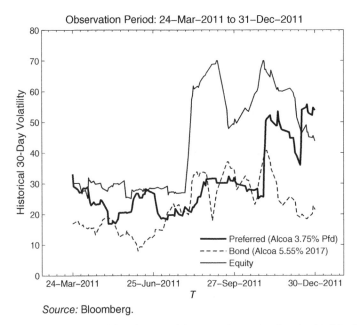

Source: Bloomberg.

Figure 1.2   Historical 30-day volatility of some of the asset classes funding the ALCOA balance sheet: equity, bonds, and preferreds.

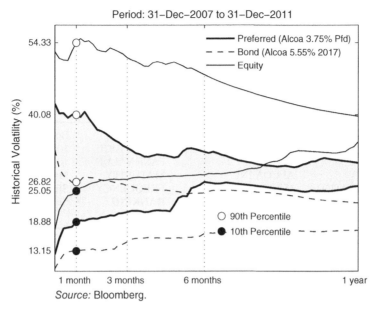

Figure 1.3   Volatility cone of a preferred, the equity, and a corporate bond issued by ALCOA. Period 2003–2013.

achieve this result, both the 90th and the 10th percentiles for each of these rolling windows are connected on a graph. The volatility cone for ALCOA for the period 2003–2013 can be found in Figure 1.3. A volatility cone is an interesting graphical snapshot view of the historical volatility of an asset.

From the sample volatility cone of ALCOA, we learn that the cone and therefore the risk of the preferred share is at an intermediate level between the cone of the shares and the volatility cone of a corporate bond. For the 1-month time horizon, the 90th percentile of the realized volatility is 54.33% for shares, 26.82% for bonds, and 40.08% for preferred shares. This illustrates the higher risk of the preferred compared with a standard corporate bond from the same issuer. With the help of the volatility cone, one can look under the hood of this bond-like instrument and discover a higher level of embedded risk.

1.4 CONVERTIBLE BONDS

Another instrument within the hybrid family is the convertible bond. The total amount of outstanding convertible bonds at the writing of this book equals \$469 bn spread across 1960 different issues.[2] Basically, these instruments can be regarded as corporate bonds where the investor has the right to convert the bond into shares. This conversion right is restricted to the investor only. It is not an obligation and hence remains at the discretion of the investor. Therefore, conversion is labeled as optional. The number of shares received upon conversion is typically outlined in the prospectus and is called the conversion ratio (C_r). After conversion, the investor forgoes the remaining coupons (c) and the final cash redemption of the face value

---

[2] *Source:* UBS.

(N) of the convertible bond. The conversion price (C_P) is the embedded purchase price of the shares obtained through conversion:

$$C_P = \frac{N}{C_r} \tag{1.2}$$

ALCOA 5.25% March 15, 2014			
ISIN	US013817AT86	SEDOL	B65YPD6
ISSUE DATE	March 24, 2009	ISSUE PRICE	100%
ISSUE SIZE	575 mn	FACE VALUE	1000
STOCK	ALCOA INC	MATURITY	March 15, 2014
CONVERSION RATIO	155.4908	FREQUENCY	SEMI-ANNUAL
REDEMPTION	100.00%	RANKING	SENIOR UNSECURED
COUPON	5.25%		

In March 2009 ALCOA issued a $575 mn convertible bond distributing a semi-annual 5.25% coupon. A summary of the structure of this convertible can be found in the Table above. The bond expires on March 15, 2014. The owner of the bond has an opportunity up till this final maturity date to convert the bond into shares. If the investor skips this conversion, the final payout will be $1000 plus the final coupon of $26.25. By contrast, if the investor opts for the conversion, he receives 155.4908 shares of ALCOA with value S_T. A rational investor maximizes his final payout P_T at the expiration date T:

$$P_T = \max(C_r \times S_T, \$1026.25) \tag{1.3}$$

Similar to preferreds, this asset class blends bonds and equity into one structure. The extent to which a convertible bond behaves like a bond depends on the level of the share price. A low share price at time $t < T$ makes conversion unlikely; the investor is better off receiving coupons instead of converting the bond in cheap shares. The convertible bond has in such a case the price dynamics of a corporate bond and is sensitive to changes in interest rate and credit spread levels. The value of the convertible P_t is said "to trade close to the bond floor" (B_F). The bond floor is the corporate bond component of the convertible. It is calculated as the present value of all the cash flows embedded in the convertible bond while neglecting any possible conversion into shares. This is also often called the investment value of the convertible.

High prices of the underlying share lead to high conversion probabilities and the value of the convertible is then close to parity (P_a). Under such circumstances, the value of a convertible is definitively more a share than a bond:

$$P_t \approx P_a = \frac{C_r S_t}{N} \tag{1.4}$$

The parity or conversion value of a convertible represents the value of the amount of underlying shares received upon conversion per bond.

The convertible bond market is far from standardized. Bond structures are quite different across issues. They differ not only in basic features such as coupon structure, conversion ratio, or maturity. There is more, since each convertible bond comes with additional features impacting its price and properties. In Chapter 2, features such as calls, puts, refixes, dividend protection, etc. will be discussed in detail.

1.5 CONTINGENT CONVERTIBLES

Contingent convertibles, contingent capital, CoCos, buffer convertible capital securities, enhanced capital notes, etc. are all different names for the same kind of capital instrument issued by a financial institution. Having different names for one and the same instrument clearly adds to the confusion surrounding this new asset class. The contingent convertible market is in its infancy and lacks standardization. There is no such thing as a typical CoCo structure. In a nutshell, a contingent convertible comes down to a standard corporate bond issued by a bank that can absorb losses without triggering a default for the issuing bank. The loss absorbency is obtained by writing down a predetermined fraction of the face value of the bond or by converting the bond into shares of the underlying bank.

The market for contingent convertibles kicked off in December 2009 when the Lloyds Banking Group launched its $13.7 bn issue of enhanced capital notes. This issue was spread over a number of bonds with maturities ranging from 10 to 22 years. This first CoCo issue was set up as an exchange for existing hybrid securities issued by Lloyds. Next in line was Rabobank, which made its first entry in the market for contingent debt with a €1.25 bn issue early 2010. After this, things turned quiet until February 2011, when Credit Suisse launched its so-called buffer capital notes. This issue ($2 bn) turned out to be quite popular and was more than 12 times oversubscribed. Yield-hungry investors were lining themselves up to include this new asset class in their portfolios. The Credit Suisse issue took place against the background of the new regulatory regime in Switzerland that requires large banks to hold loss-absorbing capital up to 19% of their risk-weighted assets [58]. This capital has to consist of at least 10% in common equity and up to 9% in contingent capital.

The start of this new asset class was met with significant skepticism from market practitioners, regulators, and scholars, involving heated debates. However, the CoCo issuance in the first quarter of 2012 equaled $3.7 bn, which corresponded more or less to 30% of the convertible bond issuance over the same period. The dust is clearly settling and regulatory initiatives throughout the financial world have helped CoCo bonds to earn an accepted position in the capital structure of banks. In Europe, during the period 2009–2013, approximately $40 bn was issued of this new category of debt. In Chapter 3, the concept of contingent convertibles, their valuation, and market risks will be covered in detail.

1.6 OTHER TYPES OF HYBRID DEBT

1.6.1 Hybrid Bank Capital

Innovative Tier 1

The financial industry is quite unique as it has to adhere to restrictions and regulations when it comes to capital structure. Corporates in other sectors of the economy are free to decide to what extent they want to use leverage. When such a company over-extends its debt and runs an unhealthy balance between the amount of equity and debt, it becomes vulnerable to economic shocks. An over-leveraged company may not be able to deal with disappointing earnings following a slow-down in its business. This could possibly lead to a bankruptcy and could create some ripples within the economy if the company is large enough.

A failure of a bank, on the other hand, may easily send a real shock wave through the economic system, thereby bringing other financial institutions to the brink of collapse. The Basel Committee of the Bank of International Settlements (BIS) develops guidelines and supervisory standards in banking supervision. This committee has a clear focus on banking stability. In July 1988, the committee published its first work "international convergence of capital measurement and capital standard" [17], subsequently better known as Basel I or the Basel Capital Accord. Basel I came with two novelties: it defined the two basic building blocks of banking or regulatory capital and it laid out a minimum requirement for these components.

Regulatory capital can be decomposed conceptually into Tier 1 capital and Tier 2 capital.[3] Tier 1 capital should reflect high-quality capital that is able to absorb bank losses in a going-concern context, whereas Tier 2 capital was originally supposed to absorb losses only in a gone-concern context. The concept of regulatory capital has disappointed during the credit crisis of 2008, as its quality, consistency, and transparency showed fundamental flaws [144]. The large bank losses that materialized during the crisis highlighted the important economic differences between the Tier 1 and Tier 2 components of regulatory capital. Because Tier 2 capital (such as subordinated debt) was only loss absorbing after a bank had been declared bankrupt, banks needed to raise new equity to remain solvent notwithstanding their non-negligible stock of Tier 2 capital. Furthermore, banks disposed of surprisingly little capital that was effectively loss absorbing, despite very high reported Tier 1 capital ratios. In the end, so-called Common Equity Tier 1 (CET1) capital, a subcomponent of Tier 1 and solely composed of retained earnings and common equity, turned out to be the only loss-absorbing building block of the capital structure. Equity indeed never has to be paid back and the company has full discretion on how to reward the share holders through the distribution of dividends.

In a speech given at the American Economic Association in 2001, Andrew G. Haldane, Executive Director of the Bank of England, elaborated on the amount of Tier 1 capital and the ability of a bank to withstand a shock on the assets side of its balance sheet. It was shown how, for a group of major financial institutions which in the fall of 2008 either failed or required government support, the Tier 1 ratio[4] was increasing as the credit crunch was about to start. The signaling power of these improving Tier 1 ratios wrong-footed the market as far as these particular banks were concerned [114].

The Tier 1 bucket has never been designed to be filled with hybrid instruments only. However, because interest rate payments are tax deductible while dividend payments are not, financial engineering pushed banks to create innovative Tier 1 instruments. In fact, banks have been relying heavily over the period 1995–2008 on innovative Tier 1. These instruments are quite different from convertible bonds and contingent convertibles. The latter securities have an outspoken hybrid nature because the probability of a conversion into shares is part of the instrument setup. At expiration, the investor in these instruments will either end up with shares or with the face value of the bond. This is not the case for innovative Tier 1 instruments. These typically do not convert into shares but earn their hybrid status from the fact that the nature of these instruments is equity like: permanent character and coupon deferrability being part of these "equity" properties. To illustrate the hybrid nature of the innovative or additional Tier 1 bonds compared with more traditional forms of debt, one can take a look at two particular

---

[3] The Tier 3 category disappears in Basel III.

[4] The Tier 1 ratio relates the total amount of Tier 1 capital a bank has at its disposal to the value of the risk-weighted assets.

Table 1.2   Characteristics of a hybrid and senior bond issued by Société Générale

	Société Générale	
Bond Type	Tier 1	Senior Unsecured
Issue Date	January 26, 2005	April 20, 2011
S&P Rating	BBB	A
Maturity	Perpetual	April 20, 2016
Coupon (%)	4.196	4
Coupon Frequency	Annual	Annual
Possibile Coupon Deferral	Yes	No
Par Amount	1000	100 000
ISIN	FR0010136382	XS0618909807
Call Date	January 26, 2015	
Call Price	100%	
Step-Up Coupon	3M EURIBOR + 153 bps	
Price (%)	67.500	103.675

Source: Bloomberg. Date: April 27, 2012.

examples. In Table 1.2, there is a short description of a hybrid Tier 1 bond and a senior bond, both denominated in euros and issued by Société Générale, a French bank:

- **Senior bond**
  The senior bond received an A rating from Standard & Poor's, has a 4% annual coupon, and has a remaining maturity of almost 4 years. The coupons have to be paid by the issuer to the bond holder. Failure to do so would trigger a default of this bank.
- **Hybrid Tier 1**
  The Tier 1 bond is perpetual but comes with a first call date 10 years after the issue date. If Société Générale skips the call, the coupon structure changes and the bond turns into a floating rate note where the bank is paying 153 bps over Euribor. The hybrid carries a possibility that in case of unsatisfactory capital ratios, the interest on this debt might not be paid. Such an event does not push the issuing bank into default, however.

Studying the price returns of both bonds of Table 1.2 in the second half of 2011 reveals the equity nature of Tier 1 debt. There is no direct relationship between the Tier 1 bond and the underlying shares according to the prospectus. Nevertheless, the perpetual nature of the bond and its deep subordination make it sensitive to share price movements. In Figure 1.4, the daily log returns[5] of Société Générale's share prices are plotted against the daily log returns in the senior and Tier 1 bond. The beta[6] of the Tier 1 returns versus the share price returns is 0.25. Every percentage move on the stock therefore, on average, implies a 25 bps move on the bond. The correlation between the two time series is 42%. By contrast, the senior bond's price changes are clearly not correlated to share price changes. This example illustrates the equity character of innovative Tier 1 structures and hence also their hybrid nature.

Similar to preferreds, the coupon payments on these innovative instruments can sometimes be deferred in times of financial distress. This will act as a loss-absorbing buffer. Similar to our Société Générale example, Tier 1 hybrids often come with a call option and a corresponding

---

[5] A log return or logarithmic return of a variable X between two different dates t_0 and t_1 is given by $\log(X_{t_1}) - \log(X_{t_0})$ with $t_0 < t_1$.
[6] The beta (β) of a bond, stock, or portfolio is a number describing the volatility of this asset in relation to the volatility of a reference asset. Beta measures the sensitivity of the returns of the asset with respect to changes in the price of the reference asset.

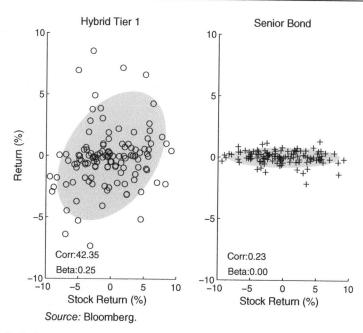

Source: Bloomberg.

Figure 1.4 Daily log returns of the share price of Société Générale versus the return of a Tier 1 hybrid and a senior unsecured bond. Observation period: June 30, 2011 to December 30, 2011.

step-up clause. If the bank does not buy back the bond on the call date, the coupon is increased with a predetermined step up. This step-up penalty would indeed create an incentive for the bank to redeem this hybrid Tier 1 on the call date. This early redemption possibility, however, is against the nature of Tier 1 instruments which should have a perpetual character. On top of this, such bonds failed to absorb losses in the 2008–2009 credit crisis. It is, therefore, no surprise that similar Tier 1 instruments with a step-up coupon have been outlawed in Basel III and lose their top-notch capital status. This has prompted financial institutions in 2012 to start buying back these hybrids and replacing them with new Basel III-compliant regulatory capital. The phasing out of this kind of hybrid debt by Basel III is going to take place gradually up to the full implementation of these new capital adequacy rules on January 1, 2019.

Tier 2

Tier 2 bonds rank above equity and Tier 1 bonds. These bonds are subordinated to senior debt and are loss absorbing on a gone-concern basis. Tier 2 has also been impacted by the August 2010 proposal of the Basel Committee regarding the loss absorbency of regulatory capital [26]. All non-common Tier 1 and Tier 2 instruments at internationally active banks must have a clause in their terms and conditions that requires them to be written off or converted into shares on the occurrence of a non-viability event. This non-viability event is the earlier of (1) the decision to make a public-sector injection of capital, without which the bank would become non-viable and (2) a decision of the national regulator to write off the debt, without which the firm would become non-viable.

A hybrid Tier 1 – such as the one we used as an example in Figure 1.4 – creates for the investor an undesired loss-absorption risk. The interest payments can indeed be canceled by

Table 1.3   Characteristics of a callable Tier 2 bond issued by Deutsche Bank

Deutsche Bank	
Bond Type	Tier 2
Issue Date	January 16, 2004
S&P Rating	BBB+
Maturity	January 16, 2014
Initial Coupon (%)	3.875
Coupon Frequency	Quarterly
Possible Coupon Deferral	No
Par Amount	1000
ISIN	DE0003933511
First Call Date	January 16, 2009
Call Price	100%
Call Notice	30 Days
Step-Up Coupon	3M EURIBOR + 88 bps
Price (%)	97.90

Source: Bloomberg. Date: April 25, 2012.

the issuer. This is a **deferral risk**. There is another type of risk that will be explained in this book: **extension risk**. This is the risk that the company will not call back the bond on the first call date. Because of this, the life of the bond is extended at least till the next call date (if any). This would push the repayment of the redemption amount further into the future. A Tier 2 bond issued by Deutsche Bank will be taken as a case study to illustrate the risks of buying such a callable bond while ignoring its hybrid nature. The characteristics of the bond have been defined in Table 1.3. The total issue size of the bond is €1 bn.

The call notice for the bond was 1 month. This implies that the company had 30 days to let the investors know whether or not it was going to call. Deutsche Bank had as issuer of this bond up till December 16, 2008 to make up its mind, given the fact that the first call date of the bond was January 16, 2009. The market was clearly expecting Deutsche Bank to call the bond and pay back €1 bn. The price of the bond was indeed smoothly converging to the call price and seemed to be immune to the turmoil in the financial markets in the fall of 2008. This is illustrated in Figure 1.5. Deutsche Bank's decision not to call back the bond generated a 10% loss for the investors holding this particular bond in their portfolio at the moment Deutsche Bank decided not to call. Investors had been valuing the bond on the basis that the first call date would indeed be the maturity date of the bond when they would receive the full par amount. Their assumption was based on the belief that Deutsche Bank would be facing a step up in the interest payments if they skipped the call. In case of such a call, the initial coupon of 3.875% would be replaced by a quarterly floating Euribor rate with a spread of 88 bps.

Rationally, Deutsche Bank did the right thing not calling the bond. As a financial institution it was, like other banks, witnessing a flight to quality during the 2008 credit crisis. Investors preferred government bonds above bank debt. The share price of Deutsche Bank suffered and the CDS spreads increased (see Figure 1.6). Therefore, it became more expensive for an investor to buy insurance on the CDS market against a default on bonds issued by Deutsche Bank. On December 17, 2008 the CDS spread was 244.62 bps.[7] If Deutsche Bank had to call

---

[7] A basis point on a credit default swap protecting €10 mn of debt from default for a period of 5 years is equivalent to €1000 per year.

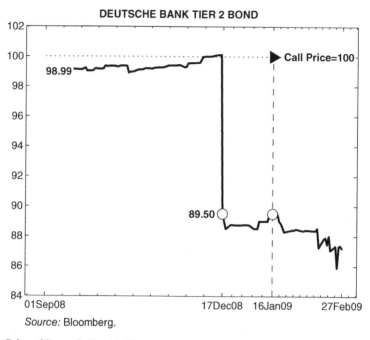

Figure 1.5   Price of Deutsche Bank's Tier 2 bond and the impact of skipping the first call date.

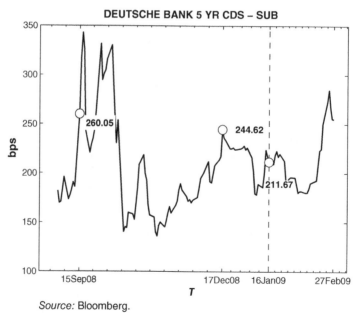

Figure 1.6   5-Year CDS rate for Deutsche Bank's subordinated debt.

back the issue and refinance the total amount of €1 bn, it would pay much more than the extra cost of facing the step up in the coupon.

1.6.2   Hybrid Corporate Capital

A corporate hybrid is a long-dated, deeply subordinated debt instrument with cancelable coupons issued by a non-financial institution. Sometimes this debt instrument has one or more embedded issuer calls. If the issuer forgoes the call and keeps the bond alive, the post-call-date coupon structure changes. For the issuer, there is an interest rate charge increase with a predefined step up. During the month of January 2013 there was a record $14 bn issuance of corporate hybrids. One hybrid issued by EDF, a major French utility, had an issue size of $4 bn. Corporate issuers seek, through hybrids, benefits for the funding of their balance sheets. Corporates typically protect the rating of senior notes through the issuance of lower-rated hybrid instruments in order to obtain "cheap equity" [135]. A credit analyst will welcome the fact that a new source of funding has been used which is deeply subordinated to senior debt. A wide variety can be observed in the corporate hybrids that have been issued so far. The differences between these corporate hybrid bonds can be organized along three different axes: coupon payments, permanence, and subordination.

- **Coupon payments**
  Most hybrids come with a coupon, the payment of which can be skipped at the discretion of the management of the company (**optional deferral**). A **mandatory deferral** corresponds to a case where a breach of a financial ratio would trigger the non-payment of the coupon. The deferrals on the coupon payments can be **cumulative** or **non-cumulative**. In the first case, the issuer has to deal with the coupon payments that were deferred in the past before any new coupons or dividends can be paid out. There is also a connection between the payment of the dividends on the common stock and the coupon payments on hybrid debt. A **dividend or coupon pusher** would force hybrid coupon payments if a dividend payment on common stock had taken place. In some cases a **lookback period** is combined with a coupon pusher. Coupon payments are pushed to the holder of the hybrid if the issuing company has rewarded its equity investors with a dividend payment during this lookback horizon. The opposite case is that of a **dividend stopper**, where the deferral of a coupon payment on a hybrid bond eliminates any dividend payment on common stock.
- **Permanence**
  The equity nature of a hybrid bond increases with the maturity of the bond. A rating agency will typically view the absence of a specific maturity date, such as in the case of a perpetual bond, as a factor to give more equity credit to a hybrid bond [164]. The existence of a call date with a step-up coupon would weaken the equity profile as this could force the issuer to redeem the structure prematurely in order to walk away from the higher interest charge on the bond. For the investor, the mere existence of an issuer call introduces uncertainty regarding the final maturity date of the bond. This uncertainty is labeled "extension risk." An example of this kind of risk was illustrated in Figure 1.5 when we covered an unexpected extension of a hybrid bond issued by Deutsche Bank. In the space of corporate hybrids we find a similar example in Nufarm, an Australian company specializing in the development and marketing of crop-development products. In November 2011 it decided not to call back its hybrid bond on the first call date. What was originally a 5-year security immediately shifted into a perpetual bond with a semi-annual call. The company accepted to pay the step-up percentage of 2%.

Table 1.4   Characteristics of a hybrid bond issued by Bayer

	Bayer
Bond Type	Hybrid
Issue Date	July 29, 2005
S&P Rating	BBB−
Maturity	July 29, 2105
Initial Coupon (%)	5.00
Coupon Frequency	Annual
Optional Coupon Deferral	Yes
Mandatory Coupon Deferral	Yes
Par Amount	1000
ISIN	XS0225369403
First Call Date	July 29, 2015
Call Price	100%
Step-Up Coupon	3M EURIBOR + 280 bps
Price (%)	99.71

Source: Bloomberg. Date: April 30, 2012.

- **Subordination**

  The subordination is another factor when it comes to categorizing the equity nature of a hybrid security. Deeply subordinated debt will receive more equity credit.

An example of a hybrid bond issued by a corporate is the 100-year €1.3 bn bond issued by Bayer in 2005 (see Table 1.4). This bond is callable after 10 years with a step-up feature. The bond carries a deferral risk on the coupon payments. This interest payment deferral is both optional and mandatory:

- Optional deferral. At the discretion of Bayer, the issuing company, the coupon payments can be omitted. This deferral is cumulative.
- Mandatory deferral. On a so-called cash flow event, the issuing company is not allowed to distribute the coupon payments on this bond. The issuer can then voluntarily decide to make up such unpaid interest within 1 year following the suspension of the coupon payment. The cash flow event would occur if the consolidated cash flow of the issuer is less than 7% of the revenues of the company.

There is no standardization at all in corporate hybrids. There is an extreme range of structuring possibilities when it comes to designing the optimal bond structure. This results in a wide variety of issued hybrids. There is a continuum that ranges from the very bond-like structures with a fixed maturity to the more equity-like perpetual structures with non-deferrable coupons.

1.6.3   Toggle Bonds

A toggle bond is a debt instrument where the failure to pay a coupon will be compensated by increasing the size of the future coupons. This hybrid instrument has a very high junk-bond status and contains compensation for the investor that can take place in two different ways.

- **Cash**

  The coupon will be increased when the upcoming coupon payment cannot be made in time. This is where toggle bonds deserve their junk-bond status. A company is literally allowed to fill up a hole while digging a bigger one.

- **Payment in kind (PIK)**

  The PIK bond gives the issuer the flexibility to allocate more bonds to the investor in case the debt schedule cannot be made. The deferred coupon payment is added to the balance of the bond. The default rate of this kind of debt was very high during the 2008 subprime crisis. The post-2008 deals carry outspoken limits that specify to what event new debt can be issued to make up for the missed coupon payments.

1.7 REGULATION

National regulators have been implementing new regulations after the credit crunch, much of this under the leadership of international bodies such as the Basel Committee or the FSB. As explained in Section 1.5, CoCos are an example of an offspring of these new laws and rules that came into being after 2009. Central banks all over the world had to bail out banks using tax-payers' money. Since then, regulators have been under ongoing pressure from the public to make sure this never happens again. Two options were available to the policy makers [105]. First of all they could impose measures to make the bankruptcy of a bank less likely. A second measure would focus on making the impact of such a default on the financial system as small as possible. The failure of Lehman Brothers in September 2008 triggered an avalanche of financial distress throughout the world. This is the contagion risk that regulators need to deal with going forward.

1.7.1 Making Failures Less Likely

The failure of a bank can be made less likely by reducing the likelihood that the bank will incur large losses on its operations. An investment bank running a complex portfolio of structured products likely runs a higher risk than a retail bank following a traditional banking model where it produces moderate but stable returns. The Volcker rule is a specific section of the Dodd–Frank act named after Paul Volcker, a former chairman of the Fed, that deals with this specific risk. This rule restricts banks in their proprietary operations and prevents them from owning large stakes in hedge or private equity funds. A similar initiative has been taken in the UK following the publication of the report of the Independent Commission on Banking (ICB), chaired by Sir John Vickers. This so-called Vickers report [123] proposes ring-fencing, a clear separation and segregation between the retail business of a bank and its trading operations.

The Basel Committee on Banking Supervision has made, in its Basel III proposal, a push for a higher minimum regulatory capital. Not only the minimum capital for banks was to be increased, but also the quality of the required capital had to be higher. The Basel Committee made it clear that a capital instrument could only be considered as regulatory capital if it was truly loss absorbing [26]. All of the Basel III initiatives aim to make government-led bail-outs less likely.

1.7.2 Making Failures Less Disruptive

In March 2008, investors were watching very closely the difficult situation in which Bear Stearns, a US investment bank, had landed itself. The questionable liquidity of the assets on the balance sheet of Bear Stearns fed rumors that the Bear had cash problems. Meanwhile the share price had been sliding down for over a year, going from $164.06 on February 1, 2007 to $57 on March 13, 2008 – the day before its earnings announcement. When the share price of Bear Stearns lost another 50% after this announcement, the Federal Reserve Bank of New

York stepped in. Their actions led to the take over of the ailing investment bank by JP Morgan Chase. On March 17, 2008 JP Morgan Chase had offered to acquire Bear Stearns at a price of $2 per share, a fraction of its value a month earlier. The bid was subsequently increased to $10 per share and the acquisition was concluded on April 8, 2008. To make the deal attractive to Jamie Dimon, the CEO of JP Morgan Chase, the Federal Reserve (the "Fed") had agreed to take $30 bn of the losses on the worst assets of Bear Stearns [178]. The Bear Stearns tragedy was absorbed very well by the market and the financial system seemed resilient enough when it came to absorbing losses. Only 6 months later, the market turned out to be less able to deal with the failure of a big international player. The bankruptcy of Lehman Brothers sent shock waves throughout the financial system. The aftermath of the default of Lehman Brothers extended beyond the United States. In fact, it was the administration process in Europe which proved to be most difficult. The US part of the Lehman business had been acquired by Barclays, while the administrators of the European business of Lehman Brothers, with its headquarters in London, had a most difficult time sorting things out [128]. The administrators had to understand the business and operational workflow first, before they were able to make decisions. This was an almost impossible task given the complex structure of the bank, the complexity of the assets on its portfolio, and primarily because most ex-Lehman staff were landing jobs at other financial institutions. Those who knew and could help were not around any more . . . Cleaning up the Lehman debris took a very long time. Major banks are now working with their regulators to produce so-called "living wills" [56]. These are road-maps to explain how to orderly wind down the bank in case of a bankruptcy. As such, a living will also explains the different relationships within the same banking group.

1.8   BAIL-IN CAPITAL

When a bank is bailed out with tax-payers' money, external funds are used to recapitalize the bank or to cover its losses. This rescue operation can take place by relying on an external resolution fund (RF) or a deposit guarantee scheme (DGS). In both cases this is a form of state aid. A deposit guarantee reimburses a limited amount of the deposits to depositors whose bank has failed. In the member states of the European Union the cap on a DGS payout is €100 000. The safety of the deposits is guaranteed by a national agency in the home country of the bank. Examples of such institutions are the Federal Deposit Insurance Corporation (FDIC) in the USA and the Financial Services Compensation Scheme (FSCS) in the UK. One could argue that a country using a DGS introduces a moral hazard in its banking system. Banks know that whatever the outcome of their actions, the deposits will be guaranteed by the government. The existence of such a bail-out mechanism could stimulate them to take excessive financial risks in order to achieve higher returns. Without a DGS, in contrast, investors would only open a deposit with the safest banks of their country.

Bail-in capital is a different solution since it will force bond holders to take their burden of the bank's losses. A bail-in bond can be written down or converted into shares immediately before the financial institution reaches a state of bankruptcy. This is a more extreme construction than a contingent convertible, where the haircut or conversion only takes place when the bank is still a going concern. CoCos recapitalize the bank when its capital ratios are considered too weak, not when the bank is on the brink of collapse.

Bail-in bonds would impose the burden on the bond holders not on the tax payers. At the same time that the bonds are bailed in, the regulators can take other forceful measures: the existing equity of the bank can be wiped out and the management of the failing bank can be

Table 1.5 Bail-in losses in Ireland

Bank	Date	Amount (EUR mn)	Loss (%)
Anglo Irish	20-Oct-10	$1600	80–95
Bank of Ireland	8-Jun-11	$2600	80–90
Allied Irish	11-May-11	$2600	77.5–90

Source: Barclays.

replaced. The regulator might even force the bank to sell some of its assets. Such a bail-in mechanism would allow the bank to continue to operate, thereby avoiding any disruption to the financial system. Bailing in bonds is a harsh but swift solution. A customer of a bailed-in bank is not supposed to notice a difference on a Monday morning when the bail-in mechanism was applied during the weekend. Paul Calello, the former head of the investment banking business of Credit Suisse, and Wilson Ervin, its former chief risk officer, examined how a bail-in might have been applied in the case of Lehman [47]. They came to the conclusion that Lehman might have been saved if its subordinated bonds had been bailed in and converted into shares together with a smaller haircut imposed on the senior bonds.

Anybody taking a first glance at the bail-in solution will advocate that bond holders are forced to take their share of responsibility whereas a bail-out solution would keep the same bond holders alive thanks to tax payers' money. Is the use of bail-in bonds therefore a big plus? There are strings attached to the bail-in solution. Some tax payers will still be picking up part of the bill when a bail-in is used to save a bank. These individuals will find out, for example, that they have nevertheless been hit by the bail-in because their pension fund had some of its assets invested in bail-in bonds. Tax payers' money might not have been used directly but the bottom line remains the same.

An example of a bail-in can be found in some Irish banks, where this punitive solution was imposed on some of the bonds of Allied Irish, Bank of Ireland, and Anglo Irish during the Irish banking crisis in the period 2010–2011. The losses ranged from 80% for Lower Tier 2 (LT2) bonds to 95% of the principal for the Tier 1 (T1) bond of Anglo Irish Bank (see [148]). Senior debt was, in this bail-in exercise, left out of the burden sharing. A summary can be found in Table 1.5.

1.9 RISK AND RATING

1.9.1 Risk

The source of the market risk inherent in the category of hybrid instruments is directly linked to their ranking within the balance sheet. Hybrid capital instruments rank just above equity. The recent turmoil in the financial markets has been a very good example to illustrate the risk profile of this kind of debt. The year 2008, and especially the last 3 months of that year, was a period where the credit crunch left a scar on multiple portfolios. In the spring of 2011, a new crisis erupted. This second crisis, a sovereign debt meltdown, started in Europe with Greece and soon spread out all over Italy, Spain, and Portugal. In the bear market years (2008 and 2011), hybrids were doing particularly badly. Their deep subordination and high equity content pushed their returns clearly close to where the equity markets were performing in those periods. In Table 1.6, one can find an overview of the returns of four categories of hybrid

Table 1.6   TIER 1: Markit Iboxx Tier 1 Index, TIER 2: Markit Iboxx Lower Tier 2 Index, SENIOR: Markit Senior Bank Index, PREFERRED: S&P US Preferred Index, CONVERTIBLE: BofA Merill Lynch Global Convertible Index, MSCI: MSCI World Index

| | FINANCIALS | | GENERAL | | | |
Year	TIER 1	TIER 2	SENIOR	PREFERRED	CONVERTIBLE	MSCI
2008	−36.39%	−4.97%	4.83%	−29.61%	−29.35%	−40.11%
2009	40.54%	17.15%	12.73%	25.64%	36.34%	22.82%
2010	10.86%	2.89%	3.31%	5.72%	11.73%	7.83%
2011	−12.63%	−6.71%	2.13%	−8.20%	−5.66%	−7.56%
2012	29.76%	31.01%	13.67%	11.23%	13.44%	13.07%

Source: Markit Partners, Bloomberg, and MSCI.

instruments compared with the performance of the equity markets (MSCI Index) and senior financial bonds in particular. Within the financial hybrids, the Tier 2 bonds outranked the Tier 1 securities in the two crisis years of 2008 and 2011. In 2008, for example, an investor would have lost 4.97% on Tier 2 bonds whereas investments in Tier 1 securities would have yielded on average 7 times more losses (−36.39%).

1.9.2   Rating

Because of the higher investment risk associated with hybrid securities, these bonds receive a lower rating compared with senior debt issued by the same entity. Rating agencies typically lower hybrid debt a couple of notches below this senior issue. S&P, for example, lowers a hybrid security one notch for subordination and one to two notches more depending on the specifications of the coupon deferral [135].

1.10   CONCLUSION

The following chapters provide a deeper analysis of each of the different categories of hybrid capital introduced in this first part of the book. The very few examples covered in this introductory chapter have already illustrated the complete lack of standardization in the hybrid space. No two instruments are the same, making comparison not straightforward.

2
Convertible Bonds

Convertible bonds have been around more than a century and their origin can be linked to the history of the American rail roads. The railroad magnate J.J. Hill needed, in 1881, an innovative way to finance one of his new projects. The convertible bond market has evolved enormously since this first issue more than a century ago, but the principle of mixing debt and equity in one single instrument remains the same. This chapter provides an overview of the different kinds of convertible bonds, some specific instrument features, and an introduction to the terminology used.[1]

2.1 INTRODUCTION

Table 2.1 contains an overview of the outstanding convertible bonds as of May 1, 2012. This table illustrates the importance of the US convertible bond market both in size and number of convertible bonds issued. The convertible bond market is significantly smaller than the corporate bond market. The $492 bn outstanding convertible bonds display, however, a wider variety of different features. Each of these features has an impact on the valuation and price dynamics of the convertible bond. Layers of complexity are combined and stacked upon each other. This lack of standardization is an important challenge for a newcomer to the convertible bond scene. The job of a convertible bond analyst does not start with the selection of a suitable pricing model. Instead, the first step is always a thorough reading of the prospectus where all the specific characteristics are described at length.

Some of the elements in the prospectus might not have any direct influence on the payoff of the convertible bond, but will still have a clear impact on the risk and hence the price of the convertible. In the section of the prospectus dealing with take-overs, for example, the potential investor is informed about any possible changes in the instrument's anatomy if the underlying company of the convertible bond were to be acquired by another corporate. These change-of-control features could, for example, change the conversion ratio of the bond in case of a take-over. This improvement in the terms and conditions is called a ratchet clause. Any ignorance from an investor in setting up a convertible bond position could, however, lead to a loss. An equity investor will always greet a take-over of one of his stocks with enthusiasm. This is not necessarily the case for convertible bond investors. Only those investors or analysts who did their homework and crawled through the lengthy prospectus will be rewarded. For those failing to do so, convertible bond investing is not a safe pair of hands and may lead to unpleasant surprises.

Table 1.6 already clearly illustrated that the convertible bond market took its share of damage during the financial storm that hit the market during the subprime crisis in 2008. The Bank of America Merrill Lynch Convertible Bond Index, for example, dropped 29.35% in 2008. The MSCI World Index – a popular benchmark for equity investors – lost 10% more than this convertible bond index. The hybrid nature of the average convertible bond protected investors

---

[1] We refer readers who want to gather a deeper understanding of convertibles to our previous work on this topic [67].

Table 2.1 Global convertible bond universe (May 1, 2012)

Region	$ bn	No. issues
USA	215	792
Europe	125	295
Japan	36	97
Asia ex Japan	79	637
Other	37	290
Total	**492**	**2111**

Source: UBS.

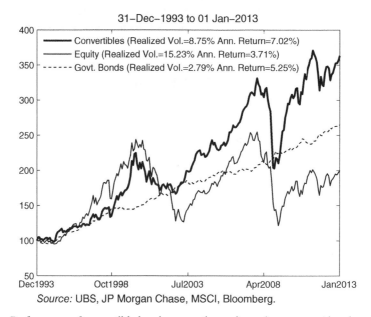

Figure 2.1 Performance of convertible bonds versus the equity and government bond markets.

more than those holding a diversified international equity portfolio with the MSCI World Index as benchmark.

In Figure 2.1 we extend the comparison of convertible bonds versus other asset classes to a horizon of 19 years covering the period 1993–2013.[2] The period observed in this graph contains three outspoken bear market periods.

- **2000–2002**

  This stock-market downturn started with the bursting of the internet bubble and witnessed periods of high volatility such as in the weeks following the September 2001 attacks. Investor confidence suffered after an outbreak of several accounting scandals (Enron, WorldCom), which further accelerated the fall of the markets.

---

[2] The equity markets are represented by the MSCI World Index, the government bond market by the JP Morgan Global Government Bond Index, and as the benchmark of the convertible bonds we used the UBS Global Convertible Bond Index.

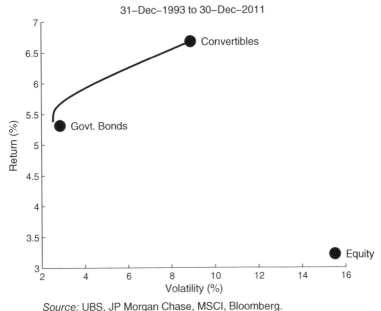

31–Dec–1993 to 30–Dec–2011

Source: UBS, JP Morgan Chase, MSCI, Bloomberg.

Figure 2.2   Efficient frontier for a portfolio of convertible and government bonds.

- **2008**

  The equity markets lost as much in 2008 as they lost in the two previous crisis
  years combined (2001–2002). Equity levels were pushed considerably downward following
  the subprime debt crisis, which led investors to shy away from risky investments. Financials
  in particular were leading the decline. The largest drop came in September–October 2008
  when Lehman Brothers filed for bankruptcy and the markets slipped almost 30% lower in
  this 2-month period.

- **2011–May 2012**

  The markets slipped into another bear market period. The banks had barely repaired their
  balance sheets when a European sovereign debt crisis spooked the investors. Fears over
  a possible bankruptcy of Greece and the risk of further contagion drove equity levels
  substantially lower.

The safest investment over this 19-year horizon consisted of a diversified portfolio of
government bonds returning on average 5.32% per year with an annualized realized volatility
of 2.79%.[3] Convertible bonds returned more, but their annualized return of 7.02% entailed a
higher realized volatility of 8.75%. Figure 2.2 depicts an efficient frontier[4] combining these two
asset classes. It illustrates at the same time the disappointing results for an equity investment.
This asset class, represented by the MSCI World Index, carried more risk and generated lower
returns.

---

[3] The annualized volatility was calculated as the standard deviation of the daily log returns over the full horizon. A logarithmic
or log return of two consecutive asset prices A_i and A_{i+1} is calculated as $\log(A_{i+1}) - \log(A_i)$. In the assumption that there are 250
trading days in a calendar year, the standard deviation of the daily log returns was annualized using the multiplier $\sqrt{250}$.

[4] The efficient frontier connects the different portfolio combinations offering the highest return for a given level of volatility. The
efficient frontier is a concept in modern portfolio theory introduced by Harry Markowitz and others [90].

2.2 ANATOMY OF A CONVERTIBLE BOND

2.2.1 Final Payoff

The final payoff and value of a convertible bond (P_T) at the maturity date $t = T$ is written as:

$$\max(N, C_r \times S_T) \tag{2.1}$$

The holder of a convertible has the right, at the maturity date, to exchange the face value N of the bond for C_r shares with price S_T. C_r is the conversion ratio. In case there is a final coupon payment C at the maturity date T, the payoff function changes:

$$\max(N + C, C_r \times S_T) \tag{2.2}$$

Rewriting Equation (2.2) and making abstraction of the fact that the convertible pays a coupon allows us to strip the convertible bond into a bond with face value N and C_r European call options on the underlying share:

$$P_T = N + C_r \times \max(0, S_T - C_P) \tag{2.3}$$

The strike of each call option is equal to the conversion price C_P of the convertible bond:

$$C_P = \frac{N}{C_r} \tag{2.4}$$

Applying put–call parity, it can then be shown that holding such a European-style convertible bond is economically the same as holding C_r shares combined with a European put option to sell this amount of shares against the face value N of the convertible bond:

$$P_T = C_r \times S_T + \max(N - C_r \times S_T, 0) \tag{2.5}$$

We note that the conversion price can sometimes be modified during the life of the convertible bond. This can, for example, occur as a result of a corporate action such as a stock split, the breach of a dividend threshold, or whenever a ratchet clause is applied in a take-over situation.

Splitting a convertible bond into a bond and a European option is only possible if the conversion right is restricted to the maturity date of the convertible bond. In reality, convertible bonds almost always allow for a conversion during the life of the bond. This makes our European convertible bond example somewhat hypothetical.

2.2.2 Price Graph

Equation (2.5) represents the cash flow paid out to the convertible bond holder at the final maturity date T. The investor has to make a choice between receiving either C_r shares or the face value of the bond including the final coupon. Determining the value of a convertible bond P_t on a date $t < T$ is less straightforward. It depends on the chosen valuation model and typically involves parameters such as expected dividend yield, volatility of the underlying stock, credit default swap data of the issuer, and the interest levels of the different currencies involved. The latter is a topic which will be covered in detail in Chapter 6.

Figure 2.3 shows the price graph of a convertible bond as a function of the underlying stock price. Although the price function depends on the specific valuation model, it reveals already

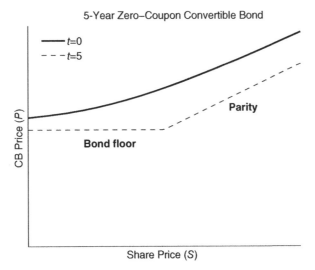

5-Year Zero–Coupon Convertible Bond

— $t=0$

– – – $t=5$

Parity

Bond floor

CB Price (P)

Share Price (S)

Figure 2.3 Price graph of a convertible bond at maturity $t = 5$ and at the issue date $t = 0$.

some model-independent properties. This graph shows, for example, how the convertible bond develops a linear behavior for high share price levels. The convertible's value seems to be driven by the value of the amount of the underlying shares received on conversion. This is the **conversion value** or **parity** (P_a). When the underlying share price is high, the convertible bond is clearly more sensitive to share price movements.

The same figure illustrates how the convertible loses some of its stock price sensitivity when the share price is low. At these share price levels, the holder of the convertible has no economic interest to convert the bond. The value of the convertible bond converges in this case to the present value of the cash flows (coupons C and face value N) generated by the bond features of the convertible. This discounted value is called the **bond floor** (B_F). In layman terms and cutting corners short, one could summarize the properties of a convertible bond as an instrument that behaves like a stock in good times and converges to the bond floor in bad times.

The convertible bond can therefore be of interest for a fixed-income investor, and on the other side of the spectrum where the price of the convertible converges to parity, one will find an equity investor having a similar interest in the instrument. Both points of view provide us with respectively P_a and B_F, which are a boundary condition to the value of a convertible bond.

2.2.3 Quotation of a Convertible Bond

The market makers active at the convertible desks of investment banks quote bid and offer prices for convertible bonds and express these as a percentage of the bond's face value. These quoted prices are typically **clean prices**: one has to add the **accrued interest** to calculate the total cash amount for the transaction. The **dirty price** of a convertible is the sum of its clean price and the accrued interest. The accrued interest is the interest that has been accumulated since the issue date, or since the previous coupon payment. As an example of a bond that quotes

Table 2.2   Characteristics of the convertible bond issued by Euronav

EURONAV 6.5% January 31, 2015			
ISIN	BE6000351286	SEDOL	B41X9B9
ISSUE DATE	September 9, 2009	ISSUE PRICE	100%
ISSUE SIZE	150 mn	FACE VALUE	100 000
STOCK	EURONAV	MATURITY	January 31, 2015
CONVERSION RATIO	4316.1882	COUPON FREQUENCY	SEMI-ANNUAL
REDEMPTION	100.00%	SENIORITY	SENIOR UNSECURED
COUPON	6.5%	CURRENCY	USD
CALLABLE	yes		

Source: Prospectus.

"clean" and as a percentage of its face value, we took the USD-denominated convertible bond issued in 2009 by EURONAV, a Belgian shipping company (see Table 2.2).

Case Study: Buying a EURONAV Convertible

On Friday May 4, 2012 a market maker provides a bid–offer quote for the EURONAV convertible bond equal to 85.90%–86.90%. An interested buyer wants to lift the offer and seeks to purchase $5 mn of this issue. What would be the total cash amount to be paid?

The bond settles on $T + 3$, which means that the cash is paid out three business days after the purchase date. Since the dealing date in this example is on a Friday, the bond settles on the Wednesday of the following week:

- Trade Date: May 4, 2012.
- Settlement Date: May 9, 2012.
- Previous Coupon Date: January 31, 2012.
- Coupon: 6.50%.
- Coupon Frequency: Semi-annual (S/A).
- Day Count: 30/360.

There are exactly 99 days between the settlement date and the previous coupon date, during which the bond accumulated interest. The accrued interest for a $5 mn USD transaction is equal to $89 375:

$$\text{Accrued interest} = \$5\,000\,000 \times 6.5\% \times \frac{99}{360} = \$89\,375$$

The total cash amount paid by the investor to the market maker's bank account is hence $4 434 375:

$$\text{Total cash amount} = \$5\,000\,000 \times 86.9\% + \$89\,375 = \mathbf{\$4\,434\,375}$$

The EURONAV example covers the majority of convertible bonds. Prices are in general being quoted in clean terms and as a percentage of the face value. The main exception to this rule are the French convertible bonds where the prices are quoted in dirty terms. Moreover, the price is a cash price, never a percentage. In this case, there is no need to add the accrued interest to the quoted price in order to figure out the cash amount on the settlement date. An example of such a bond is described in Table 2.3. This convertible has been issued by CAP GEMINI, a French computer and management consulting company.

Table 2.3   Characteristics of the convertible bond issued by Cap Gemini

CAP GEMINI 3.5% January 1, 2014			
ISIN	FR0010748905	SEDOL	B3R5BP0
ISSUE DATE	April 20, 2009	ISSUE PRICE	34
ISSUE SIZE	575 mn	FACE VALUE	34
STOCK	CAP GEMINI	MATURITY	January 1, 2014
CONVERSION RATIO	1	COUPON FREQUENCY	ANNUAL
REDEMPTION	34	SENIORITY	SENIOR UNSECURED
COUPON	3.5%	CURRENCY	EUR

Source: Prospectus.

Case Study: Selling a Cap Gemini Convertible

A portfolio manager of a convertible bond fund wants to unwind his stake of 120 000 bonds in the CAP GEMINI 2014 convertible bond. The bond is quoted in dirty terms: 38.09–38.30. What is the cash amount the portfolio manager will receive?

This two-way price means that the market maker is willing to pay €38.09 per bond and would sell the bond at a price of €38.30. The portfolio manager owns 120 000 bonds and would hence receive €4 570 800 (= 120 000 × €38.09) on the settlement date.

2.2.4   Bond Floor (B_F)

The bond floor or the investment value is the value of the convertible if it were to be stripped of the possibility to convert into the underlying shares. It is the bond component of the convertible. This value equals the sum of the discounted cash flows distributed by the convertible bond. These cash flows are typically discounted using a discount rate r_b:[5]

$$B_F = \sum_{i=1}^{N_c} C_{t_i} \exp\left(-r_b t_i\right) + N \exp(-r_b T); \quad t_i = \text{time in years till the } i\text{th coupon} \quad (2.7)$$

Here, N_c is equal to the number of upcoming coupons, C_{t_i} is the coupon paid out at time t_i, and N is the face value of the convertible bond which is redeemed at the maturity date T. The discount rate r_b is equal to the risk-free rate r to which a credit spread cs is added.

Case Study: Bond Floor Calculation of EURONAV

To illustrate the calculation of a bond floor, we consider again the example of the EURONAV convertible bond specified in Table 2.2. To discount the USD-denominated cash flows, we use an interest rate of 0.67%.[6] The credit spread to be added on top of this risk-free rate is

---

[5] In this book we will favor the use of continuous interest rates when performing fixed-income calculations. The equivalent notation using the more traditional actuarial discount rate r'_b would be:

$$B_F = \sum_{i=1}^{N_c} \frac{C_i}{(1+r'_b)^{y_i}} + \frac{N}{(1+r'_b)^T} \quad (2.6)$$

[6] This discount rate uses a day count basis of actual/365 (A/365).

1700 bps. This is a high value and reflects the precarious financial situation of this shipping company early 2012.

Date	Years (A/365)	Cash Flow ($)	Discount Factor
July 31, 2012	0.24	3 250	0.962
January 31, 2013	0.75	3 250	0.886
July 31, 2013	1.24	3 250	0.817
January 31, 2014	1.75	3 250	0.753
July 31, 2014	2.24	3 250	0.694
January 31, 2015	2.75	103 250	0.640
		Calculation Date	May 4, 2012
		Present Value	79 416.871
		Accrued	1 787.50
		BF (%)	**77.63%**

The bond floor takes the same quotation convention as the price of the convertible bond. In the example above, it is therefore calculated as a clean price. The bond floor of the convertible is 77.63%. A graphical presentation of the bond floor, parity, and the convertible bond prices observed in the period 2009–2012 for the EURONAV convertible can be found in Figure 2.4.

If the convertible were to be issued with a put clause, granting the right to the investor to sell back the bond to the issuer on a particular date, the bond floor only includes the cash flows up till the put date. The put feature is covered in depth in Section 2.4.2.

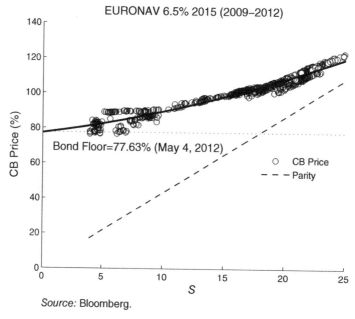

Source: Bloomberg.

Figure 2.4   Price graph of the EURONAV 2015 convertible bond.

Starting from the notion of a bond floor and the price P of the convertible bond, one can define the **investment premium (%)** as:

$$\frac{P - B_F}{B_F} \tag{2.8}$$

This is an indication of how much an investor is willing to pay for the option embedded in the convertible. Another name for the same metric is **premium to the bond floor**. The investment premium is typically calculated as a percentage of the bond floor, but can also be expressed as an absolute difference or points (pts). In this case the investment premium is expressed as:

$$P - B_F \tag{2.9}$$

2.2.5 Parity

Parity (P_a) is the value of the shares one would hold if the bond were to be immediately converted. This equals the conversion ratio times the value of the share and is expressed as a percentage of face value if the bond is trading as a percentage of face value:

$$P_a = \frac{S \times C_r}{N}$$
$$= \frac{S}{C_P} \tag{2.10}$$

When the bond is trading in units such as in the CAP GEMINI convertible, parity will be:

$$P_a = S \times C_r \tag{2.11}$$

The **premium to parity (%)** relates the market price of the convertible to parity. It is given by:

$$\frac{P - P_a}{P_a} \tag{2.12}$$

Parity is expressed as a percentage. It is the percentage one is willing to pay above the current market price of the share for a future ownership of these shares through holding the convertible. The premium can be explained by those features of the convertible structure that make it advantageous to hold the convertible over an outright investment in the underlying shares. The convertible might distribute a coupon, which could be higher than the dividends paid out by the shares for example. Such a yield advantage increases the value of the premium.

The bond floor provides a lower boundary of the convertible's theoretical price P for low share prices. When the share price increases, the convertible will move away from its bond floor and converge to the conversion value of the bond. Parity is hence a lower boundary for the convertible's theoretical value in such a case.

2.2.6 Convexity

The price graph in Figure 2.4 displays the positive convexity of the convertible bond with respect to the underlying share price. The price $P(S)$ of a convertible bond as a function of the share price is an increasing convex function. In other words, its second derivative with respect to S is positive. This positive gamma, as it is sometimes called, is a core property of the convertible bond:

$$\frac{\partial^2 P}{\partial S^2} > 0 \qquad (2.13)$$

The positive (equity) gamma indicates that the equity sensitivity ($\Delta = \frac{\partial P}{\partial S}$) of the convertible increases when the value of the underlying stock appreciates and decreases when the share price drops:

$$\frac{\partial \Delta}{\partial S} > 0 \qquad (2.14)$$

The convertible behaves more and more like a share when the stock price is doing well. In the opposite case, when the share is not performing at all, its value will slip more toward the bond floor. One could consider the following simple boundaries:

$$\lim_{S \to \infty} \Delta = \lim_{S \to \infty} \frac{dP}{dS}$$

$$= \frac{d}{dS} \lim_{S \to \infty} P$$

$$= \frac{d}{dS} \frac{S \times C_r}{N}$$

$$= \frac{C_r}{N} \qquad (2.15)$$

$$\lim_{S \to 0} \Delta = 0 \text{ (assuming no default)} \qquad (2.16)$$

Value of Positive Convexity

An investor with a good understanding of the dynamic behavior of a convertible clearly has an edge over his or her competitors. Understanding how the bond behaves when it trades close to the bond floor ($P \approx B_F$) demands a good understanding of fixed-income mathematics. On the other side of the spectrum, when the CB[7] is very much in the money and the premium to parity very small, the convertible behaves like a stock ($P \approx P_a$). The gray area is right in the middle. Between these two extreme situations, the CB is of a more complex nature. This is where the convexity or the non-linearity can work for or against an investor. Understanding convexity is key when working with convertibles. The convexity or gamma is the change of the equity exposure (Δ) for a small change in the value of the underlying share of the convertible. A positive convexity means that the more the underlying share appreciates in value, the more one's convertible portfolio will be exposed to such stock price changes. The opposite happens if the value of the share drops. The equity risk of the convertible will, in such a case, diminish. The more the share price goes down, the more the convertible becomes a bond and the more it will protect the investor from share price changes.

Let's assume that we have a valuation model to calculate the theoretical price of a convertible bond P for a given share price S. The precise nature of the function $P(S)$ is not relevant at this point. It could be a closed-form formula or maybe even derived using a Monte Carlo

---

[7] Convertible bond.

simulation. At this point in the book, the precise model does not really matter. We can apply a Taylor series expansion of $P(S)$ around the current share price S_0 and the corresponding convertible price $P(S_0)$:

$$P(S) = P(S_0) + (S - S_0)\left(\frac{\partial P}{\partial S}\right)_{S=S_0} + \frac{1}{2}(S - S_0)^2 \left(\frac{\partial^2 P}{\partial S^2}\right)_{S=S_0} + \ldots \quad (2.17)$$

or

$$P(S) = P(S_0) + (S - S_0)\Delta_{S_0} + \frac{1}{2}(S - S_0)^2 \Gamma_{S_0} + \ldots \quad (2.18)$$

where Δ_{S_0} is the delta at S_0 and similarly Γ_{S_0} is the gamma at S_0. In what follows, we will denote this by Δ and Γ for simplicity. The changes in the value of the convertible bond δP when we are dealing with small fluctuations in the share price $\delta S = (S - S_0)$ can hence be approximated as:

$$\delta P = P(S) - P(S_0) \approx \Delta \delta S + \frac{1}{2}\Gamma(\delta S)^2 \quad (2.19)$$

Part of the equity exposure of the convertible can now be eliminated by selling a quantity of Δ shares at a price S_0. The portfolio is now "delta-neutral." The portfolio has a value Π and consists, after executing the hedge, of a long position in the bond and a short exposure in Δ shares. The portfolio is hence considered to be "delta-hedged":

$$\Pi = P - \Delta \times S_0 \quad (2.20)$$

The changes $\delta \Pi$ in the value of this delta-hedged portfolio depend solely on the convexity Γ and the square of the share price change:

$$\delta \Pi = P(S) - P(S_0) - \Delta \times (S - S_0) = \delta P - \Delta \delta S = \frac{1}{2}\Gamma \delta S^2 \quad (2.21)$$

Keeping other parameters such as time, interest rates, etc. unchanged, clearly results in a positive expected portfolio change when $\Gamma > 0$:

$$\mathbb{E}[\delta \Pi] = \frac{1}{2}\Gamma \mathbb{E}[\delta S^2] > 0 \quad (2.22)$$

In Equation (2.22) $\mathbb{E}[\delta S^2]$ illustrates the randomness of the share price S. It measures the range or the volatility[8] with which S fluctuates around the current share price S_0. The wider this range and the larger the positive convexity (Γ), the better the expected portfolio changes will turn out to be. A portfolio with only positive convexity is considered to be "long gamma." The more volatile the stock, the higher the expected benefit for the holder of such a portfolio.

Without any doubt, positive convexity can create value. This makes a convertible instrument interesting to hold on a delta-hedged basis. This investment style is the bread and butter of convertible arbitrage specialists. Equation (2.22) is the best way to explain why volatility is an important component in the pricing of convertibles. Recall for the moment that we have not chosen any pricing model at all. No assumptions have been made regarding the stochastic process of the underlying share. A straightforward back-of-the-envelope calculation showed us that the volatility of the stock will be a main ingredient in the pricing formula.

---

[8] In the strict mathematical sense, the volatility of a stock price S is equal to the standard deviation of the log returns.

Table 2.4   Characteristics of the convertible bond issued by Renewable Energy

RENEWABLE ENERGY 6.5% June 4, 2014			
ISIN	NO0010543457	SEDOL	B4WVR85
ISSUE DATE	October 13, 2009	ISSUE PRICE	100%
ISSUE SIZE	320 mn	FACE VALUE	50 000
STOCK	RENEWABLE ENERGY	MATURITY	June 4, 2014
CONVERSION RATIO	11058.9655	CURRENCY	EUR
REDEMPTION	100%	SENIORITY	SUBORDINATED
COUPON	6.5%	COUPON FREQUENCY	QUARTERLY

Source: Prospectus.

By contrast, we can also consider a portfolio with a negative convexity. Here it is in the interest of the investor to have an underlying share price which is not volatile at all. The less the stock moves, the better. A delta-hedged position with negative gamma on a very volatile share is indeed a recipe for disaster. Nobody wants to own negative convexity unless one is fairly compensated to be exposed to this kind of market risk. Owning positive convexity therefore must come at a cost; no free lunch in the world of convertible bonds. The positive expected payoff of a delta-hedged convertible bond portfolio with a gamma that is positive for a large range of share prices needs to be paid for. This is the reason why the coupon on convertible debt is lower than the coupon of a corporate bond issued by the same issuer. The lower coupon compensates for the optionality and the resulting positive convexity packaged into the bond.

Convertibles Double-Signed Gamma

A real-world convertible bond example will show that blending theory and practice together is easier said than done. The convertible bond issued by the Renewable Energy Corporation will be a perfect guide in our quest to fully understand convertible bond convexity. The characteristics of this convertible can be found in Table 2.4. The Renewable Energy Corporation (REC) is a Norwegian solar energy company. The price chart of this convertible covering the period 2010–2012 is shown in Figure 2.5.

On this price graph, two 4-month periods have been singled out. The first one covers the period from September 4, 2010 to January 4, 2011. During this period the volatility of the convertible bond and the corresponding underlying share was moderate. The second period from June 19 to October 19, 2011 has been much more difficult for the solar energy company. The solar equipment maker missed out on its earnings release in the second quarter of 2011. The share price plunged and drove the convertible bond's price down. The value of the bond had almost halved during this particular period. A graph where the convertible bond price is plotted against the underlying share price for these two periods is illustrated in Figure 2.6. The statement that an investment in a convertible bond provides downside protection seems to be unrealistic. The textbook idea that investing in convertibles is participating in the upside while taking no down-side risk is not correct. The idea of a smooth convergence to the bond floor for falling share prices, as illustrated in Figure 2.4, seems to be a fallacy. In the case of this particular bond, the collapse of the share price has pushed the credit spreads upward. As a consequence of this, the bond floor itself is pushed lower and lower. Figure 2.6 illustrates the "normal" convertible bond behavior from September 2010 to January 2011. There is positive

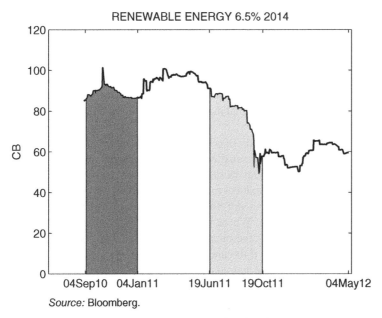

Source: Bloomberg.

Figure 2.5   Price graph of the Renewable Energy convertible bond.

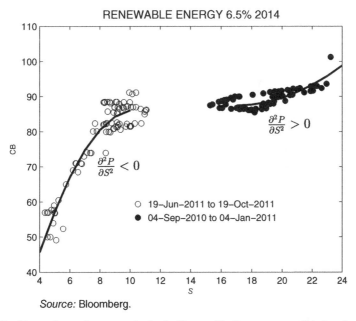

Source: Bloomberg.

Figure 2.6   Positive and negative convexity in the Renewable Energy convertible bond.

convexity during these months. The opposite is true during the summer of 2011. In this gloomy period, the convertible has negative gamma. The equity exposure is indeed increasing for a decrease in the share price. The lower the share price, the more an investor in this convertible seems to be exposed to it. The Renewable Energy example reveals the true complex nature of a convertible bond. It is an instrument that can display a double-signed gamma. Positive convexity can sometimes change into negative convexity, which becomes very dominant when share prices are extremely low. In normal market circumstances, however, the positive gamma prevails.

This is the Jekyll and Hyde property of convertible bonds. Convertibles seem to have a split personality when it comes to equity sensitivity; positive gamma on the way up and negative gamma on the way down. This real-world behavior makes a convertible bond price very challenging to quantify in a mathematical model. The story that a convertible bond is a simple blend of a bond and an option does not hold any more, and ignoring the fact that negative gamma can appear is dead wrong. Where positive convexity increases the theoretical price of a bond, negative convexity goes the other way. It should lower the price one is willing to pay for the convertible. Especially if the underlying stock is very volatile, one cannot dismiss negative gamma. Ignoring negative gamma will lead to an overestimation of the theoretical price of the convertible.

In Figure 2.7 we represent the density function of the share prices for the two periods. A lognormal density function has been fitted to the observed share prices. There is a density plot for each of the two sample periods. Figure 2.7 reveals how the period where the convertible

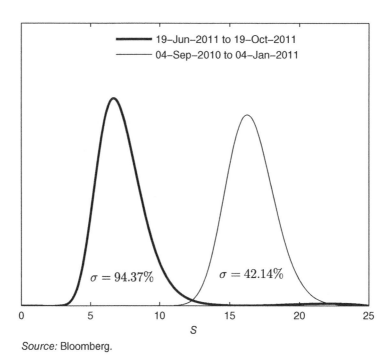

Source: Bloomberg.

Figure 2.7   Positive and negative convexity comes with different volatility levels (Renewable Energy convertible bond).

bond displayed negative gamma (June to October 2011) corresponded to the situation where the realized volatility of the underlying share price was high. During this 4-month period, REC's share price had an annualized realized volatility of 94.37%. This was more than twice the volatility of the other observation period. In this initial period from September 4, 2010 to January 4, 2011, the gamma was positive. This is a perfect illustration why one cannot ignore negative gamma. We observed negative gamma in distressed periods when the stock price was very volatile. In this example the volatility took extreme values when the gamma was negative. The same example showed how the lower realized volatility matched a period when the gamma was positive, which is exactly the opposite of the desired behavior. An investor hopes for a volatile stock price when the gamma is positive, and a stock price threading calm waters when the bond has negative gamma. A low volatility for share price levels when the gamma is positive and high equity volatility when the gamma is negative therefore has to lower the theoretical value of the bond. A pricing model constructed on a Black–Scholes foundation, which is assuming a constant volatility, cannot cope with this kind of complexity. Simple diffusion processes, where share price changes are modeled through a geometric Brownian motion, ignore the fact that volatility can change during the life of the option. Any possible dependence of the level of the volatility on the level of the share price is ignored in such models. The observation in this paragraph makes a real case to use, for example, stochastic volatility models.

2.2.7 Optional Conversion

The holder of a convertible bond has the option to end the bond's existence prematurely by converting it into shares. This right is the **optional conversion**. As long as this option to convert is not exercised by the investor, the bond continues to exist. On the maturity date, two events can happen: either the face value N and a final coupon C are paid out or the bond converts into C_r shares with value S_T:

- **Final redemption**
  This is the case where the investor decides not to convert into shares, but opts instead to receive the final coupon C and the face value of the bond. This happens when:

$$N + C > S_T \times C_r \qquad (2.23)$$

- **Final conversion**
  The bond holder converts when the market price of the share S_T is high enough:

$$S_T > \frac{N + C}{C_r} \qquad (2.24)$$

Example: Optional Conversion

Consider a convertible bond that has been issued 4 years ago and is now 1 year away from its final maturity date. Each bond has a face value N equal to 100, distributes no coupons, and can be converted to 0.7 shares. The conversion price is hence 142.86. The current share price is 283.65 and the 1-year continuous interest rate r equals 2.96%. Should we convert the bond right now or keep the bond alive for another year, till the final maturity date is reached? At the maturity date the bond is then either converted or redeemed into cash.

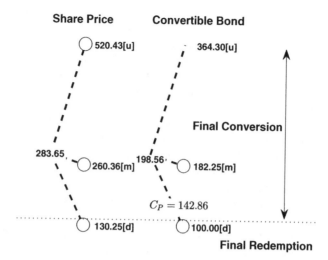

Figure 2.8   Optional conversion of a convertible bond.

In order to answer this question, we need a model. We assume that starting from the current share price, the share can reach three different states ([u], [m], and [d]) at the maturity date (see Figure 2.8). This simplified model allows for three possible values S_T originating from the current share price. Each of these final states or "nodes" has a corresponding probability. The upper and lower nodes [u] and [d] can be reached with a probability equal to $\frac{1}{6}$. The probability of reaching the middle node [m] where the share price $S_T = 260.36$ is $\frac{2}{3}$. This simplified model offers a first introduction to trinomial trees, a numerical technique we will work out in detail in Chapter 6.

The convertible bond matures at one of the three possible states and the value of the convertible P_T at the maturity date is given by:

$$P_T = \max(N, C_r \times S_T) = \max(100, 0.7 \times S_T)$$

- **Node [u]: Probability $\frac{1}{6}$**
  The share price goes up to node [u] and reaches at that point a value of 520.43. This node corresponds to a final conversion. A rational investor will maximize his wealth and convert the bond into shares. The value of the bond at this point is $364.30 = 0.7 \times 520.43$.
- **Node [m]: Probability $\frac{2}{3}$**
  The share price drifts lower to node [m] where $S_T = 260.36$. This is another point where the bond holder will opt for a final conversion into shares. The terminal value of the bond in this state is equal to 182.25.
- **Node [d]: Probability $\frac{1}{6}$**
  The share price has more than halved after it drops to 130.25 when it reaches the node [d]. This final node is lower than the conversion price and the bond holder will prefer to receive the face value of the bond. Hence $P_T = 100$.

Starting from our current stock price and a simple stock price simulation, we now know what values the convertible can take after another time step of exactly 1 year. The expected value of the bond at the maturity date given our current share price is:

$$\mathbb{E}(P_T \mid S = 283.65) = \frac{1}{6} \times 364.30 + \frac{2}{3} \times 182.25 + \frac{1}{6} \times 100 = 198.88 \qquad (2.25)$$

Assuming there is no bankruptcy risk, one can discount the cash flow to today's node. This discounted expected cash flow is the **continuation value** P_c of the convertible bond in the starting node:[9]

$$P_c = \exp(-r) \times \mathbb{E}(P_T \mid S = 283.65) = 193.08 \qquad (2.26)$$

The value of the convertible at time t is denoted as P_t. This theoretical value is not necessarily equal to P_c because the investor has the option to convert the bond into shares. The conversion value or parity P_a depends on the level of the share price S_t and is equal to $C_r \times S_t = 198.56$. The value on conversion is higher than the continuation value obtained in Equation (2.26):

$$P_t = \max(P_a, P_c) = 198.56 \qquad (2.27)$$

In this educational example, the investor will go for an early optional conversion because $P_a > P_c$. This rational choice will deliver a larger payoff than keeping the convertible bond alive till the final maturity date.

2.2.8   Forced Conversion

The investor can also be forced into an early conversion of the convertible. This could happen if the convertible bond is called by the issuer. If the bond gets called, the issuer pays the investor the call price K. This is the early redemption amount and does include, depending on what is specified in the prospectus, accrued interest. If parity is high enough, the convertible bond will be too far in the money for the investor to give this advantage away. The investor will in this case – after having received the call notice from the issuer – convert the bond into shares. Forced conversion will take place when $P_a > K$. The current value of the convertible P_t has to include such a forced conversion. This changes Equation (2.27):

$$P_t = \max(P_a, \min(K, P_c)) \qquad (2.28)$$

In Section 2.4.1, we cover the issuer call and its impact from a valuation and risk perspective in much more detail.

2.2.9   Mandatory Conversion

A mandatory convertible bond always redeems into shares, never into cash. As an example we cover one particular kind of convertible out of the wide range of mandatory convertible bonds: **PEPS**. This acronym stands for Participating Equity Preferred Stock. Another name for the same instrument is **PRIDE** (Preferred Redeemable Increased Dividend Securities) or **DECS** (Debt Exchangeable for Common Stock). This instrument comes with a double conversion

---

[9] In this example no reference is made to risk-neutral valuation.

ratio, therefore has two conversion prices, and is mandatory convertible. At maturity the investor always ends up with a certain amount of shares. There is a lower conversion price $(C_{P,L})$ and a higher conversion price $(C_{P,H})$. The value of the share price at the expiration date of the PEPS convertible specifies the conversion ratio and the amount of shares an investor will receive:

$$\text{Number of Shares} = \begin{cases} C_{r,L} & \text{with } C_{r,L} = \dfrac{N}{C_{P,L}} \text{ if } S_T < C_{P,L} \\ C_r & \text{with } C_r = \dfrac{N}{S_T} \text{ if } S_T \geq C_{P,L} \text{ and } S_T \leq C_{P,H} \quad (2.29) \\ C_{r,H} & \text{with } C_{r,H} = \dfrac{N}{C_{P,H}} \text{ if } S_T > C_{P,H} \end{cases}$$

As an example, we considered a PEP-like mandatory convertible on a share that distributes no dividends and has a volatility equal to 40%. Using a 3% interest rate, the mandatory was priced at two different moments in time: 6 months and 1 month before the final maturity date. The curve of the theoretical price for a wide range of share prices can be found in Figure 2.9. The convertible distributes no coupons and has a dual-strike structure with conversion price equal to 80 and 120.

In case of a disappointing share price performance where S_T would be lower than 80 at the maturity date, the investor will receive more shares than if the share price were above 120. The amount of shares received on expiration depends clearly on the share price performance. This introduces unmistakably a double convexity into the payoff profile of the mandatory convertible bond: negative gamma in an area where $S_t \approx 80$ and positive gamma if $S_t \approx 120$. The closer to the final maturity date, the more visible this difference in convexity. This motivates practitioners to price these kinds of mandatories with two volatilities. A high volatility for the lower conversion price and a low volatility for the higher share price levels.

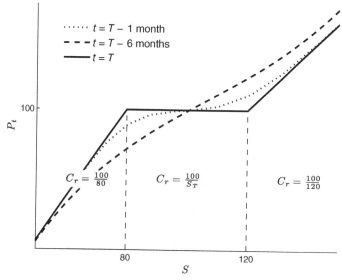

Figure 2.9 Mandatory convertible bond with two conversion prices: 80 and 120.

Table 2.5   Characteristics of the mandatory convertible issued by Cliffs Natural Resources

CLIFFS NATURAL RESOURCES 7% February 1, 2016			
ISIN	US18683K4085	SEDOL	B9C9HG2
ISSUE DATE	February 1, 2013	ISSUE PRICE	25
ISSUE SIZE	29 mn shares	FACE VALUE	25
STOCK	CLIFFS NATURAL RESOURCES	MATURITY	February 1, 2016
LOW C_P	29.00	HIGH C_P	35.53
CURRENCY	USD		
COUPON	7%	FREQUENCY	QUARTERLY

Source: Prospectus.

An example of such a mandatory preferred is the bond issued by Cliffs Natural Resources early 2013 (Table 2.5). The two conversion ratios are 0.7037 and 0.8621, corresponding respectively to the higher and lower conversion price.

2.3 CONVERTIBLE BOND ARBITRAGE

2.3.1 Components of Risk

Linear Components of Risk

Earlier in Equation (2.19), we linked the changes in the convertible bond price δP to changes in the underlying share price δS. We now test this assumed linear relationship on a real-world example. Such a practical test should reveal how important equity prices are, when it comes to understanding the market risk of a convertible bond. For this particular case study, we take the Archer Daniels convertible bond (Table 2.6) and graphically represent the weekly share price changes versus corresponding changes in the price of the convertible bond. The observation period is limited to the year 2011 and these $n = 52$ weekly observations are mapped in Figure 2.10. Using n historical price changes δS_i and δP_i for respectively the share and the convertible bond, we can determine the slope $\hat{\Delta}$ that fits best the data set $\{\delta S_i, \delta P_i\}_{i=1,...,n}$. This is a straightforward application of ordinary least squares:

$$\hat{\Delta} = \underset{\Delta}{\operatorname{argmin}} \sum_{i=1}^{n} (\delta P_i - \Delta \delta S_i)^2 \tag{2.30}$$

Table 2.6   Characteristics of the mandatory convertible issued by Archer Daniels

ARCHER DANIELS 0.875% February 15, 2014			
ISIN	US039483AV49	SEDOL	B1RVDW5
ISSUE DATE	February 15, 2007	ISSUE PRICE	100
ISSUE SIZE	$1 150 mn	FACE VALUE	1000
STOCK	ARCHER DANIELS	MATURITY	February 15, 2014
C_r	23.30		
CURRENCY	USD		
COUPON	0.875%	FREQUENCY	SEMI-ANNUAL

Source: Prospectus.

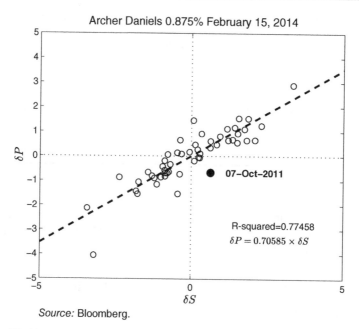

Source: Bloomberg.

Figure 2.10 Weekly share price changes versus changes in the price of the Archer Daniels 2014 convertible bond observed during 2011.

In this particular case, the slope $\hat{\Delta}$ fitting the linear model to the data is equal to 0.706. The R-squared (R^2) or coefficient of determination[10] obtained from applying such a single-factor linear model is 77.5%. This number implies that using the linear model described in Equation (2.19), share price changes δS only explain 77.5% of the price movements δP in the particular case of the Archer Daniels convertible.

[10] The coefficient of determination, a number between 0 and 1, is used in the context of statistical models where a model f is used to estimate the value of a particular variable y. Suppose we have n values for the variable we want to model. For each value y_i, there is a corresponding modeled value f_i. This leaves us to define the following variances:

- **Total variance:** SS_T

$$SS_T = \sum_{i=1}^{n} (y_i - \bar{y})^2 \tag{2.31}$$

with

$$\bar{y} = \frac{1}{n} \sum_{i=1}^{n} y_i \tag{2.32}$$

- **Unexplained variance:** SS_U

$$SS_U = \sum_{i=1}^{n} (y_i - f_i)^2 \tag{2.33}$$

R^2 is defined as:

$$R^2 = 1 - \frac{SS_U}{SS_T} \tag{2.34}$$

This hands-on exercise tells us that relying solely on one single risk component such as share price changes to explain the dynamic behavior of the convertible is far from perfect. The R-squared of 77.5% reveals that other elements will intervene in the valuation of the convertible. Equity risk is certainly not the only thing, and there are in this particular convertible several anomalies that deserve our attention. For example, the 7-day period from September 30 to October 7, 2011 illustrates how an increase in the share price from \$24.98 to \$25.45 failed to lift the price of the Archer Daniels convertible. The convertible price in this specific week even decreased from 99.64 to 98.97. This observation indicates the need to construct a multi-factor valuation model that also takes into account other components such as, for example, credit spread volatility or interest rate volatility.

Non-linear Components of Risk

The Archer Daniels example pointed out how share price changes drive changes in the convertible bond price. In this single-factor model, we limited ourselves to a linear model:

$$\delta P = \widehat{\Delta} \delta S \tag{2.35}$$

A natural extension to this would be to take convexity into account:

$$\delta P = \widehat{\Delta} \delta S + \frac{1}{2} \widehat{\Gamma} \delta S^2 \tag{2.36}$$

Again we can use least squares to fit the data to the model described in Equation (2.36). This time we have to find values for both $\widehat{\Delta}$ and $\widehat{\Gamma}$ that minimize the error between the modeled price changes of the convertible and its observed price changes δP_i:

$$(\widehat{\Delta}, \widehat{\Gamma}) = \operatorname*{argmin}_{\Delta, \Gamma} \sum_{i=1}^{n} (\delta P_i - \Delta \delta S_i - \frac{1}{2} \Gamma (\delta S_i)^2)^2 \tag{2.37}$$

The R-squared from this non-linear model improves marginally from 77.5% to 77.9% (Figure 2.11). Hence, incorporating gamma offers a minor improvement.

Two Linear Risk Components

A natural extension to a single-factor model would be to include interest changes δr. Such an approach builds further on the linear model of Equation (2.19). The sensitivity of the convertible bond price to interest rate changes is given by *rho*:

$$\delta P = \frac{\partial P}{\partial S} \delta S + \frac{\partial P}{\partial r} \delta r + \dots \tag{2.38}$$

with

$$\Delta = \frac{\partial P}{\partial S}$$

$$rho = \frac{\partial P}{\partial r}$$

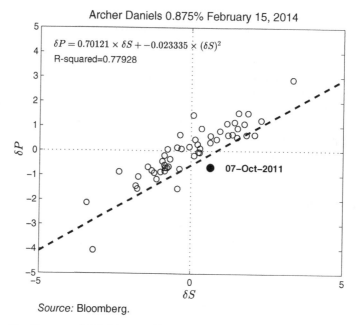

Source: Bloomberg.

Figure 2.11 Non-linear model linking weekly share price changes to changes in the price of the Archer Daniels 2014 convertible bond observed during 2011.

Fitting the historical weekly observations of share price, bond price, and interest rate changes $\{\delta S_i, \delta P_i, \delta r_i\}_{i=1,\dots,n}$ to the linear model described in the equation above can again be realized using a least-squares approach:

$$(\hat{\Delta}, \widehat{rho}) = \underset{\Delta, \rho}{\arg\min} \sum_{i=1}^{n} (\delta P_i - \Delta \delta S_i - rho \delta r_i)^2 \tag{2.39}$$

The obtained linear fit is represented in Figure 2.12 and shows the negative impact of increases in the interest rate ($\delta r > 0$) on the price of the convertible bond. This linear two-factor model brings us a value of R-squared which is marginally higher (79.4%) than in the previous statistical fit. In the case of Archer Daniels, a linear two-factor model has more explanatory power than a non-linear single-factor model based only on share price changes while excluding any other parameter.

Two Non-linear Risk Components

Finally, we can combine Δ and *rho* into a setting where the convexity of the convertible bond's price versus the two factors S and r is taken into account:

$$\delta P = \frac{\partial P}{\partial S} \delta S + \frac{\partial P}{\partial r} \delta r + \frac{1}{2} \frac{\partial^2 P}{\partial S^2} (\delta S)^2 + \frac{1}{2} \frac{\partial^2 P}{\partial r^2} (\delta r)^2 + \frac{\partial^2 P}{\partial r \partial S} \delta S \delta r + \dots \tag{2.40}$$

The non-linear fit is represented in Figure 2.13. An overview of the different regression methods and their corresponding values for R-squared is given in Table 2.7. The Γ component

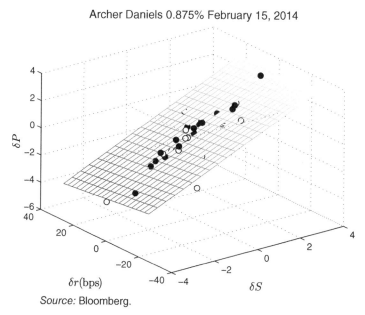

Source: Bloomberg.

Figure 2.12 Weekly share price and interest changes versus changes in the price of the Archer Daniels 2014 convertible bond observed during 2011. $\widehat{\Delta} = 0.72$ and $\widehat{rho} = -0.015$.

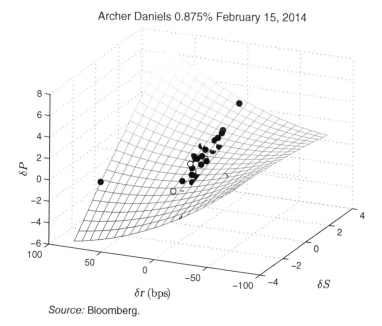

Source: Bloomberg.

Figure 2.13 Weekly share price and interest changes versus changes in the price of the Archer Daniels 2014 convertible bond observed during 2011.

Table 2.7 Values of R-squared obtained for the different regression methods

R-squared (%)	Δ	Δ, Γ
Single factor: S	77.5	77.9
Two factors: S, r	79.0	82.0

also contains cross-terms such as $\frac{\partial^2 P}{\partial r \partial S}$. This table carries the main conclusion that single-factor models lag multi-factor models in explanatory power.

2.3.2 Delta

The most important and probably most looked at risk component of a convertible bond is its underlying equity risk. This is measured by the delta. Delta (Δ), as previously defined, is the first derivative of the price of the convertible P with respect to the price of the underlying common stock S:

$$\Delta = \frac{\partial P}{\partial S} \tag{2.41}$$

The delta is a linearization of the convertible bond's equity exposure. We use a real-world example to further illustrate this concept better. In Table 2.8, one can find the characteristics of the Ryland convertible which will be used as a calculation example. On June 1, 2012 the mid-market price P_0 of this convertible was equal to 97.48% and the share price was $20.45. Given these market data, the theoretical Δ obtained from a pricing model is equal to 1.76. The delta is the slope of the convertible's price curve for a particular value of S. This linearization of the convertible's price is often applied in practice. This is the so-called **dollar nuking** or **dollar neutral pricing**, which is given by the following equation:

$$P = P_0 + \Delta \times (S - S_0)$$
$$P = 97.48 + 1.76 \times (S - 20.45) \tag{2.42}$$

If the share price were to move from 20.45 to 20.65, the price of the convertible would increase to 97.83% (Equation (2.42)). This equation allows a practitioner to estimate the price change on a convertible bond for a given change in the price of the underlying share without having to rely on a valuation model. There is a caveat attached to the concept of dollar neutral

Table 2.8 Characteristics of the convertible bond issued by the Ryland Group in 2012

RYLAND 1.625% May 14, 2018			
ISIN	US783764AQ64	SEDOL	B8DG8G2
ISSUE DATE	May 14, 2012	ISSUE PRICE	100%
ISSUE SIZE	225 mn	FACE VALUE	1000
STOCK	RYLAND GROUP	MATURITY	May 14, 2018
CONVERSION RATIO	31.2168	COUPON FREQUENCY	SEMI-ANNUAL
REDEMPTION	100.00%		
COUPON	1.625%	CURRENCY	USD

Source: Prospectus.

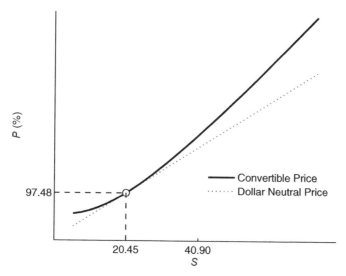

Figure 2.14   Price plot of the Ryland convertible bond. Pricing date: June 1, 2012.

pricing, however. The convexity of the position is ignored and dollar neutral pricing also assumes nothing happens to volatility levels, credit spreads, or interest rates. In Figure 2.14 the error resulting from the dollar neutral pricing is illustrated. A linear model will always under estimate the price of the convertible for a given change in the underlying share price.

For ever-increasing share prices, the delta converges:

- When the convertible's price is expressed as a percentage of the face value N:

$$\lim_{S \to \infty} \Delta = \frac{100 \times C_r}{N}$$

- For a convertible where the price is expressed as a cash amount:

$$\lim_{S \to \infty} \Delta = C_r$$

For high share prices, the convertible's price converges to parity and the convertible bond adopts equity-like behavior. The maximum value that the Ryland convertible's Δ can obtain is equal to $3.12(= \frac{100 \times 31.2168}{1000})$, as illustrated in Figure 2.15. When the share price drops far below the conversion price, the fixed-income component of the convertible will prevail and the delta is close to zero. The value of the convertible is equal to the bond floor and in this case the theoretical gamma should move to zero as well.

Convertible bond practitioners often use the delta percentage $\Delta_{\%}$ instead of Δ when dealing with the equity sensitivity of a convertible bond. $\Delta_{\%}$ ranges from 0% to 100% and is given by the following equation:[11]

$$\Delta_{\%} = \frac{\Delta \times N}{C_r \times 100} \tag{2.43}$$

---

[11] If the convertible were to trade in cash terms, $\Delta_{\%} = \frac{\Delta}{C_r}$

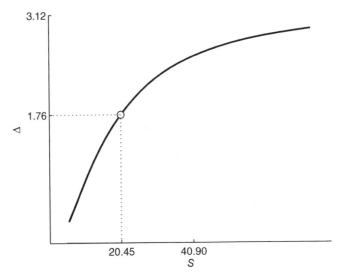

Figure 2.15   Δ of the Ryland convertible bond. Pricing date: June 1, 2012.

When calculating the corresponding $\Delta_\%$ for the Ryland convertible with $\Delta = 1.76$:

$$\Delta_\% = \frac{1.76 \times 1000}{31.2168 \times 100} = 56.38\% \qquad (2.44)$$

In Figure 2.16 the evolution of the $\Delta_\%$ is graphed.

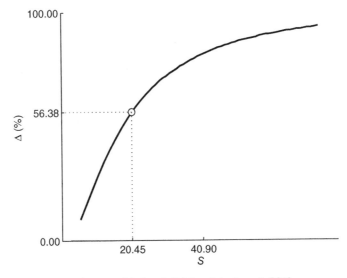

Figure 2.16 $\Delta_\%$ of the Ryland convertible bond. Pricing date: June 1, 2012.

2.3.3 Delta Hedging

On June 1, 2012 the closing price of the share is equal to $20.45. The Δ of the Ryland convertible is 1.76. A trader can now immunize the equity risk of a holding in this convertible bond by using an offsetting short position in shares. For each convertible bond a certain number of Δ_S shares has to be sold short. The position is delta-neutralized:

$$\Delta_S = \Delta \times \frac{N}{100} = \Delta_\% \times C_r = 17.6 \text{ shares} \qquad (2.45)$$

Another notion of the equity sensitivity of a convertible bond is the so-called cash delta $\Delta_\$$. It stands for the cash or dollar amount of Δ_S:

$$\Delta_\$ = \Delta_S \times S \qquad (2.46)$$

Given a share price of 20.45, the corresponding cash delta is $17.6 \times 20.45 = \$359.9$.

The dollar value of this hedged convertible bond portfolio Π is insensitive for small share price movements. We hence have that $\frac{\partial \Pi}{\partial S} = 0$ when $S = 20.45$. When the share price now moves further away from its current level, the delta-neutrality is no longer valid. For small share price movements, however, the losses and gains on the short equity position are offset by equivalent gains and losses on the convertible bond holding.

2.3.4 Different Notions of Delta

In the previous sections we encountered different notions of the delta of a convertible bond: Δ, Δ_S, and $\Delta_\%$. Each of them expressing the same thing: the equity exposure of one single convertible bond. Table 2.9 gives a summary and allows us to move quickly from one notion to the other. There is a difference depending on whether the bond is quoted in percentage terms or as a cash amount. These different definitions sometimes get mixed up and lead to obvious confusion.

Table 2.9 Overview of different deltas

| Delta | Bond Quotation | |
	Percentage	Amount
$\Delta =$	$\dfrac{\partial P}{\partial S}$	$\dfrac{\partial P}{\partial S}$
$\Delta_S =$	$\Delta \times \dfrac{N}{100}$	Δ
$\Delta_\% =$	$\dfrac{\Delta}{C_r} \times \dfrac{N}{100}$	$\dfrac{\Delta}{C_r}$
$\Delta_\$ =$	$\Delta_S \times S$	$\Delta_S \times S$

2.3.5 Greeks

Along the same lines of thought, we can define other sensitivities with respect to the different pricing parameters:

Rho	$\dfrac{\delta P}{\delta r}$	Price sensitivity of the convertible for a change in interest rates.
Vega	$\dfrac{\delta P}{\delta \sigma}$	Sensitivity for a change in the overall level of the model volatility. The measure is usually scaled toward a 1% absolute increase in the volatility level.
Theta Θ	$-\dfrac{\delta P}{\delta(T-t)}$	Price change of the convertible with the passage of time. This parameter is not a real measure in the sense of risk. Time will pass by and the convertible will expire. Option traders keep a wary eye on this greek because it is linked to the gamma of the portfolio they manage. The theta most often measures the change in value of the optional component in the convertible only. This is the option theta. The daily interest rate accrual is not taken into account.
Epsilon	$\dfrac{\delta P}{\delta q}$	Price impact for a change in the dividend yield. The dividend yield impact is in practice determined using a 10% increase in those yields.
Psi	$\dfrac{\delta P}{\delta b}$	Price impact for a change in the borrow cost of the underlying share.
Omicron	$\dfrac{\delta P}{\delta CS}$	Price impact for an increase in the credit spread CS. Typically this measure is based on a 1 bps increase in the level of the credit spread. Practitioners also call this sensitivity the Credit DV01.

The greeks are calculated as if the price function of the convertible $P(S)$ is a known and continuous function of S. The absence of closed-form formulas sometimes imposes the use of a numerical method to calculate the greeks. The value of every greek is then obtained using a finite difference approach:

$$Delta \approx \frac{P(S+h) - P(S)}{h}$$

or

$$\Delta \approx \frac{P(S+h) - P(S-h)}{2h} \tag{2.47}$$

and

$$\Gamma \approx \frac{P(S+2h) - 2P(S) + P(S-h)}{h^2} \tag{2.48}$$

In the limit where $h \to 0$, the numerical approximations of Δ and Γ converge to the correct value. The other greeks are in practice typically calculated using the following set of equations:

Rho	$P(r+0.01) - P(r)$	The yield curves are shifted upward by 100 bps.
Vega	$P(\sigma+0.01) - P(\sigma)$	The volatility in the model is bumped upward by 100 bps.
Theta	$P(t+1\ \text{day}) - P(t)$	The convertible P is priced twice. Once using today's valuation, a second time the following day $(t+1)$.
Epsilon	$P(q+0.1) - P(q)$	A 10-bps absolute shift is applied on the dividend yield of the underlying share.
Psi	$P(b+1\text{bps}) - P(b)$	Impact of charging 1 bp more in the stock borrow fee b.
Omicron	$P(CS+1\text{bps}) - P(CS)$	The credit spreads CS are increased by 1 bp.

2.4 STANDARD FEATURES

2.4.1 Issuer Call

The issuer sometimes embeds a call into the convertible bond structure. This feature grants the right to the issuer to call back the convertible bond and pays the investor an early redemption amount K. The early redemption amount K is the strike of the issuer call. The exact amount K received by the investor on the call date can be modified slightly in case of a coupon-bearing convertible bond (Section 2.4.3). After receiving a call notice, the investor can still opt to forgo the cash payment K and convert the bond into shares. There are two distinct types of issuer calls:

- **Hard call**
  A hard call makes the convertible bond unconditionally callable by the issuer. The rational issuer will in principle call back the bond if the early redemption amount K is lower than the continuation value P_c of the convertible.
- **Soft call**
  A soft call would only allow a convertible to be called back if the parity P_a reaches a particular threshold. This level is also known as the **call trigger** $(K_\%)$. As long as this trigger is not breached, the convertible cannot be called and the holder of the bond cannot be forced into conversion. The trigger condition on the parity boils down to imposing a minimum level above the conversion price C_P above which a call might be possible:

$$P_a > K_\% \tag{2.49}$$

$$S > K_\% \times \frac{N}{C_r}$$
$$S > K_\% \times C_P \tag{2.50}$$

The bond becomes callable if the share price is higher than a predetermined percentage above the conversion price. Very often this soft call condition needs to be valid for n out of m consecutive trading days. Only when this condition is met, can a call notice be sent to the investor. In this case Equation (2.28) can be used to determine the value of the convertible P_t.

Case Study: Value of the Call Feature
A call feature makes the convertible less attractive for the investor. Instead of further enjoying a steady cash flow from the coupons combined with an upside equity exposure to the underlying share, the life of the bond may be abruptly stopped. To illustrate the impact of a call feature on the theoretical value of a convertible bond, we fall back on a practical example. Consider the convertible bond issued by Shire plc, a pharmaceutical company based in the UK. The details of the convertible are summarized in Table 2.10. This convertible can be called back from May 23, 2012 onward but only if the parity reaches a level higher than 130%. If such a soft call takes place, the bond's coupon stream stops and the bond holder will have to choose between receiving the shares or the early redemption amount K. The redemption amount is, for this particular bond, equal to par. What would happen if the call clause were to be omitted from the prospectus? How much would the theoretical price of this particular convertible bond increase if the call simply did not exist at all?

Table 2.10   Characteristics of the convertible bond issued by Shire plc

SHIRE PHARMACEUTICALS 2.75% May 9, 2014			
ISIN	XS0299687482	SEDOL	B1WTP17
ISSUE DATE	May 9, 2007	ISSUE PRICE	100%
ISSUE SIZE	1100 mn	FACE VALUE	1000
STOCK	SHIRE PLC	MATURITY	May 9, 2014
CONVERSION RATIO	30.4599	CURRENCY	USD
REDEMPTION	100%	SENIORITY	SUBORDINATED
COUPON	2.75%	COUPON FREQUENCY	SEMI-ANNUAL
SOFT CALL FROM	May 23, 2012	SOFT CALL TRIGGER	130% (20 out of 30 days)
CALL PRICE (K)	100%		
PUT DATE	May 9, 2012	PUT PRICE %	100

Source: Prospectus.

The answer can be found in Figure 2.17, where the price graph has been plotted for the convertible once with and once without the call feature. The Shire convertible is denominated in USD, hence the conversion price is in USD as well:

$$C_P = \frac{1000}{30.4599} = \$32.83$$

The trigger level $K_\%$ from which the convertible becomes callable is \$42.68 or 2725 pence.[12] Figure 2.17 shows how the value of the callable version snaps back to the parity line for high enough levels of the share price. For a share price equal to 2725 pence, there is a 7.52% price difference compared to a bond without such a call feature.[13] This difference in theoretical price between the callable and the non-callable variant of the Shire convertible becomes smaller when the share price moves lower and further away from the conversion price.

The Shire 2014 convertible bond became callable 5 years after the issue date in May 2007. There was hence a period during which the bond was protected from an issuer call. Such a period is labeled a **call protection** and is part of most convertible bond structures with a call feature. Typically, bonds are as a matter of fact never made callable immediately after the issue date.

Issuers also tend to wait until parity is well above the trigger level before sending out the call notice. The reason for this is that investors often have between 30 and 90 days to make up their mind to convert into shares or to opt for the cash amount K. This is the **notice period**. Investors tend to wait as long as possible to inform the issuer about their choice taken. An issuer calling back his bond therefore runs the risk that after the expiration of the notice period, the conversion value is lower than the early redemption amount. In such a case, the issuer would have to pay out the investor an amount which is higher than the conversion value.

Calling an issue too soon, even when $P_a > K$, can go very wrong. In February 2001 VNU, a leading international publishing and information company, announced the call back of its convertible bonds at par. The real expiry date of the convertible was 4 years later but the issuer decided to redeem its convertible prematurely. On the announcement date of the decision to call back the bond, parity was 117.80%. This was a safe amount above the call price and

---

[12] Using the GBP/USD rate of 1.566 on May 24, 2012.

[13] This example was priced on May 24, 2012 using an equity volatility σ equal to 24% and a credit spread of 100 basis points.

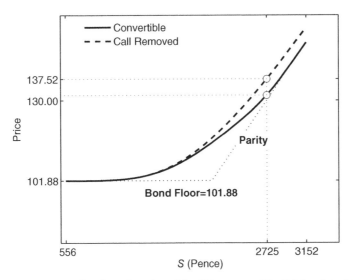

Figure 2.17   Impact of the soft call on the value of the Shire convertible. Pricing date: May 24, 2012.

implied a very high probability that the investors were going to opt for a conversion into shares. Bad luck for VNU, because after the announcement of the call the shares dropped by more than 20%. This price decline took place during the notice period of the call. Finally, on April 17, 2001 parity reached 92.5%. Of course every rational investor now responded to the call notice by not accepting a forced conversion into shares. Instead, they all went for the early redemption amount. This created an unexpected cash drain for the company. The issuer had to pay the convertible bond holders a total amount of €340 mn. To get out of this liquidity trap, VNU had to issue a new convertible to pay back the old one [93].

Modeling the fact that issuers will not call too soon can be done by adding a **call cushion** ΔK into Equation (2.28):

$$P_t = \max(P_a, \min(K + \Delta K, P_c)) \tag{2.51}$$

This call cushion is chosen arbitrarily by the convertible bond analyst modeling a particular convertible bond issue. However, the choice of such an arbitrary input can be circumvented by properly modeling the effect of the notice period on the convertible bond price [112]. Specifically, after receiving the call notice, the investor has a limited amount of time (δt) to choose either the early redemption amount K or the C_r shares. The notice period, which starts at time t, brings the investor to a comfortable position of being allowed to pick the largest of two possible payoffs at the end of the notice period ($t + \delta t$):

$$\max(C_r S_{t+\delta t}, K)$$

The equation above tells us how the call notice puts the investor long C_r shares combined with a put on these shares. The strike of this put option is the early redemption amount. This corresponds to the final payoff at $t + \delta t$ of a convertible bond CB with face value K and conversion ratio C_r. The theoretical value at time t of such a convertible is denoted $CB_{t,t+\delta t,C_r,K}$. So, when the issuer calls the bond, the early redemption amount is not K but the value of this short-dated convertible $CB_{t,t+\delta t,C_r,K}$. The issuer should base the decision to call or not on the value of this short-dated convertible bond. Instead of including an arbitrary call cushion, one can incorporate the effect of the notice period in Equation (2.51):

$$P_t = \max(P_a, \min(CB_{t,t+\delta t, C_r, K}, P_c)) \tag{2.52}$$

The rational investor will base his decision on the length of the notice period δt and parameters such as the volatility of the underlying share price. A volatile stock price, for example, will increase the value of $CB_{t,t+\delta t, C_r, K}$ and make an early redemption less likely. The issuer will probably refrain from calling back the bonds, something which would not be done if the underlying share had no volatility at all.

2.4.2 Put

A convertible bond sometimes comes with a put clause. This additional feature allows the investor to sell the bond back to the issuer at a predetermined price. This is the put price or put amount P_v. A put makes the convertible bond more attractive for a potential investor. It "sweetens" the deal and reduces the downside risk. The put does not necessarily enforce a hard floor or support under the value of a convertible bond. A put on the convertible bond issued by a low-rated company can turn out to be nothing else than a paper parachute. The impact of the put depends, as a matter of fact, on the credit quality of the issuing company. To illustrate the financial mechanics involved when a put is embedded into a convertible bond structure, we go back to the example discussed in Section 2.2.7.

Example: Put Feature

The convertible priced in Section 2.2.7 has been issued 4 years ago and is now 1 year away from its final maturity date. Each bond has a face value N equal to 100, distributes no coupons, and can be converted into 0.7 shares. The conversion price is therefore 142.86. Presently we assume that the current share price S_t in this example is equal to 74.09. The 1-year continuous interest rate r equals 2.96%. Should we put back the bond to the issuer or not?

From the current share price our model incorporates four different states possible to arrive at the final maturity date 1 year from now. Contrary to the example in Section 2.2.7, we will allow a small probability of the bond defaulting. This default probability is 1% and if such a default were to occur, the value of the convertible bond is expected to be equal to a recovery value of $30. On such a default event, we assume the stock price will drop to zero and stay there. A creditor, in contrast, would indeed still be able to recover some of the assets of the company, and recovers $30 for the convertible. This is the recovery rate π. In Figure 2.18 the four nodes to which the share price S can jump in a time step of 1 year are plotted next to the corresponding convertible bond values. The nodes $[u]$, $[m]$, and $[d]$ have a corresponding conditional probability of respectively 16.5%, 66.0%, and 16.5%. Furthermore, there is a 1% probability of a default.

The current value of the convertible P_t is given by:

$$P_t = \max(P_c, P_a, P_v) \tag{2.53}$$

- **Put amount**: $P_v = \$100$
- **Parity**: $P_a = C_r \times S = 0.7 \times 74.09 = \$51.86$

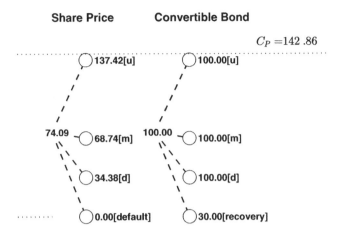

Figure 2.18   Puttable convertible bond.

- **Continuation value:** P_c is the discounted value of the expected value of the convertible in the following node $t = T$, given the fact that the current share price S_t is 74.09. This conditional expectation is:

$$E(P_T \mid S = 74.09) = 0.165 \times 100 + 0.66 \times 100 + 0.165 \times 100 + 0.01 \times 30 = \$99.40$$

From discounting this cash flow, we can determine the value of P_c:

$$P_c = \exp(-0.0296) \times \$99.40 = \$96.4$$

Using Equation (2.53), we find:

$$P_t = \max(P_c, P_a, P_v) = \max(\$96.4, \$51.86, \$100) = \$100 \tag{2.54}$$

The current value P_t of the convertible bond is equal to $\$100$ and right now we conclude that we have to put the convertible back to the issuer if we want to maximize our economic interest.

Case Study: A Put Increases the Value of a Convertible Bond

We demonstrate this on a real-world example. For this purpose consider the convertible bond issued in April 2012 by the China Hongqiao Group. The bond can be put against par in 2015, 3 years after the issue date. The characteristics of this convertible are summarized in Table 2.11.

The convertible is denominated in USD whereas the underlying share price is quoted in HKD. The closing price of the share on May 25, 2012 was 3.59 HKD. The value of 1 HKD expressed in USD is given by the exchange rate $FX_{HKD,USD} = 0.12925$. The parity of the convertible on the pricing date is equal to:

$$P_a = \frac{FX_{HKD,USD} \times C_r \times S}{N} = 52.89\% \tag{2.55}$$

Using a volatility of 25% for the underlying share and a credit spread of 900 bps, the price graph of the theoretical value of the China Hongqiao convertible has been given in Figure 2.19. There are two graphs: one for the convertible as defined in the prospectus and a second graph

Table 2.11   Characteristics of the convertible bond issued by China Hongqiao

CHINA HONGQIAO 6.5% April 10, 2017			
ISIN	XS0764303813	SEDOL	B7JMLL3
ISSUE DATE	April 10, 2012	ISSUE PRICE	100%
ISSUE SIZE	150 mn	FACE VALUE	200 000
STOCK	CHINA HONGQIAO	MATURITY	April 10, 2017
CONVERSION RATIO	227 967.945	CURRENCY	USD
COUPON	6.5%	COUPON FREQUENCY	SEMI-ANNUAL
SOFT CALL FROM	April 10, 2015	SOFT CALL TRIGGER	130% (20 out of 30 days)
CALL PRICE (K)	100%		
PUT DATE	April 10, 2015	PUT PRICE	100%

Source: Prospectus.

where the put feature has been eliminated from the instrument setup. The theoretical value of the convertible would drop from 93.83 to 89.87 if the put were to be removed given the current stock price level. The same figure also illustrates how the bond floor B_F is increased through the inclusion of the put.

Put and call features are often combined into one and the same convertible. The China Hongqiao convertible illustrates this. The put makes the structure more attractive for the investor, whereas a call has the opposite effect. Determining the value of a convertible bond P_t when both a call and a put are active can be realized by modifying Equation (2.28) or (2.53) into:

$$P_t = \max(P_a, P_v, \min(K, P_c)) \tag{2.56}$$

If none of the call or put features are adding more value than P_c, the convertible is kept alive. This corresponds to a situation where $P_c < K$ (the issuer will not call) and $P_c > P_v$ (the bond holder will not put the convertible) and $P_c > P_a$ (there is no optional conversion).

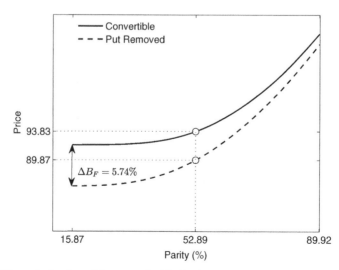

Figure 2.19   Theoretical value of the put embedded in the China Hongqiao convertible bond. Pricing date: May 25, 2012.

2.4.3 Coupons

Next we bring the coupons C_i distributed by the convertible on dates t_i into the valuation problem. Adding these cash flows or the accrued interest can be realized through a straightforward modification of Equation (2.56). This will be handled later in this book. In this section, we emphasize the economic impact of the accrued interest (Acc). The way accrued interest gets handled differs from convertible to convertible. Three different cases are to be considered:

- **Accrued on conversion $[\mathbf{1}_{(Conversion)} = 1]$**
  The bond holder receives accrued interest on conversion.
- **Accrued on put $[\mathbf{1}_{(Put)} = 1]$**
  The bond holder receives the amount P_v plus the accrued interest Acc when putting the bond back to the issuer.
- **Accrued on early redemption $[\mathbf{1}_{(Call)} = 1]$**
  The early redemption amount K is increased with the accrued interest Acc earned between the previous coupon date and the day the convertible gets called.

Equation (2.56) therefore changes to:

$$P_t = \max\left(P_a + Acc \times \mathbf{1}_{(Conversion)}, P_v + Acc \times \mathbf{1}_{(Put)}, \min(K + Acc \times \mathbf{1}_{(Call)}, P_c)\right)$$
(2.57)

Another difference can appear on the coupon date itself. Suppose, for example, that on a coupon date t, a coupon amount C is paid out to the bond holder. Then the accrued interest Acc logically drops to zero and starts accruing again from the next business day onward. The investor holds on this date a cash amount C and the value of the convertible bond. Equation (2.57) now reads a lot simpler on a coupon date:

$$P_t = C + \max(P_a, P_v, \min(K, P_c))$$
(2.58)

It is not uncommon to deal with convertible bonds where the coupon C is not paid out when the issuer calls the bond on the coupon date itself. This particular case changes Equation (2.58):

$$P_t = \max(P_a + C, P_v + C, \min(K, P_c + C))$$
(2.59)

What at first sight seems to be a minor change for anyone browsing through the prospectus can have significant valuation consequences. The timing of the coupons, the convention concerning what happens to the accrued interest on a call date or during an optional conversion, can make a large difference. Convertible bond investing requires much more than keying parameters into a valuation model. The prospectus or term sheet of any convertible bond issue needs to be sliced and diced before any valuation attempt is undertaken. Anyone not doing so exposes the entire convertible bond portfolio to documentation risk. Having a state-of-the-art numerical model to price convertible bonds is meaningless, when the input data are flawed…

Case Study: Dealing with Coupons

Two portfolio managers – let's call them A and B – have the same convertible bond in their respective portfolios. Manager A is clearly of the more lazy type, spending more time on the golf course than at the trading desk. He has made a significant investment in a fully-fledged trading system with real-time valuation and position keeping of his convertible bond investments. This trading infrastructure gives the portfolio manager a feeling of safety. But sloppiness clearly sets in, because too many of the tasks are automated. The most important source of information, the convertible bond's prospectus, remains unfortunately often unread. The data fed into the models is therefore often wrong: garbage in, garbage out. Manager B cannot rely on the same trading tools of his competitor and is clearly lagging behind from this perspective. This portfolio manager is compensating his competitive disadvantage by hard work. Indeed, where his competitor has only a limited interest in the prospectus, manager B does his homework thoroughly. He is browsing through every paragraph of the lengthy prospectus in order to get a grip on all the specific features of any particular convertible issue. This is where things go terribly wrong for portfolio manager A…

The convertible bond in which they are both invested has 6 more months to go before reaching the final maturity date. The bond has a face value of $100, a conversion ratio C_r equal to 0.7, distributes a 10% coupon, and has a soft call trigger equal to 105%. The early redemption amount K is 108% of face value. The last coupon payment was 6 months ago, which brings the current accrued interest to $5. The current trading price of the convertible is $112. Today's share price S is $150, which just meets the soft call condition. The continuous interest rate is equal to 2.96%.

The prospectus clearly states that on conversion the bond holder will be entitled accrued interest ($1_{(Conversion)} = 1$). A couple of paragraphs further, the prospectus also mentions: "… The bonds may be redeemed at the option of the issuer in whole (but not in part only) at 108% of the principal amount but will not include accrued interest. Relevant notion of this shall be given to the bond holders …" Manager A has not picked up this particular sentence from the prospectus. He assumes that accrued interest will be paid out on a call: $1_{(Call)} = 1$. However, the real condition is $1_{(Call)} = 0$.

Because of this subtle difference in instrument setup, both managers will have a different theoretical value for the same convertible bond. Moreover, they will have different views on its call risk and on top they will have a different Δ. Manager A will have it wrong, despite having the better trading tools. In this example, we will study how ugly it can get. Portfolio manager B correctly understood the fact that the accrued is not going to be paid out whenever the issuer calls the bond back, a fact which his competitor ignored.

- **Theoretical price**

  From its current price level and given a volatility of 40%, the share price can move to three different states at expiration date T: $S_T \in \{\$241.6, \$147.98, \$90.6\}$. The corresponding terminal values for the convertible bond are: $P_T \in \{\$169.12, \$110, \$110\}$. All of this happens with transition probabilities respectively equal to 16.58%, 66.34%, and 16.58%. Both managers also model the same probability of 0.50% that the stock goes into default in the final 6 months up to the maturity of the convertible bond. The recovery value is $30. The different possible share prices and convertible bond values are represented in Figure 2.20. The continuation value P_c on today's date is therefore equal to:

$$
\begin{aligned}
P_c &= \exp(-r(T - t))E(P_T \mid S = 150) \\
&= \exp(-r(T - t)) \times (0.1658 \times 169.12 + 0.6634 \times 110 \\
&\quad + 0.1658 \times 110 + 0.0050 \times 30) \\
&= \exp(-0.0296 \times 0.5) \times 119.40 \\
&= \$117.65
\end{aligned} \tag{2.60}
$$

Share Price   **Convertible Bond**

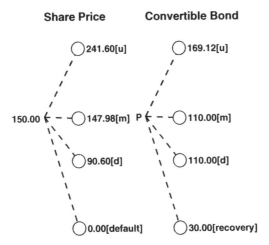

Figure 2.20   Convertible bond 6 months before the maturity date.

The convertible cannot be put ($P_v = 0$), parity P_a is equal to \$105 and in the table below a summary of the calculation of the convertible bond's price P_t can be found. P_t is given by Equation (2.57):

	Manager A Assumes that the accrued interest is added to the early redemption amount.	**Manager B** Has read in the prospectus that the early redemption amount is equal to \$108. No accrued interest will be added.
Accrued on call	$1_{(Call)} = 1$	$1_{(Call)} = 0$
Accrued on conversion	$1_{(Conv)} = 1$	$1_{(Conv)} = 1$
P_a	105	
K	100	
Acc	5	
P_t	$\max(P_a + Acc, \min(K + Acc, P_c))$ \$113	$\max(P_a + Acc, \min(K, P_c))$ \$110
Issuer call	Yes $(K + Acc < P_c)$	Yes $(K < P_c)$
Forced conversion	No $(P_a + Acc < K + Acc)$	Yes $(P_a + Acc > K)$

The calculation results in a different theoretical value P_t for the convertible bond. The portfolio manager A, who did not put enough effort into the reading and interpretation of the prospectus, obtained a theoretical price equal to \$113. He considers that the bond is trading too cheap in the market, given the fact that the current market price of the convertible is equal to \$112. His competitor, manager B, has a fair value of \$110 for the convertible.

- **Forced conversion**

  The differences in valuation for one and the same convertible bond are one aspect resulting from a lack of understanding of the convertible's documentation. Manager A has as outcome that the bond will be called by the issuer as of today. The soft call condition is satisfied and the early redemption amount $K + Acc$ is smaller than the continuation value P_c of the bond. From the mindset of this portfolio manager, the convertible carries no equity exposure. The bond will be called and the investor will receive the early redemption amount equal to $113. Hence, $\Delta = 0$.

This is a result that clearly differs from the perspective of the other portfolio manager. Manager B arrives at the correct conclusion that there will be a forced conversion at this point in time. Converting the bond into shares is the correct answer to the issuer call. At this point, holding a convertible has the same exposure as holding C_r shares: $\Delta = 0.7$.

2.4.4 Dividends

If the shares received on conversion are existing shares, the dividend entitlement is passed on immediately to the holder of these shares. The day after conversion, the investor owning those shares has the right to any dividends declared and paid out after the conversion date. But when the conversion is into new shares, that have yet to be created, the dividend entitlement comes with the necessary caveats. For some convertibles, the dividend entitlement only starts for the fiscal year during which the bonds have been converted.

An example of this particular dividend entitlement can be found in the prospectus of the convertible bond issued in 2009 by the Publicis Group, a French advertising services company (see Table 2.12). The prospectus reads:

"…The new shares issued upon conversion of Bonds shall be subject to all provisions of the Company's by-laws (statutes) and will carry dividend rights as from the first day of the fiscal year in which the Exercise Date of the Conversion/Exchange Right falls. Such shares will give holders the right, in respect of such fiscal year and subsequent fiscal years, to the same dividend (on the basis of the same nominal value) as that paid in respect of other shares with equivalent dividend rights …"

The paragraph above from the prospectus is not an easy read. An example will show clearly what is at stake. The fiscal year of the Publicis Group runs from January 1 to December 31. If an investor were to convert, for example, the bond into shares on June 8, 2012 these shares would only be entitled to dividends from the year 2013 onwards. This is the fiscal year when the dividends resulting from Publicis's profits earned during the year of conversion (2012) would be paid out to the share holders. The following case study on the Publicis convertible is a suitable exercise to get a better grip on the impact of the timing of the dividends and the dividend entitlement of the convertible bond. The dividend schedule containing the previous and scheduled ex-dividend dates and dividend payments of Publicis is given in Table 2.13.

Table 2.12   Characteristics of the convertible bond issued by Publicis

PUBLICIS 3.125% July 30, 2014			
ISIN	FR0010771899	SEDOL	B5ZR5L6
ISSUE DATE	June 24, 2009	ISSUE PRICE	27.90
ISSUE SIZE	718 mn	FACE VALUE	27.90
STOCK	PUBLICIS GROUP	MATURITY	July 30, 2014
CONVERSION RATIO	1.0030	COUPON FREQUENCY	SEMI-ANNUAL
CALL DATE	July 30, 2012	CALL TRIGGER	36.27
COUPON	3.125%	CURRENCY	EUR

Source: Prospectus.

Table 2.13   Dividend schedule of Publicis

	Publicis Dividend
Date	D (€)
June 27, 2012	0.70
June 30, 2011	0.70
June 30, 2010	0.60

Source: Bloomberg.

Case Study: Converting the Bond or Not?

The main characteristics of the Publicis convertible are summarized in Table 2.12. On Friday June 8, 2012 an investor is holding the Publicis convertible which is priced at €37.48. Like most French convertibles this is a dirty price and represents an all-in amount including the accrued interest. The price of the underlying share is, on the same date, equal to €37.8. Should the investor convert or not at this stage?

It is important to point out that the price of the stock is trading above the call trigger, which is set at €36.27. The call protection is still active, however, and only from July 30 will the bond be callable by the issuer of the bond. A forced conversion or early redemption on June 8 is therefore out of the question. Deciding whether to convert or not is based on the comparison of the conversion amount or parity with the value of the convertible. The theoretical value of the convertible on June 8, 2012 is given by:

$$P_t = \max(P_a, P_c) \tag{2.61}$$

On optional conversion no accrued interest will be paid out in this particular case. Since $P_a = C_r \times S = 1.0030 \times 37.8 = 37.91$, an investor might jump to the wrong conclusion to convert. The current market price of the bond is lower than the amount received on conversion, but using this observation to decide to convert the bond into shares would be wrong. On conversion the bond holder does not receive existing shares S trading currently at a price of €37.8, but new shares S_N. The new shares will not be entitled the dividend of €0.7, which is scheduled for June 27, 2012 and will be paid on July 2, 2012 (Table 2.13). The value of S_N is equal to S minus the present value of this dividend payment. After the ex-dividend date and assuming Publicis will not pay any further dividends in 2012, there will be no difference between the existing shares and the shares created on conversion in 2012:

- **Before June 27, 2012**

$$S_N = S - \frac{D}{1 + r \times \frac{(t_D - t)}{360}} \tag{2.62}$$

with

$$D = \text{Dividend: €0.7}$$
$$t_D = \text{Dividend Payment Date: July 2, 2012}$$
$$t = \text{Pricing Date: June 8, 2012}$$
$$r = \text{Interest Rate: 0.6\%}$$
$$S_N = S - 0.6997$$
$$= \text{€37.10}$$

- **From June 27, 2012 onwards**

$$S_N = S$$

Using the value for S_N we obtained above, P_a is equal to €37.211, a value which is lower than the price of the bond. The investor is therefore better off not converting and should keep earning interest on the bond till the next coupon payment date at an annual rate of 3.125%. After the ex-dividend date and before the start of the new fiscal year, there is no economic difference any more between the value of the new shares S_N created on conversion and the existing shares S. They carry the same dividend entitlement.

2.5 ADDITIONAL FEATURES

2.5.1 Dividend Protection

A convertible bond investor participates in the price appreciation of the underlying shares. This embedded option nevertheless puts the investor at a disadvantage compared with an equity investor, for an increase in the dividend payout is passed on to the equity investor but not to the holder of the convertible. The theoretical value of the convertible bond actually decreases when the issuer announces an improvement to the dividend schedule, for the increased dividends cause the share price to drop more on the ex-dividend date. Convertible bonds tend therefore to be issued with dividend protection features, protecting the financial interests of the convertible bond investor in case of a dividend increase during the life of the convertible. One such feature is a so-called **dividend pass through**, where any dividend payout above a threshold is passed on to the bond holder. Most often this will be realized through an adjustment of the coupon payments. The most common intervention in the terms and conditions of the convertible bond to protect the bond holder from dividend increases is handled through an **improvement of the conversion terms**. The threshold level T_D that triggers a change in the conversion ratio can be specified as an absolute cash amount or as a dividend yield. A dividend payout that does not breach T_D can in some cases be carried forward to the next dividend payment date. In such a case it will be combined with the new dividend in order to verify any possible changes to the conversion price.

Absolute Threshold

The conversion ratio is increased from C_r to C_r^*. The corresponding change in the conversion price is given by the following formula:

$$C_P^* = C_P \times \frac{S - \max(D - T_D, 0)}{S} \qquad (2.63)$$

The share price level S in the formula above is usually taken on the ex-dividend date. The change in the conversion ratio depends on the difference between the dividend D and the threshold T_D. A practical example that examines step by step a conversion price change because of a dividend is given in the following case study.

Case Study: Dividend Protection on the NYRSTAR 2014 Convertible
The characteristics of the convertible bond issued in 2009 by Nyrstar, a mining and metals company, can be found in Table 2.14. The dividend threshold $T_D = 0$, which implies that any dividend payout entails a change of the conversion price.

Table 2.14 Characteristics of the convertible bond issued by Nyrstar

NYRSTAR 7% July 10, 2014			
ISIN	BE6000211829	SEDOL	B3NVT25
ISSUE DATE	July 10, 2009	ISSUE PRICE	100
ISSUE SIZE	129 mn	FACE VALUE	50 000
STOCK	NYRSTAR	MATURITY	July 10, 2014
CONVERSION RATIO	8103.7277	COUPON FREQUENCY	SEMI-ANNUAL
CALL DATE	July 10, 2012	CALL TRIGGER	150%
COUPON	7%	CURRENCY	EUR
DIVIDEND THRESHOLD	0		

Source: Prospectus.

On July 13, 2011 the company declared a dividend of €0.15. The scheduled ex-dividend date was a few weeks later on August 9. The share price S on the ex-dividend date was equal to €7.13 and the previous conversion price was equal to €6.30. The new conversion price is calculated as:

$$C_P^* = 6.30 \times \frac{7.13 - 0.15}{7.13} = 6.17$$

The conversion ratio increased from 7949.125 to 8103.728.

Percentage Threshold

When the dividend protection specifications are stated in terms of a dividend yield, the change in the conversion price is triggered by the difference in the dividend yield q and a predetermined dividend yield threshold T_D, which is also expressed as a percentage:

$$C_r^* = C_r \times \left(1 + \max(q - T_D, 0)\right) \tag{2.64}$$

2.5.2 Take-Over Protection

A holder of a convertible bond is to a certain extent protected if the underlying share were to be the target of a take-over. A cash bid for the underlying share would take all the volatility out of the share price S. The convertible bond price P would therefore collapse to parity P_a, which could give rise to a large loss for the convertible bond investor. The prospectus deals with this particular risk. Two basic measures can be foreseen by the issuer to protect the financial interests of the convertible bond holder:

- **Change of control put**
  A change of control put will enable the convertible bond holder to return the bond back to the issuer and receive a redemption value for it. The change of control put is of course only useful when the bond is trading below this redemption amount or when the credit quality of the acquiring company is low.
- **Conversion enhancement**
  In some cases the prospectus will grant the holder of the convertible better conversion terms if the stock were to be taken out by a take-over bid. The conversion ratio will be increased according to a predefined schedule or formula. This is a so-called **ratchet** and is covered extensively in [67].

Take-over situations can be perilous when a long position in a convertible is hedged through a short position in the underlying shares. Such a hedged position can lose a lot of value since the increase of the underlying share price is not necessarily met with an equivalent improvement in the terms of the convertible bond. In such a case the losses on the short equity hedge will be larger than the gains on the convertible bond.

2.5.3 Refixes

Convertibles can also contain "reset" or "refix" features. Here, the conversion price can be revised downward. Such an event would take place in the case of disappointing stock prices. Lowering the conversion price and the resulting increase in the conversion ratio works against the interest of the share holders. They see their stake in the company diluted and are, as a matter of fact, punished twice with these kind of convertibles: once through the devaluation of the value of their shares and a second time when they are hit with the dilution.

There are two different kinds of refix possible. The first category are the **snapshot resets** where the fixing of the new conversion price takes place on one single day. The second category, known as **window resets**, is more common. Here, the resetting of the conversion ratio is based on the average closing price of the stock during a particular time frame (the window). In some converts there is an annual refixing of the conversion ratio scheduled. More information on these instruments and their pricing can be found in [196]. The initial conversion price C_P gets changed to a new price C_P^* on the reset date T_R. The change from C_P to C_P^* is based on the level of the share price S_{T_R} observed on T_R. The refixing into a new conversion price is based on the level of the share (S_{T_R}) on the reset date and its relative value compared with the two trigger levels αC_P and βC_P ($\alpha > \beta$):

$$C_P^* = \begin{cases} \alpha C_P & \text{if } S_{T_R} > \alpha C_P \\ S_{T_R} & \text{if } \beta C_P \leq S_{T_R} \leq \alpha C_P \\ \beta C_P & \text{if } S_{T_R} < \beta C_P \end{cases} \tag{2.65}$$

The new conversion price is capped by the factor α. It cannot rise above this level and it imposes a minimum level on the corresponding conversion ratio. In case of a bad share performance, the new conversion price will be lower, but will be floored by a factor β. Between those two trigger levels the parity of the convertible remains equal to one. If, for example, $\alpha = 1$ and $\beta = 0.8$, a downward reset is limited to 80% of the current conversion price. Given the cap on the conversion price, the conversion ratio cannot decrease. We have further the following extreme cases:

- $\alpha = \infty$
  There is no cap applied on the new conversion price. The higher the level of the share price S_{T_R} at the moment of the refix, the higher the new conversion price C_P^* and the lower the new conversion ratio C_r^*. The current share holders in the issuing entity are better off. They are less diluted in the case of a good share performance.
- $\beta = 0$
  There is no floor in the refixing. The more the share price falls the higher the conversion ratio. The current share holders are facing an unlimited dilution.

Table 2.15   Characteristics of the convertible bond issued by the Mingfa Group

<table>
<tr><td colspan="4" align="center">MINGFA GROUP 5.25% May 23, 2016</td></tr>
<tr><td>ISIN</td><td>XS0596873520</td><td>SEDOL</td><td>B3SXFL7</td></tr>
<tr><td>ISSUE DATE</td><td>May 23, 2011</td><td>ISSUE PRICE</td><td>100</td></tr>
<tr><td>ISSUE SIZE</td><td>1 460 mn</td><td>FACE VALUE</td><td>1 mn</td></tr>
<tr><td>STOCK</td><td>MINGFA GROUP</td><td>MATURITY</td><td>May 23, 2016</td></tr>
<tr><td>CONVERSION RATIO</td><td>315 656.563</td><td>COUPON FREQUENCY</td><td>SEMI-ANNUAL</td></tr>
<tr><td>CALL DATE</td><td>June 23, 2013</td><td>CALL TRIGGER</td><td>142%</td></tr>
<tr><td>PUT DATE</td><td>June 23, 2013</td><td>NUMBER OF RESETS</td><td>1</td></tr>
<tr><td>START RESET</td><td>January 27, 2012</td><td>END RESET</td><td>February 27, 2012</td></tr>
<tr><td>RESET DATE</td><td>March 10, 2012</td><td>RESET FLOOR (β)</td><td>0.625</td></tr>
<tr><td>COUPON</td><td>5.25%</td><td>CURRENCY</td><td>HKD</td></tr>
</table>

Source: Prospectus.

- $\alpha = \infty$ and $\beta = 0$

  There are no bounds set on the new conversion ratio. At the reset date the convertible is reset to an at-the-money level. The new conversion ratio satisfies:

$$C_r^* = \frac{N}{S_{T_R}} \tag{2.66}$$

Case Study: MINGFA 5.25% 2016 Convertible ($\alpha = 1$ and $\beta = 0.625$)
A practical example of a convertible bond with a reset will allow us to get a better understanding of this relatively exotic instrument feature. The convertible bond issued in May 2011 by the Mingfa Group, a Chinese property developer, contains one single reset. The changing of the conversion price to C_p^* was scheduled to take place on March 10, 2012. The initial conversion price C_p was equal to HKD 3.168. The other characteristics of the Mingfa convertible can be found in Table 2.15. The reset mechanism is based on the weighted average share price $\overline{S}_{T_R}$ observed during the reset window that covers the period January 27 to February 27, 2012. Only an increase can be applied to the conversion ratio. Moreover, according to the terms and conditions of the prospectus, this refix schedule is only allowed if $\overline{S}_{T_R} < 0.8333 \times C_P = 2.64$ HKD.

The new conversion price was reset on March 10 to the volume weighted average price observed during the reset window. A change in C_P was only allowed to take place if $\overline{S}_{T_R} <$HKD 2.64 and could never be lower than a floor of HKD 1.98 ($= 0.625 \times 3.168$). The new conversion price C_p^* turned out to be equal to HKD 2.61, marginally below the required level of HKD 2.64. The conversion ratio increased with 67 485.19 shares per convertible to 383 141.75 $=$ (1 000 000/2.61).

Case Study: Death Spiral Risk
For a convertible bond arbitrageur, used to managing a delta-hedged portfolio of convertible bonds, a reset increases risk. The increase of the conversion ratio forces this portfolio manager to increase the short position of shares held against a long holding in the convertible bond. The higher the level of the new conversion ratio C_r^* compared with C_r, the more shares need to be sold. In the case of a reset window, the rebalancing of the short equity hedge will typically be performed on a daily basis from the starting date to the final date of the refix window. The

market impact on the share price will be a lot smaller than a reset, where the refixing of the conversion ratio is an adjustment that takes place on one single day only.

We note that a convertible bond with a reset carries negative convexity because the Δ of the convertible will appreciate when the share price moves lower. This is caused by the fact that a decrease in S will push C_r^* upward. Negative gamma can push the share price lower during the refixing process. A lot will depend on the liquidity of the shares. If the amount of shares added to the conversion ratio is large compared with their average daily trading volume, the impact of the delta-hedging adjustment will be very visible. In such a case the adjustment of the delta hedge will push the share price further down, which will thereby increase C_r^* even more. Not surprisingly, these convertibles are called "death spiral convertibles." This nickname suggests that a firm that issues a convertible with a reset feature can be doomed. The setup and the design of the instrument might be an open invitation to short sellers who could push down the price of the equity. In [120] the negative feedback effect on a company's share price after it decides to issue a convertible with a reset is discussed at length. The authors studied over 487 convertible bonds with a refix during the period 1995–1998 and concluded that the share price of the underlying shares of these convertibles dropped on average 34%. This is a substantial negative impact, especially if one considers that the MSCI Word Index increased by 94% over the same horizon. Most of the companies studied in this sample were small cap companies and the majority of the convertible bonds had no floor on C_P^* ($\beta = 0$).

2.6   OTHER CONVERTIBLE BOND TYPES

2.6.1   Exchangeables

An exchangeable is a convertible where the issuer is not the same company as the one in which bond holders receive shares upon conversion. No new shares are being created and there is therefore no dilution on the existing share holders. These instruments are important for a corporate (e.g., News Corp) that has a large stake in another company (e.g., BSkyB) and wants to reduce its holding going forward. Using a convertible bond, the corporate actually enters into a forward sale of this stake, for the underlying share can be sold against the conversion price of the convertible. In the example of the exchangeable defined in Table 2.16, News Corp can sell its stake in BSkyB to the market by issuing this exchangeable bond. The actual ownership of the shares, however, will only change once this bond is converted by the investor. Until this date, News Corp will keep receiving dividends on its stake in BSkyB. Regardless of this

Table 2.16   Characteristics of the exchangeable into BSkyB issued by News Corp

BSkyB/News Corp 0.750% March 15, 2023			
ISIN	US65248V3042	SEDOL	2491334
ISSUE DATE	March 18, 2003	ISSUE PRICE	100%
ISSUE SIZE	1655 M		
STOCK	BSKYB	ISSUER	NEWS CORP
STOCK CURRENCY	GBP	BOND CURRENCY	USD
CONVERSION RATIO	77.09	FACE VALUE	1000
REDEMPTION	100.00%	MATURITY	March 15, 2023
COUPON	0.75% (30/360)	FREQUENCY	SEMI-ANNUAL

Source: Prospectus.

Table 2.17 Characteristics of the synthetic convertible on Vivendi issued by Natixis

NATIXIS 0.25% April 7, 2014			
ISIN	XS061024528	CURRENCY	EUR
ISSUE DATE	April 7, 2011	ISSUE PRICE	100%
ISSUE SIZE	1655 M		
STOCK	VIVENDI	ISSUER	NATIXIS
CONVERSION RATIO	2347.969	FACE VALUE	50 000
REDEMPTION	100.00%	MATURITY	April 7, 2014
COUPON	0.25%	FREQUENCY	ANNUAL

Source: Prospectus.

conversion happening or not, News Corp has already received the proceeds of this sale upfront through the issue of this convertible. The credit risk of this instrument is determined by the issuer, not the underlying share. A bankruptcy could make a delivery of the underlying shares impossible. This convertible structure can also become attractive from a credit risk point of view for the investor. When the underlying shares are ring-fenced and hence isolated from the issuing company, they are protected from any claim on the issuing company in case of default. Thus, default of the issuing company will have no impact on the parity of the convertible.

2.6.2 Synthetic Convertibles

A synthetic convertible bond is a package consisting of a bond to which a warrant or an option on an underlying share is attached. Such a convertible is typically structured by an investment bank to meet the needs of an interested investor base. The maturity, conversion price, coupon structure, etc. have been tailor-made to match the particular requirements of the investors. A synthetic convertible is an equity-linked structure, its credit risk is tied to the quality of the issuing bank while the equity exposure is coming from the underlying share.

An example of such a convertible is the €10 mn synthetic convertible bond on Vivendi issued by Natixis, a French bank (Table 2.17). The structure is driven by the particular needs of a professional investor. It is the task of the structuring desk of the investment bank to come up with terms and conditions that suit the potential buyer. In most cases, the initiative comes from a professional investor looking to buy exposure to a company through a tailor-made synthetic convertible bond. These investors forward their investment request to several competing trading desks; the best offer wins and gets the deal.

Example: Constructing a Synthetic Convertible
On May 18, 2012 an investment bank is contacted by a fixed-income investor seeking to purchase a short-dated bond that is convertible into shares of Apple (Table 2.18). The investor manages a bond portfolio and has a clear investment mandate that prohibits him from owning a direct investment in shares or warrants. Convertible bonds would be allowed, however. Unfortunately, no convertible bond had been issued so far with Apple as underlying stock. A synthetic convertible will help the fund manager to steer around this cliff.

The main ingredient to engineer a solution for the fund manager's problem is most likely the call warrant on Apple shares issued by Sociéte Générale in November 2011. The price of the warrant is $1.85 on May 19, 2012. The warrant expires on December 21, 2012. This short

Table 2.18   Characteristics of a European call warrant on Apple, issued by Sociéte Générale

APPLE CALL WARRANT 500 December 21, 2012

ISIN	FR0011153634	CURRENCY	USD
ISSUE DATE	November 22, 2011	ISSUE PRICE	10.73
ISSUE SIZE	5 M		
STOCK	APPLE	ISSUER	SOCIÉTÉ GÉNÉRALE
STRIKE	500	SHARES/WARRANT	0.025
PRICE	1.85	MATURITY	December 21, 2012

Source: Bloomberg.

maturity of 217 days fits perfectly the requirements of the potential client, who made clear that his intentions were to acquire a short-dated synthetic convertible bond. Assuming a face value for each of the bonds of $100, the first step in this case study is to determine the number of shares C_r in which the synthetic convertible can be converted if the warrant described in Table 2.18 is going to be incorporated in the package. The final payoff of the synthetic convertible depends on the value S_T of the Apple shares on the maturity date and is given by:

$$P_T = \max(\$100, C_r S_T) \tag{2.67}$$

$$= \$100 + C_r \times \max\left(S_T - \frac{\$100}{C_r}, 0\right)$$

The equation above shows how the synthetic convertible consists of a zero-couponbond and C_r European call warrants with strike $100/C_r$. Because the strike of the warrant is $500, the conversion ratio of the bond is:

$$C_r = \frac{100}{500} = 0.2 \tag{2.68}$$

Hence a zero-coupon bond with a face value of $100 needs to be combined with 0.2 call warrants, where one share of Apple can be purchased for $500. The Apple warrant issued by Sociéte Générale only gives 0.025 shares per warrant. This implies that each synthetic needs to be combined with eight of the warrants into one package. This corresponds to an investment of $14.8. Using an interest rate of 1.06%, the value of the zero-coupon component of the synthetic convertible is:

$$\frac{\$100}{(1 + 0.0106 \times \frac{217}{365})} = \$99.37 \tag{2.69}$$

The fair value of the synthetic convertible with a face value of $100 and a conversion ratio of 0.2 shares of Apple is **$114.17** (=14.8 + 99.37).

2.6.3   Cross-Currency Convertibles

Convertible bonds are international securities. The currency denomination of the convertible bond is not necessarily limited to the currency of the underlying shares. The exchange rate between the stock and the bond currency is given by FX_{SB}. This is the number of units of the bond currency one has to pay to own one single unit of the stock currency. The underlying share price expressed in the bond currency (S_B) is given by:

$$S_B = \frac{S}{FX_{BS}} = S \times FX_{SB} \qquad (2.70)$$

The cross-currency convertible incorporates currency risk within the convertible bond structure. The parity P_a of the convertible bond is the value of the underlying amount of shares and this amount clearly depends on the level of the exchange rate:

$$P_a = \frac{C_r \times S \times FX_{SB}}{N} \qquad (2.71)$$

An investor holding a cross-currency bond is not only long in shares but also holds an implied long position in the currency of the underlying stock versus the currency of the bond. Since the conversion ratio is fixed, the value of the shares received appreciates when the stock currency increases versus the bond currency. Next to a delta for the equity exposure, there is in the particular case of a cross-currency bond also a delta (Δ_{FX}) measuring the impact of a change in FX_{SB} on the theoretical value of the convertible:

$$\Delta_{FX} = \frac{\partial P}{\partial FX_{SB}} \qquad (2.72)$$

$$= \frac{\partial P}{\partial S_B} \times \frac{\partial S_B}{\partial FX_{SB}}$$

$$= \Delta_S \times S$$

$$= \Delta_\$$$

The long exposure in the underlying currency of stock versus the currency of the bond is given by $\Delta_\$$. This currency exposure is equal to the cash equity delta of the convertible bond. This is a dynamic exposure; the currency exposure increases for increasing share prices and moves to zero with the convertible bond price approaching the bond floor.

Example: Cross-Currency Exposure

An example of a cross-currency bond is the Premier Oil convertible. The bond issued by this international oil and gas exploration company is denominated in USD, but the underlying share is denominated in GBP. The characteristics of this bond are given in Table 2.19.

Table 2.19   Characteristics of the convertible bond issued by Premier Oil

PREMIER OIL 2.675% June 27, 2014			
ISIN	XS0304206161	SEDOL	B1Z7615
ISSUE DATE	June 6, 2007	ISSUE PRICE	100%
ISSUE SIZE	250 mn	FACE VALUE	1000
STOCK	PREMIER OIL	MATURITY	June 27, 2014
CONVERSION RATIO	149.3976	CURRENCY	USD
COUPON	2.675%	COUPON FREQUENCY	SEMI-ANNUAL
SOFT CALL FROM	July 11, 2012	SOFT CALL TRIGGER	130%
CALL PRICE (K)	100%		

Source: Prospectus.

On June 8, 2012 the stock closed at a price of 353 pence and the $\Delta_\%$ of the convertible under a certain model was equal to 43%. What is the currency exposure resulting from a position of 500 of these convertible bonds?

The investor is long GBP (stock currency) versus the USD (bond currency). The delta cash from a holding of 500 bonds is equal to this implied currency exposure. From Equation (2.73):

$$\Delta_{FX} = \Delta_\$ = 500 \times \Delta_\% \times C_r \times S = 113\,385.31 \text{ GBP} \tag{2.73}$$

The investor would need to sell 113 385.31 GBP against USD in order to immunize this cross-currency risk. The number of shares that would need to be sold short against this long convertible bond position is $\Delta_\% \times C_r \times 500 = 32\,120$ shares. This represents the same cash amount in GBP as the currency exposure calculated in Equation (2.73). Both currency and equity exposure have the same cash amount, equal to 113 385.31 GBP. In risk terms, the equity exposure is, in this example, more important than the embedded currency risk. The historical volatility of the GBP/USD exchange rate was, on the calculation date of this example, 5 times smaller than the historical equity volatility observed over the same horizon.

2.6.4 Reverse Convertibles

Reverse convertibles are bonds where the investor is reimbursed with either a number (C_r) of shares (S) or the face value (N). This choice is in the hands of the issuer, not the investor. Contrary to the convertible bonds, it is the issuer who has the right to convert the bond at the expiration date into shares, not the investor. An optional conversion prior to the maturity date is not part of a reverse convertible bond. The holder of the reverse convertible typically receives periodic coupons. The payoff at maturity is given by:

$$\min(N, C_r \times S) \tag{2.74}$$

Rearranging the terms in the equation gives:

$$N - \max(0, N - C_r \times S) \tag{2.75}$$

The reverse convertible is therefore the sum of a bond with face value N and a short put option on C_r underlying shares. The strike of the put is the face value of the bond. Because of the embedded short put, the price of the reverse convertible is lower than the price of an equivalent bond having the same face value and coupon structure. The buyer of such an instrument has sold a put option on the underlying shares. The proceeds of this put option lower the price of the bond but can force the holder of the reverse convertible to accept delivery of the underlying shares. The proceeds of the short put are used by the issuer to generate a higher yield than in the case of the ordinary bond yield.

The issuer of a reverse convertible is typically an investment bank with the capability to hedge the risk of this instrument because of their trading desk's access to the options market. The more expensive the embedded put, the higher the embedded coupon in the deal. These instruments were issued in large amounts in 1998 when the market witnessed its very first important increase in implied volatility levels after the LTCM collapse. In some jurisdictions, however, they were banned for a while because inexperienced retail investors were reimbursed in cheap shares instead of being redeemed the face value of the bond. Often investors were misled by the large coupon and did not fully understand what they were investing in.

Table 2.20   Characteristics of the convertible preferred issued by Monarch Financial Holding

MONARCH 7.8%			
ISIN	US60907Q2093	SEDOL	B4QRWJ5
ISSUE DATE	March 3, 2009	ISSUE PRICE	$25
ISSUE SIZE	800 000 SHARES	MATURITY	PERPETUAL
STOCK	MONARCH FINANCIAL HOLDING	CURRENCY	USD
CONVERSION RATIO	3.125	FACE VALUE	25
CALL TRIGGER	$10.4	CALL PRICE	5
COUPON	7.8%	FREQUENCY	QUARTERLY

Source: Prospectus.

2.6.5   Convertible Preferreds

The conversion feature can also be blended into a preferred stock. Such a combination leads us to a convertible preferred. An example of such a preferred security is the perpetual issued by Monarch Financial Holding, a bank holding company headquartered in Chesapeake, VA. The 7.8% coupon paid out quarterly by this preferred structure is non-cumulative and can therefore be skipped. Such an event would not trigger a default of the issuer. Each preferred has a face value of $25 and can be converted by the investor into 3.125 shares. This convertible preferred contains an issuer call as summarized in Table 2.20.

2.6.6   Make-Whole

In some cases a make-whole feature is added to the convertible bond setup. This provision makes the convertible more attractive to the buyer. A make-whole provision softens the relatively harsh effects of an issuer call where the investor either accepts the early redemption amount K or converts the bond into C_r shares. In the case of a make-whole feature the early redemption amount is increased by a make-whole premium M. This supplementary cash flow could, for example, be equal to the present value of all the coupon payments that would be received if the issuer had not decided to call back the bond. The value of the convertible bond P_t at time t can be obtained by modifying Equation (2.56):

$$P_t = \max(P_a, P_v, \min(K + M, P_c)) \tag{2.76}$$

The make-whole provision can also be achieved without increasing the early redemption amount K. Upon a call, the conversion ratio could for example be improved. This raises the amount of shares the bond holder would receive on a forced conversion, while the conversion ratio for the optional conversion remains unchanged.

2.6.7   Contingent Conversion

The contingent conversion feature specifies that the conversion by the holder can only happen under certain conditions. These conditions may refer, for example, to particular periods in the year when conversion would be allowed or to certain minimum share price levels.

2.6.8   Convertible Bond Option

A convertible bond option is used by market participants who want to strip the convertible bond of its credit exposure. These options are also called Ascots. Through a convertible bond option, the credit risk of the convertible is considerably reduced. On default of the underlying convertible, only the premium of the bond option is lost. An investment in the convertible bond instead would result in a much larger loss. Ascots are covered in depth in [67].

2.7   CONVERTIBLE BOND TERMINOLOGY

2.7.1   144A

Convertible bonds in the United States fall like any other capital-raising instrument under the Securities Act of 1933. This act is there to protect the investors against fraud. Any company in the United States that wants to issue bonds, convertible bonds, or shares must register this intention with the SEC. This public registration process is long and would blur any attempt by the issuer to quickly raise convertible debt whenever the market circumstances would be perfect to do so. This is where the 144A rule offers, since 1990, a fast-track process for companies looking to raise capital. These 144A bonds can only be sold to qualified investors and are kept initially off-limit for the retail public. Once the bond gets registered, individual investors are also free to trade in these securities.

2.7.2   Fixed-Income Metrics

Over the years, the convertible bond terminology has inherited a large set of derivative risk measures from derivative traders, having moved into the convertible bonds scene. These metrics, that measure the sensitivity of the convertible bond's price to a change in the pricing parameters, have been covered in Section 2.3.5. Managers of corporate bond portfolios also have a keen investment interest in convertible bonds. These investors invaded convertible bond desks with their own typical fixed-income language. Fixed-income investing is indeed all about yield and duration. These risk measures need to be carefully interpreted in the convertible bond space since they are based on the notion that a convertible bond can be reduced to a stream of cash flows: N_c coupons C and the face value N. The optionality and corresponding possible conversion into shares is ignored in this concept. Since fixed-income metrics such as yield and duration have been around a long time, long before the Black–Scholes equation and its "greeks" surfaced on convertible bond desks, it should not be a surprise to see how a lot of investors still deal with convertibles solely using these corporate bond concepts. The different yield measures are going to be explained by taking the Micron Technology bond described in Table 2.21 as an example. On June 15, 2012 the mid-market quote P for the bond was 85% and its accrued interest Acc equaled 0.56%.

Current Yield ($CY = 1.76\%$)   Value of the annualized coupon (C) divided by the price P of the convertible:

$$CY = \frac{1.5}{85} = 1.76\% \tag{2.77}$$

Yield To Maturity ($YTM = 2.50\%$)   Discount rate needed to make the present value of all the cash flows coming from the convertible (coupons (C) and final redemption N) equal to the dirty price of the convertible ($P + Acc$). The convertible is treated as a pure debt instrument and the embedded option to convert the bond into shares is ignored. The

Table 2.21   Characteristics of the convertible bond issued by Micron Technology

MICRON TECHNOLOGY 1.5 % August 1, 2031			
ISIN	US595112AL74	SEDOL	B6WCYG9
ISSUE DATE	August 1, 2011	ISSUE PRICE	100%
ISSUE SIZE	345 mn	FACE VALUE	1000
STOCK	MICRON TECHNOLOGY	MATURITY	August 1, 2031
CONVERSION RATIO	105.2632	CURRENCY	USD
COUPON	1.5%	COUPON FREQUENCY	SEMI-ANNUAL
SOFT CALL FROM	August 5, 2015	SOFT CALL TRIGGER	130%
CALL PRICE (K)	100%	PUT DATE	August 1, 2018

Source: Prospectus.

YTM is the rate of return for which the dirty price of the convertible P equals all the resulting cash flows earned by owning the convertible:

$$P + Acc = \sum_{i=1}^{N_c} \frac{C_{t_i}}{(1 + YTM)^{t_i}} + \frac{N}{(1 + YTM)^T} \tag{2.78}$$

The yield to maturity has been represented graphically in Figure 2.21. It shows how an initial investment in one convertible accrues from an investment of $855.6 to a final payout of $1007.5 (1000 + final coupon of 7.5). From the purchase date onward a regular stream of semi-annual coupons ($7.5) will also be collected by the convertible bond holder.

Yield To Put ($YTP = 4.17\%$)   This yield is calculated based on all the cash flows till the date of the next put. The convertible bond issued by Micron Technology is puttable by the investor on August 1, 2018. Including a final coupon of $7.5, this corresponds to a cash flow of $1007.5 and yields 4.17%.

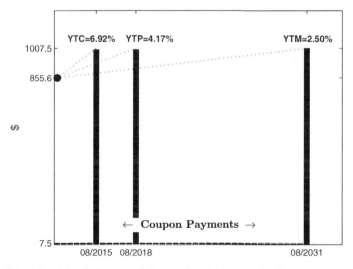

Figure 2.21   Schedule of the different cash flows when the Micron Technology convertible is called, put, or kept until the final maturity date.

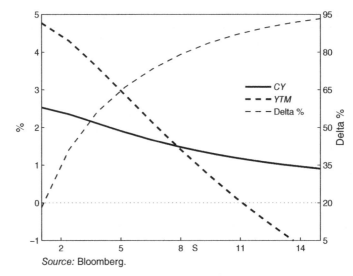

Source: Bloomberg.

Figure 2.22 Yield to maturity (*YTM*) and current yield (*CY*) for different share price levels for the Micron Technology convertible.

Yield To Call ($YTC = 6.92\%$)   This yield calculation uses all the cash flows up till the call date, which is in our example, August 5, 2015. This yield is higher here than the yield to put and the yield to maturity. Given the current price of the convertible, a rational issuer will indeed not call back the bond. Such a decision would offer the highest yield to the investor.

Yield To Worst ($YTW = 2.50\%$)   This is the lowest yield of the three previous yield definitions.

Blended Yield ($BY = 1.99\%$)   Using yields in convertible bond valuation can easily lead to wrong decisions. This is a zone with financial quicksand. Figure 2.22 is a perfect illustration of this. An increasing share price S increases the value of the embedded option within the convertible bond. Convertibles with high deltas are much more than vanilla fixed-income investments. Here the concept of yield to maturity becomes blurred. In the case of the Micron Technology convertible, and using market data as of June 16, 2012, Figure 2.22 shows how the yield to maturity becomes negative when $S > \$10.9$. For a high-delta convertible, the concept of current yield still has value, however. The convertible bond investor keeps collecting the $\$7.5$ coupon every 6 months and the current yield (CY) hence corresponds to the annualized return on the price of the convertible bond if all market parameters such as share prices, interest rates, etc. remain unchanged.

For convertibles where the share price is trading far below the conversion price, the delta is low and using a yield to maturity makes much more sense. The difference between the convertible and a straight corporate bond has almost vanished at this share price level. This leads to the concept of a blended yield BY, where current yield and yield to maturity are combined into one singe number. In the particular case of the Micron Technology bond, $\Delta_\% = 67.34\%$ and the blended yield BY is equal to 1.99% (calculation date: June 15, 2012):

$$BY = \Delta_\% \times CY + (1 - \Delta_\%) \times YTM \tag{2.79}$$

Macaulay Duration ($D_{Mac} = 16.35$ years)   The standard textbook definition of the Macaulay duration [121] tells us that D_{Mac} measures the weighted average number of years we have to wait for the cash flows to be paid out from a convertible bond structure. The cash flows consist of the face value N and the coupons C. If the bond were to distribute no coupons at all, the Macaulay duration would be equal to the remaining maturity T of the convertible bond. Macaulay duration is again a risk measure inherited from the fixed-income world which ignores any embedded equity optionality. The duration of the Micron Technology convertible on June 16, 2012 was equal to 16.35 years but ignored the fact that the bond can be put and called respectively 6.13 and 3.12 years from the pricing date.

Modified Duration ($D_{Mod} = 16.29$ years)   The modified duration D_{Mod} measures the percentage price change ($\frac{\delta P}{P}$) of the bond for a change in the yield δY:

$$D_{Mod} = -\frac{1}{P}\frac{\partial P}{\partial Y} \tag{2.80}$$

Macaulay duration and modified duration are both termed "duration." Because of this, the two concepts very often end up mixed. It is important to keep in mind the conceptual distinctions between them. Macaulay duration is a time measure with units in years, whereas the modified duration is a sensitivity measure. In the case of continuous yields, both durations are equal in value. The calculation of the Macaulay duration for a convertible with a continuous compounded yield Y is given by:[14]

$$D_{Mac} = \sum_{i=1}^{N_c} t_i \left[\frac{C_{t_i} \exp(-Y \times t_i)}{P} \right] + T \left[\frac{N \exp(-Y \times T)}{P} \right] \tag{2.81}$$

The continuous yield Y is the yield to maturity obtained by applying a continuous compounding in Equation (2.78):

$$P + Acc = \sum_{i=1}^{N_c} C_{t_i} \exp(-Yt_i) + N \exp(-YT) \tag{2.82}$$

From the definition of the modified duration:

$$\frac{\delta P}{P} = -D_{Mod} \times \delta Y \tag{2.83}$$

$$= \frac{1}{P}\frac{\partial P}{\partial Y}\delta Y$$

$$= \left[\sum_{i=1}^{N_c} -t_i C_{t_i} \exp(-Y \times t_i) - TN \exp(-Y \times T) \right] \frac{\delta Y}{P}$$

$$= -D_{Mac} \times \delta Y$$

Equation (2.83) illustrates the fact that for continuous yields both duration concepts are equal in value. Equation (2.83) also illustrates the opposite behavior of yield and bond

---

[14] Practitioners sometimes prefer to calculate the duration of the bond floor only. In Equation (2.81) the symbol P is replaced by B_F, the value of the bond floor.

prices: if one goes up, the other will go down and vice versa. This relationship is a linear view of a fixed-income investor of the yield sensitivity of a convertible bond. A similar linear simplification existed in the mindset of a derivative trader when applying dollar neutral pricing on a convertible bond (Equation (2.42)).

Dollar Duration ($DV01$)   Dollar duration or DV01 is the absolute change δP in the value of a bond for a unit change in the yield Y:

$$DV01 = \frac{\partial P}{\partial Y} \tag{2.84}$$

It is connected to the concept of modified duration because:

$$DV01 = -D_{Mod} \times P \tag{2.85}$$

Suppose we want to quantify the impact of a 25 bps increase on the market price of the Micron Technology convertible. The current market price P is 85.0 and D_{Mod} equals 16.29. An increase of 25 bps ($\delta Y = 0.0025$) lowers the bond price by 3.46%:

$$\delta P = -16.29 \times 85 \times 0.0025 = -3.46 \tag{2.86}$$

Case Study: VaR Calculation of Micron Technology 1.5% 2031
Suppose that one wants to do a back-of-the-envelope calculation of the Value at Risk (VaR) of a portfolio with one single investment: a Micron Technology convertible bond. The VaR needs to be calculated for a holding period of 1 month and a confidence level of 99%. The obtained VaR number reflects the maximum loss the portfolio can encounter with a probability of 99% given a holding period of 1 month. There is only one chance out of a hundred that the loss could be bigger than this VaR number. The VaR$_M$ for a holding period of 1 month is obtained by applying the $\sqrt{T}$-rule on the annual VaR:

$$\text{VaR}_M = \sqrt{\frac{1}{12}} \text{VaR} \tag{2.87}$$

Several VaR methods exist, but we will use the parametric VaR model as explained in [67]. The parametric VaR is founded on the concept that the price returns of the parameters driving the value of the financial instrument follow a normal distribution.

A fixed-income investor would consider only one source of risk driving the price of the convertible: the yield Y. The link between the increase in the yield and the decrease in the bond is the duration D_{Mod}. In his eyes the VaR would depend exclusively on the annual volatility of the yield (σ_Y). For a 99% confidence interval, the investor will apply shocks of $2.33 \times \sigma_Y$ on the value of Y.[15]

The equity investor has a different view on risk. This investor considers the convertible as equivalent to a number of shares and relies solely on the Δ of the convertible bond,

---

[15] $2.33 = N^{-1}(0.99)$, with $N(x)$ the cumulative normal distribution function.

whereas a corporate bond investor would use duration in the VaR calculation. A summary of the calculations is given in below:

	View on Risk	
	Equity Investor	Bond Investor
Formula	$\delta P = \Delta \times \delta S$	$\delta P = -D_{Mod} \times P \times \delta Y$
Parameters	$\sigma_S = 47.34\%$	$\sigma_Y = 59.20\%$
	$S = 5.89$	$Y = 2.47\%$
	$\Delta_\% = 67.3\%$	$C_r = 105.2632$
Sensitivity	$\Delta = \frac{\Delta_\% \times C_r \times 100}{N} = 7.09$	$D = 16.29$
VaR	$\text{VaR} = \Delta \times S \times 2.33\sigma_S$	$\text{VaR} = D \times P \times Y \times 2.33\sigma_Y$
	$\text{VaR} = 46.06\%$	$\text{VaR} = 47.18\%$
	$\text{VaR}_M = \sqrt{\frac{1}{12}} \times \text{VaR}$	$\text{VaR}_M = \sqrt{\frac{1}{12}} \times \text{VaR}$
	$\text{VaR}_M = 13.30\%$	$\text{VaR}_M = 13.62\%$

The equity investor sees the maximum drop of the bond over the next month being as large as 13.30%. A decrease larger than this drop from a current value of 85% to 71.7% would occur with a probability of 1%. The value at risk calculated from the viewpoint of the bond investor leads to a 13.62% drop. Yield and delta-based risk measures are very different in nature.

Fugit   This is the expected average life of the bond. This output is dependent on the model used and will hence be subject to the assumptions taken in the model. If there were to be a 100% probability that the bond will not be called by the issuer, nor put by the investor, the fugit equals the remaining time till the final maturity date.

Yield Advantage   The yield advantage is the difference between the current yield of the convertible and the dividend yield of the underlying share.

2.8   CONVERTIBLE BOND MARKET

2.8.1   Market Participants

There are more people involved in the convertible bond market than just the buyers and the sellers. Each of these accommodating participants fulfills a very particular role.

Lead Manager

The lead manager is the investment bank taking responsibility to arrange the terms and conditions of the issue and assist the corporate issuer in setting the terms of the convertible bond. This bank gets awarded the mandate by the issuer to do this. The lead manager will sometimes form a syndicate with other banks willing to underwrite the issue.

Trustee

The terms and conditions in the prospectus will be looked after by the trustee. The trustee is appointed by the issuer but stands up for the rights of the bond holders. The trustee watches, for example, over the fact that the coupons are being paid out. It is a purely administrative task in which the trustee will also keep a record of the bond holders. This administrative task becomes a very operational one, if the issuer were to default on the debt. In such a case the role of the trustee gets more important.

Paying Agent

The hybrids we discussed so far make regular payments. These payments are never made directly by the issuer. The regular coupons of the convertible bond, for example, will be paid by the paying agent to the investors on behalf of the issuer.

Market Makers

A majority but not all convertibles are quoted on an official stock exchange. By no means would this listing be a guarantee for a liquid trading environment. The listing is most often needed for regulatory reasons in order for the convertible bond to be able to be sold to institutional investors that can only invest in listed securities. The actual transaction is an over-the-counter deal through market makers. Market makers quote constantly intraday bid and offer prices for the convertibles they are active in. This is based on the pricing models of the firms they work for and their own assumptions regarding the credit and equity risk of the bond. The profit for the market makers consists of the bid–offer spread applied on the convertible price. These quotes are made available through electronic information systems such as Bloomberg or Reuters. Traders and portfolio managers can act on this information to buy or sell a convertible bond.

2.8.2 Investors

Outright Investors

This category of investors is also named "long only" and stays away from the hedging of the larger part of the convertible bond exposures in the portfolio. Currently, these investors represent the larger part of the convertible bonds' investor base. Their allocation of capital to a particular bond issue is based on their conviction in the underlying shares, the attractive yield of the bond, the inclusion of the bond in a convertible bond index, etc.

Convertible Bond Arbitrageurs

The so-called arbitrageurs will buy the convertible bond and strip the risk into different components. Those components that are considered too risky or overvalued are sold off. The remainder of the convertible bond, its unhedged risk, is kept in the portfolio. This is the typical investment style of hedge funds that are very active in this market.

The word "arbitrage" is definitively a wrong choice. An arbitrage is a risk-free trade that generates a return above the risk-free rate. Traders have a tendency to have a looser definition of the word arbitrage. In convertible arbitrage there is financial risk involved. A portfolio manager sizing up the portfolio to get higher returns from such an "arbitrage" plays a risky game. It can be seen as picking up nickels in front of a steam roller [80]. In the convertible arbitrage world, there are a lot of variations on this theme. The possibilities are endless. Most of the time the arbitrage focuses on the mechanical link between the bond and its underlying

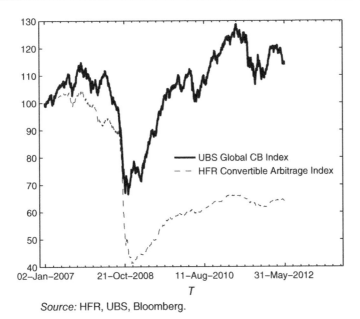

Source: HFR, UBS, Bloomberg.

Figure 2.23   Comparison of the performance of the convertible bond arbitrage strategy (using the HFR CB Arb Index) versus the performance of the UBS Global Convertible Bond Index.

share. Sometimes the credit component is hedged away together with the volatility risk. A traditional example is one where, after the convertible is bought, the investors execute some or all of the following trades:

- **Hedging the default risk** by buying protection through a credit default swap[16] on the same corporate that issued the convertible.
- **Hedging the interest rate risk** embedded in the bond. The interest rate part is hedged out by selling bond futures or by entering into an interest rate swap in the currency of the convertible bond. The swap will typically be one where the investor pays fixed coupons and receives floating interest rate.
- **Hedging the volatility risk** through equity options on the underlying stock. The convertible has an embedded option and the more volatile the underlying stock, the more valuable the embedded option. A loss in value can occur through an unexpected decrease in volatility and can be hedged by selling a listed call option on the underlying stock.
- **Hedging the equity risk** by selling a certain quantity of underlying shares. This momentarily freezes the equity sensitivity of the convertible holding.

In Figure 2.23 the performance of a convertible bond arbitrage strategy for the period 2007–2012 is compared with the returns of an outright investment into convertible bonds. The outright or long-only approach has delivered a better return than the convertible bond arbitrage strategy, which never seemed to have recovered from the sell-off in 2008.

---

[16] A credit default swap on a bond is a financial instrument where the buyer pays a quarterly fee "the spread" to the seller. In case of default of the underlying bond, the buyer of the CDS has the right to give this bond to his counterparty on the CDS and receive the face value for it.

2.9 CONCLUSION

This part of the book has given a general introduction to convertible bonds, offering a good entry point for any investor who is confronted for the first time with a prospectus of such a financial instrument. Every reader who has got a grip on the different features explained will have climbed further on the learning curve. The next chapter deals with contingent convertibles, which we will explore further using the convertible bond terminology introduced in this chapter.

3

Contingent Convertibles (CoCos)

Contingent convertibles are the newest member in the family of hybrid financial instruments and deserve everybody's attention. After a reluctant start, yield-hungry investors were very keen early 2013 to invest in these bonds. This chapter provides a detailed anatomy of the structure of these bonds, their inherent risks, and the regulatory climate in which they were conceived.

3.1 INTRODUCTION

Contingent convertible notes (CoCos) made a very modest entry into the financial landscape in November 2009, when the Lloyds Banking Group offered the holders of some of its hybrid debt the possibility to swap these holdings into a new bond with contingent conversion features [68]. A CoCo stands for a bond that will be converted into equity or suffers a write-down of its face value as soon as the bank gets into a situation where it might, for example, not have enough regulatory capital. This feature encompasses the loss-absorbing capacity of the CoCo bond. As soon as such a situation occurs, the mechanism is automatically triggered. Triggering the conversion of the bond into shares or activating the write-down of the face value takes place when the bank is still a going concern. This constitutes a major difference from bail-in capital, where the loss absorption kicks in when the bank fails. Contingent capital is a going-concern solution whereas bail-in capital is a gone-concern instrument.

This conversion into shares creates a dilution for the existing share holders. The solvency of the bank is improved under circumstances where it would typically be difficult if not impossible to go to the capital markets directly and try to raise equity. Regulators have advocated the use of CoCos since the conversion into shares or the write-down of the face value absorbs losses and keeps the bank alive without the use of tax payers' money. This is because CoCos have been designed to be truly loss absorbing, in contrast to other regulatory instruments such as hybrid Tier 1 bonds which failed during the near collapse of the financial system early 2009. Banks were unwilling to cancel the coupons on these hybrid Tier 1 structures and tax payers ended up bailing out banks.

CoCos had a rather humble start. In 2010 only one bank followed the example of Lloyds and issued contingent debt. This initiative was taken by the Dutch Rabobank. The hesitant launch of this new asset class was mainly due to the regulatory framework that was far from ready. Only after the Basel Committee made public the new set of capital requirements for banks at the end of 2010 did CoCos gain more credibility. The Basel Committee made it clear that the loss absorbency of regulatory capital was at the top of its agenda. The structure and pricing of CoCos was initially a topic of lively debate between regulators, issuing banks, rating agencies, investors, and trading desks around the globe. Gradually the dust settled and in 2011 some regulatory bodies, such as the European Banking Authority (EBA) and the Office of the Superintendent of Financial Institutions Canada (OSFI), laid out some key guidelines in the design of contingent capital notes. The EBA even went as far as designing a proper CoCo term sheet in December 2011 [91]. Regulators turned into structured product designers. Contingent capital has the possibility to be converted into shares, but this does not turn these bonds into yet another kind of convertible bond. There are similarities but also a lot of important differences between convertible bonds and CoCos. Hence, we cannot rely on traditional convertible bond pricing models to quantify the market risk of CoCos. In this book several possible pricing methods will be worked out at length. Before CoCo bonds made their first appearance in banks, insurance companies had already issued similar instruments. These instruments offered the insurance industry the possibility to provision for big one-time losses [2].

3.2 DEFINITION

At the time of writing this book, it still remains difficult to come up with a clear-cut definition for this instrument. Three years after the first CoCo issue, standardization has not yet set in. The lack of standardization reflects the uniqueness of the circumstances in which contingent capital is being issued. Some banks will issue contingent debt to respond to a particular requirement from the national regulator (UBS or Credit Suisse). Banks may issue CoCos to repay previously received state aid (KBC). Every financial institution has its own rationale [117].

Banks and regulators have been using different names for one and the same asset class. This adds to the overall confusion. What the Swiss called contingent convertibles is, for example, labeled buffer convertible capital securities (BCCS) in the member states of the European Union. The common denominator for all these instruments is their loss-absorption capacity. This is obtained by incorporating a possible conversion into shares or by having the face value of the bond written down. Through this conversion or write-down, the bond holders face a loss and this decreases the outstanding debt load for the issuing banks. An example of a CoCo bond where conversion in shares can be forced is the bonds issued by Lloyds. An example of a write-down CoCo is one of the CoCos issued by Rabobank.

- The **Lloyds** ECNs, as these CoCos were labeled, did not involve raising new capital. They were concerned with a mere swap of existing hybrid capital into this new contingent convertible. Lloyds had received state aid from the UK government and the acceptance of this state aid did not allow holders of hybrid capital to receive coupons. The only way for investors to keep receiving a steady income stream was to swap the hybrid bonds they were holding into one of the new series of CoCos issued by the Lloyds Banking Group. These instruments were issued in November 2009 and benefited from a high coupon as compensation for the risk of being converted into equity as soon as the bank's Core Tier 1 capital dropped below the trigger level of 5%.[1] The early investors in this first ever CoCo issue were 30% hedge fund investors [37].
- **Rabobank** issued a write-down CoCo bond early 2010. A trigger of this CoCo would result in a write down of 75% of the bond's face value. Rabobank was not a listed company and hence a write down is more natural than a conversion into equity. The trigger was set at a capital ratio of 7% and these contingent notes carried a non-deferrable coupon of 6.875%. The Rabobank note was very well received by the market and was twice oversubscribed.

---

[1] In Basel III this corresponds more or less to a Core Tier 1 ratio of 2.5% [9].

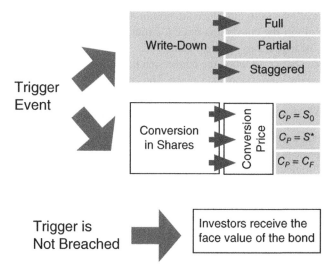

Figure 3.1   Anatomy of a CoCo.

3.3 ANATOMY

The anatomy of a CoCo bond is determined by three key components: (1) the loss-absorption mechanism, (2) the trigger event that sets the whole loss-absorbing mechanism in motion, and (3) the host instrument into which this mechanism has been embedded. See Figure 3.1.

3.3.1 Loss-Absorption Mechanism

On the appearance of a trigger event at a trigger moment t^*, the bond can be either converted into shares or receive a haircut on its face value N.

Conversion into Shares

The number of shares received per converted bond is the conversion ratio C_r. The conversion price (C_P) of a CoCo with face value N is the implied purchase price of the underlying shares on the trigger event:

$$C_P = \frac{N}{C_r} \tag{3.1}$$

If the bond is converted into shares, the loss for the investor (L_{CoCo}) depends on the conversion ratio (C_r) and the value S^* of the shares at time t^* when the trigger materializes:

$$
\begin{aligned}
L_{CoCo} &= N - C_r \times S^* \\
&= N\left(1 - \frac{S^*}{C_P}\right) \\
&= N(1 - \pi_{CoCo})
\end{aligned}
\tag{3.2}
$$

The equation above allows us to introduce the notion of a recovery rate for a particular CoCo bond (π_{CoCo}). The closer the conversion price C_P matches the market price of the shares S^* at the trigger date, the higher this recovery ratio.

A CoCo investor is better off when the conversion price is low. In such a case, more shares will be created when the conversion takes place. The current share holders, on the other hand, will prefer a higher conversion price. They want as little dilution as possible of their equity stake in the bank. We discuss three possible choices for C_P [70].

- **Floating conversion price: $C_P = S^*$**
  The conversion price is set equal to S^*, this is the share price observed at the trigger moment t^*. The value S^* logically corresponds to a low share price since the trigger logically takes place at depressed share price levels. This particular choice for C_P leads to a 100% recovery for the CoCo investor. The share holders bear the brunt of the trigger event while the CoCo holders do not take part in any of the losses because the shares are obtained at market price. So far no CoCo bond has been issued with this conversion price mechanism. From a regulatory point of view these CoCos are not accepted because they are not truly loss absorbing and dilution is unbounded.
- **Fixed conversion price: $C_P = S_0$**
  S_0 is the share price of the bank on the issue date of the contingent convertible. The number of shares created upon conversion is known and fixed at the issue date of the CoCo bond. This is in sharp contrast to the previous possibility where there was no limit on the number of shares created. This conversion mechanism has been the choice of Lloyds Bank and was incorporated in their series of contingent convertibles in December 2009 (Figure 3.2). For the Lloyds CoCos $S_0 = C_P = 59$ GB pence (GBp) (Table 3.1).

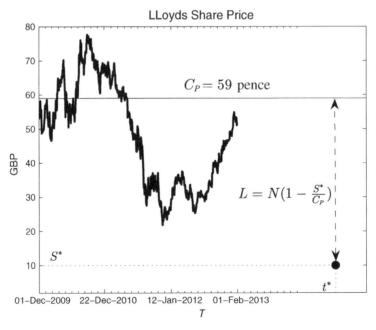

Figure 3.2   If a Lloyds CoCo bond triggers when $S^* = 10$ GBp, the CoCo investor would face a loss equal to 83% ($= 1 - \frac{10}{59}$).

Table 3.1 Summarized description of the Lloyds ECNs and the Credit Suisse BCN

	Lloyds	Credit Suisse
Full Name	Enhanced capital notes	Buffer capital notes
Issue Size	GBP 7 bn (32 Series)	$2 bn
Issue Type	Exchange	New Issue
Issue Date	December 1, 2009	February 24, 2011
Maturity	10–20 year	30 year
Yield at Issue	Libor +7–8%	Libor + 5.22%
Callable		Callable on August 24, 2016. On this call date the coupon is reset at the 5-year USD swap rate + 522 bps
Coupon	1.5–2.5% increase of the coupon of the hybrid capital the bond was exchanged for	7.875%
Coupon Deferral	None	None
Conversion Price	59 pence (=share price at issue of the ECN)	$\max(20\,USD, 20\,CHF, S^*)$
Trigger Level	5% Core Tier 1 (Basel II)	7% CET1 (Basel III)
Non-Viability Trigger	No	Yes

Source: Prospectus.

- **Floored conversion price:** $C_P = \max(S^*, S_F)$
  This conversion price offers a compromise between the two previous solutions. The conversion price is set equal to the price S^* observed at the moment the bond gets triggered into conversion, but is not allowed to drop below a certain floor S_F. This was the choice of Credit Suisse when it designed, in February 2011, its first contingent convertible. Credit Suisse does not allow the conversion price C_P to drop below either 20 CHF or 20 USD. The floor on the conversion price puts a cap on the conversion ratio. Later in the same year, the Canadian regulator (OSFI[2]) came up with a set of principles governing the design of non-viability contingent capital. It also favored a conversion method that includes a limit on the number of shares issued when the trigger event takes place [157] (Table 3.1).

Write-Down

For a bank like Rabobank, that has no listed shares, the write-down of the face value of the bond is an alternative way to impose losses. However, a bank which has its shares trading on a regulated stock exchange may also opt for a similar write-down mechanism to absorb losses. This has been the approach of UBS, Barclays, and KBC (Table 3.2). In the case of KBC, this was done because under no circumstances did one want to further dilute the strategic share holders of the bank and jeopardize their majority.

Further, there is the fact that an equity conversion could indeed constitute a disadvantage for an investor. A portfolio manager of a corporate bond fund may, for example, not be allowed to own shares. This could make a possible investment in CoCo bonds, that possibly convert into shares, very difficult. In addition, there is also the concern of the equity investors that

---

[2] Office of the Superintendent of Financial Institutions Canada.

Table 3.2 Examples of write-down convertibles

	Barclays	Rabobank	ZKB
Issue Size	$3 bn	€1.25 bn	590 mn CHF
Issue Date	November 21, 2012	March 12, 2010	January 31, 2012
Maturity	10 year	10 year	Perpetual
Yield at Issue	Libor + 6.2%	Libor + 3.5%	Libor + 2.9%
Coupon	7.625%	6.875%	3.5%
Callable	—	—	Every year starting on June 30, 2017. The call price is 100. After the first call date the coupon is equal to the 5-year swap rate + 298 bps and is reset every 5 years.
Coupon Deferral	None	None	Yes
Dividend Stopper	None	None	Yes
Write-Down	Full (100%)	Partial (75%)	Staggered (in multiples of 25%)
Trigger	CET 1 ratio	Equity capital/RWA	CET 1 Ratio
Trigger Level	7%	7%	7%
Non-Viability Trigger	Yes	No	Yes

Source: Prospectus.

after a trigger event CoCo investors own a controlling stake in the bank [161]. Both reasons may push a bank to opt for contingent capital with a write-down of the face value instead of a conversion in shares.

Three write-down mechanisms are possible:

- **Full write-down**
  In this particular kind of CoCo bond, the face value will be completely wiped out in case the bank's capital ratio fails to remain above the minimum threshold. The CoCos issued by KBC and Barclays are applications of this mechanism.
- **Partial write-down**
  The first CoCo bond with a write-down feature incorporated a haircut of 75%. This was the contingent convertible issued by Rabobank. The investor is reimbursed 25% of the face value at the trigger.
- **Staggered write-down**
  The Zuercher Kantonalbank (ZKB) is a Swiss state-owned bank that has no listed shares outstanding. From this perspective ZKB found itself in the same situation as Rabobank when designing its CoCo bond. This Swiss bank launched, in January 2012, a CoCo bond with a flexible write-down mechanism. The novelty in this issue was the fact that the investor would be imposed losses up to the point where the breach on the capital trigger was solved. The haircuts can only occur in multiples of 25%. The ZKB CoCo bond is the first example of a contingent convertible with a staggered write-down mechanism.

Some regulatory instances are open to consider CoCos that allow the decimated face value to be written up again [57]. A write-down is therefore not necessarily the end of the world since the face value does not have to be lost forever. A CoCo bond is a going-concern solution. The

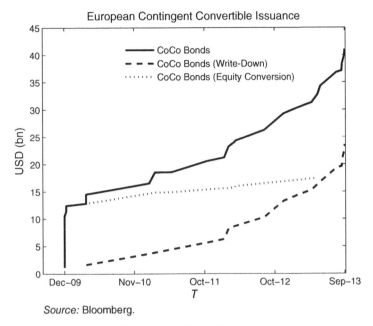

Figure 3.3 Issuance of write-down CoCos vs. CoCos with an equity conversion.

bank has been given more room to breathe after the CoCo investors absorbed some of the losses. A write-down/write-up CoCo allows investors to recover some of these losses whenever the bank is profitable again.

Write-Down Issuance

The launch of this young asset class was mainly driven by CoCos where the loss-absorption mechanism was a conversion into shares. CoCos with a write-down were initially less common. A conversion into shares gives a CoCo investor a possible compensation when the trigger is breached. The CoCo investor becomes a share holder and participates in any future price appreciation of the shares. The conversion into shares might, in contrast, become a problem for a bond investor who does not have the mandate to participate in issues with a possible conversion into equity. The conversion feature hence reduces the marketability of the instrument and it should therefore not be a surprise that we witnessed in 2013 more issuance of write-down CoCos than bonds with an embedded equity conversion. The write-down feature is also regarded as more transparent. The investor knows beforehand how much a possible loss absorption can cost. Figure 3.3 illustrates that since September 2013 there have been more write-down CoCos in Europe than CoCos with a conversion feature.

3.3.2 Trigger

Accounting Trigger

CoCo bonds with an accounting or capital ratio trigger have a loss-absorption mechanism linked to the healthiness of the bank's balance sheet. A capital ratio makes a comparison

Table 3.3 Accounting triggers of different CoCo structures compared with the reported CET1 levels. The fully loaded CET1 level corresponds to a situation where the bank's capital structure is Basel III compliant

	Trigger Level	Reported CET1	Fully Loaded CET1
Barclays	7.0	10.9	8.2
Credit Suisse	7.0	15.6	8.1
KBC	7.0	13.8	10.8
Lloyds	5.0	11.9	7.7
UBS	5.0	19.0	9.8

March 2013.
Source: JP Morgan.

between the amount of regulatory capital and the assets a bank carries on its balance sheet. These assets are weighted using a particular scheme. The highest weight goes to the riskier portion of the asset pool. This risk weighting is crucial and takes place under the supervision of the national regulator of a financial institution. On an international level, organizations such as the Bank of International Settlements and its Basel Committee play a crucial role. Their proposals help to create a level playing field amongst the internationally active banks with respect to the definition and calculation of their capital ratios.

Under Basel III, which will be covered in Section 3.5, the CET1 ratio has been put forward as a key health indicator of a financial institution. The higher the ratio, the more common equity a bank has available to deal with any unpleasant surprises in its investments (government bonds, corporate bonds, loans, etc.). The absolute minimum level of this ratio is 4.5% and it should therefore not come as a surprise that all CoCo bonds have a trigger level above this ratio. An overview of some accounting triggers that have been used and the reported CET1 levels can be found in Table 3.3.

Regulatory or Non-Viability Trigger

The presence of a non-viability clause means that the national supervisor has discretion whether or not to trigger the bond [26]. The Basel Committee's proposal to use a debt write-down or equity conversion provision in the terms and conditions of new Tier 1 and Tier 2 instruments puts emphasis on the use of such a regulatory trigger. It is sometimes argued that this discretion could reduce the marketability of a bond. The opponents of non-viability triggers claim they are a blank cheque written out to the financial authorities.

In [157], the OSFI laid out several principles to which contingent capital should adhere. Canadian contingent debt comes mandatory with a non-viability trigger. The regulator has offered some information on the circumstances that will set the trigger. The OSFI will, for example, quantify to what extent the assets owned by the bank offer enough protection to its depositors and creditors. Other elements that will be taken into consideration are a possible difficulty in rolling over short-term funding or the impossibility of raising capital to adequate levels.

Market Trigger

A market trigger is a trigger based on an observable issuer-related metric reflecting the solvency of this issuer. A natural candidate for such a metric is the share price level or the credit spread. In the academic world there is often a tendency to favor the use of market-based triggers in the construction of the contingent convertible notes. One of the arguments often held against the use of market triggers is the fact that they are thought to be prone to manipulation. An obvious example of this problem is the so-called flash crash[3] on the US stock market on May 6, 2010. In [54] the authors propose a conversion from debt to equity if the share price of a financial institution declines by, for example, more than 40% over a 1-month period. This proposal is based on the assumption that a similar correction has to result from a proper reflection of the economic health and solvency of the financial institution.

Multi-Variate Trigger

The conversion of the CoCo bond into shares could also be structured in such a way that it does not depend on one single trigger condition. One could, for example, go a step further and extend the use of an accounting trigger to also include a universal systemic trigger. The Squam Lake Working Group on Financial Regulation [179] has proposed the use of such a multi-variate trigger. The latter has bank-specific characteristics but also takes the state of the economy as a whole into account. The supervisor declares in a first step a state of emergency and accepts thereby the existence of a systemic crisis. This is the macro trigger. The second condition, a micro trigger that needs to be fulfilled simultaneously to have a conversion into shares, is that the bank itself must have a capital ratio falling below a preset standard. This dual trigger would ensure a recapitalization of problematic banks in a situation where the financial industry is facing tough times as well. In good times, banks would be allowed not to write down any of their contingent debt even when the capital ratio falls below the specified trigger level.

Solvency Trigger

On March 5, 2013 Swiss Re placed a $750 mn contingent convertible bond. The order book was more than seven times oversubscribed. The bond offered an annual 6.375% coupon, but the investor suffers a full write-down of the face value (and outstanding coupons) in case of a trigger event. This trigger event is linked to a breach of a predetermined solvency ratio, which has been set at 125% of the Swiss Solvency Test (SST). The SST is a risk-based capital standard for insurance companies in Switzerland. It has been in force since 2006 and measures to what extent an insurance company has enough capital to deal with 99% of the liabilities at the end of the year.

---

[3] In the afternoon of May 6, 2010 during a 20-minute period, the stock prices of almost all of the 8000 individual equity securities traded in the United States suffered an aggressive price correction and a quick reversal. Over 20 000 trades across more than 300 securities were executed at prices more than 60% away from their values just moments before. This crash disappeared as quickly as it appeared and was labeled the "Flash Crash," earning a spot in the hall of fame of previous stock market crashes such as the "Great Crash" of 1929 or "Black Monday" of 1987. There was blood on the streets because some market participants had sold assets at extremely low prices. The SEC[4] and CFTC[5] were scrambled in and published, in September 2010, a lengthy report finger-pointing a large mutual fund. The sell order of this fund for $4.1 bn of mini-futures on the S&P destabilized the market, which was already nervous and thin. All of this happened with the European sovereign debt crisis on everybody's trading screens earlier that day.

[4] Securities and Exchange Commission.

[5] Commodity Futures Trading Commission.

3.3.3 Host Instrument

Coupon Bond

Almost all contingent convertibles have been structured around traditional coupon-bearing debt. Most of the time the coupon rate is fixed and in the case of a callable issue such as ZKB (Table 3.2), the host of the CoCo bond turns into a floating-rate instrument after the call date.

Convertible Bond

The Bank of Cyprus gave a new twist to the structure of a contingent convertible by structuring the forced conversion in case of a trigger event around a traditional convertible bond. This allows investors to profit from a strong share performance. The forced conversion following a possible trigger is here combined with an optional conversion which is at the discretion of the investor. The bank announced its intention in February 2011 – and finally issued on May 28, 2011 – a total of €890 mn of this new kind of debt. These convertible enhanced securities, as they were marketed by the Bank of Cyprus, were very quickly dubbed **CoCoCos** by the financial industry [132, 156]. Thanks to the combination of forced and optional conversion, the bank could offer loss-absorbing debt. Otherwise, the issuance of new debt would have been prohibitively expensive for the Bank of Cyprus. The incorporation of an optional conversion offers some upside potential for investors. It offers at the same time an advantage to the issuer because the inclusion of the optional conversion reduces the overall interest rate charge. The Bank of Cyprus's CoCoCo bond had two conversion prices (Table 3.4):

- **Optional conversion price**
  The conversion price is set at €3.3 per share. The investor has the right to convert the bond into shares against this embedded purchase price. Given the fact that the face value N of this issue is equal to €1, the conversion ratio C_r equals 0.303.
- **Forced conversion price**
  The forced conversion is a fact when the CET1 ratio drops below 5%. The conversion price equals 80% of the weighted average share price S^* observed in the 5-day period preceding

Table 3.4 CoCoCo bond issued by Bank of Cyprus

	Bank of Cyprus
Issue Size	€890 mn
Issue Date	May 28, 2011
Maturity	Perpetual
Yield at Issue	6.5%
Coupon	6.5%
Callable	After 5 years. From this first call date onward the coupon is reset to 6-month Libor + 3%
Coupon Deferral	Yes (non-cumulative)
Optional Conversion Price	3.3
Forced Conversion Price	$\max(0.8 \times S^*, 1)$
Trigger	CET 1 ratio
Trigger Level	5%
Non-Viability Trigger	Yes

Source: Prospectus.

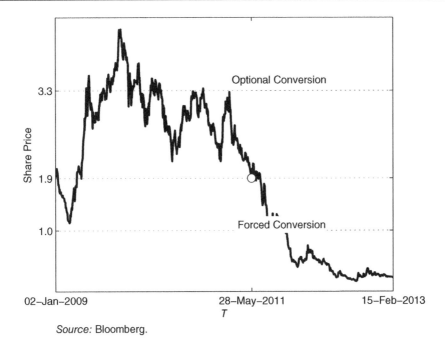

Source: Bloomberg.

Figure 3.4   Two conversion price levels for the Bank of Cyprus CoCoCo issued on May 28, 2011.

this trigger. This conversion mechanism imposes a floor C_F on the conversion price. C_P is not allowed to drop below €1:

$$C_P = \max(0.8 \times S^*, 1) \qquad (3.3)$$

where

$$S^* = \frac{S_{t1} + S_{t2} + S_{t3} + S_{t4} + S_{t5}}{5} \qquad (3.4)$$

$t1, \ldots, t5$ are the five trading days before the trigger takes place.

The two conversion price levels for the optional and the forced conversion have been illustrated in Figure 3.4.

3.4   COCOS AND CONVERTIBLE BONDS

3.4.1   Forced vs. Optional Conversion

In Figure 3.5 the price graph of a sample contingent convertible has been plotted. Before the trigger takes place, the bond displays a negative convexity with respect to the share price. Once the trigger is hit, the bond is converted into shares.

The possible conversion into shares is a property which CoCos share with traditional convertible bonds. However, this does not allow an investor to label these instruments as yet another convertible bond variety. CoCos are a totally different asset class. An owner of CoCo bonds exposes himself to a mandatory conversion in shares. The investment feature embedded

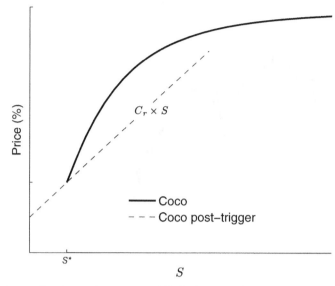

Figure 3.5   Price profile of a contingent convertible before and after the trigger event.

within standard convertible bonds is most of the time optional at the sole discretion of the investor. The investor decides whether to convert or not.

3.4.2   Negative vs. Positive Convexity

In Figure 3.6 the graphs of the theoretical price (P) of a standard convertible and a contingent convertible are represented together. The convertible bond has an obvious positive convexity

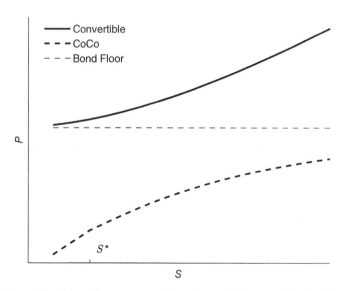

Figure 3.6   Price profile of a contingent convertible and a standard convertible bond.

with respect to the share price level ($\frac{\partial^2 P}{\partial S^2} > 0$). The convertible bond converges to the bond floor as the share price loses ground and converges to parity when the share price moves far above the conversion price. The CoCo bond has the opposite behavior since the convergence to the underlying parity occurs for depressed share price levels. Close to the trigger level, the CoCo investor will be fully exposed to share price movements. This sensitivity fades away when the share price, for example driven by the profitability of the bank, reaches a higher level. This is a clear illustration of negative convexity.

3.4.3 Limited vs. Unlimited Upside

CoCo bonds do not offer an unlimited exposure to the positive performance of the underlying shares. On the contrary, the payout potential of a contingent convertible is limited to the coupons C and the face value N. This stream of cash flows is the **bond floor** for a standard convertible bond and provides, in the absence of credit risk, a lower boundary to its theoretical price. CoCo bonds have a so-called **bond ceiling**. This represents the maximum theoretical price that can be obtained by the contingent convertible. This bond ceiling limits the upside potential of a CoCo. This price level could be reached in case of a very distant accounting trigger.

The fact that some traditional convertible bonds are issued with a so-called "CoCo feature" unfortunately adds to the confusion. This particular convertible bond feature only points to the fact that the convertibility of the bond is contingent on the level of the share price [131]. This unfortunately blurs the boundary between standard convertible bonds and CoCos.

The CoCo bond has a larger downside compared with the standard convertible. For low share price levels the convertible bond, in the assumption that the issuer does not default, converges to the bond floor. The CoCo bond will, under these circumstances, face a write-down of the face value or an expensive conversion into cheap shares.

3.4.4 Similarity to Reverse Convertibles

CoCos share the possibility of a forced conversion with reverse convertibles (Figure 3.7). These are bonds with an embedded short put option (Section 2.6.4). The difference from reverse convertibles is twofold, however. In the case of a reverse convertible, the conversion into shares takes place at the final maturity date only. A CoCo investor, on the contrary, may be forced into conversion at any point in time before the expiration of the bond. A second difference is the fact that in case of a reverse convertible, the issuer's decision to redeem the bond in shares depends solely on the share price level at the maturity of the bond. There is no involvement of an accounting or regulatory trigger.

3.5 COCOS AND REGULATIONS

3.5.1 Introduction

Regulators have been simultaneously working on two different fronts in the aftermath of the 2008 crisis. First, they wanted to reduce the impact of a single bank failure on the rest of the economy. Second, they aimed to reduce the probability of a bank failure taking place. This second goal can be achieved by making sure that banks are better equipped to weather a financial storm. Banks need to be more loss absorbing. This can be achieved by increasing

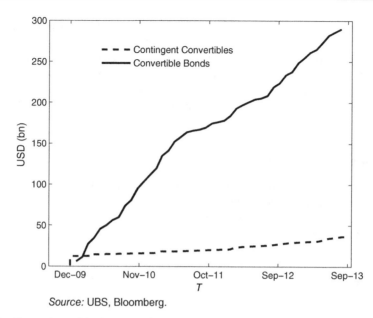

Source: UBS, Bloomberg.

Figure 3.7 Comparison of the issuance of convertible bonds and contingent convertible (2010–2013).

the amount of regulatory capital and the loss-absorbing capacity of this capital base. This is where contingent convertibles are considered to add value. In this section we elaborate on how the different regulatory initiatives impact the way financial institutions will have to think about their regulatory capital. This new legal background has an impact on what can and what cannot be done when designing and structuring contingent debt.

3.5.2 Basel Framework

The Basel Committee ("the Committee") was founded in 1975 and its members come from Argentina, Australia, Belgium, Brazil, Canada, China, France, Germany, Hong Kong, India, Indonesia, Italy, Japan, Korea, Luxembourg, Mexico, the Netherlands, Russia, Saudi Arabia, Singapore, South Africa, Spain, Sweden, Switzerland, Turkey, the United Kingdom, and the United States. The Committee's Secretariat is located at the Bank for International Settlements in Basel, Switzerland and is staffed mainly by professional supervisors on temporary secondment from member institutions. The Committee is wrongfully seen as a super-regulator imposing minimum requirements on every bank's capital, regulating the reporting and weighting of its market risk, imposing methods to calculate its counterparty risk, etc. The Committee imposes none of these. It only proposes general supervisory principles. Doing so, the Committee stimulates the creation of a level playing field amongst the internationally active banks. In between each of these financial institutions and the Basel Committee, we find the national regulators. A regulator will transform proposals coming from the Basel Committee into national law. It is at this level that minimal capital requirements for a bank are imposed [144]. The original capital accords have been proposed by the Basel Committee and are better known as the Basel I, II, and III capital accords. Many aspects of the Basel Committee's role have changed in the many years it has been around. One of the main differences is the recent political and time pressure placed upon the decision-making process [55].

It is helpful to wander through the complete sequel from the Basel I to the Basel III capital accords, in order to get a good understanding of what regulatory capital is all about. A summary of Basel I and II will increase our understanding of the latest set of minimum capital requirements proposed in the Basel III accord. CoCo bond solutions have their roots firmly planted in the last edition of this framework.

3.5.3   Basel I

In July 1988, the Committee published a seminal work "International convergence of capital measurement and capital standard" [17], which subsequently became known as Basel I or the Basel Capital Accord. Basel I introduced two novelties: it defined the two basic building blocks of banking capital and it laid out a minimum requirement for this capital [68].

The main novelty of this first capital accord was the fact that it proposed a minimum capital ratio for every bank. This ratio consisted of the amount of total regulatory capital over the value of the risk-weighted assets held by the bank. The fundamental rule here was that a bank should have at least a ratio of 8%. This ratio was called the "Cooke ratio," after P.W. Cooke, the chairman of the Committee from 1977–1988. The 8% minimum requirement was there to prevent internationally active banks from excessive risk taking.

According to Basel I, a bank having risk-weighted assets of $100 bn needed $8 bn of regulatory capital to fund its operations. Therefore, a bank could in fact leverage itself 12.5 $(= \frac{100}{8})$ times while adhering to the minimum requirement of Basel I. For every dollar of capital, it could indeed spend 12.5 times this amount on assets.

To make a distinction between the riskiness of the assets, the Committee came up with a weighting scheme, however. A bank holding government bonds would need less capital than a competitor investing mainly in loans and corporate debt. The weighting scheme was rule based, very straightforward, and originated from the type of debt a bank owned. Government debt on the balance sheet received a better treatment than corporate debt. A second ingredient was the origin of the debt; the OECD[6]-originated debt required less regulatory capital, for example. The Basel 1988 Capital Accord eventually led to the use of five weights: 0, 10, 20, 50, and 100%.

- **0%**: Cash and OECD government debt
- **10%**: Loans extended to domestic public-sector entities
- **20%**: Loans given to banks incorporated in a OECD country
- **50%**: Loans fully secured by a residential property
- **100%**: Loans to the private sector, non-OECD banks, real-estate investments, etc.

The weighting scheme illustrates that Basel I had an outspoken focus toward credit risk. It insufficiently covered risk taking when banks started to change their business model and boosted the size of their derivative operations and structured product portfolios. Basel I was too easily arbitraged . . .

---

[6] Organization for Economic Cooperation and Development (34 countries).

3.5.4   Basel II

Basel II was released by the Basel Committee in June 2004, with a scheduled implementation starting in January 2007 [18]. The definition of qualified capital and the required 8% total capital of the first Basel accord did not change. The new accord introduced more fine tuning regarding the risk weighting of the assets. The risk weights used in the first Basel accord were considered as being far too simple and too distant from economic reality. A bank was better off from a regulatory point of view extending a loan to a risky bank in the OECD than to a well-established and solid financial institution in a non-OECD country. In the first capital accord, there was no room for diversification either. The total capital requirement for a bank was the sum of all the requirements for every position on a standalone basis.

In Basel II, three categories of risk were now recognized: credit risk, market risk, and operational risk. Every single one of these components is now adding up to the total required minimum capital a bank should hold. The previous OECD/non-OECD split to categorize the credit risk of the assets was replaced by an approach where external or internal ratings could be used to categorize assets on the balance sheet. The "standardized approach," however, provided thinking along the lines of Basel I but allowed for external ratings to be applied on the credit positions held by the bank according to three different categories: sovereigns, banks, and corporates (Table 3.5). More important was the fact that Basel II also provided a framework for the risk weighting to be applied to securitized assets. Where a AAA-rated mortgage-backed security in Basel I received a 50% risk weighting, Basel II would see this particular risk weighting drop to 20% in the standardized approach. For some, this is where the seeds of the banking crisis of 2008 were planted. A bank now had the possibility of piling on more risk and simultaneously lowering the risk-weighted assets. An illustration of this is the eagerness with which financial institutions began to invest in collaterized debt obligations (CDOs) on a large scale. The external rating assigned to these complex instruments was not too punitive from a capital perspective. As it turned out, this credit rating did not reflect the real financial risk and the regulatory capital held as a loss-absorbing safety buffer was not adequate at all. Financial innovation had swiftly outflanked the new barriers raised by regulators in Basel II. Some commentators [48] put the blame for the 2008 meltdown on the Basel I camp, however. They would argue that the subprime crisis started at a point in time when the Basel II proposals were far from being fully implemented on a national level.

One of the major innovations introduced by this first Basel update was the so-called "three-pillar" structure. The first pillar stands for the minimum capital requirement, the second pillar is the interaction of the bank with its national supervisors, and the third pillar is the market discipline. The last pillar deals with the regular disclosure of capital requirements, risk

Table 3.5   Summary of the risk weighting for the credit risk according to Basel II, based on S&P ratings (standardized approach)

External Rating	Risk Weights		
	Sovereigns	Banks	Corporates
AAA to AA−	0%	20%	20%
A+ to A−	20%	50%	50%
BBB+ to BBB−	50%	50%	100%
BB+ to B−	100%	100%	100%
Below B−	150%	150%	150%
Unrated	100%	50%	100%

weightings, with the market. This last pillar assumes that the market rewards those banks that have a healthy risk–return profile and punishes those that don't.

Another often-heard complaint about the Basel II accord in connection with the financial crisis is its pro-cyclical nature. In an economic downturn financial institutions will need, as a matter of fact, to raise more capital. The average credit rating of the financial assets held by the bank will deteriorate when the economy enters into a recession. This could dramatically change the risk weighting of these assets and the capital ratio would drop below the minimum level as a result of this. Unfortunately, raising capital at this point in the economic cycle is going to be very difficult. To make matters worse, competing banks with the same business model will simultaneously face the same issue and will also be scrambling for new capital. In this respect, if there is a crunch, Basel II will definitively deepen it further [111]. A counter-cyclical regulation would deal with this fallacy since it would force the banks to increase their capital in booming times but allow them to run a reduced inventory of regulatory capital in a harsher economic environment.

The capital requirement calculations behind Basel II are complex and not transparent at all. This weakens both Pillars II and III according to Andrew G. Haldane, Executive Director at the bank of England: "... For what the market cannot observe, it is unlikely to be able to exercise discipline over. And what the regulator cannot verify, it is unlikely to be able to exercise supervision over ..."

3.5.5 Basel III

Introduction

Less than 20 years after the inception of Basel I, recurring financial crises still remained a hallmark of the modern financial system. Central bankers, regulators, kept fixing loopholes in the regulation after every crisis. In July 2009, Basel 2.5 was brought into action. This amendment contained a fix to the Basel II package in order to prevent a 2008 crisis from happening again [19]. Those aspects that did not work properly during the crisis were dealt with. Later in the same year, in December 2009, the Committee turned another page and revamped the Basel II accord completely. The Basel Committee announced a package of proposals for deeper reforms [125, 20] to make the banking sector more resilient from a capital and liquidity perspective. These proposals laid out the principles around which the upcoming Basel III accord was constructed. This third capital accord can be seen as one component out of a wide range of global measures agreed at the G20 meeting in Pittsburgh (September 2009). The leaders of the world's largest economies made it clear at this international forum: "... To make sure our regulatory system for banks and other financial firms reins in the excesses that led to the crisis. Where reckless behavior and a lack of responsibility led to crisis, we will not allow a return to banking as usual ..." [136].

Before coming up with a new regulatory proposal, the Basel Committee always starts with an initial release of a consultative document. Banks are then allowed to respond to this draft and comment on the proposal. A total of 272 market participants decided to respond during the 4-month period following the initial disclosure of the proposals for the new Basel III framework.[7] After this consultative period, the Basel Committee finally disclosed in September 2010 the new minimum capital ratios [22]. The final Basel III proposal [25] has not been embraced

---

[7] All of the responses, some of which are anonymous, are available at the website of the Bank of International Settlements: http://www.bis.org/publ/bcbs165/cacomments.htm.

overwhelmingly by all the parties involved. After all, the Basel II reform had not even been rolled out completely. The final Basel III proposal impacts the regulatory capital of a bank on different fronts.

Boosting the Quality of Regulatory Capital

The regulatory capital in Basel II was very fragmented. A top executive of the Bank of International Settlements would declare: "... We had Tier 1 capital, Innovative Tier 1, Upper and Lower Tier 2, Tier 3 capital, each with their own limits which were sometimes a function of other capital elements. The complexity in the definition of capital made it difficult to determine what capital would be available should losses arise ..." [115]. Basel III simplified the structure of regulatory capital:

- Tier 3 has been banned as a category of regulatory capital in the new accord. Basel III has also disallowed some other components on the balance sheet from being incorporated in Tier 1. Innovative capital instruments such as some hybrid bonds, which were previously permitted in a limited amount as part of Tier 1 capital, are no longer allowed and will have to be phased out. Specifically, every year starting from 2013, the amount of these hybrid bonds that can count as Tier 1 capital will be reduced by a further 10%.
- No distinction will be made between Upper or Lower Tier 2 capital. Only one category of Tier 2 debt will prevail in a Basel III setting. This category consists of subordinated debt.
- The new capital accord also added more focus to common equity and defined Common Equity Tier 1 (**CET1**)[8] [107] as top-quality capital since it has the largest loss-absorbing capabilities. This component of the regulator capital withstands a shock while the bank continues to function normally. Common Equity Tier 1 is going-concern capital. Tier 2 capital has only loss-absorption capabilities when the bank becomes insolvent. This is gone-concern capital. Basel III has brought common equity to the front stage so that it has got every bank's attention. Simultaneously, the Basel Committee has left room for non-Core Tier 1 instruments that are nevertheless loss absorbing: this is the category of Additional Tier 1. CoCos can be part of this Additional Tier 1 bucket.

Capital Conservation Buffer

One of the other Basel III novelties is the introduction of a minimum **capital conservation buffer** (2.5% of the risk-weighted assets), which needs to be entirely held in common equity. This capital conservation buffer (CCB) is intended to make sure that banks have a minimum amount of capital to absorb losses in periods of financial distress. A bank that fails to meet the requirement regarding this 2.5% CCB buffer will have to face restrictions on discretionary capital distributions such as dividends and bonuses.

Counter-Cyclical Buffer

With the aim of reducing the pro-cyclical nature of the previous capital accord, the Basel Committee introduced a so-called **counter-cyclical buffer**. The minimum level of this buffer is set at the national level and should account for 0% to 2.5% of the total risk-weighted assets

---

[8] Common Equity Tier 1 and Core Equity Tier 1 share the same abbreviation: CET1. Core Equity 1 is a concept introduced by the European Banking Authority (EBA). These two concepts are somewhat different in the detail, although not that far removed in their impact [85]. In this book we will always refer to the Basel III definition of CET1.

[21]. This buffer consists, just like the capital conservation buffer, entirely of common equity. The aim here is clearly to force financial institutions to build up a war chest of capital in periods of excessive credit growth. Such bull market periods are often associated with a system-wide build-up of risk against which protection is needed.

Dealing with Large Banks

Basel III is also trying to put an end to the "too-big-to-fail" problem where a default of one large financial institution brings the whole financial system to the brink of collapse. Therefore the Basel Committee and the Financial Stability Board imposed extra capital charges for a **systemically important financial institution** (SIFI). To deal with the too-big-to-fail issue, the Financial Stability Board (FSB) drafted a list of 29 internationally active banks earning the label of being globally systematically important [159]. SIFIs are subject to an extra capital surcharge ranging from 1 to 2.5% of their risk-weighted assets, with a possibility to go as high as 3.5% [27]. This top 3.5% bucket leaves the door open for the FSB to discourage banks from becoming even more systemically important.

There had been much speculation regarding the role of CoCos in this capital surcharge for SIFIs. Certain central banks such as, for example, the German Bundesbank were clearly in favor of adopting CoCos in the SIFI package [77]. The Basel Committee somehow popped this ambition and did not allow contingent capital to be used by SIFIs to meet this extra surcharge. Banks needed to use capital of the highest quality, Common Equity Tier 1, to meet the SIFI surcharge requirement.

A More Conservative Risk Weighting of Assets

In the period running up to the 2008 crisis, banks were reporting very small changes in their risk-weighted assets. Nevertheless, the total assets owned by these institutions had increased considerably [115]. There seemed to be a disconnect between the financial exposure taken by a bank and the risk weighting attached to it. It was therefore not a surprise to see that Basel III refined the risk weightings once more. Banks can still use their own internal models to produce a risk weighting of the assets [190], however. One of the implemented changes was the requirement that banks now have to hold capital to protect against mark-to-market losses due to the deterioration of the credit quality of a counterparty to an OTC transaction. This is the implementation of credit valuation adjustments (CVA). Other changes were the use of stressed value at risk and a capital charge for less liquid, credit-sensitive assets.

Higher Minimum Capital Ratios

1. **Minimum capital requirement: 8%**

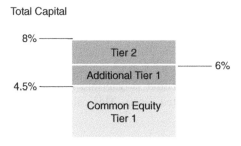

At first sight, banks need to hold the same amount of capital as in the previous Basel II capital accord: a mere 8% of the risk-weighted assets. Basel III is more stringent than its predecessors. The 8% requirement in Basel II was founded on a thin layer of 2% common equity. On top of this, there was considerable room left for Tier 2 or Tier 1 bonds in the capital structure of a bank. This changes the new capital accord, where Tier 2 can now only take up a maximum of 2% and Additional Tier 1 is allowed up to 1.5%.

2. **Capital conservation buffer: 2.5%**

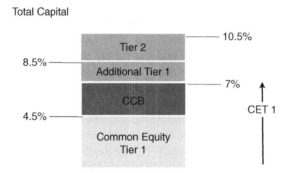

The capital conservation buffer needs to consist entirely of Common Equity Tier 1 (CET1). In Basel III, the minimum amount of common equity therefore moves up from 2% to 7%. The common equity ratio of a bank now seems to be increased by a factor of 3.5 compared with the Basel II capital accord, where it was required to be above a minimum level of 2%. In reality, the minimum amount of common equity increases by a factor of 7, because of the much tighter definition of capital in Basel III [115].

3. **Counter-cyclical buffer: 0.0%–2.5%**

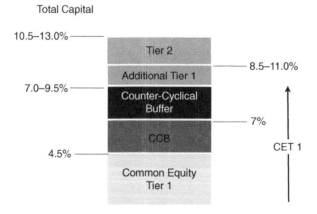

The size of the counter-cyclical buffer is determined by the national regulator and can go up to 2.5% of the risk-weighted assets. This can take the CET1 requirement up to 7.0–9.5%.

4. **SIFI surcharge: 1.0%–3.5%**

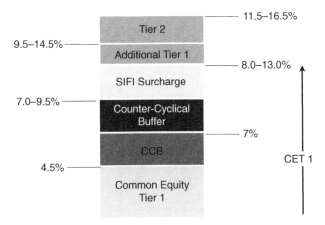

In a Basel III setting, an internationally active and systematically very important bank could see its minimum capital requirement increase to up to a total percentage of 16.5% of the risk-weighted assets.

Phased Implementation

An immediate implementation of the full Basel III proposal on January 2013 would have pulled the rug from under many financial institutions. The timing of the Basel III project was not ideal, for the announcement of this new capital accord coincided with the unfolding of a major financial crisis in Europe. Furthermore, the financial problems in Greece, Spain, and Portugal made the future of the euro as a single currency uncertain. Many banks had to deal with undercapitalized balance sheets after suffering write-downs on their holdings in European government debt. The minimum capital required for Basel III was simply not there. Not in the quantity nor in the quality needed. Banks were granted time to implement this new standard, which led to a transitional arrangement from January 2013 till January 2019 (Figure 3.8) [160]. The European Banking Authority [168] quantified in 2012 that an immediate and full implementation of Basel III would have created an overall capital shortfall of €550 bn. The largest shortfall was in the category of common equity.

Tier 2 and Additional Tier 1

The regulatory capital base has become loss absorbing in Basel III [24]:

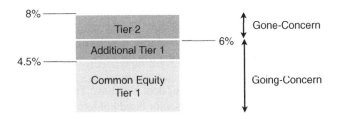

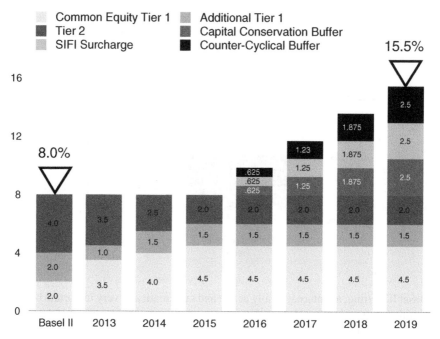

Figure 3.8 Implementation scheme of Basel III for a large internationally active bank, assuming that the national regulator imposed a 2.5% counter-cyclical buffer and that the bank classifies for a SIFI surcharge of 2.5%. The bank has a 6-year time frame to increase its minimum total capital from 8.0% to 15.5%.

- **Tier 1 capital**

  Tier 1 consists of Common Equity Tier 1 and Additional Tier 1. These two elements are considered going-concern because an impact on their value or their inability to pay the expected coupons will not generate a default event. The financial institution can still continue its activities on an ongoing basis.

  The Additional Tier 1 bucket is taking over from what was previously known as innovative Tier 1 instruments. This old category is gradually being phased out. The main characteristics of Additional Tier 1 are its perpetual nature, the possibility of a coupon deferral at the discretion of the issuer, the fact that coupons need to be paid out of distributable profits, and its subordination to senior and subordinated debt (Tier 2). An issuer call is allowed but the call provision cannot contain an incentive to redeem. On top of this, the issuer call needs to be approved by the national regulator. The amount of capital that is redeemed early must also be replaced with capital of the same quality or better.

  The loss absorption of Additional Tier 1 is such that the trigger level for conversion or write-down must be at least a Common Equity Tier 1 ratio of 5.125%. The aggregate amount to be written down or converted into shares must be at least the amount needed to immediately bring the bank's CET1 ratio to the trigger level.

- **Tier 2 capital**

  Tier 2 capital ranks below deposits and senior debt but above Tier 1 capital. Tier 2 debt has been designed to isolate the depositors and senior bond holders from any negative effect. It is there to absorb losses when the Tier 1 base has been wiped out. Under Basel III, Tier 2 capital ensures loss absorption in case of liquidation (gone-concern) [28].

In order to qualify as Tier 2 capital, the instrument must be subordinated to depositors and general creditors. Tier 2 debt can be neither secured nor guaranteed. The minimal original maturity has to be at least 5 years. An issuer call is allowed, but only after the first 5 years. In Basel III there is no longer a distinction between Lower and Upper Tier 2.

Leverage Ratio

A lack of regulatory capital was not the only worry of the Basel Committee. The Committee has also focused on liquidity and leverage in Basel III, which makes this last Basel version very different from the previous ones. Imposing capital requirements with respect to the risk-weighted assets had proved not to be strong enough. The original risk buckets of Basel I were straightforward. A bank clerk could perform the back-of-the-envelope calculations [114]. With the introduction of Basel II, this process evolved to a risk-weighting system based on sophisticated risk models. It should not come as a surprise that different banks, using their respective internal models, could evaluate the risk of the same pool of assets very differently. In 2009, the FSA[9] constructed a hypothetical portfolio based on 64 externally rated corporate, bank, and sovereign exposures. Banks were then asked to use their internal models to calculate the capital required to be held against this portfolio. The outcome of this simulation was striking and pinpointed one of the main weaknesses of Basel II. For wholesale exposures to banks, the calculated capital requirements differed by a factor of over 100%, for corporate exposures 150%. For sovereign exposures, the results differed by a factor of up to 280% [114].

The weakness of relying the stability of the banking system on the amount of regulatory capital held against risk-weighted assets was illustrated by Philipp M. Hildebrand, former chairman of the Governing Board of the Swiss National Bank. He illustrated how, using risk-weighted assets, the two largest Swiss banks were among the best-capitalized banks in the world in 2008 [119]. Using leverage as a measure, however, these institutions were among the worst-capitalized banks and a ticking time bomb. A leverage number is the ratio of capital over the total amount of assets. Since the latter is not using any risk weighting at all, its value does not depend on any internal model. There are no adjustments made for the varying degrees of risk. Corporate loans, customer loans, bonds, or toxic mortgages are all treated the same.

Basel III introduces a restriction on leverage. Leverage is the ratio of the capital of the bank over its assets, irrespective of the riskiness of these assets. The definition of the leverage ratio is given by:

$$\text{Leverage Ratio} = \frac{\text{Tier 1 Capital}}{\text{Assets}}$$

This leverage ratio does not replace the other capital requirements, which are all relative to the pool of risk-weighted assets. It is seen by some as the only way to backstop those banks trying to circumvent risk-based capital requirements. Proponents regard it as a simple measure which is hard to manipulate. In the proposal, the minimum ratio has been set at 3%, meaning that a bank could leverage up to a factor of 33.3. In the United States, the FDIC included in its implementation of Basel III a much higher ratio for its banks. Top US lenders will have

---

[9] Financial Services Authority.

to meet a leverage ratio of 6%, which is twice the Basel number. This proposal has been met with a lot of disbelief from the banks regarding the leverage ratio as a crude measure [34].

Liquidity

The experience of the Committee has always been in the area of capital requirement regulation. Since Basel I, this was done with respect to a particular risk weighting. In Basel III, the measures have been extended using a 100% risk weighting when introducing the leverage ratio. Another novelty in Basel III was the fact that liquidity now became an integral part of the international regulatory framework. A bank needs both enough capital and liquidity in order to remain in business. Capital on its own is not enough. A bank's fate is tied to both capital and liquidity. Imagine, for example, a conservative retail bank with a very solid regulatory capital base consisting only of equity. The rest of the funding comes from deposits. The bank invests primarily in high-quality but long-dated government bonds. The quality of the regulatory capital, and the low risk weighting of the financial assets held by the bank, will make it look good from a Basel II or Basel I perspective. The bank will expose itself to a serious nightmare if it faces an important drawdown on its deposits. The liquidity profile of the government bonds it is holding on its balance sheet could be insufficient to match the outflow generated by the deposit holders. Basel III dealt with this shortcoming and defined two liquidity metrics in the new proposal. The committee introduced a **net stable funding ratio** (NSFR) and a **liquidity coverage ratio** (LCR).

- **Liquidity coverage ratio**
  The liquidity coverage ratio is a measure for the amount of high-quality and liquid assets an institution holds that can be used to offset the net cash outflows it would encounter under a 30-day stress scenario. This could, for example, be a run on the bank by all the deposit holders amplified by a simultaneous drawdown of the credit lines granted by the bank to its corporate clients. The liquidity coverage ratio is defined as:

$$\text{LCR} = \frac{\text{Amount of Highly Liquid Assets}}{[\text{Cash Outflows} - \text{Cash Inflows}]_{\text{30-day funding scenario}}}$$

  Through the LCR, a bank is now forced to hold enough unencumbered high-quality assets that can easily be sold and converted into cash. The specification about what exactly is to be considered as liquid assets has been the subject of a good amount of lobbying of the banking industry. Basel III had to relax its initial stance following a hard-fought lobbying process. In January 2013, the Committee drafted the final proposal regarding this ratio [30]. A gradual phase-in of this requirement, starting in January 2015, means that the banks have to reach in January 2019 a LCR of 100%.
- **Net stable funding ratio**
  The NSFR is a complement to the LCR and stimulates banks to have the right balance between the liquidity profile of the assets and the approach to fund these assets. This measure is part of the Basel III framework in order to avoid banks funding long-term assets such as, for example, mortgages with only short-term borrowing. An example of a bank that faced such a liquidity trap was Northern Rock in the UK. In the period 1999–2007 the bank doubled the size of its balance sheet to GBP 32 bn and financed this mortgage business with short-term wholesale funding [45]. This forced Northern Rock to continuously roll over this short-term debt from one maturity date to the following one. In 2007 this funding

mechanism stopped abruptly. In the middle of the credit crisis, Northern Rock was not able to sell enough of these mortgages in order to reduce the size of the asset pool and hence its funding requirements. Moreover, there was no available source of stable funding. Northern Rock could also not rely on any prearranged liquidity lines. In February 2008, the bank was finally nationalized by the UK government.

The NSFR is a ratio that measures how much stable funding a financial institution has at its disposal to survive a year-long liquidity crisis on the financial markets. This metric stimulates banks not to rely solely on short-term funding even when this is easily available. The NSFR metric, which needs to be larger than 100%, is defined as:

$$\text{NSFR} = \frac{\text{Available amount of stable funding}}{\text{Required amount of stable funding}}$$

The required amount of stable funding depends on the nature of the liquidity of the assets held by the bank. For this purpose, each asset class has been assigned a so-called requirement factor in the Basel III proposal. For equity and gold this factor equals 50%. As a consequence of this, a $100 investment in an equity portfolio forces the bank to have at least $50 stable funding. The stability of a funding source has also been specified by the Basel Committee. Regulatory capital has the largest funding stability. It is there forever and has been assigned an availability factor of 100%. Relying on wholesale funding is less stable and corresponds to an availability factor of 50%.

As an example, we can consider an investment bank that has $5 bn in assets all invested in equities. The liability side of the bank consist of $1 bn in common equity while the rest is short-term wholesale funding. The NSFR ratio is equal to 1.2:

$$\text{NSFR} = \frac{1 \times 100\% + 4 \times 50\%}{5 \times 50\%} = 1.2 \tag{3.5}$$

Liquidity regulation being a new line of action means that the Committee adopted a more careful approach while stressing its commitment to global liquidity standards. Using the words of Nout Wellink[10]: "... We want to make sure we get it right..." [191]. The enforcement date of this part of the Basel III regulation will be in 2019, 4 years later than originally expected.

3.5.6   CoCos in Basel III

Delay on the Implementation

At the end of 2012, right before the start of the phasing in of the Basel III rules, only three-quarters of the member states had completed the full implementation of the previous Basel II capital accord edition. The new Basel III proposals have to be adopted by the different member states and have to be written into national law. This legal process is not taking place overnight. Instead, a gradual transition has been proposed by the Committee. This is starting in January 2013 and reaching full implementation in January 2019. The three new measures covering leverage, the too-big-to-fail surcharge, and liquidity will be phased in from 2015 onwards.

While the rules of Basel III came into effect on January 1, 2013, only 8 out of the 27 jurisdictions had issued final regulations at that point in time: Australia, China, Hong Kong, India, Japan, Saudi Arabia, Singapore, and Switzerland. The consequence of this delay meant that just 20% of the 29 global systemically important banks will be subject to Basel III

---

[10] Chairman of the Committee and President of the Dutch Central Bank.

regulations from this agreed start date [29]. Early 2013, US banks were even still continuing to disclose their capital requirements on the Basel I framework. In June 2013, the FRB,[11] FDIC,[12] and OCC[13] issued three joint proposed rules enhancing the regulatory capital requirements for US banks, hereby implementing Basel III in the USA.

Contingent Capital in Basel III

This initial delay has not put a backstop on the issuance of new CoCo bonds, as can be seen in Figure 3.7. It has indeed been made very clear for the banks where and how CoCos can be used. CoCos do not belong to the CET1 category of a bank's capital and hence they do not get the label of being top-quality capital. In the aftermath of the launch of the Basel III proposal, there was some confusion however. Early 2011, there was for example a fair amount of speculation that CoCos could be used to meet the SIFI surcharge. This idea never materialized, and the portion of the regulatory capital where these bonds can be put to work has been restricted to Tier 2 and Additional Tier 1. These components are allowed to take up, respectively, 2% and 1.5% of the risk-weighted assets.

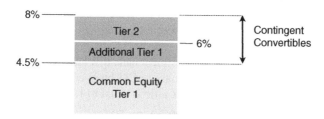

In January 2011, the Basel Committee specified that a debt instrument can only be part of the regulatory capital if losses can be absorbed in such a way that tax-payers' money is not going to be needed to bail out banks [14]. This loss absorption is triggered by an event that forces the bond to be either converted into common equity or written off. According to the Basel Committee, the trigger event is the earlier of:

- The decision by the relevant authority to use public funds and inject these into the bank, without which this bank would become non-viable.
- The decision by the same relevant authority that the bank is no longer viable without a write-off on its debt.

In both cases the trigger is in the hands of a regulatory body that supervises the bank. This trigger mechanism is called a non-viability or regulatory trigger and is a standard component of any Tier 2 or Additional Tier 1 instrument issued in the Basel III framework. On top of this non-viability trigger, contingent debt has an automatic trigger mechanism through the incorporation of an accounting trigger in its terms and conditions. When implementing Basel III into European law, CRDIV[14] has, for example, laid out a minimum level of 5.125% of CET1. Table 3.6 illustrates some contingent convertibles belonging to either Additional Tier 1 or Tier 2.

---

[11] Federal Reserve Board.
[12] Federal Deposit Insurance Corporation.
[13] Office of the Comptroller of the Currency.
[14] CRDIV is a European directive implementing Basel III.

Table 3.6 CoCo bonds belonging to either Tier 2 or Additional Tier 1

		ADDITIONAL TIER 1						
Issuer	Country	Issue Date	Maturity	Call Date	Trigger Level	Coupon	Issue (mn)	
RABOBANK	Netherlands	Jan-11	Perpetual	July-16		8.375	2000	USD
RABOBANK	Netherlands	Nov-11	Perpetual	June-17		8.4	2000	USD
ZKB	Switzerland	Jan-12	Perpetual	June-17	7.00	3.5	590	CHF
BBVA	Spain	May-13	Perpetual	May-18	5.125(*)	9	1500	USD
SOCGEN	France	Aug-13	Perpetual	Nov-18	5.125	8.25	1250	USD
		TIER 2						
Issuer	Country	Issue Date	Maturity	Call Date	Trigger Level	Coupon	Issue (mn)	
CREDIT SUISSE	Switzerland	Feb-11	Feb-41	Aug-16	7.00	7.875	2000	USD
UBS	Switzerland	Feb-12	Feb-22	Feb-17	5.00	7.25	2000	USD
CREDIT SUISSE	Switzerland	Mar-12	Mar-22	Mar-17	7.00	7.125	750	CHF
UBS	Switzerland	Aug-12	Aug-22		5.00	7.625	2000	USD
BARCLAYS	UK	Nov-12	Nov-22		7.00	7.625	3000	USD
KBC	Belgium	Jan-13	Jan-23	Jan-18	7.00	8	1000	USD

(*) The BBVA CoCo has a set of multiple accounting triggers.

The \$1.5 bn additional Tier 1 issue from the BBVA, a Spanish bank, has been met with a large oversubscription coming from investors hunting for yield. It was the first CRDIV-compliant contingent convertible ever. The 9% coupon on this perpetual security covers different levels of risk that deserve our attention (see also Table 3.7):

- **There is no incentive to pay a coupon**
  The issuer has full discretion over the payment of a coupon. There is no dividend stopper such that the non-payment of a coupon on the CoCo bond restricts dividend payments on the underlying stock. Any deferral is going to be non-cumulative. A coupon that is not

Table 3.7 Additional Tier 1 CoCo bond issued by BBVA

	BBVA
Issue Size	\$1.5 bn
Issue Date	May 9, 2013
Maturity	Perpetual
Yield at Issue	Libor + 8.26%
Coupon	9%
Callable	Every year starting on May 9, 2018. The call price is 100. After the first call date the coupon is equal to the 5-year swap rate + 826 bps.
Coupon Deferral	Yes (non-cumulative)
Dividend Stopper	None
Dividend Pusher	None
Conversion Price	$\max(S^*, \$5)$
Trigger	Multiple accounting triggers
Non-Viability Trigger	Yes

Source: Prospectus.

paid, is lost for ever. The discretion also comes with the absence of any dividend pusher. This Spanish bank can honor its shareholders with a dividend without having to meet the scheduled interest payment on this contingent capital bond.

- **Perpetual maturity and absence of any incentive to redeem early**
  The bond is deeply subordinated and long dated but becomes callable 5 years after the issue date on May 10, 2018. After this date the bond is yearly callable and switches from a fixed-coupon bond to a floating-rate note paying 826 bps above the 5-year USD swap rate. This spread on top of the floating interest rate does not contain a step-up. It corresponds to the credit spread of the CoCo bond prevailing at its issue date. The existence of a supplementary step-up in the coupon after the call date would be seen as an incentive for the issuer to redeem the bond early. The absence of such an incentive is important for a bond to earn the status of Additional Tier 1.
- **Loss absorption**
  On a trigger event the bond is converted into shares, the conversion is equal to the weighted average share price five business days before the trigger occurred. Similar to the Credit Suisse structure and in line with CRDIV, there is a limit on the number of shares created on conversion. This introduces a floor of $5 on the conversion price of this CoCo bond.
- **Combining multiple accounting triggers into one**
  Next to the non-viability trigger held by the regulator, there are a multiple of accounting triggers. This mechanism allows the bond to qualify in different jurisdictions at the same time as regulatory capital such as Additional Tier 1 under CRDIV (Basel III). The trigger levels are respectively 5.125% of CET1 under CRDVI, 6% of Tier 1 under Basel II, and 7% of the capital principal ratio under the Bank of Spain's regulation.

The issuance and warm reception of the BBVA contingent convertible is important to the European banking universe [193]. This was the first CRDIV-compliant loss-absorbing bond earning a qualification as Additional Tier 1. It was immediately expected that multiple banks would follow suit.

Under Basel III, the minimum trigger level was set at 5.125% and as a result there has been a trend toward issuing CoCo bonds with a trigger level matching this particular ratio [32]. This is illustrated in Figure 3.9.

3.5.7   High and Low-Trigger CoCos

A distinction needs to be made between high and low-trigger contingent capital. This notion was introduced in 2010 by the Swiss regulator. The high-trigger CoCos are to have a 7% trigger and the 5% trigger level holds for the low-trigger contingent convertibles. It should not come as a surprise that Switzerland was the first country with a dedicated contingent capital framework [68]. The banking business is a very important pillar of the Swiss economy. Without any doubt, the 2008 global economic crisis has illustrated Switzerland's vulnerability. Its banking industry was, and still is, dominated by two large banks: Credit Suisse and UBS. Between the fourth quarter of 2007 and the third quarter of 2009, the combined losses of these two banks amounted to CHF 59 bn. This is a respectable number for a country with a GDP of CHF 450bn. Switzerland was maybe too small to deliver an implicit state guarantee for these two banking giants it was hosting on its national territory. In November 2009, the Federal Council of Switzerland mandated a commission of experts to examine how to limit the risks posed by these important banks. This resulted in a report which went a lot further in its proposals than what Basel III was aiming for [58].

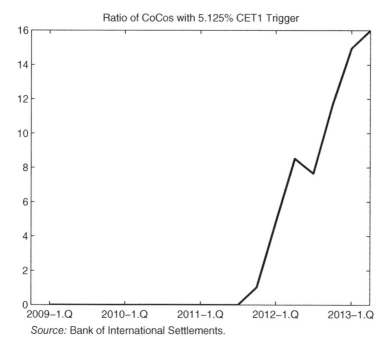

Source: Bank of International Settlements.

Figure 3.9   Issuance of CoCos with a 5.125% trigger level.

Whereas Basel III would result in a minimal capital requirement of 10.5%,[15] Credit Suisse and UBS are going to have to face by the end of 2018 a total capital requirement of 19%, of which at least 10% in common equity. In this so-called "Swiss Finish," the regulator has also left a front-stage role for CoCos. The 19% requirement is, in this Swiss proposal, divided into three components:

- **Minimum requirement: 4.5%**
  The minimum requirement of 4.5% needs to be held in common equity.
- **Buffer: 8.5%**
  This buffer has been imposed in order to allow a bank to absorb major losses without any disruption to its normal business operations and without suffering any loss of confidence amongst the creditors or depositors. This 8.5% buffer needs to consist of at least 5.5% of common equity and up to 3% of contingent capital with a 7% trigger.
- **Progressive component: 6%**
  The progressive component is the extra layer of capital imposed on Swiss banks carrying a large systemic risk. The magnitude of this depends on the market share and the total assets of the bank. This results in a 6% requirement for both Credit Suisse and UBS. This third component consists entirely of CoCos with a 5% common equity trigger.

The proposal allows UBS and Credit Suisse to issue up to 9% of their risk-weighted assets in CoCos: 6% in low-trigger CoCos and up to 3% in high-trigger contingent debt.

---

[15] Including the capital conservation buffer.

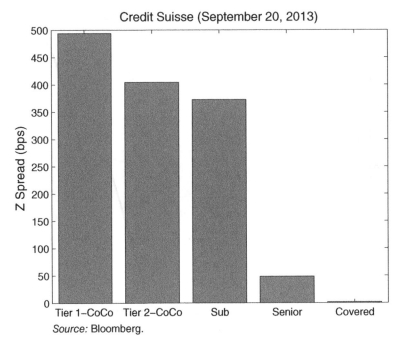

Figure 3.10   Z spread for different bonds issued by Credit Suisse.

3.6 RANKING IN THE BALANCE SHEET

The investors will obviously demand a higher yield from CoCos that are likely to trigger first. The yield of contingent capital will therefore be logically higher than the yield of senior debt issued by the same financial institution. An overall illustrative overview has been provided in Figure 3.10, where the credit spread for different balance sheet components of Credit Suisse has been provided.

3.7 ALTERNATIVE STRUCTURES

One of the earlier academic contributions to the development of contingent capital is the work of Raviv [165]. The author works out the benefits of having debt-for-equity swaps in the capital structure of a bank. The conversion of debt into equity takes place as soon as a well-defined capital ratio falls below a specified threshold. This work was built on the earlier research of Flannery [98, 99], where the trigger event was based on parameters that are continuously observable (unlike the regulatory ratios, such as core Tier 1). The conversion mechanism is, in this particular case, linked to the ratio of the market value of equity over the book value of the outstanding debt.

Another alternative structure is the so-called COERC or call option enhanced reverse convertible designed by Pennacchi, Vermaelen, and Wolff [158a]. This particular instrument uses a market-based trigger such as a share price but the instrument can be split into two components. There is first of all the bond that converts automatically into equity once the share price drops below a particular trigger level. The conversion price is set significantly below the trigger price. The second component embedded into the structure is the call option owned by the equity holders of the bank. Through this call option, the investors can buy back the newly created shares from the bond holders. The strike price of this call option is the conversion price of the COERC. This process involves no regulatory intervention and allows the share holders to avoid a massive dilution.

3.8   CONTINGENT CAPITAL: PRO AND CONTRA

3.8.1   Advantages

- **Automatic strengthening of the bank's balance sheet with common equity**
  The bank is shoring up its capital base without having to start a road show to issue new capital or to consider a rights issue to increase its equity base. History has indeed taught us how difficult it can be for a financial institution to convince new investors to invest, when the bank is facing turbulent times. Contingent capital has the merit of reinforcing the balance sheet in an automatic way. The high coupon earned by CoCo bond holders can be seen as an insurance premium paid by the issuer to have at any time these investors on standby to inject common equity or participate in a write-down when the trigger is hit.
- **Incentive for the management to raise capital beforehand**
  The management of a bank would impose an important dilution on its equity investors if new equity were to be created as a result of a forced conversion of a CoCo bond. Management is now clearly incentivized to deal with this issue beforehand and to make sure that its solvency is strong enough to weather a possible financial storm and to fend off the loss absorption.
- **The liquidity profile of the bank is automatically improved in times of stress**
  The write-down of the CoCo bond, or its conversion into shares, reduces the debt service payments for the bank. The coupons and the face value no longer need to be repaid. This reduces the debt burden of the bank in an orderly way without generating a default event.

CoCo Bonuses

CoCos can also be put to work in aligning the risk-taking initiatives of the management with the fate of the share holders of the bank. The bonus policy in a bank is such that trading staff will participate on the upside but will not pick up a portion of the bill on the downside. The banking crisis that started in 2008 cannot be attributed solely to the bonus culture that prevailed in those days. There is a long list of other causes that have brought the financial system to the brink of collapse [178]. However, remunerating the management of a bank in CoCos instead of cash bonuses would have changed this a lot. In the United Kingdom, the capital ratios of the banks would have been 1 percentage point higher in 2007 if half of the bonuses were to be paid out in CoCos [114].

3.8.2   Disadvantages

More Interconnectedness

The default of an investment bank such as Lehman Brothers illustrated how the fate of one bank was linked to the health of each of its counterparties. Banks were deeply interconnected on an international level and this facilitated the 2008 financial crisis to spread quickly and contaminate the whole financial world. In [167] the Financial Stability Oversight Council[16] argues how the creation of contingent debt can create a risk of contagion. As soon as banks start to invest in each other's CoCo bonds, it is straightforward to imagine how a trigger event in, for example, a European CoCo would bring a US bank into trouble.

A report on the issuance of CoCo bonds appeared in the Quarterly Review report of the Bank of International Settlements [32]. This report argues that the bulk of the demand for contingent convertibles came from retail investors and small private banks. Insurance companies and banks remained on the sidelines so far. According to the BIS report, private banks and retail investors were responsible for 52% of the overall demand. Asset management companies accounted for 27% of the overall volume, whereas hedge funds took 9% of the issue size. Banks and insurance companies each took the remainder of the volume. This observation points to the fact that the loss absorption is not transferred to other financial institutions. The retail public is carrying the majority of this risk.

Accounting Triggers

- **Lack of transparency**
  A trigger should be defined in such a way that an investor can price the financial risk embedded within contingent debt [54]. A CoCo holder should be able to understand and quantify the probability of being forced to face a conversion into shares or a write-down. A non-viability trigger that can be activated by a regulator or a trigger that depends on a capital ratio does not offer the same transparency as triggers based on observable variables. This point of view is shared by most rating agencies.

- **Triggering too late**
  The loss absorption of contingent debt could be triggered too late when an accounting trigger is used. This could occur when a financial institution has been too creative in the calculation of its risk-weighted assets. In that case the capital ratios do not reflect at all the real state of the bank's solvency. These capital ratios do not guarantee a timely advance warning of an impending solvency issue. Determining these regulatory measures is model dependent and is therefore not error free. This point has been made very clear by Andrew Haldane, Executive Director of the Bank of England, when he addressed the American Economic Association in Denver on January 9, 2011 [114]. His story is that of two groups of banks in the United Kingdom: "crisis banks" and "no-crisis banks." The first group consists of banks that did benefit from a government intervention during the credit crunch that brought down the financial system. The no-crisis banks did remain solvent throughout this difficult period without any injection of capital from the government or the delivery of a state guarantee. The reported capital ratios between the two sets of banks where largely indistinguishable, however. According to Andrew Haldane, the crisis banks looked even slightly stronger in the period preceding the crisis based on the regulatory capital ratios. This observation is definitively food for thought. It justifies to some extent the widespread criticism regarding the use of these data to warn the financial system of impending solvency problems. Market-based measures can in that perspective add more value when it comes to constructing an early warning system to trigger contingent capital.

---

[16] The Financial Stability Oversight Council was created in the United States under the Dodd–Frank act. The FSOC has a statutory mandate to identify risks and respond to emerging threats to the financial stability of the United States' banking system.

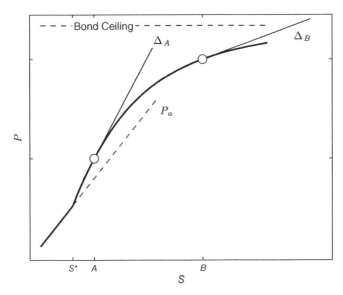

Figure 3.11   Theoretical price P of a contingent convertible vs. the price of the underlying share S.

Death Spiral

The possible conversion into shares of a CoCo bond introduces a mechanical dependence on the value of this instrument on the level of the share price. Encountering a trigger will indeed happen at depressed share prices. The investor will be forced to accept cheap shares when a trigger materializes. The probability of such a conversion will increase when the share price S reaches depressed levels, even if the trigger is linked to, for example, a capital ratio. The CoCo converges to parity P_a in this case. Parity is the value of the amount of shares received when the trigger event takes places and is defined as [67]:

$$P_a = C_r \frac{S}{N} \tag{3.6}$$

where S is the current stock price.

This move of the price of the CoCo P toward P_a is illustrated in Figure 3.11. This figure provides a graphical representation of the theoretical CoCo price and is based on the assumption that a trigger will take place when the share price reaches the value S^*. The same figure also shows that for high values of the share price, the value of the CoCo converges away from parity toward the bond ceiling.

Figure 3.11 illustrates how the equity sensitivity of the CoCo increases when the share price moves lower: $\Delta_A > \Delta_B$. This is negative convexity because the CoCo investor gets longer in shares in the case of falling share prices. In the opposite case, when all is fine for the underlying financial institution and the share price is performing well, the CoCo is moving further away from the danger zone. The negative convexity is visualized in Figure 3.12, where for one of the Lloyds CoCos the bond price has been plotted against the share price. The graph illustrates the somehow opposite behavior of a contingent convertible with respect to standard convertible debt. The negative gamma of a CoCo will have an impact on the hedging of contingent debt. Especially when the underlying shares have limited liquidity, the share price could suffer

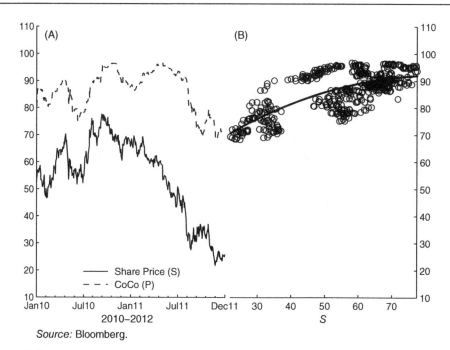

Source: Bloomberg.

Figure 3.12 (A) Share price and CoCo price during the period 2011–2012. (B) Scatterplot where the CoCo price is plotted against the share price.

a serious deterioration. The equity exposure of a contingent convertible increases when the share price moves lower. An investor looking to immunize the equity risk in the contingent convertible has to sell more shares when the share price weakens ($\Delta_A > \Delta_B$). This selling activity could push the share price further down, which in turn would even induce more shares to be sold by the investor. Such a share price collapse is called the "death spiral."[17] The death spiral risk has often been the topic of lively debate between opponents and proponents of contingent debt. The bottom line is that the issue size of a CoCo bond must be determined while taking into account the liquidity of the underlying shares. Only a sufficient amount of shares trading in a liquid market can avoid a collapse of the share price. In [71] a proposal is worked out where contingent debt is structured with multiple trigger levels instead of one capital ratio that sets the conversion into shares. The effect of a coupon cancelation from this perspective is investigated in [60].

3.8.3 Conclusion

This chapter has provided a general introduction to contingent debt. The basic building blocks of these loss-absorbing instruments have been explained at length in order to be able to deal with the valuation and risk analysis of these instruments in a subsequent chapter.

---

[17] The concept of death spiral risk has been studied at length in the case of convertible bonds with a reset mechanism [120].

Table 3.8 Table comparing the asset swap spread of a CoCo bond issued by Lloyds against a CoCo bond issued by Credit Suisse

February 26, 2013	Lloyds	Credit Suisse
ISIN	XS0459091236	XS0595225318
Trigger	5%	7%
Regulatory Trigger	No	Yes
5-Yr CDS Subordinated (bps)	332	167
Asset Swap Spread (bps)	534	564

Tax Issues

At the time of writing this book, the issuance of contingent debt occurred in Europe. The contingent convertible train was driven by European financials, but the main investment interest came from Asia. The United States was not present on the CoCo scene. In June 2012, the Financial Stability Oversight Council (FSOC) published a CoCo–related study required by the Dodd–Frank Act [167]. The goal of the report was to study the feasibility, benefits, costs, and structure of contingent capital for US financial companies. No specific guidance came out of this required report that would start off CoCo issuance in the USA. A possible show stopper is the fact that under the current Treasury guidance, interest rate charges for convertible debt is not tax deductible.

Regulation

The Basel III capital accord has been particularly instrumental in the rise of this new asset class. CoCos offer the loss-absorption property that the Basel Committee demands from regulatory capital. Different countries have, however, responded in different ways on how to introduce contingent debt in the capital structure of their banks. There is, for example, no worldwide standardization on trigger levels or conversion mechanisms. Comparing a CoCo from one jurisdiction to another needs to be done carefully.

An example is set out in Table 3.8. There, we start with the initial observation that the default swap spread on 5-year subordinated debt from Credit Suisse (167 bps) is much lower than Lloyds (332 bps). This makes sense and reflects the better health of Credit Suisse compared with Lloyds. When turning our attention to the spreads on contingent debt, we observe how the CoCos share similar asset swap spread levels. The bonds issued by Credit Suisse have a higher trigger and on top of this, they have a non-viability clause. These two facts bring the loss absorption risk of this Swiss CoCo closer to its UK counterpart.

Bond Indices

The inclusion of contingent debt in a popular bond index might provide a boost to contingent capital. For the moment, CoCos are not included in any of the fixed-income reference indices such as those compiled by Bank of America Merrill Lynch and Barclays Capital. The consequence is that investors who use those indices as benchmarks do not invest in contingent debt. The Barclays Capital Index Product Group has made it clear [106] that contingent capital is – similar to other mandatory convertibles – not eligible to be included in the broad-based investment-grade Barclays capital bond indices. There could be a spot, however, for contingent capital in some of the convertible bond indices.

Corporate Hybrids

4.1 INTRODUCTION

In the introductory chapter we defined a corporate hybrid as a long-dated, most of the time even perpetual, debt instrument. Very often a set maturity is missing. Through their perpetual nature, these bonds earn an equity status. Hybrids are deeply subordinated and carry a cancelable and variable coupon stream. Because of their subordination in the capital structure, hybrids have as good as no recovery value in case of default. In addition, this debt instrument often has one or more embedded issuer calls. The latter grants the right to the issuer to redeem the security before the scheduled maturity date, if any. In case the issuer of the hybrid bond skips the call and keeps the bond alive, the post-call-date coupon structure changes. Not calling back the bond on the call date often creates a higher interest rate charge for the issuing company, as the coupon stream could be increased with a predefined step-up percentage.

Hybrid bonds are located at the intersection of debt and equity. The fact that these bonds carry regular predefined interest payments makes them bond-like. Further, like coupons on corporate debt, the coupons of the hybrid are generated from the pre-tax income of the company. The interest rate charge is as such tax-deductible for the issuing company. This is in contrast to dividend payments on equity, since these come out of the post-tax income.

The mere fact that the coupons can be deferred without triggering a default event makes a hybrid security look like an equity-like instrument.[1] This is in full analogy with the flexible character of dividend payments to the equity investors. A company has full discretion over the dividend payments to its share holders. There is very often a link between the attribution of dividends to equity and the payment of coupons on hybrid debt issued by one and the same corporate. This happens through features such as dividend-stoppers or dividend-pushers, which will be covered later in this chapter.

4.2 ISSUER OF HYBRID DEBT

The issuing companies can be split into two broad categories: investment-grade companies and lower-rated companies [147]. The investment-grade hybrids are labeled "safe haven hybrids," whereas their lower-rated equivalents are better known as "high beta hybrids." For an issuer there are several advantages attached to the issuance of hybrid debt. There is first of all the tax-deductibility advantage we mentioned before. In addition, this equity-like financing takes place without any direct dilution for the share holders. The hybrid debt does not receive voting rights either. Another advantage of issuing hybrid debt is the credit support for the senior bond holders as the insertion of a hybrid layer puts senior bond holders in a more comfortable position. The flip side of the medal is of course that hybrids are more expensive than senior

---

[1] In some cases the non-payment of interest on an outstanding hybrid bond can lead to default. Some hybrid issues contain a clause where non-payment of deferred interest after a certain number of years constitutes a proper default event. An example of such an issue is the REXAM 6.75% 2067 hybrid bond.

bonds in terms of interest rate charge. A corporate should also not be carried away by the fact that it can, at least in theory, defer coupon payments unpunished. A coupon deferral will hurt investors, and exactly those investors will think twice before ever committing resources again to a new bond issue coming from the same corporate issuer.

4.3 INVESTING IN HYBRID DEBT

For an investor interested in investments offering a higher yield, hybrid bonds offer an interesting alternative. This explains the popularity of hybrid debt in a low-interest-rate environment. A top-quality issuer has only a moderate yield to offer compared with government bonds. Investors desiring higher yields have to move to lower-rated bonds from different issuers. The pick-up in yield is justified by the higher default risk of lower-rated corporate debt. The mere existence of hybrids offers the investor the possibility to stay away from such lower-rated issuers while still earning a high coupon. It is therefore sometimes argued that the higher coupons of hybrid debt, issued by an investment-grade issuer, offer a better alternative. It always remains to be seen what is best: investing in hybrid bonds from a top-quality issuer or buying senior bonds from a sub-investment-grade company.

It should also remain very clear that the higher yields offered by hybrids are a result of the particular risk embedded within the hybrid security. The coupons can, for example, be deferred by the issuer. Furthermore, a credit default swap does not offer protection against such a deferral since such a dividend cancelation does not constitute an immediate default event. Figure 4.1 is an illustration of the extra yield offered by a hybrid bond. Bayer, a major pharmaceutical

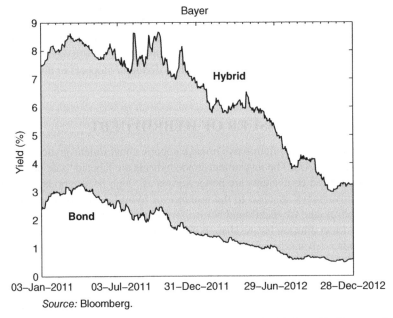

Source: Bloomberg.

Figure 4.1 Comparison of yields offered on hybrid and non-hybrid debt issued by Bayer, an investment-grade issuer.

company, has a single A rating[2] for its long-dated straight bonds. As an example, we consider a senior bond issued by this investment-grade issuer. This security[3] carries a coupon of 4.625% and there are no calls attached to this debt instrument. Such an instrument is often labeled straight debt, because it is debt in its simplest form: a final redemption and a stream of fixed coupons. The same issuer has also issued a long-dated hybrid bond. This hybrid security differs from straight debt because it is callable and because its coupons are cancelable. This extra risk justifies the fact that the average yield difference between the hybrid and the straight bond amounted to 297 bps during the period 2011–2012. This is the reason why some regard investing in hybrid bonds as a way to get better spreads from better companies [130].

4.4 STRUCTURE OF A CORPORATE HYBRID BOND

There is an enormous range of possible corporate hybrid structures, allowing us to find a compromise that suits both the requirements of the issuers and the demands from investors. The subordination of the hybrid bond carries a risk premium. The other constitutive elements can turn the hybrid into an overly complicated instrument in the eyes of some investors. The fact that the large rating agencies do not share a common view on the treatment of hybrid debt is an illustration of this problem. We will explore the structure of a typical hybrid bond around the following dimensions: subordination, coupon structure, replacement capital covenant, and issuer calls.

4.4.1   Coupons

Optional Deferral

The optional deferral of hybrid coupons at the discretion of the issuer increases the financial risk of the bond holder, who therefore needs to be compensated by a higher yield.

The same type of flexibility in renumeration toward investors can be found in common stock. In practice, companies do not like to use this opportunity to cut or cancel dividend distributions to their share holders. A dividend cut is considered as a negative signal regarding the future financial performance of the firm. An example of a firm avoiding such a cut was Enron Corporation, an S&P 500 energy company that filed for bankruptcy on December 2, 2001. Enron kept desperately paying dividends and did not even cancel the September 2001 dividend a couple of months before the unavoidable default. Research from Standard & Poor's illustrates that the same holds true for coupon payments on hybrid debt. Not paying out the coupon does not trigger a default event. Yet, most firms prefer not to defer any of these interest rate payments even if they are entitled to it according to the prospectus. Out of the 90 companies investigated in the research from S&P, 49 actually defaulted without ever having deferred a coupon payment [130]. Issuers of hybrid debt, that run into financial difficulties, will often elect to honor their obligations and pay the coupons. They judge that – even if they are legally entitled to defer coupons – they are better off not to do so. Sooner or later, they

---

[2] Standard & Poor's – April 9, 2013.
[3] ISIN XS0420117383.

have to face the credit markets again. At that moment, having a history of coupon cancelations would drive up the cost of new debt.

As mentioned before, an example of such an issuer was TUI, a large international travel group. When TUI canceled a scheduled dividend payment on its common stock on December 14, 2006, it still continued to pay out the coupon on its callable perpetual bond on January 30, 2007.

Mandatory Deferral

In case there is a possibility of mandatory deferral, the coupon payment is linked to well-determined conditions. There is a wide variety in possible covenants. We mention some of them:

- **Leverage ratio**
  Hybrids can have covenants in place that put a halt to any of their coupon payments if the net debt of the issuer[4] is too large compared with the EBITDA.[5] The EBITDA is a metric of the financial performance of the corporate. It is basically equal to the net income with taxes, depreciation, and amortization added back to it [189]. The payment of the coupon is linked to the ratio net debt/EBITDA remaining below a specified level.
- **Interest rate coverage**
  The interest rate coverage of a company links its earnings power (through, for example, EBITDA) to the cost of servicing its debt. In case of an insufficient interest rate coverage ratio, the coupon payment can be mandatorily halted. There are a myriad of possibilities in mandatory deferral covenants. The mandatory coupon deferral of a hybrid security issued by Siemens, a German engineering and manufacturing company, has a mandatory deferral linked to the interest coverage. The details of the bond can be found in Table 4.1. For this Siemens hybrid the coupon payments stop, as soon as the ratio $(CF + I)/I$ is less then 3.0[6] with:

$$CF = \text{net income} + \text{minority interest} + \text{amortization, depreciation, and impairments}$$
$$I = \text{interest expense}$$

(Non)-Cumulative

If the deferral is non-cumulative, a deferred coupon is lost forever. In the cumulative case, coupons are not lost. They become due as soon as the issuer starts paying coupons again. In some cases, the investors may even be offered interest on the deferred coupon amounts. Only after the cumulative amount of the canceled coupons has been compensated for, can the coupon schedule be reactivated. A further distinction has to be made between cash and non-cash cumulative interest. In the latter case, the missed coupons can be settled in a different way through a so-called alternative cash settlement mechanism (ACSM). The ACSM foresees raising the necessary amount of equity to raise cash to pay back the hybrid investor or alternatively allows a distribution of shares to the holders of hybrid debt.

---

[4] Net debt = short-term liabilities + long-term liabilities − cash(equivalents).
[5] EBITA = earnings before interest rate, taxes, depreciation, and amortization.
[6] For the fiscal year 2012, this index ratio was 7.2.

Table 4.1 Characteristics of a hybrid perpetual bond issued by Siemens

SIEMENS

Par Amount	1000	
ISIN	XS0266838746	
Issue Date	September 14, 2006	
Issue Size (mn)	900	
Currency	EUR	
Maturity	September 14, 2066	
Initial Coupon (%)	5.25	
Coupon Frequency	Annual	(Quarterly after the first call date)
Optional Coupon Deferral	Yes	Cumulative
Mandatory Coupon Deferral	Yes	Non-cumulative
Call Date	September 14, 2016	(Quarterly afterwards)
Call Price	100%	
Coupon after Call	3M EURIBOR + 225 bps	
RCC	Yes	

Source: Bloomberg.

Fixed to Floating

On the first call date, the bond's stream of fixed-coupon payments usually gets modified. The bond often switches into a floating-rate security offering a predetermined spread above a reference rate. This spread sometimes has an embedded step-up or interest rate "penalty." In that case the fact that the issuer decides not to call the bond will increase the future interest rate charges. As an example, we consider a perpetual bond issued by TUI, a European travel organization, in December 2005 (Table 4.2). TUI decided not to call back the bond on the first call date in January 2013 and hence opted for an extension till at least the next quarterly call date scheduled on April 30, 2013. The post-call coupon structure is linked to the 3-month interbank Euribor rate. The spread added on top of this reference rate equals 730 bps. The table on the next page summarizes the mechanics involved in the determination of the new

Table 4.2 Characteristics of a hybrid perpetual bond issued by TUI

TUI

Par Amount	1000	
ISIN	DE000TUAG059	
Issue Date	December 9, 2005	
Issue Size (mn)	300	
Currency	EUR	
Maturity	Perpetual	
Initial Coupon (%)	8.625	
Coupon Frequency	Annual	(Quarterly after the first call date)
Optional Coupon Deferral	Yes	Cumulative
Mandatory Coupon Deferral	No	
Call Date	January 30, 2013	(Quarterly afterwards)
Call Price	100%	
Coupon after Call	3M EURIBOR + 730 bps	

Source: Bloomberg.

coupon. Similar to swaps, the fixing of the reference rate takes place two business days before the coupon date on January 30, 2013.

Date	EURIBOR 3M	
January 30, 2013	23.0	Coupon Date
January 29, 2013	22.6	
January 28, 2013	22.4	Fixing Date
Spread	**730.0**	
New Coupon		
Start Date	January 30, 2013	
End Date	April 30, 2013	
Coupon (bps)	**752.40**	

The new coupon of 752.40 bps is in any case lower than the initial coupon of 862.5 bps. This reduction is linked to the fact that the reference rate has dropped almost 2% since the issue date of this hybrid bond and the first call date.

Dividend Stoppers and Pushers

Through the terms and conditions of the hybrid bond, the corporate can be forced to make a connection between the dividend schedule for the share holders and the interest rate payments on the hybrid debt. This was covered in Section 1.6.2. In case of a dividend-stopper, a coupon deferral on the hybrid stops any further dividend payments or share buy backs on common equity. A dividend-pusher is slightly different. If dividends are paid on common equity, the coupon payments on hybrid debt are automically "pushed" and reactivated.

4.4.2   Replacement Capital Covenant

The issuer can make a statement in the prospectus of the hybrid regarding his intention to fund a possible early redemption of the hybrid. It is a declaration of intent to use new proceeds or issue a new hybrid to redeem the existing one. Doing so, there will be no negative impact on the senior bond holders. Such a statement, however, is not an obligation and is not enforceable in a court of law. The replacement capital covenant (RCC) is a covenant in the terms and conditions of the bond that goes a step further. This legally binding agreement specifies that the hybrid can only be called back and redeemed by the issuer with funds coming from either a newly issued hybrid or new equity capital. This covenant clearly protects the senior bond holders and is therefore appreciated by the rating agencies [172]. The corporate issuer has the obligation to preserve the credit quality of the issuer's senior bond holders.

If the issuer does not call back the bond at the earliest occasion, the coupons usually will be increased with a step-up. In return, the existence of such a step-up will increase the likelihood of an early call and repayment of the bond. Such a repayment works against the interest of the senior bond holders. The RCC then comes to their rescue since the layer of subordinated debt will have to be replaced by a similar amount of deeply subordinated capital. This explains the fact that rating agencies advocate the inclusion of a capital replacement covenant in the prospectus of the hybrid bond. Doing so, the issuer protects the rating attributed to its outstanding senior debt. Through the RCC feature the issuer shows his intention to have a constant permanent layer of hybrid debt in the liability pool. A practical example of a replacement capital covenant can be found in the hybrid bond issued by Siemens in 2006 (Table 4.1). Through this feature the issuer points out to the investor that in case the bond will be redeemed prematurely on a call date, this redemption will be financed through either the issuance of new shares or the placement of new hybrid bonds. These new hybrid bonds are replacement securities and this replacement has, in the case of Siemens, to take place 6 months before the redemption date.

4.4.3   Issuer Calls

Corporate hybrid debt can be called back by the issuer. This right kicks in on a particular date: the call date. Very often, there is more than one date on which the bond can be called back. The period before the first call date is known as the call protection period.[7] The longer the call protection; the higher the equity nature of a hybrid bond. The possible early exit and repayment of the face value is pushed further into the future in case of a longer call protection.

A call feature has to be studied in combination with the coupon structure and the existence of an RCC in the terms and conditions of the bond.

- **Coupon structure**

  Let's start with a simplified example where there is only one call date which is, at the same time, a coupon step-up date. If the issuer decides not to call the bond, he will normally face an increase Δc in the coupons c after this call date. This is the so-called coupon step-up feature. As discussed before, the probability of calling back the bond is tied to the level of the coupon step-up. This increased interest rate charge needs to be compared with the cost of capital of the firm on the call date. The firm might be facing harsher credit conditions to finance new debt. This might lead to a situation where the firm is better off forgoing the call and accepting the coupon step-up. Through the embedded issuer call, the investor has sold an option to the issuer to terminate the hybrid bond at the call date. Under the assumption there is only one call date, we can already come up with a framework to value the embedded optionality. Suppose the bond has a maturity T with a first call date at T_c, $T_c < T$. The bond has face value N and carries the following coupon structure:
  - Before call date $0 < t \leq T_c$: coupon $= c$
  - After call date $T_c < t \leq T$: coupon $= c + \Delta c$

  The hybrid can be seen as the sum of two components:
  - **Long a (floating rate) corporate bond**

    The bond expires on the first call date T_c and pays a coupon c.
  - **Short a put option on a corporate bond**

    The put option expires on T_c and has strike N. The underlying asset is a corporate bond with maturity $T - T_c$ that starts at $t = T_c$ and pays a coupon $c + \Delta c$. In our simplified example, this put option is a European option and grants the issuer the right to extend the debt with a higher coupon. The holder of the hybrid bond holds the short put option and is forced to accept delivery of this bond, albeit with an increased coupon.

  The hybrid bond issued by Siemens (Table 4.1) has a step-up of 100 bps. The spread of the bond to the swap rate on its issue date in September 2006 is called the issue spread and was equal to 125 bps. The coupon after the first call date is increased with this 100 bps step-up and is hence equal to 3-month Euribor + 225 bps.

---

[7] A bond which is not callable during, for example, the first 5 years will be labeled as "NC5."

- **RCC**

  If there is a replacement capital covenant (RCC) established before the first call date, then the issuer will be more reluctant to call the bond. In this case, the early redemption has to be refinanced through either the issuance of new shares or similar hybrid debt.

  The RCC clause, laid out in the prospectus, might only be active after the call date. In this case, the issuer is not tied to any obligation at all to replace the hybrid when calling it back. Through the call feature, the bond can be terminated before the coupon structure is altered and before the replacement capital covenant kicks in.

- **Call structures**

  The sequence of call dates and coupon step-ups differs from hybrid to hybrid. Standardization is absent in both the structure of the coupons and the organization of the different call dates. Calls and coupons are tied together, however, which does not allow us to skip any of these structural elements in our analysis. The combination of the coupon payments and their step-up, the RCC and the layout of the call dates will impact the likelihood for an issuer to redeem the bond prematurely.

  In Figure 4.2, we illustrate the coupon stream and call date(s) for three different hybrid bonds:

  – **Deutsche Borse**

    This 100-year bond was structured with two coupon resets: one 5 years and one 10 years after the issue date. Initially, the bond starts with a fixed annual coupon of 7.5%, which changes after 5 years into a new annual coupon. This coupon is reset at the 5-year swap rate, to which the issue spread of 285 bps has been added. This spread corresponds to the difference between the yield of the bond and the 5-year swap on the issue date. The spread is changed another time on the second reset date from 285 bps to 385 bps. The

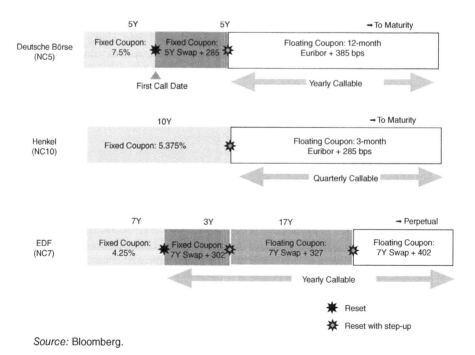

Source: Bloomberg.

Figure 4.2   Coupon and call structures for three different hybrids.

bond now transforms into a floating-rate callable security. The coupon is fixed every year and will be equal for the remaining life of the bond to 12-month Euribor plus 385 bps. The step-up coincides with the activation of the call and has an impact on a possible early redemption. If the issuer cannot finance itself cheaper than Euribor + 385 bps, it will prefer to extend the bond for at least another year.

– **Henkel**

The hybrid bond issued by Henkel has a more simple structure than the previous example. There is only one interest rate reset. The first period of 10 years after the start date of the bond is followed by a 90-year period during which the bond is a floating-rate note. The floating rate is refixed every quarter and is equal to 3-month Euribor + 285 bps. This spread contains a 100 bps step-up compared with the spread at issue.

– **EDF**

The issue of EDF is both the largest and most complex of the three examples of Figure 4.2. There are three resets in the coupon stream: one after 7, one after 10, and one after 27 years. The second reset has a step-up of 25 bps while the last reset has a 100 bps step-up compared with the spread at issue. The bond is callable on a yearly basis after 7 years.

4.5   VIEW OF RATING AGENCIES

Hybrid debt will be lower rated than senior secured debt issued by the same issuer. The rating is typically 2 to 3 notches lower in case of an investment-grade issuer (Table 4.3). For non-investment-grade debt, the notching of hybrid debt can be 3 to 4 points below senior debt [184]. The three major rating agencies (Fitch, S&P, and Moody's) each have their own proprietary process to assign a rating to a particular hybrid bond. In this book we will not go into detail on these processes designed by the rating agencies. Each agency has its own approach. The frameworks they developed share some common points, however. The common denominator is the equity character of a bond. The overall question a rating agency will ask itself when working on a particular hybrid debt issue is: "... how equity-like is this bond?..." The more it is equity-like, the lower its rating will be. The equity-like character depends on the deferral mechanism of the coupons, the inclusion of an RCC, the size of the coupon step-up on the call date, etc. For example, in most cases a mandatory coupon deferral is considered as being risker than an optional coupon deferral. Hence, such a deferral mechanism will work against the rating level.

Table 4.3   Example of the difference in ratings between hybrid and senior debt for some European issuers

Issuer	Hybrid	Senior	Difference in Notches
Bayer	BBB−	A−	3
Deutsche Borse	A+	AA	2
Henkel	BBB	A	3
Rexam plc	BB	BBB−	2
RWE	BBB−	BBB+	2
Scottish & Southern Energy	BBB	A−	2
TUI	CCC	B−	2

Source: Standard & Poor's. Date: March 1, 2013.

4.6 RISK IN HYBRID BONDS

The coupon of hybrid debt is higher than that of senior debt from the same issuer. This might at first sight generate an attractive pick-up in yield. However, this yield is a compensation for the financial risks embedded in the bond: the bond is perpetual, subordinated, its coupons can be deferred, and the issuer is granted the right to call back the bond. The hybrid investor has to offset the value of the higher yield against the additional risk.

4.6.1 Subordination Risk

Subordination risk is considered by market practitioners [130] as the most important component of the overall risk. The fact that hybrid debt ranks far below senior debt, and just above equity, implies that it will have a very small recovery rate compared with senior debt. It is widely assumed that this recovery rate π_{Hybrid} is close to nothing. The following relationship then connects the yields of both hybrid and senior debt issued by the same issuer:[8]

$$\text{Yield Hybrid Debt} \approx \frac{\text{Yield Hybrid Debt}}{1 - \pi_{Hybrid}} = \frac{\text{Yield Senior Debt}}{1 - \pi_{Senior}} \tag{4.1}$$

The extra yield earned on a hybrid compensates the investor for going down the capital structure, away from high-quality senior debt.

4.6.2 Deferral Risk

The deferral can be either mandatory or optional. In the case of an optional deferral, such an event will typically take place when the credit quality of the firm has been eroded. Indeed, a sound and cash-rich firm will not cancel a scheduled coupon payment on its outstanding hybrid debt. It will only do so when in trouble.

4.6.3 Extension Risk

This is the third component of risk for which the investor will seek compensation through a higher yield. The issuer has the right to extend the debt and force the investor to accept delivery of a longer maturity. Such an extension will happen when the credit conditions for a new issue create a higher interest rate charge than with the coupon after the step-up.

4.7 CONVEXITY IN HYBRID BONDS

4.7.1 Case Study: Henkel 5.375% 2104

In times of low interest rates and rising equity markets, the high yield offered by hybrid debt attracts new players. Both equity and bond investors are then tempted to invest in this asset class. Every one of these investors looks at the embedded market risk in a particular way.

Bond investors will, for example, rely on traditional measures such as duration and yield. We elaborate further as to why traditional bond measures fail to truly reveal the risk of a hybrid bond. Very often market practitioners will model a hybrid bond as a standard bond with a fixed

---

[8] In Chapter 13 we will analyze this relationship in more detail.

maturity. Corners are clearly being cut here and ignoring the extension risk of a hybrid bond is a dangerous practice. There is, of course, the fact that an important step-up in the coupon after the first call date increases the probability of an early redemption. Not calling the bond could increase the issuer's funding cost. It might therefore be better to call the hybrid security and issue a new one. For some, this is an open invitation to model the hybrid as a bond maturing on the first call date. The example of Deutsche Bank,[9] that unexpectedly decided not to call back an outstanding hybrid, clearly illustrated the importance of the extension risk. There is indeed an embedded optionality at work in the hybrid bond. The issuer has the choice to either pay back the bond at a call date or keep the bond alive and accept an increased interest rate because of the coupon step-up. As already indicated, the financial position of the investor can be seen as a combination of a bond expiring at the call date and a short put option on a new bond with a higher coupon starting on this call date. The strike of this option granted to the issuer to sell debt to the investor is the par amount N of the bond. The hybrid will be extended if the issuer decides to exercise this embedded option. This extension will depend on the credit spread of the issuer-related debt prevailing at the call date and the new increased coupon if the call were to be skipped by the issuer. The optionality is on the yield y of the hybrid security. The issuer is long gamma and the investor is short gamma with respect to the yield y. This is a first major difference between hybrid debt and fixed-maturity bonds. This last category only has a positive convexity toward the underlying yield:

$$\left(\frac{\partial^2 P}{\partial y^2}\right)_{\text{Callable Hybrid Debt}} < 0$$

$$\left(\frac{\partial^2 P}{\partial y^2}\right)_{\text{Fixed-Maturity Debt}} > 0 \tag{4.2}$$

The yield of a debt instrument is the sum of two components: the interest rate r and the credit spread cs. The yield y earned on a bond depends on the interest rate term structure of the currency in which the bond is denominated and the credit quality of the issuer:

$$y = r + cs \tag{4.3}$$

The yield is the discount rate to be applied on the cash flows generated by the bond in order for their present value to be equal to the market price P of the debt instrument. As far as hybrids are concerned, market practitioners use the yield to maturity (YTM) or the yield to call (YTC). The YTC only uses the cash flows up till the call date(s), whereas the YTM assumes the coupon stream of the hybrid security beyond all the call dates up till the final maturity date. The yield to worst (YTW) is the minimum of either YTC or YTM. In what follows we will use a practical example to illustrate how the yield volatility σ_y and the level of the yield determine the risk of ignoring the extension risk of the bond.

Our real-world example below shows what is at stake when modeling a callable hybrid bond as a fixed-maturity instrument. Our case study evolves around the hybrid bond issued by Henkel, a German industrial conglomerate, in 2005. We have used this bond earlier in Section 4.4.3 when illustrating different types of issuer calls. This bond is quarterly callable from November 25, 2015 onward. On this first call date, the bond transforms into a floating-rate bond with a 285 bps spread on top of the then prevailing 3-month Euribor. A summary of the characteristics of the bond can be found in Table 4.4.

---

[9] This example was covered in Section 1.6.

Table 4.4 Characteristics of the 100-year hybrid bond issued by Henkel

Henkel 5.375% 2104

Bond Type	Hybrid
Issue Date	November 25, 2005
Maturity	November 25, 2104
Initial Coupon (%)	5.375
Coupon Frequency	Annual
Optional Coupon Deferral	Yes (Non-cumulative)
Mandatory Coupon Deferral	Yes (Cumulative). The coupon is automatically deferred if the operation cash flow of the issuer is smaller than 15% of its adjusted debt
Par Amount	1000
ISIN	XS0225369403
First Call Date	November 25, 2015 (Quarterly call thereafter)
Call Price	100%
Step-Up Coupon	3M EURIBOR + 285 bps
Price (%)	106.870
Yield to First Call (%)	2.664%

Source: Bloomberg. Date: March 22, 2013.

Table 4.5 Calculation of the different bond prices using different yields. Calculation date: March 22, 2013. Bond price: 106.87

	YTM		YTC		YTW	
Yield	P	T	P	T	P	T
2.00	248.36	Nov 25, 2104	108.67	Nov 25, 2015	108.67	Nov 25, 2015
3.00	178.35	Nov 25, 2104	105.98	Nov 25, 2015	105.98	Nov 25, 2015
4.00	136.34	Nov 25, 2104	103.39	Nov 25, 2015	103.31	Nov 25, 2016
5.00	109.37	Nov 25, 2104	100.89	Nov 25, 2015	99.31	Nov 25, 2018
6.00	90.98	Nov 25, 2104	98.47	Nov 25, 2015	90.98	Nov 25, 2104

Source: Bloomberg.

In Table 4.5 we calculate the theoretical bond price for different yields using three different maturity assumptions.

- **Hybrid is called on November 25, 2015**

  The most obvious assumption is to consider that the bond will be called on the first opportunity that arises. The opposite assumption is to start from the idea that the bond will never be called and will expire at the final maturity date. In this latter case, when the yield equals 3% for example, the corresponding bond price is 178.35 (Table 4.5). By contrast, starting from the same yield but modeling the bond as a fixed-maturity bond expiring on the first call date in November 2015, the price equals 105.98. If the yield were to possess no volatility at all ($\sigma_y = 0$) and therefore be "frozen" at the 3% level, we could safely conclude that there is no risk in modeling this hybrid security as a fixed-income bond expiring on the first call date. A yield of 3% will force the rational issuer, seeking to minimize his liability, to buy back the full issue on the first occasion. But credit spreads and interest rates do move and the fact that the yields are stochastic changes the overall picture.

- **Hybrid is called on November 25, 2018**

  Given a yield equal to 5%, the assumption that leads to the lowest bond price corresponds to an expected maturity equal to November 25, 2018. This is 3 years beyond the first call date. It makes sense for the issuer to skip any right to call the bond in the period November 25, 2015 up till November 25, 2018 in order to maximize his wealth. Calling the bond on the first call date would, for example, lead to a bond price equal to 100.89 when using a 5% yield. This is more than the theoretical price of 99.31 considering a redemption on November 25, 2018.

- **Hybrid is never called**

  From a certain yield level onward it will be suboptimal for the issuer to call the bond. It will be more economical to bear the charge of the step-up coupon and carry the bond until the final maturity date. This is, for example, the case when the yield equals 6%. The bond price based on applying this particular yield to all the cash flows up till the final maturity date is 90.98.

The result of this exercise for yields ranging from 3% to 6% has been summarized in Figure 4.3. The graph illustrates the negative convexity of the hybrid's price with respect to changes in the underlying bond yield. As explained above, when the yield is equal to 6%, the assumption that the bond is called on the first call date becomes invalid. The fact that yields can move easily to a range where the bond will not be called at the first occasion is a clear warning signal to the popular school of thought modeling any hybrid callable bond as a fixed-maturity instrument.

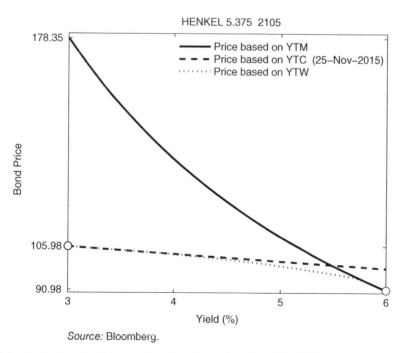

HENKEL 5.375 2105

Source: Bloomberg.

Figure 4.3 Illustration of yield convexity. Calculation date: March 22, 2013.

Table 4.6 Overview of the different dimensions of hybrid debt: maturity, subordination, and (cumulative) coupon deferral

Debt	Hybrid	Equity
Maturity		
Fixed maturity	The higher the likelihood that the bond is not going to be called back, the more the hybrid has a proper equity character. Features such as a high coupon step-up will move the hybrid away from this perpetual nature as these provide an incentive to call back early. The existence of an RCC clause which is in force before the bond can be called back has an opposite effect. It creates an increase in the equity nature of the bond.	Perpetual
Subordination		
Unsubordinated	The subordination exposes the hybrid owner more to a cyclical downturn in the business of the issuing company. This will make the hybrid bond more volatile than senior debt.	Deeply subordinated
Coupon Deferral		
Not allowed	The fact that through an optional coupon deferral the issuer has full discretion over the payment of the coupons attributes a very dividend-like nature to the interest rate renumeration of hybrid bonds. The presence of a mandatory deferral shifts the hybrid further in the direction of equity.	Allowed
Cumulative		
Yes	A non-cumulative coupon deferral turns the hybrid away from being a debt instrument. Once the coupon is unpaid, it will be lost forever. Non-cash cumulative coupons also attribute a higher equity content to the instrument.	No

4.7.2 Duration Dynamics

The presence of the issuer call brought negative convexity to the table. In terms of dollar duration or DV01,[10] the adverse effects can also be felt. Straight debt has the property that the DV01 decreases for increasing yields. The more the yields rise, the less the bond will be hurt for further yield increases. Not so for hybrid callable debt. If yields rise, duration can rise as well. The issuer might, in the case where the yields have moved up a lot, prefer not to call the bond. The refinancing at the higher rate might be more economical. This extends the maturity and pushes up the duration.

4.8 EQUITY CHARACTER OF HYBRID BONDS

Table 4.6 assists in investigating to what extent a hybrid would classify as either debt or equity. The question of whether a hybrid is a bond or an equity will be answered differently by different investors. Even rating agencies will not necessarily provide similar answers to this question. The hybrid will "earn" its equity character along different dimensions: maturity, subordination, and coupon deferral.

---

[10] DV01 measures the impact on the value of a position based on a 1 bp increase in the level of the credit spread.

Bail-In Bonds

In the banking crisis that hit Cyprus early 2013, bail-in bonds were part of the solution. The concept of bail-in capital is different from the contingent convertible capital discussed in Chapter 3. In the case of bail-in, a national resolution authority will force the write-down of a specific category of debt while respecting its seniority on the balance sheet.

5.1 INTRODUCTION

The collapse of a SIFI will rock the financial markets. Similar to the Lehman collapse, its failure will be widely felt by other financial institutions. Some banks may have direct counterparty exposure to a failed institution because of outstanding uncollateralized derivative transactions. Even banks with little or no direct exposure to a failed bank will feel the heat. Creditors of such a collapsed bank may be forced to sell their assets in order to raise cash. This liquidation exercise is a real problem if the assets are not liquid. The case of Lehman Brothers shows how this ultimately led to a wave of disorderly selling, where the actions of one bank inflict losses on another bank. The financial stability of the economy as a whole was in danger again, since even banks with no direct link at all to a failed SIFI – nor holding any assets on its balance sheet similar to the ones held by the failed bank – suffer. Panic spreads throughout the whole financial market and every bank sees its funding costs increase.

In a bail-in solution the unsecured creditors of a bank provide the additional insurance to absorb the bank's losses when the outstanding regulatory capital of this institution is not large enough. To bail in or not to bail in, that is going to be the regulator's question. Some bonds will be eligible to suffer a haircut, while others are not. A bank with insufficient bail-in capital will be regarded as putting its senior unsecured bond holders at risk. In this case even its senior debt can suffer in case of severe losses. There is, of course, always the theoretical possibility that governments will bail out senior bond holders. Tax payers could indeed bail out bond holders, but after the credit crisis of 2008, many politicians argued that this is to be avoided at all cost. There seems to be a global consensus that share holders and creditors are liable first and foremost. Without a proper resolution mechanism, a bank's failure is not a standalone event. The fear of being drawn into a negative spiral similar to what took place after the Lehman collapse can put a constraint on the willingness of a financial institution to lend to corporate investors. When banks no longer lend out money, the economy stalls and quickly slips into a recession. Europe is more vulnerable to such a lending freeze because European banks have a more important role in credit intermediation than their American counterparts. Specifically, according to a study of the Institute of International Finance (IIF), 70% of the credit intermediation in Europe is in the hands of banks. In the USA, banks take up only 24.6% of the credit supply [185, 88]. This explains the difference in opinions on both sides of the Atlantic regarding bail-in solutions. The European landscape is also dominated by large domestic banks. The existence of such large national champions is yet another major difference between Europe and the USA [110]. Moreover, the combined size of

Table 5.1 Combined assets in 2009 of the top five banks compared with GDP

% GDP	
Germany	151
United Kingdom	466
France	344
Italy	138
Spain	220
Netherlands	464
Sweden	409
Japan	115
United States	58

Source: Bank of International Settlements.

the top five banks in the major European economies is large compared with their national GDP (Table 5.1). Any weakness or failure of such domestic champions is therefore likely to have a much larger knock-on effect in Europe than in the USA.

5.2 DEFINITION

A bail-in bond is a bond that can be written down or converted into equity when the authorities consider a financial institution under their supervision on the brink of collapse. This write-down feature forces the bond holders to take their share of losses when a bank is put into resolution. The bail-in absorbs the losses suffered by the financial institution and could eventually recapitalize the bank. The loss-absorption mechanism is not necessarily a contractual feature which is stipulated in the bond's prospectus. This is a major difference from a contingent convertible where the loss absorption is triggered by one or more predefined criteria. A CoCo is loss absorbing by design, a bail-in bond has no contractual loss-absorption features. In the case of bail-in bonds, the authorities are in the driving seat. They have the statutory power to force a loss on the bond holder.

This statutory power granted to a so-called resolution authority is by no means a blank cheque granted to the government. There will be a legal framework stipulating what can and should be done. The latter may include, for example, a particular order in which liabilities are bailed in. On this score, a logical first step consists of the existing share holders having their equity investment diluted or wiped out. In a second step regulatory capital such as Tier 1 or Tier 2 may be used to cover losses. Contingent convertibles belong to the additional Tier 1 and Tier 2 bucket and are therefore in theory liable to be bailed in. Next in line are the subordinated bonds to be bailed in. If these three categories of liabilities are still not large enough to bear the losses, a final and more drastic step may be taken. Such an event could eventually be the senior bond holders and depositors losing a portion of their wealth through the bail-in. The idea of extending loss absorption to senior debt has been quite controversial. One should not forget that senior unsecured bank debt has always ranked pari passu with the deposit holders of the bank. The European Central Bank's (ECB) suggestion in July 2012, to impose losses on senior creditors of Spanish banks when the Spanish financial system received its $100 bn financial injection from Europe, was therefore a surprise. Mario Draghi, the president of the ECB, was considered to have opened pandora's box when he made a

Table 5.2   Case study: bail-in applied to a bank

(1) Initial balance sheet

Assets		Liabilities	
Cash	10	Deposits	40
Securities	40	Senior debt	30
Loans	50	Subordinated debt	20
		Equity	10

(2) Balance sheet after write-down of $10 bn

Assets		Liabilities	
Cash	10	Deposits	40
Securities	40	Senior debt	30
Loans	40	Subordinated debt	20
		Equity	0

(3) Recapitalization using bail-in

Assets		Liabilities	
Cash	10	Deposits	40
Securities	40	Senior debt	30
Loans	40	Subordinated debt	10
		Equity	10

similar plea in favor of bailing in senior Spanish banking debt [38]. Where a bail-in was avoided in Spain, it was used in full force to solve the banking crisis in Cyprus 6 months later. The depositors and creditors of its two biggest banks suffered a $7.5 bn bail-in. This was as compensation for $13 bn of financial support coming from the European tax payers.

Case Study: Bail-In Applied to a Bank

An example of a hypothetical bank with a simplified balance sheet is the best way to illustrate bail-in at work. In Table 5.2, a $100 bn balance sheet of a financial institution is invested in cash, securities, and loans. These investments are financed with deposits, debt, and equity.

The first losses are always imposed on the share holders of the bank. They rank after all the other liabilities and are first in line when it comes to taking a share of the burden. The maximum loss that the bank in this example is allowed to suffer is $10 bn. If a loss of this magnitude were to occur, the equity capital would be completely wiped out. This would bring the bank to the brink of failure. Table 5.2 illustrates how a bail-in solution is applied on subordinated debt. Converting some of the subordinated debt into equity recapitalizes the bank. Subordinated debt holders lose, in this particular case, 50% of their investment but have received equity capital instead. This simplified example illustrates why bail-in is sometimes labeled as a kind of fast-track debt restructuring.

5.3 RESOLUTION REGIME

Bail-in capital is part of a wider picture better known as a resolution regime. The latter consists of a set of procedures and tools granted to resolution authorities to intervene quickly and safely in order to ensure the continued performance of a bank's systemically important functions. This is a contingency plan where a bailed-in bank should be able to pay out or transfer deposits smoothly and instantly without sending a wave of distrust or panic through the financial markets [94]. The losses are to be shared by bond holders according to their ranking in a fair and predictable way.

5.3.1 Resolution Tools

Bail-in is not a standalone solution. Writing down the face value of the bail-in bonds is only one of the many possible steps taken by the resolution authorities. When the FSB published, in October 2011, the key attributes of effective resolution regimes for financial institutions, this particular topic was emphasized [95]. According to the FSB, the statutory powers given to resolution authorities cover much more than just recapitalizing the bank or absorbing losses through a bail-in applied on subordinated debt.

The management of the failing bank could be replaced and there should be a legal framework where new shares can be issued without any need for share holder consent. This new equity capital could be awarded to bond holders in return for a bail-in on their investment. The fully written-off equity investors or subordinated debt holders could be given warrants. Such an offering leaves some room for a participation in future positive share price appreciation. Other resolution tools are, for example, the creation of a bad bank or the acquisition of the assets by another financial institution. The existence of a firm resolution plan allows a national supervisor to act promptly and swiftly when a bank enters dangerous waters. An example of this is the case of Bradford & Bingley in the UK. The UK authorities took this bank into temporary public ownership in September 2008 after its national regulator, the FSA, considered the bank no longer solvent enough [88]. The extensive contingency plan engineered by the authorities allowed them to conduct, over a single weekend, a sale of Bradford & Bingley's retail deposits, branches, and associated systems. The Bradford & Bingley branches opened for business as usual on Monday morning.

5.3.2 Timetable

Writing a chapter on bail-in bonds is similar to covering a live soccer game. The game includes many international participants: FSB, G20, International Monetary Fund (IMF), Basel Committee, European Commission, and numerous national regulators and central banks. Therefore it should not come as a surprise that new ideas, proposals, and regulations regularly make headlines in the press. All of this happend with a European sovereign debt crisis unfolding in the background. The road toward more financial stability is paved with good intentions, but regulatory decision making tends to be slow. To make matters worse, some regulatory reports contradict others.

The non-exclusive list below reflects a timetable with the main regulatory actions taken over the last several years. Each of the topics in the timetable had a material impact on the bail-in debate and the development of bail-in bonds.

1. **October 2008: G7 (Toronto)**
   In its first meeting after the collapse of Lehman Brothers, the G7 decided to take decisive action and use all available tools to support systemically important financial institutions and prevent their failure.
2. **October 2008: European Council**
   The European Council reaffirmed its commitment to preserve the stability of the financial system, to support the major financial institutions, to avoid bankruptcies, and to protect deposit holders [89].

3. **September 2009: G20 (Pittsburgh)**
   Resolution tools such as bail-in have their roots in this particular G20 meeting. The G20 leaders present at this meeting were committed to "… create more powerful tools to hold large global firms to account for the risk they take …" and, more specifically, "… to develop resolution tools and frameworks for effective resolution of financial groups to help mitigate the disruption of financial institution failures and reduce moral hazard in the future … " [86].

4. **January 2010: Bank of International Settlements**
   The Group of Central Bank Governors and Heads of Supervision, the oversight body of the Basel Committee on Banking Supervision (BCBS), met at the headquarters of the Bank of International Settlements and discussed a possible inclusion of contingent convertibles in Tier 1 and/or Tier 2 [13].

5. **June 2010: G20 (Toronto)**
   This G20 meeting supported the work of BCBS regarding contingent capital: "We support the BCBS' work to consider the role of contingent capital in strengthening market discipline and helping to bring about a financial system where the private sector fully bears the losses on their investments. Consideration of contingent capital should be included as part of the 2010 reform package." The FSB was asked to develop concrete recommendations to address the resolution of systemically important institutions.

6. **October 2010: FSB**
   The FSB responded to the previous G20 request by proposing stricter and stronger capital requirements for SIFIs. These requirements are stronger than what is proposed in the Basel III standards. The tools proposed by the FSB to reach a higher loss absorbency are the inclusion of an extra capital surcharge or the use of bail-in bonds and contingent convertibles.

7. **November 2010: G20 (Seoul)**
   The G20 meeting in Seoul resulted in an endorsement of the policy framework and timeline proposed by the FSB regarding the reduction of the moral hazard risks posed by SIFIs. The FSB was asked to build key attributes for resolution regimes by 2011. This assignment given to the FSB resulted from the fact that many jurisdictions around the globe lacked a proper national resolution authority. The majority of the countries were not at all ready and far from prepared to cope with a failure of one of their banks.

8. **December 2010: FSB**
   The FSB established a working group on bail-in. This group had as task to study the characteristics required for bail-in to become an effective loss-absorption tool.

9. **January 2011: BCBS**
   The BCBS launched a proposal demanding that all regulatory capital is loss absorbing through either a write-down or conversion into equity [14]. The trigger is determined by an injection of tax-payers' money into the bank or the observation that the bank would no longer be viable without forcing a loss on the holders of regulatory capital.

10. **July 2011: BCBS**
    The BCBS decided that systemically important banks would not be allowed to meet the additional capital surcharge with contingent capital [23]. Only common Tier 1 instruments can be used to meet this extra capital by banks with a so-called "too-big-to-fail" status.

11. **July 2011: FSB**
    The FSB published its first consultation document regarding resolution regimes [94]. Bail-in is seen as one of the possible tools embedded within a national resolution regime.

In the eyes of the FSB, bail-in is not a standalone solution. This document emphasizes, for example, the opinion of the FSB that authorities should also be given the power to replace the management of a bank, transfer its assets, or terminate and assign contracts. The FSB also makes a clear distinction between instruments with a contractual write-off or conversion, such as contingent convertibles and instruments with a statutory write-down such as bail-in.

12. **July 2011: European Commission**

   The implementation of Basel III in Europe resulted in a directive (Capital Requirements Directive 4 or CRDIV) and a regulation (Capital Requirements Regulation 1 or CRRI) [87]. The full implementation is expected by 2019. Both CRDIV and CRRI do not address the resolution of financial institutions close to failure. A provision has been made for high-trigger contingent convertibles.

13. **September 2011: ICB**

   This report is also known as the Vickers report and introduced the concept of ring-fencing the investment banking from the retail banking business in UK financial institutions. The report also proposes a **primary loss-absorbing capacity** (PLAC) of 17 to 20% of the risk-weighted assets (RWA) and commits to bail-in bonds being part of this loss-absorption capacity [88].

14. **October 2011: FSB**

   After having received comments from the industry on its consultative document (Point 11 in the timeline), the Financial Stability Board finalizes the key attributes regarding resolution regimes. The FSB imposes the jurisdictions to have resolution regimes in place where resolution authorities have a broad range of powers to resolve a non-viable financial institution [95].

15. **November 2011: G20 (Cannes)**

   The FSB presented a report to the G20 leaders regarding the progress it made in the follow-up on the recommendations made in earlier G20 meetings regarding financial stability [96]. At this meeting the FSB presented for the first time an initial list of systemically important financial institutions and received endorsement by the G20 for its publication of the key attributes regarding resolution regimes.

16. **June 2012: European Commission**

   Draft of a directive establishing a framework for the recovery and resolution of credit institutions and investment firms [88]. This was the long-awaited draft of the Crisis Management Directive (CMD). This proposal allows banks to issue specific subordinated debt instruments that would absorb losses after regulatory capital but before any senior debt.

17. **July 2012: Financial Stability Oversight Council**[1]

   The FSOC recommended the Federal Reserve and other financial regulators to continue to study the advantages and disadvantages of including contingent capital and bail-in instruments in their regulatory capital frameworks.

18. **June 2013: European Council**

   An agreement was reached by the European Council regarding the CMD a year earlier. Most important was the decision to impose a minimum amount of bail-in of 8% of the total liabilities and own funds for each financial institution in the European Union. This

---

[1] The Financial Stability Oversight Council (FSOC) was created under the Dodd–Frank Act and has a major role to identify threats and risk to financial stability within the United States.

can be considered an important deviation from the previous line of thought. The amount of bail-in capital is a function of the total assets; the notion of risk-weighted assets has here disappeared from the scene. Only when the bail-in capital of a bank has been fully written down in a loss-absorption process can further losses be imposed on senior bonds. The need for larger bail-in buffers so that the market does not consider their senior unsecured bonds as potentially loss absorbing will send the European banks on a quest to raise an estimated amount of capital of around €440 bn [186].

5.4 CASE STUDIES

5.4.1 Bail-In of Senior Bonds

Two bank defaults hit Denmark in 2011, a couple of months after a change in the Danish laws on financial stability. The old regulation, where senior bond holders were protected, had expired on September 30, 2010. This new regulation ensured that losses could also be imposed on senior bond holders. The two defaulting banks where, for the first time, senior bond holders were bailed in were Fjordbank Mors and Amagerbanken. The Danish bail-in regulation went significantly further than in other countries, where loss absorption following a bail-in had been limited to subordinated debt. The introduction of the new bail-in laws in Denmark coincided with the European Union's internal discussions on the merits of introducing burden sharing by bond holders across the whole economic region. The fact that senior bonds could be bailed in made the Danish banking system unique and at the same time uncompetitive compared with the rest of the world. The existence of a level playing field in the banking sector is important and is something the Basel Committee continuously emphasizes.

The first Danish bank that collapsed after the implementation of this new bank rescue package was Amagerbanken.[2] It failed in February 2011, 4 months after the implementation of the new bail-in regime. The senior and subordinated bond holders were bailed in [4]. This loss absorption, where senior debt received a 41% haircut, was combined with a transfer of the assets and liabilities to a new bank which was fully owned by the FSB, the Danish government's bail-out entity. In June 2011, the second bank to fail was Fjordbank Mors. In both cases senior bond holders were bailed in and could no longer profit from the safety blanket of government support. The haircut on senior debt was, in this second bail-in, only 26% [3]. The state support for Danish banks remained in line with the rest of Europe. The guarantee for deposit holders of a failed bank was equal to €100 000.

The two banks that had been wound down were relatively small and not systemically important. Nevertheless, the fact that senior bond holders lost some of their investment sent a shock wave through the market. As a consequence, and to no-one's surprise, most of Denmark's roughly 120 banks were shut out of the funding markets [92].

The idea of allowing a bail-in on senior debt moved to the background and remained there for a short while [180]. In July 2012 Mario Draghi, the chairman of the ECB, stirred the financial markets by making a surprise comment in an interview with the *Wall Street Journal* where he called also for senior bond holders of troubled Spanish banks to be part of a bail-in. Again senior debt seemed no longer untouchable. Before this particular interview, only subordinated debt and equity were considered to be part of such a Spanish bail-in plan. This bail-in program was imposed in return for a €100 mn bail-out of the Spanish banks. Without

---

[2] Amagerbanken has been nicknamed "Armageddon Bank" in the investment community.

such a bail-in plan this amount of European tax-payers' money would not be made available. The comment regarding the inclusion of senior bonds made by Mr Draghi was in sharp conflict with what the European governments had agreed so far. The mere fact that the head of the ECB even considered allowing senior bonds to be part of a bail-in had its impact on the market; an increase of the credit default swap spreads of Spanish senior bank debt was, for example, reported. The cost of insuring this particular kind of debt rose following Mr Draghi's comment [109]. Pandora's box had been opened by the chairman of Europe's central bank. This led the European investors to the point where they started even to question the perceived safety of covered bonds [78].

5.4.2 Saving Lehman Brothers

Paul Calello, the former head of the investment banking business of Credit Suisse, and Wilson Ervin, its former chief risk officer [47], examined how a bail-in might have been applied in the case of Lehman through four different steps. In each of the steps of this imaginary bail-in process, it is the national regulator taking the initiative. The balance sheet of Lehman as at the end of the second quarter (Q2) in 2008 is represented in Figure 5.1. This balance sheet is where Calello and Ervin start their bail-in exercise.

1. **Asset write-down**
   In a first step Lehman's assets would be valued at much more conservative levels, thereby eventually wiping out all the value of the equity. Exactly this bold initiative would give the bail-in exercise credibility. In the Lehman case, this write-down would amount to $26 bn (in the aftermath of the failure of the bank, it turned out that the losses were much larger than this and amounted to $150 bn).

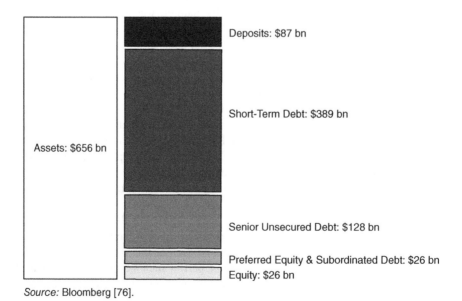

Source: Bloomberg [76].

Figure 5.1   Balance sheet of Lehman Brothers Q2, 2008.

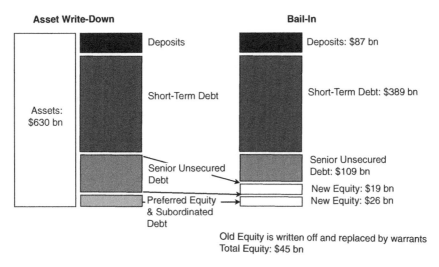

Asset Write-Down   **Bail-In**

Assets: $630 bn

Deposits

Deposits: $87 bn

Short-Term Debt

Short-Term Debt: $389 bn

Senior Unsecured Debt

Senior Unsecured Debt: $109 bn

New Equity: $19 bn
New Equity: $26 bn

Preferred Equity & Subordinated Debt

Old Equity is written off and replaced by warrants
Total Equity: $45 bn

Figure 5.2   Applying a bail-in on Lehman would have kept the bank open. The preferred equity and subordinated debt would have been converted 100% in equity. The senior debt would only have been converted for 15%.

2. **Restore equity base**
   The amount of equity needed is larger than the strict regulatory minimum. This conservative approach would help restore the confidence of the market in the financial institution.

3. **Write-down according to debt seniority**
   After wiping out the equity base of the bank, the bond holders could be bailed in. This could happen through a write-down of debt and possibly a conversion into equity of some senior bonds (Figure 5.2). Subordinated debt would be converted first and the equity conversion mechanism would crawl all the way up in the balance sheet to include senior debt. In Lehman's case the preferred stock and subordinated debt holders would come first and see their approximately $26 bn bond holdings completely written down and converted into about 58% of the equity in the new Lehman. The senior unsecured debt holders, having $128 bn Lehman debt on their books, would have to convert 15% of their bonds into Lehman equity using this Calello–Ervin scenario. They would now own $19 bn of equity after this bail-in exercise. The remaining 85% of the senior bonds would stay unaffected, similar to the deposits and the secured credit. This move would have doubled the capital base of Lehman to $45 bn. Lehman would have stayed in business and a systemic shock would have been avoided. On top of this, the remaining debt could have been better rated because of the broader equity base.

4. **Replace the management**
   The regulators would, in a final step, replace the management of the bank. Applying this four-step process shows that senior debt holders in the Lehman case study would have been better off keeping 85% of their initial investment. This is much bigger than the 20% post-bankruptcy recovery values on the debt.

The collapse of the investment bank created a wave of disorderly selling, which in the illiquid environment of September 2008 reduced the value of the assets beyond everybody's imagination. A bail-in of the bond holders would have made the liquidation of the massive asset pool of Lehman unnecessary. As a result, the contagion that touched other banks in 2008 could have been avoided according to Calello and Ervin. Lehman's equity holders would have lost all the value of their shares in this first step, but could possibly have been offered warrants that would acquire a positive value as soon as the "new" Lehman rose from its ashes and became profitable again. It is important that a bail-in process is carried out swiftly, and it needs the approval of the bank's home state regulator. This regulator needs to be able to force a write-down and possibly a conversion of the debt, similar to this Lehman example.

5.5 CONSEQUENCES OF BAIL-IN

5.5.1 Higher Funding Costs

Banks inevitably face higher funding costs when they issue bail-in bonds. Bond investors demand higher yields to reflect the removal of the implicit state support and the inclusion of the prospect of these bonds being written down or converted into equity. For European banks, the average increase in a bank's funding cost is expected to be equal to 15 bps [88]. However, cross-border differences in bail-in legislation can make its implementation very challenging for international banks.

5.5.2 Higher GDP

The European Commission has quantified the beneficial impact of a bail-in requirement on the GDP of the European member states. Having a lower probability of a full-blown banking crisis that creates a fall in GDP is a large positive effect. A bail-in resolution forces the cost of a crisis on the equity and bond holders instead of using tax-payers' money. As a consequence, European countries should feel a positive effect in their own funding costs because they no longer have to carry the state guarantee of the banks under their supervision. This positive impact on GDP is expected to be between 0.34% and 0.62% [88].

5.5.3 Availability of Bail-In Bonds

One of the concerns raised by the European Commission in its CMD, is the availability of bail-in capital. The amount of bail-in bonds determines how other funding sources may be needed to help a bank absorb losses. Such ex-ante funds are deposit guarantee schemes and resolution funds. Rating agencies will look at the available loss-absorbing cushion of bail-in bonds before attributing a particular credit quality to the senior unsecured debt of a bank. The possible lack of sufficient bail-in capital is therefore an important issue. National authorities could immediately impose a bail-in status on all subordinated and unsecured bank debt retrospectively. Such a bold move will, however, impact abruptly the funding costs of the banks and can create a wave of deleveraging across the European financial institutions. A more moderate approach has been proposed whereby the bail-in powers will be applied from January 1, 2018 onwards [12]. This gives the banks enough time to prepare to expand their pool of bail-in bonds and align their liability structure to this new European directive.

5.5.4 Paying Bankers in Bail-In Bonds

Erkki Liikanen, the Bank of Finland governor, advocated the use of bail-in bonds in bonus payments to bankers. Bankers would somehow be forced to eat their own stew. This initiative would make bankers more risk averse. The equity option schemes granted in the past to bank executives clearly missed this effect. One of the first banks to follow this suggestion was UBS. This bank announced early 2013 that their senior bankers would see their bonuses paid in bail-in bonds.

5.6 CONCLUSION

From a regulatory perspective, bail-in capital is work in process. The most important thing to retain is the fact that there is now a continuum of loss-absorbing capital instruments on the balance sheet of a bank. Starting from equity and climbing up to Tier 1 CoCos followed by Tier 2 CoCos, one ultimately arrives at a layer of subordinated bonds that are eligible to share the burden generated by extreme losses. Market participants started in the course of 2013 to realize how investing in subordinated debt implies participation in a bail-in scenario. The introduction of bail-in bonds pushes a bail-out of the banks into the background. Hereby, the established link between sovereigns and their national financial institutions is weakened.

6

Modeling Hybrids: An Introduction

6.1 INTRODUCTION

It is in our human nature to try to understand how things work. Looking back at our ancestors, we see that they were driven by the same desire to know and understand more. The Greeks modeled the cosmos as a set of spheres. The planet earth was in the center of everything. It took more than 2000 years to cancel out the geocentric model and describe the mechanics of the planets orbiting around the sun. But even when the earlier models were dead wrong, they brought comfort because they helped to understand events such as the seasons, day and night, and the appearance of the stars in the sky. In finance we try to achieve the same thing, building a mathematical description – the model – of the way asset prices move. Even after incorporating the more advanced mathematical tools, every model remains unfortunately a weak blueprint of reality. The mathematical nature of the models makes us forget that they rely on assumptions about human behavior, a large difference from the laws of physics. No financial model – however sophisticated it might be – can predict the markets with certainty [40]. One never should bet the firm on it.

In this chapter we offer an introduction to the different approaches when it comes to developing a valuation model for a hybrid security. There is unfortunately no "one-size-fits-all" solution available and it should not be a surprise that each investment bank has a particular view on how to model these complex securities. Some of the approaches are very heuristic and intuitive while others require a deep understanding of financial mathematics. Hybrids are located between debt and equity. This opens up possibilities to combine equity and interest rate derivative models to get a better understanding of the market risk embedded in a hybrid security. These are the so-called two factor models because they contain two sources of risk. Each source (equity and interest rates) comes with its own volatility describing the random behavior of these variables. A correlation ties the two stochastic processes together. All of this will be explained in Chapter 13. Before one gets exposed to these complex two-factor models, it is useful to cover as a first step the one-factor models at length. In a one-factor model, the value of a hybrid security is assumed to be driven by one stochastic process only: equity prices, interest rates, or credit spreads. A credit derivative trader tends to reduce the valuation problem of a hybrid security to the calculation of an appropriate yield. This yield should incorporate a fair compensation for the risk of a possible financial loss in case of a default or when a forced conversion into shares takes place. For an equity derivatives specialist, a hybrid security is a potential long position in shares. The latter specialist will put equity derivative models at work to price convertible debt.

Before we reach out to the fully-fledged two-factor models, we first shed light on some heuristic techniques to price hybrids. These are literally back-of-the-envelope models since they allow for quick decision making while managing a bond portfolio. The simplicity of such rule-of-thumb models comes at a cost, however, since not all the instrument features are covered. A typical example of such an approach is an investment process for a hybrid portfolio where yield-to-maturity is the main decision variable. This is a metric inherited from

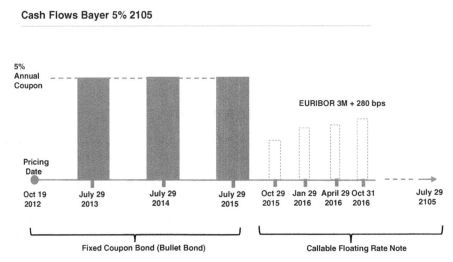

Figure 6.1   Coupon structure of the Bayer 5% 2105 bond.

the world of corporate bonds. Such a concept cannot be interpreted without risk when dealing with convertible bonds or contingent convertibles. The instrument is reduced to a stream of pure bond cash flows. It totally ignores the embedded optionality of the former instruments.

6.2 HEURISTIC APPROACHES

In general, a heuristic is an educational method in which learning takes place through discoveries resulting from investigations. A trader with a long track record would call this experience. In finance, these practical approaches are categorized as rules of thumb and there has been a great deal of mileage in their application in the world of hybrids. In the following sections we will discuss two of these techniques applied to two different segments of the hybrid asset class: corporate hybrids and convertible bonds. Using a practical example, we illustrate the shortcomings of these rules of thumb mainly because of the presence of the embedded optionality.

6.2.1 Corporate Hybrids: Yield of a Callable Bond

In Table 1.4 we described as an example the long-dated hybrid bond issued in 2005 by Bayer, a large German pharmaceutical company. The coupon structure is represented in Figure 6.1. The bond pays an annual fixed coupon of 5% during the first 10 years and is callable every quarter starting July 29, 2015. The quarterly call price is par, which corresponds in this case to a cash amount of €1000. There is a step-up feature incorporated in the coupon structure of this hybrid bond. The fixed annual 5% coupon will be paid out for the last time on the first call date and from then onward the bond becomes a floating-rate bond where 280 bps are added on top of the 3-month Euribor rate.[1] For the issuer this implies that it has an opportunity to

---

[1] Euribor stands for the Euro Interbank Offered Rate. It is a daily reference rate based on the average interest rate at which Eurozone banks lend unsecured funds to each other.

Table 6.1   Calculating the present value of the coupons using a yield of 2.62%

Coupon Date	Face Value	Coupon	Discount Factor	Present Value
07/29/2013		50.000	0.9801	49.01
07/29/2014		50.000	0.9551	47.76
07/29/2015	1000	50.000	0.9307	977.28
			Total	1074.04
			Accrued	11.92
			Bond Price	**106.21**

finance its operations at a cost of 280 basis points above the interbank interest rate level for the next 90 years following the payment of the last fixed coupon in 2015. Every quarter the issuer can call back the bond, pay back its face value, and cancel all the remaining floating coupons. This hybrid security is a perfect example to illustrate the shortcomings of traditional fixed-income measures like yield to maturity.

On Friday October 19, 2012 a fund manager is keen to invest in this particular bond. The price of the bond is 106.21 and the manager starts from the wrong assumption that the bond is certainly going to be called back by the issuing company. The call decision for the bond issued by Bayer will depend on what credit conditions the issuer can attract for funding compared with the post-call interest rate charge.

Accrued Interest

The bond has been accruing 87 days of the 5% coupon between the previous coupon date on July 29, 2012 and the next settlement date which is October 24, 2012.[2] The accrued amount per bond is €**11.92** ($=1000 \times 5\% \times 87/365$).

Yield to Call

The manager expects the bond to be called back by the issuer on the first call date and ignores any extension of the bond. The expected maturity corresponds to the date when the fixed coupon is going to be paid out for the very last time. If the issuer refrains from calling the bond on this date then the next quarterly coupon is based on a percentage that is 280 bps above a 3-month floating interest rate.

Given the current price of the bond, the cash flows up to the first call date correspond to a yield of 2.62%. The corresponding calculation can be found in Table 6.1.

Yield of Callable Debt

This yield to the call date is 242 bps above the yield on German government bonds. For our portfolio manager the yield on the 100-year hybrid seems to offer an attractive spread above corporate non-callable debt issued by Bayer. This yield difference is illustrated in Figure 6.2. The high yield on the hybrid can be explained by the fact that it offers compensation for the risk of missing out on one or more coupons and for having to deal with a possible extension

---

[2] The bond settles three business days after the purchase date.

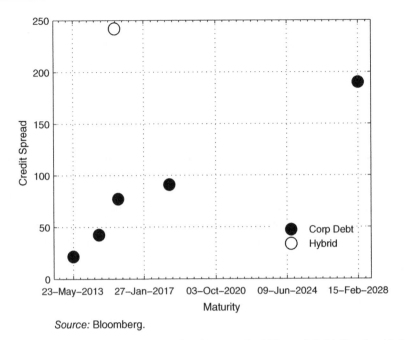

Source: Bloomberg.

Figure 6.2 Credit spread of Bayer corporate bonds versus the 100-year hybrid (October 19, 2012).

of the bond's maturity. The yield difference therefore does not suggest an immediate arbitrage opportunity. An uninformed investor will be tempted to select without any further consideration the higher-yielding hybrid into the portfolio.

6.2.2 Convertible Bonds: Break Even

Yield Advantage

The yield advantage of a convertible bond is the difference between the current yield CY of the bond and the dividend yield q on the underlying shares. To illustrate this we refer to the bond issued by Medivation in March 2012 (Table 6.2). The dividend yield q is equal to 0 for this company, active in the biomedical sector. In this particular case the yield advantage is

Table 6.2 Characteristics of the convertible bond issued by Medivation in 2012

MEDIVATION 2.625% April 1, 2017			
ISIN	US58501NAA90	SEDOL	B41R4Z0
ISSUE DATE	April 1, 2017	ISSUE PRICE	100%
ISSUE SIZE	259 mn	FACE VALUE	1000
STOCK	RYLAND GROUP	MATURITY	May 14, 2018
CONVERSION RATIO	9.7586	COUPON FREQUENCY	SEMI-ANNUAL
REDEMPTION	100.00%		
COUPON	2.625%	CURRENCY	USD

Source: Prospectus.

therefore equal to the current yield. On August 23, 2012 the closing price of the bond was 122.16. The corresponding current yield is therefore:

$$CY = \frac{2.625}{122.16} = 2.15\% \tag{6.1}$$

Break-Even Calculation

At a price of 122.16, the convertible bond trades at a premium over the value of the underlying shares $(P > P_a)$. This premium can be explained by the discounted value of the expected coupons, the embedded optionality, and other attractive instrument features. The investor is paying a cash amount $N \times (P - P_a)$ above the value of the underlying shares when investing in a particular convertible bond. Assuming that all the variables remain constant and that accordingly the share price S and hence the parity P_a do not move, the only source of income is the current yield CY of the bond. The convertible bond holder accumulates a wealth of $N \times P \times CY \times \Delta T$ over a period of ΔT years. Investing the same amount of cash $N \times P$ into shares yields an annual dividend q. The break-even period $\Delta_{\text{Break-Even}}$ is the time needed to hold a convertible bond in order to make up for the premium to parity:

$$\Delta_{\text{Break-Even}} \text{ (yrs)} = \frac{P - P_a}{P \times (CY - q)} \tag{6.2}$$

The share price on August 23, 2012 of the Medivation stock closed at \$95.19 on the Nasdaq. The break-even calculation of the Medivation convertible is given by:

$$P_a = \frac{C_r S}{N} = \frac{9.7586 \times 95.19}{1000} = 92.89\%$$

$$\begin{aligned} \Delta_{\text{Break-Even}} \text{(yrs)} &= \frac{P - P_a}{P \times (CY - q)} \\ &= \frac{122.16 - 92.89}{122.16 \times 2.15\%} = 11.14 \text{ year} \end{aligned} \tag{6.3}$$

On the calculation date of the break-even period, the bond had an effective remaining maturity of 4.61 years, which is far below the break-even time of 11.14 years. This rule of thumb might lead an investor to the conclusion to refrain from buying this particular convertible bond. The premium to parity is equal to 28.33% and is too expensive to be earned back by the coupon payments earned before the expiry of this convertible. The bond will likely expire before the break-even is achieved. However, this is a wrong conclusion as many corners have been cut. The break-even period is a simplistic rule unsuitable in the management of convertible bond portfolios. Instrument features such as a put or an issuer call are ignored using this heuristic rule.

6.3 BUILDING MODELS

6.3.1 Introduction

When approached by a trainee on the equity derivatives trading desk, a market maker may be asked what model is being put to work. The market maker may answer that trinomial trees have been successfully implemented to calculate the different hedge ratios of the portfolio. As a result, the desk knows in real time its equity exposure. This is far from a satisfactory answer, however. Trinomial trees are only a small part of a financial model. A lattice or tree model is merely a numerical technique implemented to solve for the price of a derivative product.

When being confronted with a similar question, market practitioners sometimes respond in buzzwords. They claim to use Black–Scholes, Heston, Hull–White, etc. The key issue is not the model itself, but the driving factors and assumptions on which the model has been built. A financial model is therefore a combination of four elements: a choice of one or several factors, a stochastic process, a numerical implementation, and a calibration of the model.

- **Factors**

  A factor is a source of risk driving the value of a hybrid security. A typical one-factor model is the Black–Scholes model for European equity options. Here all the parameters are deterministic apart from one: the underlying share price S. According to Bruno Dupire, founding father of the local volatility model, there is a particular process for how financial variable modeling develops: "First, people aren't aware of it. Then it's included, but as a constant. Then it's allowed to depend deterministically on some underlying variables. Finally it becomes fully stochastic"[50]. Hence, factors have been included in more advanced models and this evolved, for example, in the application of stochastic volatility models like the Heston model. These are models where the equity volatility σ_S follows a stochastic process correlated to the random process of S itself.

- **Stochastic processes**

  The stochastic process describes the random behavior and the resulting distribution function of the different factors included in the model. A typical stochastic share price process is a geometric Brownian motion where the random behavior is characterized by the equity volatility σ_S and the drift μ_S. This process is at the root of the Black–Scholes approach. For hybrid securities such as CoCos and convertible bonds, we will show that one factor is not always satisfactory. There are also one-and-a-half factor models. This is an offspring of a two-factor model where the random behavior of one particular source of risk is trimmed down by making it a function of the other remaining factor. Imagine, for example, a two-factor model based on credit default swap spreads (cds) and share price levels (S). Two stochastic processes are needed, one for each of the two parameters. In a one-and-a-half factor approach, the stochastic behavior of the cds is somehow eliminated by linking it to the share price S. Here, cds is a function of S and fully driven by the volatility of S. From historical data it has been observed that a negative correction in the share price often went hand in hand with an increase of the perceived default risk. Using $cds = f(S)$ removes one random source of risk from the model by linking it deterministically to another stochastic variable. In this way a two-factor model is reduced to a one-and-a-half factor model.

- **Numerical implementation**

  After choosing the factors in the model, linking each of them to a particular stochastic process comes first. The final step is the implementation of a numerical solution to price the hybrid security. Ideally, there is a closed-form solution available. Without any doubt, the existence of such a solution is one of the reasons for the popularity of the Black–Scholes model. Very often, closed-form formulas are easy to implement but will be rather heavy in the assumptions taken. Traders and portfolio managers sometimes drag their heels when it comes to fully acknowledging the assumptions behind the closed-form formulas they are using on a day-to-day basis. An illustration of this was the widespread reliance on the Gaussian copulas in the pricing of CDOs. Some might argue that the calculation speed of the closed-form formulas compensates for the corners being cut in the modeling approach.

This is where lattice techniques such as binomial or trinomial trees enter the stage. These approaches can handle a fair amount of instrument complexity but remain very educational. Indeed, they give us a very good understanding of the dynamic behavior of hybrids as long as one sticks to a single factor. Other possibilities to solve for the price of a hybrid instrument after having chosen a particular stochastic process are the finite difference and the Monte Carlo method. Quantitative analysts at banks and hedge funds are continuously putting a great deal of work into this implementation. This is often a technology issue, as vast amounts of computer power are being deployed. The costs of such an infrastructure can be high and need to be weighted against the benefits it offers to the trading desk.

In this book we will focus on closed-form solutions, trinomial trees, and the American Monte Carlo method. This latter method offers numerous possibilities to price hybrid debt using the more advanced stochastic processes while handling conveniently the early optional conversion into shares.

- **Calibration**
  The financial models described above are constructed around factors such as interest rates, share prices, and credit spreads. These sources of risk can be combined or used on a standalone basis. The value of a hybrid security can therefore be tied back to the market price of other instruments sharing the same underlying equity. Doing so, we can link the value of a convertible bond to corporate bonds, listed options, credit default swaps, etc. issued by the same company. This is why the approaches described above are considered to be **no-arbitrage models**: the value of the hybrid instrument fits within the market prices of other assets issued by the same firm. The process of finding those model parameters such that the market price of the instrument fits the modeled price is called calibration.

6.3.2   Martingales

Martingales

In the theory of stochastic processes, the **filtration** F_k associated with a stochastic process X records the past behavior of this process up till time k [129]. One could look at the filtration as the information about the stochastic process available up to time k. The stochastic variable X satisfies the martingale property when, for every time $t > k$, the following equation holds:

$$\mathbb{E}[X_t|\mathcal{F}_k] = X_k \tag{6.4}$$

If the above property holds for all k and t such that $t > k$, then we can say that the process X is a martingale. It is important to impose that this property needs to hold for all t and k. A martingale process carries an important intuitive meaning. If X is a martingale, any knowledge of its past is irrelevant to its future. The expected value of the next draw in the process X is equal to its current value X_k. Drawing a card from a deck of cards is, for example, not a martingale process. Any knowledge of the cards that were already chosen and displayed on the table will help to improve the odds of drawing a particular card in the next run.

Measures

When taking the expectation $\mathbb{E}$ of the outcome of a stochastic process X_t observed at a future time t, we are attaching probabilities to all the different states that this random variable can take: $\{x_1, \ldots, x_n\}$ at time t. In financial mathematics, the collection of all the possible outcomes of this stochastic process $X = \{X_t, t \geq 0\}$ is called the sample space Ω. Assigning to each of the possible outcomes of this sample space a particular probability brings us to the concept of a probability measure $\mathbb{P}$. The expectation of X is always taken with respect to a particular measure $\mathbb{P}$ and is hence denoted $\mathbb{E}_{\mathbb{P}}[X_t]$.

In derivatives pricing, the risk-neutral measure $\mathbb{Q}$ is such a probability measure. In the literature it is often known under the name "martingale measure." The concept of risk neutrality will be covered later, in Chapter 8. For the moment one just has to retain one major fact about this risk-neutral measure. The value of an asset P is, in the risk-neutral setting, equal to the expected value of the discounted future payoff. Under this risk-neutral measure the price of a financial asset at time P_t expiring at time $T > t$ is given by:

$$P_t = B_t \mathbb{E}_{\mathbb{Q}} \left[\frac{P_T}{B_T} | \mathcal{F}_t \right] \tag{6.5}$$

where B_t represents the value at time t of one unit of cash invested at $t = 0$. Hence, B_t/B_T is a discount factor. It is the time t value of one unit of cash received at time T. B_t is a process that stands for the money market or bank account that accrues over time. From time t to T, it grows from B_t to B_T. One often models the process $B = \{B_t, t \geq 0\}$ as an accrual process starting with the initial value $B_0 = 1$ and changes it according to the following differential equation:

$$dB_t = B_t r_t dt \tag{6.6}$$

The short-term continuous interest rate r_t is then allowed to be a random process as well. In such a case, the equation above turns into a stochastic differential equation. In the assumption that the continuous interest rate is constant, we have:

$$\int_t^T \frac{dB_t}{B_t} = \int_t^T r dt \tag{6.7}$$

$$\log\left(\frac{B_T}{B_t}\right) = r(T - t)$$

Hence

$$B_T = B_t \exp(r(T - t))$$

The equation above allows us to calculate the amount of cash B_T available at time T when starting at time t with a certain amount of cash B_t on the bank:

$$B_t = B_T \exp(-r(T - t)) \tag{6.8}$$

From this we obtain the discount factor B_t/B_T. Given the fact that we considered constant interest rates:

$$\frac{B_t}{B_T} = \exp(-r(T - t)) \tag{6.9}$$

6.3.3 Model Map

The purpose of this part of the book is to provide an introduction to the valuation of hybrid securities. If this was a book on the pricing of equity derivative securities only, then it would be perfectly possible to obtain a solid understanding of even the more complex derivative structures without having to read the more advanced mathematical theories on this topic. It is not a requirement at all to study Girsanov's Theorem, learn about the Radon–Nikodyn derivative, or understand the corresponding theory of a measure change to earn your stripes on an equity derivatives trading desk. This statement is more or less valid in the world of hybrid securities as long as one sticks to the less advanced one-factor models. Trinomial trees that were implemented to value American put options can indeed be rolled out easily to value CoCos or convertible bonds. As soon as we move one notch higher in the number of factors in the model, things change drastically.

To illustrate this we go back to Equation (6.5), where the theoretical value of an asset P_t was given under the risk-neutral measure $\mathbb{Q}$. Suppose that the continuous interest rate r is constant, we can hence rewrite this equation as:

$$P_t = \frac{B_t}{B_T} \mathbb{E}_\mathbb{Q}[P_T | \mathcal{F}_t]$$
$$= \exp(-r(T - t)) \mathbb{E}_\mathbb{Q}[P_T | \mathcal{F}_t] \tag{6.10}$$

Equation (6.10) tells us that under the risk-neutral measure the theoretical price of a derivative instrument is hence equal to the discounted expected payoff. A similar equation holds when those interest rates are stochastic as well. In such a case we have to stick to Equation (6.5) and incorporate both interest rate and equity volatility. Combining interest rate volatility and equity volatility in a hybrid model is like opening Pandora's box when one lacks a thorough understanding of the mathematical theory behind asset pricing. We will move in this book step by step and from example to example in order to reveal in a very practical way how to deal with these challenges when pricing hybrid debt. A map of the possible financial models combining different numerical techniques, different choices for random factors, and their corresponding stochastic processes can be found in Figure 6.3. This will be our road-map in the valuation examples we will handle in the upcoming chapters.

6.3.4   Cheapness

Theoretical values obtained for a particular instrument can be very different from the price this instrument is being traded at. An example of this is convertible bonds. For this particular member of the hybrid family, there can be a clear disconnect between the theoretical value (P) of a convertible and the price against which the bond is actually trading in the market (P_M). This leads us to the concept of cheapness, which is defined as:

$$\frac{P - P_M}{P} \tag{6.11}$$

In Figure 6.4 one can find the average cheapness of the convertible bonds in the BAML[3] convertible bond index for a period of just over 5 years. This graph confirms the practitioners' view that convertible bonds tend to trade below their theoretical value. The mere existence of this cheapness should be convincing enough to refrain from using valuation as the only decision tool while managing a convertible bond portfolio. Investing in cheap bonds in the conviction that they will move higher and eventually converge to their theoretical value is not

---

[3] This cheapness has been calculated by BAML (Bank of America Merrill Lynch) using their own proprietary models.

Map of Valuation models for Hybrids

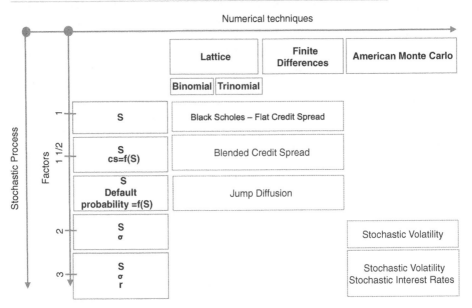

Figure 6.3   Schematic overview of no-arbitrage financial models.

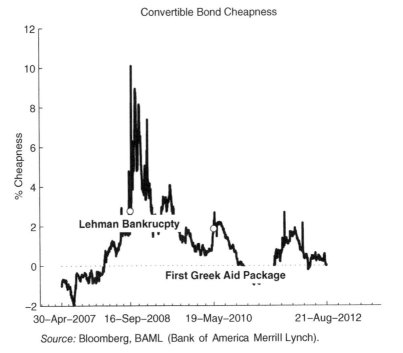

Source: Bloomberg, BAML (Bank of America Merrill Lynch).

Figure 6.4   Average cheapness of the convertible bonds in the BAML Global Convertible Bond Index.

likely to pay off. Cheap bonds can even become cheaper, or the time horizon needed for this cheapness to disappear is too long.

The persistent cheapness may result from the complex nature of this asset class, which makes arbitrage strategies difficult and costly to implement. The pricing of convertible bonds under the assumption of the existence of a perfect hedge is unrealistic. Rebalancing a delta hedge of a convertible position comes at a cost, and so does borrowing the underlying shares. An empirical study of the cheapness of convertible bonds in the French market can be found in [5]. This paper concludes that high-delta convertible bonds, where hedges are easier to set up, trade closer to their theoretical value. For these deep-in-the-money convertible bonds, the convertible exhibits the same dynamic behavior as a long position in the underlying shares. Another explanation can be found in Figure 6.4. The graph points out that the cheapness of convertible bonds is definitively linked to liquidity issues (bankrupcty of Lehman in September 2008) or to flight-to-quality situations observed in periods of distress (first bail-out of Greece in May 2010).

6.4   HOW MANY FACTORS?

A case study in Section 2.3.1 revealed that limiting a model to a single factor, such as equity prices, could fail to explain the dynamic behavior of a convertible bond. We showed that some dislocations occurred where a share price increase did not correspond to an increase in the convertible bond price. Other factors are also at work in convertible bond modeling, such as interest rates, volatility, or credit spreads. These factors are neither constant nor deterministic and can therefore be considered as additional sources of risk. Each of these can be assigned to a particular stochastic process. This phenomenon is not limited to convertible bonds only. A similar exercise on a Lloyds contingent convertible (Table 6.3) reveals the same shortcoming of single-factor equity models when dealing with contingent debt. Figure 6.5 illustrates, for example, how a decrease in the share price of Lloyds can correspond to an increase in the market price of the contingent convertible. Specifically, from February 1, 2011 to April 28, 2011, the share price of Lloyds decreased by 5 pence while the CoCo increased 7.62% over the same horizon. Such an observation does not fit the foundation of a model where a lower equity price increases the probability of a forced conversion and therefore weakens the price of the CoCo bond.

A single-factor model with only one stochastic element, such as the share price, is therefore often unsatisfactory. The model might correspond to our intuition regarding the price behavior

Table 6.3   Characteristics of a contingent convertible issued by Lloyds in 2009

LLOYDS 7.625% October 14, 2020			
ISIN	XS0459091236	SEDOL	B4N82R9
ISSUE DATE	December 1, 2009	ISSUE PRICE	100%
ISSUE SIZE	€226 mn	MATURITY	October 14, 2020
STOCK	Lloyds	CURRENCY	EUR
CONVERSION PRICE	59 GBP	FACE VALUE	1000
LOSS ABSORPTION	Conversion in shares	TRIGGER	5% Common Equity Tier 1
COUPON	7.625%	FREQUENCY	ANNUALY

Source: Prospectus.

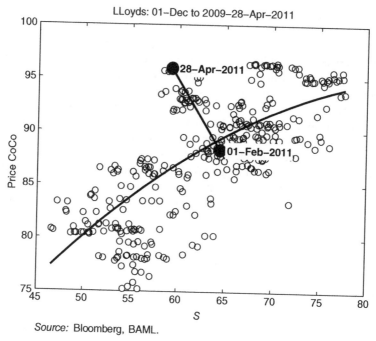

Source: Bloomberg, BAML.

Figure 6.5 Scatterplot of the share price of Lloyds (GBP) versus the price of a contingent convertible. The characteristics of the CoCo are summarized in Table 6.3.

of contingent debt, but fail to incorporate the non-deterministic nature of interest rates and credit spreads. Similar to the approach in Section 2.3.1, we can use a regression analysis on historical data to determine to what extent adding more factors to a non-linear model helps to explain the price changes of a contingent convertible. In a first step we can obtain, through ordinary least squares (OLS), the best fit between n historical weekly price changes δS_i and the changes in the market price δP_i of this particular CoCo over the same weekly period. The approach has been explained in Equation (2.36) and offers an average R-squared of only 24%. A one-factor share price model is therefore not the best technique when dealing with contingent debt. One can now broaden the exercise and throw in more factors. We can add changes in interest rates δr and credit default swap spread changes δcds and combine these with δS. A total of n weekly changes $\delta F_i = [\delta S_i \ \delta r_i \ \delta cds_i]$ can now be regressed against δP_i.

Using OLS one can determine the best fit $(\widehat{\Delta_F}, \widehat{\Gamma_F})$:

$$(\widehat{\Delta_F}, \widehat{\Gamma_F}) = \underset{\Delta_F, \Gamma_F}{\text{argmin}} \sum_{i=1}^{n} \left(\delta P_i - \Delta_F \delta F_i^T - \frac{1}{2} \delta F_i \Gamma_F \delta F_i^T \right)^2 \qquad (6.12)$$

The first estimated parameter from the regression is a row vector $\widehat{\Delta}_F$ which consists of three elements. These are the linear sensitivities of the convertible bond price changes with respect to changes in S, r, and the level of the credit default swap:

$$\Delta_F = [\Delta_S \ \Delta_r \ \Delta_{cds}]$$

The estimated parameter $\widehat{\Gamma_F}$ represents a symmetric matrix with the non-linear sensitivities of the convertible bond price:

$$\Gamma_F = \begin{bmatrix} \Gamma_S & \Gamma_{S,r} & \Gamma_{S,cds} \\ \Gamma_{S,r} & \Gamma_r & \Gamma_{r,cds} \\ \Gamma_{S,cds} & \Gamma_{r,cds} & \Gamma_{cds} \end{bmatrix} \tag{6.13}$$

The element Γ_S represents the estimate for $\frac{\partial^2 P}{\partial S^2}$ while $\Gamma_{S,r}$ estimates a so-called cross-greek: $\frac{\partial^2 P}{\partial S \partial r}$. Applying these three factors to a series of weekly data leads to the graph in Figure 6.6. The exercise is using historical price changes to estimate $(\widehat{\Delta}_F, \widehat{\Gamma}_F)$. Each time this is done using the weekly price changes over a 3-month period. The average R-squared over the interval April 2010 – August 2012 increases to 83%. The evolution of R-squared over this time frame has been represented in Figure 6.6. The explanatory power of the model clearly improved compared with the one-factor approach based on equity prices only.

On a theoretical level, there was initially not much support to incorporate multiple factors when developing equity derivative models. In 1980, Brennan and Schwartz [43] used a structural model to price convertible debt. Their approach was the first ever where stochastic interest rates were implemented. Based on a case study where the authors priced a 10-year convertible bond using a two-factor model, they concluded that the error from using a one-factor model was negligible. A more sophisticated two-factor model, where the interest rate was added as an extra source of risk, proved to change the theoretical values only slightly. Therefore, incorporating the extra factor did not justify the extra computational burden. This conclusion

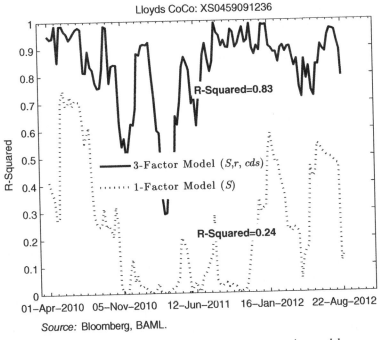

Figure 6.6 Evolution of the R-squared for different explanatory regression models.

is still a starting point for most convertible models, but needs to be handled carefully. From the same study it is clear, however, that interest rate volatility starts playing a more important role when rates are lower. In a low-rate environment, it is therefore less obvious to leave the random behavior of interest rates aside.

In a later study [133], the price impact on European options on the Nikkei 225 index, when adding stochastic interest rates to their valuation model, has been studied. The results of this exercise, which was limited to short-dated options, revealed that incorporating stochastic interest rates into stock option models does not really contribute to an improvement of the original Black–Scholes formula, which was based on constant interest rates. However, the results of this study cannot be extrapolated to the world of hybrid bonds because in this particular asset class, one is dealing with longer-dated maturities. Indeed, we are often dealing with a maturity range of 5 years and more, so that interest rate volatility cannot easily be ignored in this case.

6.5 SENSITIVITY ANALYSIS

6.5.1 Introduction

Advanced trading or portfolio management software always offers several financial models to value and hedge hybrid securities. It is rather the rule than the exception that the user of such software has the choice amongst different possible models and corresponding implementations. Numerical stability and calculation speed are important elements in this decision-making process. Such commercial packages may be well documented but often leave the user in doubt as to which one of the embedded models is best suited. Very often the model is a black box because, for reasons of brevity and clarity, the user guide cuts corners and skips much detail. Suppose that such a pricing tool gives a trader the possibility to calculate the theoretical value of a hybrid P based on a set of n inputs $X_{i \in \{1,...,n\}}$. This black box is defined by the function $P = f(X_1, \ldots, X_n)$. Global sensitivity analysis deals with the question of how the uncertainty in the theoretical price P can be linked to the uncertainty in the different input data [171]. Such an analysis may help the trader to understand which factor X_i, stochastic or not, has the largest influence on the price P. Furthermore, it does not require any knowledge at all about the pricing function in the model. Without any knowledge about the assumption behind a valuation model, this analysis will pinpoint those sources of randomness and risk that outrank the other factors and that need to be hedged first. It is always good practice to do a sensitivity analysis on an unknown valuation model for different derivative securities. Suppose that one were to find that the change in the volatility parameter σ has a large impact on the theoretical price P of a particular derivative instrument. This could be a plea to move away from a model where σ is constant and switch to a stochastic volatility model instead.

Sensitivity toward an input parameter is not a greek such as Δ, Γ, or vega. A delta (Δ), for example, informs us how the theoretical value of an option or convertible changes given a certain change in the underlying share prices S. However, there can be more risk on a low-delta option with a volatile stock as underlying than on a deep in-the-money call option on a stock that hardly moves around in price. We hence consider the sensitivity S_{X_i}. It is a normalized version of the greek $\frac{\partial P}{\partial X_i}$ because the volatility σ_{X_i} of the factor X_i is taken into account as well. The sensitivity s_{X_i} links the variance of the theoretical price σ_P^2 to the variance of the input parameter $\sigma^2_{X_i}$. In our black-box model $P = f(X_1, \ldots, X_n)$, we hence define sensitivity as:

$$s_{X_i} = \frac{\sigma_{X_i}}{\sigma_P} \frac{\partial P}{\partial X_i} \tag{6.14}$$

These sensitivities s_{X_i} may be ranked to isolate the important inputs from the less important ones. It can be shown that for a linear model [170]:

$$\sum_{i=1}^{n} s^2_{X_i} = 1$$

6.5.2 Non-linear Model

For a non-linear model we have to rely on a Monte Carlo technique to explore our black-box pricing model $P = f(X_1, \ldots, X_n)$. The Monte Carlo method, a fancy name for statistical sampling, does not have its roots in the casinos of Monaco, but in the Los Alamos National Laboratory in the United States. In the 1950s Nicholas Constantine Metropolis, a scientist working at this research institution, came up with this peculiar name. The Monte Carlo method, however, dates back to the late eighteenth century, but was seldom applied because of the labor and time it required. Only when computers became widely available was the Monte Carlo method able to make a front-of-stage appearance in physics and later in finance [116]. The Monte Carlo method consists of performing a lot of trials and calculating the outcome of every single one of these. All of this is based on random number generation by a computer.

We apply this logic to our black-box pricing model in order to understand the sensitivity of the theoretical price P regarding the n input variables $(X_1, \ldots, X_n)$. Each of these variables has a certain degree of uncertainty. Suppose that they are all independent from each other and that each X_i is normally distributed with mean μ_{X_i} and variance $\sigma^2_{X_i}$. A total N of a group of n variables $(X_1^j, \ldots, X_n^j)_{j=1,\ldots,N}$ is going to be simulated. Each data set X generated by the N Monte Carlo runs delivers us a theoretical price P_j:

$$\begin{bmatrix} X_1 \sim & N(\mu_{X_1}, \sigma^2_{X_1}) \\ \vdots & \vdots \\ X_i \sim & N(\mu_{X_i}, \sigma^2_{X_i}) \\ \vdots & \vdots \\ X_n \sim & N(\mu_{X_n}, \sigma^2_{X_n}) \end{bmatrix} \frac{\text{Random No.}}{N \text{ Runs}} \rightarrow \begin{bmatrix} X_1^1 & \cdots & X_1^j & \cdots & X_1^N \\ \vdots & & \vdots & & \vdots \\ X_i^1 & \cdots & X_i^j & \cdots & X_i^N \\ \vdots & & \vdots & & \vdots \\ X_n^1 & \cdots & X_n^j & \cdots & X_n^N \end{bmatrix} \tag{6.15}$$

$$\rightarrow \begin{bmatrix} P_1 & \cdots & P_j & \cdots & P_N \end{bmatrix}$$

Each of the N runs generates a theoretical price $P_{j \in \{1,\ldots,N\}}$. The unconditional variance of this output is:

$$V(P) = \frac{1}{N-1} \sum_{j=1}^{N} \left(P_j - \frac{1}{N} \sum_{k=1}^{N} P_k \right)^2 \tag{6.16}$$

We will now fix the value of the input variables X_i, but only one variable at a time. Freezing one of these n input variables allows us to investigate how the uncertainty of the model output is impacted. Suppose we fix a variable X_i to a fixed value X_i^*, then the variance of the theoretical price is now conditional and is equal to $V(P \mid X_i = X_i^*)$. This is the price variance due to the non-fixed remaining input parameters $X_{j,j \neq i}$. The variable X_i where this corresponding conditional variance is minimum explains most of the uncertainty in the theoretical price of the instrument.

In the extreme where a variable $V(P \mid X_i = X_i^*) = 0$, then all the other input variables have no influence on the price P using the model $f(X_1, \ldots, X_n)$. Ranking $V(P \mid X_i = X_i^*)$ in ascending order lists the sources of uncertainty of the given model in order of decreasing importance. The problem is that we do not know where to fix X_i since we do not know X_i^*. We will therefore calculate the expected value $V(P \mid X_i)$ over all the possible values of $X_i \sim N(\overline{X}_i, \sigma_{X_i}^2)$. This is $\mathbb{E}(V(P \mid X_i))$ and represents the expected variance coming from all the input factors not equal to X_i. Ordering this result in ascending order is the same as ordering $V(\mathbb{E}(P \mid X_i))$ in descending order, as summarized in the following table:

Measure	Explanation	Ranking
$\mathbb{E}(V(P \mid X_i))$	Price uncertainty coming from all the input variables different from X_i.	Ascending
$V(\mathbb{E}(P \mid X_i))$	Price uncertainty coming from X_i. This measure can be divided by the overall unconditional variance $V(P)$, which gives us a sensitivity $s_i = \frac{V(\mathbb{E}(P \mid X_i))}{V(P)} \in [0, 1]$. This is a proper metric, assisting us to rank input factors in order importance from high to low.	Descending

Case Study: Sensitivity Analysis of a Convertible Bond

In a first step the sensitivity analysis explained in the previous paragraphs is applied to a sample convertible bond. This convertible has a 5-year maturity and distributes no coupons. There are no extra instrument features either. So there are no calls, no puts, no refixes, etc. Since the expected dividend yield on the underlying share is zero, the convertible bond's theoretical price is driven by three market parameters only: the share price S, the interest rate r, and the equity volatility σ_S. This leads respectively to the following sensitivities: s_S, s_r, and s_{σ_S}. Let's assume we have a pricing model at our disposal, $P = f(S, r, \sigma_S)$, to value the convertible bond and run the N Monte Carlo simulations to perform a sensitivity analysis. The model's equity sensitivity is given by:

$$s_S = \frac{V(\mathbb{E}(P \mid S_i))}{V(P)} \quad i = 1, \ldots, N \tag{6.17}$$

In this introductory example we will show that the equity sensitivity S_S depends on the parity P_a of the convertible. It was indeed already argued in Section 2.3.2 how the convertible bond adopts equity-like behavior when parity is high. A convertible which is deep in-the-money behaves effectively as if it was a share. A second observation we want to make in this exercise is the fact that a parameter such as interest rate volatility can influence s_S as well. The more uncertainty in the interest rates, the less risk there is left to be attributed to share price movements. A total of 500 Monte Carlo simulations is run in this example. For each run we independently draw a value S_i and $\sigma_{S,i}$ from a corresponding normal distribution:

	S	σ_S
Mean	100	40%
Standard Deviation	5	3%

There is no contradiction in considering a volatility σ_S which is a lot larger than the standard deviation of S. The standard deviation refers to movements of the share price during a very short time horizon, while σ_S is an annualized volatility. For the interest rates r we consider two regimes: a high and a low volatility regime. In both cases we assume the interest rates to be normally distributed around a mean μ_r with a standard deviation σ_r: $r \sim N(\mu_r, \sigma_r^2)$:

	Interest Rate Regime	
	High Volatility	Low Volatility
Mean (μ_r)	5.00%	5.00%
Standard Deviation (σ_r)	0.60%	0.20%

We selected a certain number of conversion ratios $C_r = \{0.1, 0.3, 0.5, 0.7, 0.8, 1.1\}$. Doing so, we have different parity levels for the convertible bond. For these different levels of parity, we calculate s_S twice. Once for a regime with low interest rate uncertainty and another calculation where the interest rate volatility is high. The results are represented in Figure 6.7 and show how the equity sensitivity is smaller when the parity is lower. For the same level of moneyness, the equity sensitivity decreases when the interest uncertainty is higher. For a parity $P_a = 50$, s_S drops from 0.39 to 0.22 when interest rates switch to a high-volatility regime. This conclusion has been reached without need to calculate the greeks or have a good theoretical understanding of the model used.

Case Study: Sensitivity Analysis of a Contingent Convertible Bond

The regression analysis in Section 6.4 on the Lloyds contingent convertible already illustrated to some extent that share price movements fail to explain the larger portion of the swings in the price of this CoCo bond. Would we reach the same conclusion when applying a sensitivity analysis similar to the previous case study? As an example, we consider a 5-year zero-coupon CoCo with a face value equal to 100. The loss absorption takes place through a conversion in shares. The conversion price C_p is equal to 100, the same as the current value of the share S. We assume in this example that the underlying shares do not distribute any dividends up till the expiry of this contingent convertible. Now, suppose that we are handed a pricing model for CoCos. The model is a black box but we happen to know that this model associates the triggering of a CoCo and its conversion into shares with an event where the share price crosses a barrier S^*. This level is called the trigger level.

The pricing model $P = f(S, r, \sigma_S, S^*)$ is clearly based on an approach where a CoCo is modeled as an equity derivative. The only random source in this model is the share price S. This black-box model comes with no documentation or support to help us understand

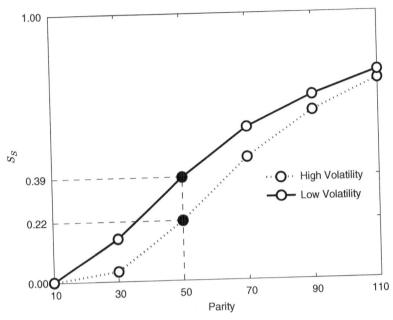

Figure 6.7 Sensitivity analysis for a 5-year convertible bond for two interest regimes.

the assumptions regarding the stochastic behavior of the share price. The interest rates r and the equity volatility σ_S are considered deterministic. But since we know that in this model the CoCo is triggered as soon as the share price drops below S^*, we can already draw two preliminary conclusions:

- **Share price is very distant from the trigger level:**
  $S \gg S^*$ In this case a trigger is very unlikely and the CoCo is very distant from a situation where losses are imposed on the investors. The contingent convertible is clearly a high-quality bond and only the level of the risk-free interest rates r impacts its theoretical value.
- **Share price is very close to the trigger level:**
  $S \approx S^*$ The CoCo is about to be triggered and the investors are close to the point where they are forced to become share holders of the issuing bank. This is a case where the contingent convertible's behavior is mainly driven by share price movements.

In this sensitivity analysis we use a Monte Carlo simulation ($N = 500$ runs) where we draw in each run i a value for S_i, $\sigma_{S,i}$, and r_i, assuming the following independent normal distributions for each of the parameters:

	S	σ_S	r
Mean	100	40%	5%
Standard Deviation	5	3%	0.4%

The different sensitivities of the pricing model have been calculated for different levels of S^* with the current share price S fixed at 100. The output of this exercise can be found in Figure 6.8 and confirms our first intuition regarding the influence of each of the parameters on

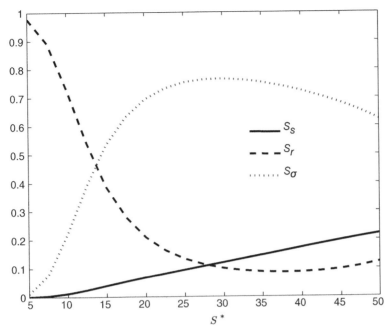

Figure 6.8 Sensitivity analysis for a 5-year zero-coupon contingent convertible bond. The sensitivity of the theoretical value generated by the model has been calculated for interest rates s_r, share prices s_S, and the equity volatility s_{σ_S}.

the theoretical value. For low values of S^* a trigger is unlikely. Here $s_r \approx 1$, which confirms one of our two preliminary conclusions. The interest rate sensitivity s_r is decreasing for increasing values of S^* and Figure 6.8 shows that very quickly the equity volatility has the largest impact on the output of our black-box pricing model: $s_{\sigma_S} > s_r$ and $s_{\sigma_S} > s_S$. This result corresponds with the output of the regression analysis done in Section 6.4, where a single-factor equity model failed to explain the larger part of the price movements of a Lloyds contingent convertible.

Modeling Hybrids: Stochastic Processes

7.1 INTRODUCTION

The value X_t is the outcome of a stochastic process X observed at time t. An example of such a stochastic process is the Brownian motion. Inevitably one tends to encounter this name very early on when studying financial calculus. The description of a Brownian motion and its properties are indeed a logical starting point of many books on derivative securities. A book on hybrids is no exception to this. In this context the story is often told of how Robert Brown (1773–1858), who was an army surgeon of the Fifeshire Regiment based in Ireland, studied pollen suspended in water [182]. Brownian motion is named after the rapid oscillatory movements of these small particles. A rather unknown protagonist when it comes to stochastic processes in finance is Jules Regnault (1834–1894). The latter was a French economist who approached the stock market in a scientific way. He based his findings on observations of share prices and concluded that the price differences of a share over a time interval tended to be proportional to the square root of the elapsed time. With this empirical observation, modern financial history was born in Paris back in 1863, more than a century before Fisher Black, Myron Scholes, and Robert Merton developed their ground-breaking formula [182]. Louis Bachelier (1870–1946) followed in the footsteps of Jules Regnault when he developed his own mathematical theory of share price movements.

7.2 PROBABILITY DENSITY FUNCTIONS

7.2.1 Introduction

The distribution of a continuous random variable X_t can be described by a probability density function $f(x;t)$. Going forward, we will always use a capital letter such as X_t to denote a stochastic variable and use, for example, the symbol x to denote the argument of a function. Where possible we will drop the subscript t to keep the equations as readable as possible. Having the probability density function $f(x;t)$ of X_t at hand allows us to calculate the probability (*Prob*) that this stochastic variable takes a value between a and b at time t:

$$Prob(a < X_t \leq b) = \int_a^b f(u)du \qquad (7.1)$$

The corresponding cumulative distribution function for X_t is such that:

$$Prob(X_t \leq x) = F(x) = \int_{-\infty}^x f(u)du \qquad (7.2)$$

From the equation above:

$$f(x) = \frac{\partial F(x)}{\partial x} \qquad (7.3)$$

The expectation of a function $k(x)$ of a variable X with density function $f(x)$ of this particular stochastic variable is:

$$\mathbb{E}[k(X)] = \int_{-\infty}^{+\infty} k(u)f(u)du \qquad (7.4)$$

The equation above sheds light on the importance of stochastic calculus in mathematical finance. Suppose we are dealing with a European call option with strike K on a share with price S. The call option is expiring at time $t = T$. The final payoff of this call option depends solely on the share price S_T observed at the expiry date and is equal to $\max(S_T - K, 0)$ or $(S_T - K)^+$. The assumption that the distribution of the share price at the expiry date S_T is determined by the density function $f(S)$ allows us to calculate the expected payout of the call option:

$$\mathbb{E}[(S_T - K)^+] = \int_{-\infty}^{+\infty} (u - K)^+ f(u)du = \int_{K}^{+\infty} (u - K)f(u)du \qquad (7.5)$$

Solving this latter equation analytically is a prerequisite to obtain a closed-form formula for the theoretical value of the option price. Solving the expected value of the payoff is one approach when it comes to derivatives pricing. An alternative, which we will encounter later, is to use stochastic calculus to develop and subsequently solve a partial differential equation. Both approaches lead, for European options, to the well-known Black–Scholes equation. In mathematical finance, the continuous process for a stochastic variable X_t is sometimes approximated by a discrete process where the variable X_t takes a finite set of values. The infinite range of possible outcomes of X_t is reduced to a limited number of state values. Each of these state values is obtained with a particular probability. Lattice methods, such as binomial or trinomial trees, are an example of this. An introductory example of such an approximation was used in Section 2.4.2 when dealing with a convertible bond with an embedded put.

7.2.2 Normal Distribution

One of the most important statistical distributions is the normal distribution $N(\mu, \sigma^2)$ with two parameters: the mean $\mu \in \mathbb{R}$ and the variance $\sigma^2 > 0$. The density function $f_N(x; \mu, \sigma^2)$ corresponding to $N(\mu, \sigma^2)$ is given by:

$$f_N(x; \mu, \sigma^2) = \frac{1}{\sqrt{2\pi\sigma^2}} \exp\left(-\frac{(x - \mu)^2}{2\sigma^2}\right) \qquad (7.6)$$

The normal distribution becomes a standard normal distribution if $\mu = 0$ and $\sigma = 1$. In this particular case the cumulative distribution function of a standard normal variable X is given by $\Phi(x)$:

$$\Phi(x) = \int_{-\infty}^{x} f_N(u; 0, 1)du \qquad (7.7)$$

The function $\Phi(x)$ is integrated in Microsoft Excel and multiple mathematical software packages. An elegant property of the normal distribution is the fact that a normally distributed variable $X \sim N(\mu, \sigma^2)$ remains normally distributed after a linear transformation to a new variable $Y = a + bX$:

$$Y \sim N(a + b\mu, b^2\sigma^2) \qquad (7.8)$$

A normal distribution holds, for example, for a random variable which is the sum of a large number of independent but identically distributed variables. This is the central limit theorem.

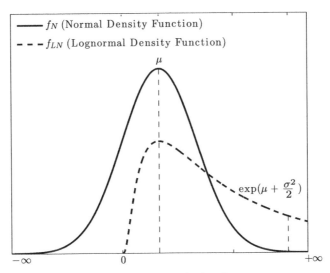

Figure 7.1 Normal and lognormal density functions sharing the same parameters μ and σ. The mean of each of the distributions has been added to the graphs.

7.2.3 Lognormal Distribution

A lognormal distribution results if the variable is the product of a large number of independent but identically distributed random variables.

If a stochastic variable X follows a normal distribution then $Y = \exp(X)$ is said to follow a lognormal distribution. In other words, if Y is lognormally distributed then $X = \log(Y)$ is normally distributed. Figure 7.1 gives a graphical representation of the normal and lognormal distributions. The probability density function of a lognormal variable Y, where the mean and variance of $\log(Y)$ are respectively μ and σ^2, is:

$$f_{LN}(x; \mu, \sigma^2) = \frac{1}{x\sigma\sqrt{2\pi}} \exp\left(-\frac{(\log(x) - \mu)^2}{2\sigma^2}\right) \qquad (7.9)$$

A summary of the major differences between the properties of these two density functions can be found in the table below:

	$f_N(x; \mu, \sigma^2)$	$f_{LN}(x; \mu, \sigma^2)$
x	$x \in (-\infty, +\infty)$	$x \in (0, +\infty)$
$\mathbb{E}[X]$	μ	$\exp(\mu + \frac{1}{2}\sigma^2)$
$Var(X)$	σ^2	$\exp(2(\mu + \sigma^2)) - \exp(2\mu + \sigma^2)$
Median	μ	$\exp(\mu)$
Kurtosis	3	$\exp(4\sigma^2) + 2\exp(3\sigma^2) + 3\exp(2\sigma^2) - 3$
Skewness	0	$(\exp(\sigma^2) + 2)\sqrt{\exp(\sigma^2) - 1}$

The shape of the two density functions is entirely defined by the two parameters μ and σ. The lognormal density function $f_{LN}(x)$ operates on the domain $(0, +\infty)$, which will make it particularly suited to model the stochastic process of the price S of a particular stock or stock index. As will be explained later in this book, the normal density function deserves its place when building a model for the log returns of these stocks. Share price log returns can indeed take any value in the domain $(-\infty, +\infty)$.

7.2.4 Exponential Distribution

The exponential distribution is a special case of the gamma distribution. Its density function depends on an intensity or rate parameter $\lambda > 0$. The density function $f_E(x; \lambda)$ corresponding to this particular probability distribution is given by:

$$f_E(x; \lambda) = \begin{cases} \lambda \exp(-\lambda x) & x \geq 0 \\ 0 & x < 0 \end{cases} \tag{7.10}$$

For the cumulative distribution function $F_E(x; \lambda)$, we have:

$$F(x, \lambda) = Prob(X \leq x) = \begin{cases} 1 - \exp(-\lambda x) & x \geq 0 \\ 0 & x < 0 \end{cases} \tag{7.11}$$

In Figure 7.2 a graphical representation of this cumulative distribution function has been given. Some key statistical parameters of the exponential distribution are listed in the table below:

	$f_E(x; \lambda)$
x	$x \in [0, +\infty)$
$\mathbb{E}[X]$	$\frac{1}{\lambda}$
$Var(X)$	$\frac{1}{\lambda^2}$
Kurtosis	9
Skewness	2

An important property of the exponential distribution is the fact that when one considers n **independent** exponentially distributed variables $X_1, X_2, \ldots, X_n$ with corresponding parameters $\lambda_1, \lambda_2, \ldots, \lambda_n$, then the minimum of these random variables will also follow an exponential distribution. We denote this minimum value $\min(X_1, X_2, \ldots, X_n)$ as X_{min}. The probability that X_{min} is above a certain value x is given by:

$$Prob(X_{min} > x) = \Pi_{i=1}^{n} Prob(X_i > x) \tag{7.12}$$

The equation above only holds because here the exponential random variables are assumed to be independently distributed. Further:

$$Prob(X_{min} > x) = \Pi_{i=1}^{n} Prob(X_i > x) \tag{7.13}$$
$$= \Pi_{i=1}^{n}(1 - Prob(X_i \leq x))$$
$$= \Pi_{i=1}^{n} \exp(-\lambda_i x)$$
$$= \exp\left(-x \sum_{i=1}^{n} \lambda_i\right)$$

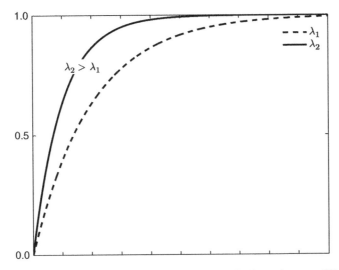

Figure 7.2 Distribution function $F(x)$ for an exponential distribution using two different parameters $\lambda_2 > \lambda_1$.

$$Prob(X_{min} \leq x) = 1 - Prob(X_{min} > x) \tag{7.14}$$
$$= 1 - \exp(-x\lambda)$$
$$\text{with } \lambda = \lambda_1 + \ldots + \lambda_n$$

The variable X_{min} hence follows an exponential distribution with an intensity parameter λ which is the sum of the intensities $\lambda_1, \ldots, \lambda_n$.

7.2.5 Poisson Distribution

A Poisson distribution is related to the class of exponential distribution functions. Unlike the exponential distribution, it is a discrete law. This discrete probability distribution gives the probability of a given number of events occurring in a fixed interval of time. These events appear independently from each other and must occur with a known rate λ. The probability that a number x of such events will actually take place is given by:

$$Prob(X = x) = \frac{\lambda^x}{x!} \exp(-\lambda) \tag{7.15}$$

The main statistical properties of the Poisson distribution $P(X)$ are given in the table below:

	$P(X)$
X	$X \in \{0, 1, 2, \ldots\}$
$\mathbb{E}[X]$	λ
$Var(X)$	λ
Kurtosis	$3 + \frac{1}{\lambda}$
Skewness	$\frac{1}{\sqrt{\lambda}}$

This distribution is sometimes called the "law of small numbers" [36]. In 1898 Ladislaus Bortkiewicz was the first to apply this distribution function to a real-world problem. He studied the number of soldiers that were killed by the unlikely event of being kicked by a horse. He applied the Poisson distribution to these data.

7.3 BROWNIAN MOTION

Brownian motion is a proper stochastic process, but it was long after Robert Brown's study of the jig-jag movement of pollen suspended in water that a rigid mathematical basis was developed. This was done by Robert Wiener (1864–1964). The latter defined four clear-cut properties that a stochastic process must possess in order to qualify as a Brownian motion [175]. A stochastic process $W = \{W_t, t \geq 0\}$ is a Brownian motion or Wiener process if:

1. **Process starts at zero**
   $W_0 = 0$.
2. **Process has stationary increments**
   The increments $W_t - W_s$ do not depend on s but on the length of the interval $\mid t - s \mid$.
3. **Process has independent increments**
   The changes in W over non-overlapping intervals are stochastically independent. For example, if we have $0 \leq t_1 < t_2 < t_3 < T_4$ then $W_{t_2} - W_{t_1}$ is independent of $W_{t_4} - W_{t_3}$.
4. **Normal distribution**
   $W_t - W_s$ follows a normal distribution $N(0, t - s)$.

The first three requirements of a process W to qualify as a Wiener process also make it a Lévy process [175]. The final requirement that the increments $W_t - W_s$ are normally distributed qualifies W as a Gaussian Lévy process.

A Wiener process possesses a number of properties. One of these is the **Markov property** that states that the future values of a random variable should only depend on the present and not on the past. This holds for a Brownian motion since the increments $W_t - W_s$ are independent of the value W_r with $r < s$.

The Brownian motion W is a **continuous process** and it has the property of **infinite variation**. To illustrate this, just imagine that we add the absolute value of all the increments dW_t together. This sum would immediately shoot away to an infinite level.

The **scaling property** of the Brownian motion means that if W qualifies as a Brownian motion then for every value $c > 0$, $\overline{W} = \{c^{-\frac{1}{2}} W_{ct}, t \geq 0\}$ is also a Brownian motion. The **shifting property** tells us that $\overline{W} = W_{t+s} - W_t$ remains a Brownian motion for all $s > 0$.

A Brownian motion is a martingale. It can indeed be shown that $\mathbb{E}(W_t | \mathcal{F}_s) = W_s$ for every $t > s$. To show this, we start by breaking up W_t into two components:

$$W_t = W_s + (W_t - W_s) \tag{7.16}$$

Taking the conditional expectation of the equation above:

$$\mathbb{E}[W_t | \mathcal{F}_s] = \mathbb{E}[W_s | \mathcal{F}_s] + \mathbb{E}[(W_t - W_s) | \mathcal{F}_s]$$
$$= W_s + \mathbb{E}[(W_t - W_s) | \mathcal{F}_s] \tag{7.17}$$

The process $W_t - W_s$ follows a normal distribution with mean 0 and variance $t - s$. Therefore, $E[(W_t - W_s)|\mathcal{F}_s] = 0$ and hence we have:

$$\mathbb{E}[W_t|\mathcal{F}_s] = W_s \tag{7.18}$$

7.4 ITO PROCESS

7.4.1 Introduction

We can incorporate the Brownian motion W_t into a more general process: the Ito process. Such a stochastic process is given by the following stochastic differential equation (SDE):

$$dX_t = A(X,t)dt + B(X,t)dW_t \tag{7.19}$$

A drift component $A(X,t)dt$ is combined with the increments of a Brownian motion dW_t. The result of this blending is illustrated in Figure 7.3, assuming constant values for A and B. The drift component makes the variable X grow proportional with time t. The Brownian motion adds "noise" on top of this linear growth. Four cases of the Ito process are worth noting:

- **Standard Brownian motion:** $A(X,t) = 0$ and $B(X,t) = 1$
- **Geometric Brownian motion:** $A(X,t) = \mu X_t$ and $B(X,t) = \sigma X_t$
  We will come back to this stochastic process in more detail because it represents the core of most equity option pricing models. An important offspring was the Black–Scholes equation for European options. The empirical observation that the variance of share price change dS depends on the level of the share price S and the elapsed time interval dt corresponds to the mathematical properties of the geometric Brownian motion.
- **Gaussian process:** $A(X,t) = \mu(t)$ and $B(X,t) = \sigma(t)$
  In this case the drift $\mu(t)$ and variance $\sigma^2(t)$ are deterministic functions of time. The change dX_t of such a random variable over the interval dt follows a normal distribution with mean $\mu(t)dt$ and variance $\sigma^2(t)dt$. The random change of X over time interval $[s,t]$ with $t > s$ is

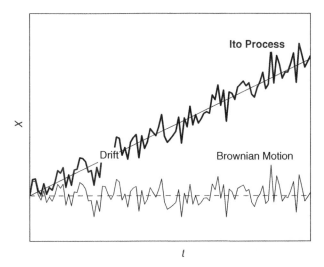

Figure 7.3   Generalized Wiener process with constant drift and diffusion term.

again normally distributed. This is because $X_t - X_s$ is equal to a sum of small increments dX_t and a sum of normally distributed variables remains normally distributed.
The mean of $X_t - X_s$ is equal to:

$$\int_s^t \mu(r)dr \tag{7.20}$$

The variance of $X_t - X_s$ is given by:

$$\int_s^t \sigma^2(r)dr \tag{7.21}$$

We could simulate the process for $X_t - X_s$ by drawing random numbers from a normal distribution $N(\overline{\mu}(t - s), \overline{\sigma}^2(t - s))$ with an average mean $\overline{\mu}$ and variance $\overline{\sigma}^2$:

$$\overline{\mu} = \frac{1}{t - s}\int_s^t \mu(r)dr \tag{7.22}$$

$$\overline{\sigma}^2 = \frac{1}{t - s}\int_s^t \sigma^2(r)dr$$

- **Gaussian process with constant parameters:** $A(X, t) = \mu$ and $B(X, t) = \sigma$
  This is a special case of the process covered above:

$$X_t - X_s \sim N(\mu, \sigma^2(t - s)) \tag{7.23}$$

7.4.2 Ito's Lemma

All the hybrid instruments discussed so far have a value which depends on one or more financial variables. This may make the price of a hybrid bond a function of interest rates, share price levels, credit default swap levels, etc.: $P(r, s, cds, \ldots)$. The parameters of this pricing function are all random variables. Ito's lemma helps us tremendously when it comes to understanding how a function $f(X)$ can be described when its input variable X is an Ito process itself. We follow the explanation of Ito's lemma given in [129]. Let X_t be an Ito process and $f(x, t)$ a twice-differentiable function, we then have that $f(X_t, t)$ is also an Ito process and that:

$$df = \frac{\partial f}{\partial t}dt + \frac{\partial f}{\partial x}dX_t + \frac{1}{2}\frac{\partial^2 f}{\partial x^2}(dX_t)^2 \tag{7.24}$$

where $(dX_t)^2$ is defined using the rules:

$$(dt)^2 = 0 \tag{7.25}$$
$$dt\,dW_t = 0$$
$$(dW_t)^2 = dt$$

Below, several studies will demonstrate the application of Ito's lemma in finance. These exercises may, at first sight, give the impression of being chosen arbitrarily and lacking any practical use. Later in this book, however, each of these cases will come back and their full applicability will be illustrated.

- **Log process**
  Suppose we are dealing with an Ito process $X = \{X_t, t \geq 0\}$, more in particular a geometric Brownian motion:

$$dX_t = \mu X_t dt + \sigma X_t dW_t \tag{7.26}$$

For the sake of simpler algebra, we assume constant parameters μ and σ in the equation above. In order to solve this equation, we make a round-trip by solving the equation in another domain. Our starting point is hence to derive the Ito process followed by the log process $Y = \{Y_t, t \geq 0\}$. We hence work with the function $Y_t = \log(X_t)$. So, $f(x,t) = \log(x)$ and:

$$\frac{\partial f}{\partial t} = 0 \tag{7.27}$$

$$\frac{\partial f}{\partial x} = \frac{1}{x}$$

$$\frac{\partial^2 f}{\partial x^2} = -\frac{1}{x^2}$$

$$dX_t^2 = (\mu X_t dt + \sigma X_t dW_t)^2 \tag{7.28}$$
$$= \mu^2 X_t^2 (dt)^2 + 2\mu\sigma dt dW_t + \sigma^2 X_t^2 (dW_t)^2$$
$$= 0 + 0 + \sigma^2 X^2 dt$$

We can therefore write:

$$dY_t = \frac{1}{X_t} dX_t - \frac{1}{2X_t^2} dX_t^2 \tag{7.29}$$

$$= \frac{1}{X_t}(\mu X_t dt + \sigma X_t dW_t) - \frac{\sigma^2}{2X_t^2} X_t^2 dt$$

In conclusion:

$$dY_t = \left(\mu - \frac{\sigma^2}{2}\right) dt + \sigma dW_t \tag{7.30}$$

$Y = \{Y_t, t \geq 0\}$ is a Gaussian process with constant parameters as covered earlier in Equation (7.23):

$$Y_t - Y_s = \left(\mu - \frac{\sigma^2}{2}\right)(t - s) + \sigma(W_t - W_s)$$

The equation above describes the change of the increment of Y between two points in time: s and t. This value change dY_t has a drift term $(\mu - \sigma^2/2)$ and a variance component σ^2. Subsequently, the solution for X can be found using $X_t = \exp(Y_t)$, the inverse of our original change of variables. Hence:

$$X_t = X_s \exp\left(\left(\mu - \frac{\sigma^2}{2}\right)(t - s) + \sigma(W_t - W_s)\right) \tag{7.31}$$

This is the solution for the geometric Brownian motion given in Equation (7.26). This solution is going to be an important building block in all of our future modeling efforts and is the basis of the so-called Black–Scholes setting.

- **Square-root process**
  A square-root process is of the form:

$$dX_t = \alpha(m - X_t)dt + \sigma\sqrt{X_t}dW_t \tag{7.32}$$

Such a process is the foundation of the Cox–Ingersoll–Ross (CIR) interest rate model [62]. It incorporates a mean-reversion property. When the value of the variable X_t moves too far away from m, it will drift back to this long-term average. The parameter α determines the

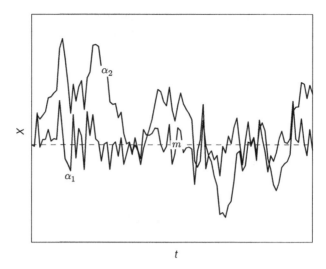

Figure 7.4   Two square-root processes sharing the same mean m and σ. There is a clear difference in the parameter governing the speed of the mean reversion: $\alpha_2 > \alpha_1$.

speed with which this reversion to the mean takes place. An illustration of this can be found in Figure 7.4.

Using Ito's lemma we can now derive the stochastic differential equation for the process Y, where Y is given by:

$$Y_t = \frac{2\sqrt{X_t}}{\sigma} \tag{7.33}$$

We hence have that $f(x,t) = \frac{2\sqrt{x}}{\sigma}$. In a first step, we determine:

$$\frac{\partial f}{\partial t} = 0 \tag{7.34}$$

$$\frac{\partial f}{\partial x} = \frac{x^{-\frac{1}{2}}}{\sigma}$$

$$\frac{\partial^2 f}{\partial x^2} = -\frac{1}{2\sigma}x^{-\frac{3}{2}}$$

Further:

$$dX_t^2 = \sigma^2 X_t dt$$

Some algebra gives us the Ito process followed by the stochastic variable Y_t:

$$dY_t = \mu(Y,t)dt + dW_t \tag{7.35}$$

with

$$\mu(Y,t) = \frac{1}{Y_t}\left(\frac{1}{2}\alpha\left(\frac{4m}{\sigma^2} - Y_t^2\right) - \frac{1}{2}\right) \tag{7.36}$$

This case study in particular shows how a change in variables of Equation (7.33) simplified the square-root process defined in Equation (7.32). The drift term got more complex after this change in variables, but the random behavior of the variable has been reduced to a Brownian motion dW_t.

If the long-term average $m = 0$, the process for Y_t is:

$$dY_t = -\frac{1}{2}\left(\alpha Y_t + \frac{1}{Y_t}\right)dt + dW_t \tag{7.37}$$

- **CEV process**
A variable X_t following a CEV process has the following stochastic differential equation:

$$dX_t = \mu X_t dt + \sigma_{CEV} X_t^{p_{CEV}} dW_t \tag{7.38}$$

The process above has, for certain values of p_{CEV}, a variance which increases when X_t decreases. The instantaneous volatility of X_t is $\sigma_{CEV} X_t^{(p_{CEV}-1)}$. This is the term in front of "$X_t dW_t$" in Equation (7.38).

When $p_{CEV} < 1$, a decrease in X_t will clearly increase its variance. This property will be applied later in this book to model the fact that the volatility of a share tends to go up when the share price moves down. The CEV model nests many different models. The CIR model of the previous case study corresponds to $p_{CEV} = 0.5$, whereas a geometric Brownian motion materializes when $p_{CEV} = 1$.

In this particular case study we apply Ito's lemma to the variable X_t after changing it into a new stochastic variable Y_t:

$$Y_t = \frac{X_t^{1-p_{CEV}}}{1 - p_{CEV}}$$

Applying Ito's lemma and thereby following a similar approach as in the two preceding case studies, we obtain the following result:

$$dY = \left(\mu X^{1-p_{CEV}} - \frac{p_{CEV}}{2}X^{p_{CEV}-1}\sigma_{CEV}^2\right)dt + \sigma_{CEV}dW_t \tag{7.39}$$

or

$$dY = \left(\mu Y(1 - p_{CEV}) - \frac{p_{CEV}\sigma_{CEV}^2}{2Y(1-p_{CEV})}\right)dt + \sigma_{CEV}dW_t \tag{7.40}$$

7.4.3 Share Prices as Geometric Brownian Motion

The geometric Brownian motion of Equation (7.26) is often used to model the stochastic behavior of the share price $S = \{S_t, t \geq 0\}$:

$$dS_t = \mu_S S_t dt + \sigma_S S_t dW_t \tag{7.41}$$

We have demonstrated before that the solution of this stochastic differential equation is:

$$S_t = S_s \exp\left(\left(\mu_S - \frac{\sigma^2}{2}\right)(t - s) + \sigma_S(W_t - W_s)\right) \tag{7.42}$$

The drift and volatility can also be specified as deterministic functions of time, in which case Equation (7.42) modifies into:

$$S_t = S_s \exp\left(\int_s^t \left(\mu_S(u) - \frac{\sigma^2(u)}{2} \right) du + \int_s^t \sigma_S(u) dW(u) \right), s \leq t \qquad (7.43)$$

Starting from the share price S_s, all the future share prices S_t will be positive and depend on S_s only. What happened to the share price S before time s does not really matter. This observation is the Markov property of the geometric Brownian motion. Equation (7.42) shows that the share price S_t is lognormally distributed. The log return $L_{S(s,t)}$ of S between time s and t therefore follows a normal distribution:

$$L_{S(s,t)} = \log(S_t) - \log(S_s) \sim N\left(\left(\mu_S - \frac{\sigma_S^2}{2} \right)(t-s), \sigma_S^2(t-s) \right) \qquad (7.44)$$

In case the drift and variance are not constant over time:

$$L_{S(s,t)} = \log(S_t) - \log(S_s) \sim N\left(\int_s^t \left(\mu_S(u) - \frac{\sigma_S^2(u)}{2} \right) du, \int_s^t \sigma_S^2(u) du \right) \qquad (7.45)$$

When a stock follows a geometric Brownian motion, its share price will be lognormally distributed because we can rewrite Equation (7.44) as:

$$S_t = S_s \exp(Z) \qquad (7.46)$$

with

$$Z \sim N(\mu^*, \sigma^{*2})$$
$$\mu^* = \left(\mu - \frac{\sigma^2}{2} \right)(t-s)$$
$$\sigma^{*2} = \sigma^2(t-s)$$

From the table in Section 7.2.3 we can derive that if we model a share price as a geometric Brownian motion, it will have the following mean $E(S_t)$ and variance $Var(S_t)$ given a current share price level S_s:

$$E[S_t \mid S_s] = S_s \exp\left(\mu^* + \frac{1}{2}\sigma^{*2} \right) \qquad (7.47)$$
$$= S_s \exp(\mu(t-s))$$

$$Var(S_t \mid S_s) = S_s^2(\exp(2(\mu^* + \sigma^{*2})) - \exp(2\mu^* + \sigma^{*2}))$$
$$= S_s^2(\exp(\sigma^2(t-s)) - 1)(\exp(2\mu(t-s)))$$

Incorporating the assumption of logarithmic returns into a valuation and pricing model immediately introduces a fallacy. In fact, the appearance of extreme events is very unlikely in a normal distribution. It is a peace-time shape of the financial world; the market behavior is certainly much more erratic than what we implied using the bell-shaped curve.

Case Study: Apple

On January 3, 2011 a portfolio manager holding a large portfolio of Apple shares expects an annual return on these shares of 10% ($\mu = 0.1$). The volatility estimate made by this investor for the share is 14.96% ($\sigma = 0.1496$). The closing price of the Apple stock on the date of this case study was $329.57. The portfolio manager has the following fundamental question: "... What is the expected range for the share price of Apple the next 2 years while only allowing a 1% probability that Apple will trade out of this boundary?"

We continue on the work done before and assume that the share price follows a geometric Brownian motion. As a consequence of this assumption, the logarithmic share price return is normally distributed. A 99% confidence interval for such a random variable can be constructed using a range of 2.58 standard deviations around the expected log return. (Indeed, $\Phi(2.58) = 0.005$.) There will hence be an upper boundary and a lower boundary given by the following equations:

$$\text{Upper boundary} = S \exp\left(\left(\mu - \frac{1}{2}\sigma^2\right)t + 2.58 \times \sigma\sqrt{t}\right) \tag{7.48}$$

$$\text{Lower boundary} = S \exp\left(\left(\mu - \frac{1}{2}\sigma^2\right)t - 2.58 \times \sigma\sqrt{t}\right)$$

$$S_0 = 329.57$$

$$\mu = 0.1$$

$$\sigma = 0.1496$$

The result of this exercise is illustrated in Figure 7.5 and shows how the share price of Apple stayed for a long time within the estimated range but broke out of this envelope on March 13, 2012. Share prices cannot easily be confined to a Brownian motion-like stochastic process.

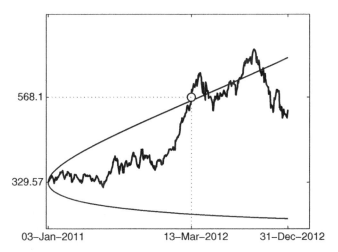

Figure 7.5 A 99% confidence interval constructed for Apple on January 3, 2011. On March 13, 2012 the share price breaks out of the confidence interval.

7.5 POISSON PROCESS

7.5.1 Definition

A stochastic process $N = \{N_t, t \geq 0\}$ is a Poisson process with intensity $\lambda > 0$ if the following holds:

1. **Process starts at zero**
   $N_0 = 0$.
2. **Process has stationary increments**
   $N_t - N_s$ only depends on the length of the interval $\mid t - s \mid$.
3. **Process has independent increments**
   The changes in N over non-overlapping intervals are stochastically independent. For example, if we have $0 \leq t_1 < t_2 < t_3 < T_4$ then $N_{t_2} - N_{t_1}$ is independent of $N_{t_4} - N_{t_3}$.
4. **Increments of N are Poisson distributed**
   The increment $N_t - N_s$ follows a Poisson distribution with intensity $\lambda(t - s)$. The probability that there are going to be k ($k \in \{0, 1, 2, \ldots\}$) events "counted" in the interval $[t, s]$ is $Prob(N_t - N_s = k)$ and is given by:

$$Prob(N_t - N_s = k) = \frac{\lambda^k(t - s)^k}{k!} \exp(-\lambda(t - s)), s \leq t \qquad (7.49)$$

The first three conditions are shared with the Wiener process and specify that a Poisson process belongs to the family of Lévy processes. It can be shown that the Poisson process is a pure jump or counting process because the jump size is equal to one. Therefore, it is often used to count the arrival of certain events. One could imagine these events to consist, for example, of skipped dividend payments, a failure to meet a debt payment, etc. Each event or jump arrives at a time τ. If the process N produces m jumps in a particular observation period, then $\tau_1, \tau_2 - \tau_1, \ldots, \tau_m - \tau_{m-1}$ are the times elapsed between each jump and the arrival of the next jump. The time between the two consecutive jumps can be shown to follow an exponential distribution with parameter λ. From this we derive that the average arrival time of such an event is $\frac{1}{\lambda}$.

Properties

There are two properties of a Poisson process N which we are going to use later on:

- $\lim_{t \to 0} \frac{Prob(N_t \geq 2)}{t} = 0$
  The intuitive meaning of this property is that in a small interval we can have at most one jump.
- $\lim_{t \to 0} \frac{Prob(N_t = 1)}{t} = \lambda$
  In a small interval t the probability of encountering one jump is approximatively equal to λt.

From Equation (7.49) we can derive the probability of having to deal without the occurrence of any event at all up till time t. This will later be called the survival probability and refers to the fact that a survival corresponds to a situation where the default event τ, which is the first time N jumps, occurs after t:

$$Prob(t < \tau) = \exp(-\lambda t) \qquad (7.50)$$

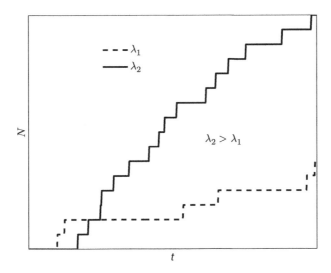

Figure 7.6   Two Poisson processes with different intensities: $\lambda_2 > \lambda_1$.

The survival probability looks very much like a discount factor used when discounting cash flows. Therefore, the intensity λ acts very much like a credit spread or yield. This will come in very handy when integrating intensity-based modeling in fixed-income mathematics [127].

The probability of having to deal with at least one event is the complementary of the equation above:

$$Prob(\tau \leq t) = 1 - \exp(-\lambda t) \tag{7.51}$$

Along the same lines of thought, the probability that a particular event occurs between time s and t conditional on the fact there was no occurrence of a jump before s is given by the difference of two survival probabilities:

$$Prob(s < \tau \leq t \mid s < \tau) = \frac{Prob(s < \tau) - Prob(t < \tau)}{Prob(s < \tau)} \tag{7.52}$$

Using Equation (7.50) this can be rewritten as:

$$Prob(s < \tau \leq t \mid s < \tau) = \frac{\exp(-\lambda s) - \exp(-\lambda t)}{\exp(-\lambda s)} \tag{7.53}$$

$$= 1 - \exp(-\lambda(t - s)) \tag{7.54}$$

In Figure 7.6 a Poisson processes is illustrated with two different intensity factors λ.

Case Study: First Coupon Loss

A manager of a pension fund with a significant exposure to hybrids is holding a position in preferred securities of three different issuers. Every single one of these preferreds distributes dividends that can be canceled. A skipped dividend payout is also non-cumulative. The issuer never has to make up for coupons that were skipped in the past. The manager wants to quantify the likelihood that there is going to be at least one failure on a coupon payment in the next

6 months by any of the three preferreds. In order to do the calculus for this case study, the following two assumptions are made:

1. **Independent events**

    The failure to pay a coupon by one of the three preferreds is assumed not to trigger or influence a dividend cancelation by either of the other two issuers. The manager believes this is a fair assumption given the fact that the issuers are active in three different business sectors. If all three of the issuers were to be active in, for example, the financial sector, this assumption would be wrong. The bankruptcy of Lehman Brothers in 2008 is a perfect example of how one default event contaminated many other financial institutions.

2. **Poisson process**

    The three counting processes $N_{1,2,3}$ that track the number of non-paid coupons for each of the three preferreds are modeled through a Poisson process. A jump event corresponds to a failure to pay the dividend on the preferred security. The three different assumed intensities are: $\lambda_1 = 0.1$, $\lambda_2 = 0.125$, and $\lambda_3 = 0.2$. The arrival time of a new event in each of these three Poisson processes is exponentially distributed according to these intensities. The average time to expect the first failure to pay the coupon is equal to $(\frac{1}{\lambda})$. For the three different preferreds this is respectively 10, 8, and 5 years. The probability of having to deal with a skipped coupon payment on the three preferreds over a time frame of 6 months can be calculated using Equation (7.51):

$$\text{Preferred } 1 = 1 - \exp\left(-\frac{0.1}{2}\right) = 4.88\%$$

$$\text{Preferred } 2 = 1 - \exp\left(-\frac{0.125}{2}\right) = 6.06\% \tag{7.55}$$

$$\text{Preferred } 3 = 1 - \exp\left(-\frac{0.2}{2}\right) = 9.52\%$$

The first arrival time of any of these three events is also modeled by an exponential distribution. As seen before in Equation (7.15), the minimum of a set of independent exponentially distributed random variables indeed follows an exponential distribution. In this case, the intensity of the distribution is $\lambda = \lambda_1 + \lambda_2 + \lambda_3 = 0.425$. The probability that we are going to deal with a non-coupon payment in this portfolio containing three preferreds during the next 6 months is 19.14%:

$$= 1 - \exp\left(-(\lambda_1 + \lambda_2 + \lambda_3) \times \frac{1}{2}\right) \tag{7.56}$$

$$= 1 - \exp\left(-\frac{0.425}{2}\right)$$

$$= 0.1914$$

7.5.2 Advanced Poisson Processes

So far, the intensity λ has been a constant. A Poisson process using such a constant intensity is called a **time-homogeneous** Poisson process. A **time-inhomogeneous** process deals with a deterministic time-varying intensity function $\lambda(t)$. The calculation of the survival

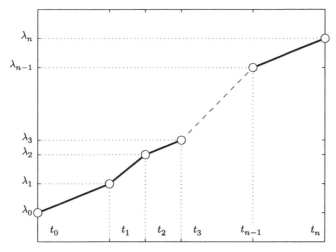

Figure 7.7   Intensity as a piecewise linear function.

probabilities is slightly different from Equations (7.50) and (7.54), where a constant intensity was used.

- Survival probability up till time t:

$$Prob(t < \tau) = \exp\left(-\int_0^t \lambda(u)du\right) \tag{7.57}$$

- Probability of an event taking place between s and t, when no such event took place before time s:

$$Prob(s < \tau \le t \mid s < \tau) = 1 - \exp\left(-\int_s^t \lambda(u)du\right) \tag{7.58}$$

Suppose we are dealing with a piecewise linear function $\lambda(t)$ as illustrated in Figure 7.7. The intensity takes the following expression:

$$\lambda(t) = \begin{cases} \lambda_0 & t < t_0 \\ \lambda_0 + \frac{\lambda_1 - \lambda_0}{t_1 - t_0}(t - t_0) & t_0 \le t < t_1 \\ \vdots & \\ \lambda_{n-1} + \frac{\lambda_n - \lambda_{n-1}}{t_n - t_{n-1}}(t - t_{n-1}) & t_{n-1} \le t < t_n \end{cases} \tag{7.59}$$

Using Equation (7.58) and the analytic expression of $\lambda(t)$ specified in the equation above, we can determine the probability that an event takes place in the interval $[t_{n-1}, t_n]$ conditional on the fact that no such event occurred before time t_{n-1}:

$$Prob(t_{n-1} < \tau \le t_n \mid t_{n-1} < \tau) = 1 - \exp\left(-\frac{(t_n - t_{n-1})(\lambda_n + \lambda_{n+1})}{2}\right) \tag{7.60}$$

When the intensity itself starts to become stochastic, we are dealing with a **Cox process** or a **doubly stochastic process**. This latter name is an indication of the double stochastic nature of the Poisson process. The jumps appear in a random way and the intensity of such a jump event is a random variable itself. An example of such a random intensity is based on the work of Cox, Ingersoll, and Ross studying interest rate dynamics [62]:

$$d\lambda_t = \kappa(\eta - \lambda_t)dt + \zeta_\lambda \sqrt{\lambda_t} dW_t \tag{7.61}$$

The stochastic behavior of the intensity λ_t is based on a Brownian motion W_t where the volatility of the process is governed by the variable $\zeta > 0$. In this Cox process, λ_t displays a mean-reverting behavior. The process starts at an initial intensity value $\lambda_0 > 0$ and when the intensity drifts too far away from the long-term intensity level $\eta > 0$, the value of λ_t will be pulled back to this level. The speed with which this reversion to the mean takes place is controlled by the parameter $\kappa > 0$.

7.5.3   Conclusion

This chapter has provided an overview of the different stochastic processes and their possible application in financial models. We retain the use of Poisson processes to model events such as defaults and the geometric Brownian motion to describe share price movements. A process such as the constant elasticity of variance (CEV) will demonstrate its use in valuation problems for instruments that require an adequate modeling of fat-tail risk, like CoCo bonds.

Modeling Hybrids: Risk Neutrality

8.1 INTRODUCTION

The geometric Brownian motion is the starting point for most equity derivative models:

$$dS_t = \mu S_t dt + \sigma S_t dW_t \tag{8.1}$$

The equation above describes the changes dS_t in the value of the share price and illustrates the dependence of those changes on the expected return μ of the stock at its volatility σ. From Equation (7.31) we know that the possible values for S_t at a future time t, starting from the current value S_s at the current time s, are given by:

$$S_t = S_s \exp\left(\left(\mu - \frac{\sigma^2}{2}\right)(t - s) + \sigma(W_t - W_s)\right), \quad t \geq s. \tag{8.2}$$

The random component driving the stock price from S_s to S_t is the Brownian motion $W = \{W_t, t \geq 0\}$. One factor in the equation above is investor-dependent. Investors will indeed have different values for the drift component μ in the equation above. An investor with a bullish mindset will have a very positive value for μ opposed to more moderate values for the investors taking a bearish stance on the stock. We now want to calculate the price of a derivative security P whose value depends on the future price path followed by the underlying share price S. How can we eliminate the different assumptions regarding μ? This is where a risk-neutral setting enters on stage, which allows derivative pricing independent from the individual investor's views. We start illustrating the possibility to hedge away any equity risk from a security with price P through the construction of a portfolio with a long position in this derivative security and a short position of Δ shares. If such a risk-free portfolio were to exist, it would earn the risk-free interest rate r. This risk-free portfolio would accrue like a money market account from B_s to B_t. If not, there would be an arbitrage possibility.

Let us first start in a simplified world where, if we push the share forward from time s to time t, there are only two different outcomes possible: this is the one-step binomial tree. The future share price S_t is either $S_s \times u$ or $S_s \times d$. The multipliers u and d, respectively increase (through an up move) or decrease (through a down move) the initial stock price S_s. The two new stock prices at time t have the corresponding values P_u and P_d for the derivative security. This is the binomial representation of Equation (8.1).

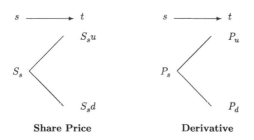

Share Price   **Derivative**

Next to the assumption that we live in an arbitrage-free world where risk-free portfolios should earn the risk-free rate, there are two additional elements which we have to add to our hypothesis:

- There are no transaction costs involved in setting up the risk-free portfolio.
- It is possible to sell short the shares needed to hedge the equity risk present in the long position of the derivative security. The absence of the possibility to perform such a short sale forbids the construction of a hedged portfolio.

The number of shares held short against holding a position in one derivative security from time s to t is the delta (Δ). The appropriate Δ eliminates all the equity risk from the portfolio and whatever price path we have, an up or a down move, one should obtain the same value:

$$P_u - \Delta S_s u = P_d - \Delta S_s d \tag{8.3}$$

Hence the required hedge must satisfy:

$$\Delta = \frac{P_u - P_d}{S_s(u - d)} \tag{8.4}$$

Selling short the shares immunizes the portfolio from the impact of having the share price go up or down. Owning such a hedged portfolio is similar to having a bank account accruing risk free from B_s to B_t:

$$\text{Time } s \rightarrow \text{Time } t$$
$$P_s - \Delta S_s \rightarrow P_u - \Delta S_s u \tag{8.5}$$

is similar to

$$B_s \rightarrow B_t$$

Hence:

$$\frac{B_t}{B_s} = \frac{P_u - \Delta S_s u}{P_s - \Delta S_s} \tag{8.6}$$

We can rewrite the equation above to find a first expression for the current (unknown) value of the derivative security P_s at time s:

$$P_s = \frac{B_s}{B_t}(P_u - \Delta S_s u) - \Delta S_s \tag{8.7}$$

Replacing Δ with Equation (8.4) we obtain:

$$P_s = \frac{B_s}{B_t}\left(P_u - \frac{P_u - P_d}{(u - d)}u\right) - \frac{P_u - P_d}{(u - d)} \tag{8.8}$$

which can be simplified to:

$$P_s = \frac{B_s}{B_t}(pP_u + (1 - p)P_d) \tag{8.9}$$

with

$$p = \frac{\frac{B_t}{B_s} - d}{u - d} \tag{8.10}$$

Note that $0 < p < 1$ if $d < \frac{B_t}{B_s} < u$, which is a natural condition because otherwise arbitrage would be possible.[1] Equation (8.9) can be given an intuitive meaning. The parameter p can clearly be seen as some kind of probability. If one sees it as the probability of arriving in an "up state" and receiving P_u for the derivative security at time t, then the expected value of P_t at time t is $pP_u + (1 - p)P_d$. This and the discount factor $\frac{B_s}{B_t}$ show how the current value P_s is the expected value of a discounted payoff. In other words:

$$P_s = B_s \mathbb{E}_Q \left[\frac{P_t}{B_t} \right] \tag{8.11}$$

We use the operator $\mathbb{E}_Q$ to denote that the expectation is taken in a risk-neutral world using p as the probability of moving up. We can apply this to the share price S_s and in the case of a constant risk-free interest rate:

$$S_s = \frac{B_s}{B_t} \mathbb{E}_Q[S_t] = \exp(-r(t - s))\mathbb{E}_Q[S_t] \tag{8.12}$$

Hence, solving for $\mathbb{E}_Q[S_t]$:

$$\mathbb{E}_Q[S_t] = \exp(r(t - s))S_s \tag{8.13}$$

From this equation we learn that, in a risk-neutral world, the share price is expected to grow at the risk-free rate r.

A similar argument can be made in the geometrical Brownian motion setting. Actually, the one-step binomial argument can be repeated in a multi-step binomial setting. By taking the number of steps to infinity and using the central limit theorem, we arrive at the geometric Brownian setting. One can further repeat the hedge argument and $\Delta = \frac{\partial P}{\partial S}$. The geometric Brownian motion process of the share price S is then driven by:

$$dS_t = rS_t dt + \sigma S_t dW_t \tag{8.14}$$

When dealing with a share that distributes a continuous dividend yield q, we have:

$$dS_t = (r - q)S_t dt + \sigma S_t dW_t \tag{8.15}$$

and

$$\mathbb{E}_Q[S_t] = \exp((r - q)(t - s))S_s \tag{8.16}$$

The equation above is going to be the starting point for the different numerical techniques going forward. Using this risk neutrality, the price of a derivative security P_s at time s is equal to the discounted value of its expected payoff. The discounting can be done at the risk-free rate and there is no intervention of any risk premium at all.

---

[1] If, for example, $u > d > \frac{B_t}{B_s}$ even the down case would give a return above the risk-free rate. Hence, everybody would borrow money from the bank to buy stock. If $d < u < \frac{B_t}{B_s}$, shorting stock would lead to a similar arbitrage.

8.2 CLOSED-FORM SOLUTION

8.2.1 Introduction

Finding a closed-form formula for the price of a derivative security is ideal from a practical perspective when trying to understand the valuation and risk of a hybrid security. Such a formula can easily be implemented in a portfolio management system and allows for an almost real-time portfolio valuation and hedging. Very often the speed and ease of use of such a solution comes at a cost because of the assumptions that have to be taken. In 1973, Fisher Black, Myron Scholes, and Robert Merton built their Nobel Prize-winning formula for European call and put options on the following assumptions [33]:

- **There is only one source of risk**
  The Black–Scholes model belongs to the family of single-factor models. The only source of risk is the share price, which is assumed to follow a geometric Brownian motion. For all the other parameters the main idea here is that their value does not change in a random way. Dividend yields, interest rates, and volatilities are deterministic. Forcing the valuation of some hybrids into a Black–Scholes framework is absolutely not ideal. In Figure 6.8 we already illustrated the sensitivity of a contingent convertible with respect to the different input factors. For the contingent convertible examined in this particular case study, a change in the equity volatility had the biggest impact on the price of a CoCo. Assuming a constant volatility here is a step in the wrong direction. This observation underscores the importance of stochastic volatility models such as the Heston model [118]. This model offers, however, only a semi-closed-form solution for European equity options for two sources of risk: the share price S and the equity volatility σ.

- **No early exercise**
  The closed-form formula engineered by Fisher Black and Myron Scholes only works for European options. A reverse convertible is an example of a hybrid security where such a closed-form solution can be put to work. In some particular cases, such as barrier and lookback options, closed formulas have been developed as well. Closed-form solutions for barrier options will come in handy later in this book when breaking up a contingent convertible into a package of barrier options. The music stops, however, when there is a possible early conversion, a change in the conversion ratio, a dividend protection, etc. In these cases, working out an analytic solution is out of the question.

- **Frictionless market**
  The underlying asset of the derivative security can be traded in a perfect world. This is a market where there are no bid–offer spreads, no transaction costs, and no borrow fees. In reality, these assumptions do not hold at all. Some turnarounds to deal with this imperfection have been introduced. Traders very often add a borrow fee b to the dividend yield q when using a Black–Scholes model. Transaction costs can also be captured somehow through a volatility adjustment. Leland [137] developed a fudge for the volatility σ. A new volatility $\overline{\sigma}$ is introduced based on a proportional transaction fee k:

$$\overline{\sigma} = \sigma\sqrt{1 + A} \qquad (8.17)$$

with

$$A = \sqrt{\frac{2}{\pi}}\frac{k}{\sigma\sqrt{\delta t}} \qquad (8.18)$$

The idea to plug this volatility into an option pricing formula developed in a Black–Scholes world seems flawed, but remains useful [197]. The parameter δt is the time interval between two subsequent acts of hedging the equity exposure of the hybrid security. A positive convexity – the traditional convertible convexity, for example – needs a lower model volatility to calculate the price of the bond: $\overline{\sigma} < \sigma$. The buyer of the convertible will pay less for the security because of the presence of transaction costs. Hedging the equity risk of this convertible security comes at a cost. Fudging the volatility is a way to get this done even when using a formula that is using a totally different assumption. For a short gamma position the volatility has to be adjusted upward: $\overline{\sigma} > \sigma$. Whalley and Wilmott [195] include the sign of the convexity in Leland's corrected volatility number:

$$\overline{\sigma} = \sigma\sqrt{1 - sign(\Gamma)A} \qquad (8.19)$$

A practical example explains best the impact of transaction costs. A portfolio manager wants to invest in a convertible bond with an emerging market stock as underlying share. He intends to run a delta-neutral position on this convertible for a while. The bond is currently very cheaply priced and should be trading at par ($P = 100$) according to his analyst. The portfolio manager agrees and therefore expects the value of the convertible to increase and converge to this higher level. The convertible's implied volatility is 30%, the underlying stock is very illiquid, and executing a trade is therefore expensive. Each hedge costs 50 bps in transaction costs ($k = 0.5\%$). The vega ($\frac{\partial P}{\partial \sigma}$) of the convertible is 0.24. How much should the theoretical price P of the bond be impacted if it is the manager's intention to delta hedge this holding every week? Applying Equations (8.18) and (8.19) on following market data yields the new volatility $\overline{\sigma} = 28.52\%$ to be plugged into the pricing model:

 – $\sigma = 30\%$
 – $\delta t = \dfrac{7}{365}$
 – $\Gamma > 0$
 – $k = 0.5\%$

The impact δP on the price of the convertible is given by:

$$\delta P = \text{Vega} \times (28.52 - 30) = -35 \text{ bps}$$

The adjusted fair value of the convertible bond is therefore $P = 100 - 0.35 = 99.65\%$.

• **Stock prices are lognormally distributed**
The lognormal distribution of share prices is a direct consequence of the assumption that stock prices follow a geometric Brownian motion (Equation (7.41)). Moving away from this assumption makes it harder to come up with a closed-form solution for derivative securities. An example of such a more complex approach is the closed-form solution in [143] for European options on underlying assets whose stochastic behavior is modeled through a variance gamma process [174]. Without going into too much detail, one could describe the variance gamma process as yet another Lévy process; it starts at zero and has stationary and independent increments. It differs from other members of the Lévy family because its increments follow a variance gamma law. The existence of a closed-form solution for European options comes with the advantage that the parameters of the stochastic process can be calibrated against prices of listed options for a wide range of strikes and maturities.

8.2.2 Black–Scholes Solution

In a Black–Scholes world, the partial differential equation for European options is:[2]

$$\frac{\partial P}{\partial t} + \frac{\sigma^2 S^2}{2} \frac{\partial^2 P}{\partial S^2} + rS \frac{\partial P}{\partial S} = rP \tag{8.20}$$

Deriving this equation in line with the assumptions and solving it in order to find the theoretical price of a European call or put is the merit of Robert Merton, Fisher Black, and Myron Scholes. Their achievement in 1973 rocked the financial world, and since that moment we have all witnessed the enormous growth of the derivatives market. Their break through paved without any doubt the progress of derivatives and structured products as a new asset class. Equation (8.20) also holds for hybrids with a European nature such as, for example, a reverse convertible where the payoff depends entirely on the value of the share price at the expiration date. This has been explained in Equation (2.75). Solving the Black–Scholes equation for a reverse convertible is only slightly different because of coupon payments and because of particular boundary conditions.

A partial differential equation such as Equation (8.20) binds the different price sensitivities of the theoretical price P of a European option together in one single line. Using the definition of the greeks in Section 2.3.5, the Black–Scholes equation can be rewritten as:

$$\Theta + \frac{\sigma^2 S^2}{2} \Gamma + rS \Delta = rP \tag{8.21}$$

Before looking into the general solution of this particular differential equation, it is worthwhile coming to grips with the physical meaning of the equation above. We can now drill a bit deeper into Equation (8.21) and consider the example of a long position in a zero-coupon reverse convertible. Suppose we find ourselves at a boundary condition where the share price is high. The owner of the reverse convertible is long a zero-coupon bond because the short embedded put option has no value in this particular case ($S \gg N/C_r$). The linear (Δ) and non-linear (Γ) equity sensitivities of the reverse convertible are accordingly close to zero. Equation (8.21) can hence be simplified to:

$$\Theta = rP \tag{8.22}$$

or

$$\frac{\partial P}{\partial t} = rP \tag{8.23}$$

Integrating this partial differential equation:

$$\log(P_T) - \log(P_t) = r(T - t) \tag{8.24}$$

Using the fact that P_T is equal to the face value N since the reverse convertible will not be redeemed into shares, we find the theoretical value P_t of the reverse convertible in this boundary case:

$$P_t = N \exp(-r(T - t)) \tag{8.25}$$

---

[2] The Black–Scholes equation formulated here is defined in a setting where the dividend yield q is equal to zero for simplicity.

Solving the Black–Scholes equation delivers us, in this particular boundary case, the formula for a risk-free zero-coupon bond priced at time t and expiring at T. This is exactly what we expected.

Suppose that the reverse convertible is not out-of-the-money and hence has a certain amount of equity exposure ($\Delta < 0$). A portfolio manager who owns this bond now decides to neutralize the equity exposure of this reverse convertible and sells $|\Delta|$ shares. The value of this delta-neutral portfolio is Π and also satisfies the Black–Scholes equation. Given the obtained delta neutrality ($\frac{\partial \Pi}{\partial S} = 0$), we have:

$$\Theta_\Pi + \frac{\sigma^2 S^2}{2}\Gamma_\Pi = r\Pi \tag{8.26}$$

This equation brings us back to Section 2.2.6, where we already discussed in an intuitive manner the convexity Γ_Π of a derivatives portfolio. From the equation above we now learn that the value Π of a delta-hedged portfolio with a high convexity will be suffering from a higher time decay than a portfolio with a smaller gamma:

$$\Gamma_\Pi \uparrow \quad \text{hence} \quad \Theta_\Pi \downarrow \tag{8.27}$$

8.2.3   Solving the Black–Scholes Equation

The Black–Scholes partial differential equation can be solved in a general way. The zero-coupon example we solved in the previous paragraph was a boundary case. The analytical expression we obtained was only valid for far out-of-the-money reverse convertibles. The closed-form solution for a European call and put will not be derived in this work. We will go straight to the results, since this has been done already numerous times in the financial literature. The interested reader is referred to the work of John Hull [121]. The theoretical price of a European call ($P_{t,Call}$) and a European put ($P_{t,Put}$) option on time t with strike K and maturity T is given by:

$$P_{t,Call} = S\exp(-q(T-t))\Phi(d1) - K\exp(-r(T-t))\Phi(d2)$$
$$P_{t,Put} = K\exp(-r(T-t))\Phi(-d2) - S\exp(-q(T-t))N(-d1)$$

with

$$d1 = \frac{\log(S/K) + (r - q + \sigma^2/2)(T-t)}{\sigma\sqrt{(T-t)}}$$

and

$$d2 = d1 - \sigma\sqrt{(T-t)}$$

$$
\begin{aligned}
q &: \text{Continuous dividend yield} \\
r &: \text{Continuous interest rate} \\
\sigma &: \text{Volatility}
\end{aligned}
\tag{8.28}
$$

The function $\Phi(x)$ has been defined in Equation (7.7). As an example, we consider a 5-year at-the-money call option on a share with a price equal to \$100. The share has a volatility of 40% and distributes a 2% dividend yield. The 5-year interest rate is equal to 5%:

$$
\begin{aligned}
&\textbf{Parameters} \\
&S && = 100 \\
&K && = 100 \\
&\sigma && = 0.4 \\
&r && = 0.05 \\
&q && = 0.02 \\
&T && = 5 \\
&\textbf{Intermediate results} \\
&d1 && = 0.6149 \\
&d2 && = -0.2795 \\
&N(d1) && = 0.7307 \\
&N(d2) && = 0.3899 \\
&N(-d1) && = 0.2693 \\
&N(-d2) && = 0.6101
\end{aligned}
\tag{8.29}
$$

This results in the value of the European call and put: $P_{t,Call} = 35.75$ and $P_{t,Put} = 23.14$.

8.2.4   Case Study: Reverse Convertible

Through Equation (2.75) we learned that a reverse convertible is equal to a bond combined with a short put option on C_r underlying shares. The strike K of the put option is equal to N/C_r and the bond distributes n coupons $c_{i=1,\dots,n}$ at times $t_{i=1,\dots,n}$. Ignoring any default risk for the moment, the price P_t of the reverse convertible is given by the following equation:

$$
P_t = \sum_{i=1}^{n} c_i \exp(-r(t_i - t)) + N \exp(-r(T - t)) - C_r \times P_{t,Put}
\tag{8.30}
$$

The value of the put option is retrieved from Equation (8.29) after substituting K with N/C_r. Equation (8.30) is the starting point of an exercise where a reverse convertible is constructed from scratch. Just imagine a sales person working on the structuring desk of an investment bank. This investment bank has a very high rating and can fund itself in the interbank market at an interest rate of 2% for a 5-year maturity. In order to satisfy client demand for a product with a high coupon, the structurer might revert to a reverse convertible to meet this particular need. Having a target price equal to par for the reverse convertible, there are two different approaches possible:

- **Target coupon of 12%**
  The reverse convertible can be constructed around a particular target coupon. The investor has, for example, laid out that he is aiming for a yield of around 12% which is of course a lot higher than the 2% interest rate that could be offered by the bank. The structurer will consider as possible underlying equity of this reverse convertible two stocks A and B with initial price 100. Each of these stocks does not distribute a dividend ($q = 0$). A and B only differ in their volatility. Stock A is expected to be twice as volatile as stock B: $\sigma_A = 40\%$ and $\sigma_B = 20\%$. Using $r = 2\%$, a face value $N = 1000$, and a 12% annual coupon, the value

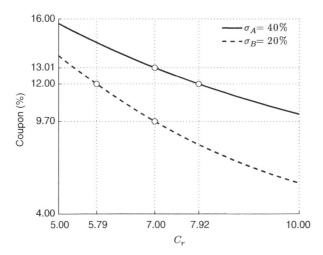

Figure 8.1 Annual coupon for a reverse convertible for different conversion ratios C_r and for two different stocks A and B.

of the 5-year corporate bond is equal to 135.25%:

$$1352.49 = 120 \times (\exp(-0.02) + \exp(-0.02 \times 2) + \ldots \tag{8.31}$$
$$\exp(-0.02 \times 3) + \exp(-0.02 \times 4) + \ldots$$
$$\exp(-0.02 \times 5)) + 1000 \exp(-0.02 \times 5)$$

This price is above the target price of 100% and the investor will need to add some short put options to the corporate bond to reduce the price from 135.25% to par. Figure 8.1 assists us in finding the short put options to be embedded in the convertible bond structure. The conversion ratio for a reverse convertible with share A is equal to 7.92, while it is 5.79 for share B. This choice of the conversion ratio C_r results in a reverse convertible with a 12% coupon. In the first case, the investor is short 7.92 put options with strike 126.26 (= 1000/7.96). For the other possibility, where share B would have been chosen, the short put options are even more in-the-money since they have a strike of 172.71. Only when $C_r > 10$ can we reduce the conversion risk to the extent that we have out-of-the-money options in the reverse convertible.

- **Target conversion ratio of 7**
  The structuring of the reverse convertible can also be handled from a different perspective. Here the investor proposes a conversion ratio of 7. This corresponds to a conversion price or strike K equal to 142.86. The highest coupon can be achieved in the case of share A, given its higher volatility. For A and B the obtained annual coupons are 13.01% and 9.70%. In both cases the value of the reverse convertible is very close to par ($P_t = 100$), as shown below:

	Stock A		Stock B
Coupon (%)	13.01		9.70
Corporate Bond Value ($)	1390		1267
C_r		7	
Strike		142.86	
Put Option ($)	55.71		38.09
Total (P_t)	**100.00**		**100.04**

The short put option is the key building block of the reverse convertible bond. The higher the volatility of the underlying share and the higher the strike of the put, the more expensive the embedded put option. The more expensive the put that can be shorted, the higher the coupon that can be assigned to the reverse convertible.

8.3   TREE-BASED METHODS

8.3.1   Introduction

Binomial and trinomial trees belong to the larger group of lattice models. The common approach in this numerical technique is to constrain the outcome of a continuous stochastic process X_t to a limited number of states observed over a finite set of times $t_0, t_1, \ldots, t_n$. A binomial tree allows a financial variable such as a share price to move to two possible states after a time step Δt, whereas a trinomial tree allows three possible values for $X_{t+\Delta t}$ starting from the current value X_t. In a previous work [67], we even approached the valuation problem of convertible bonds through heptanomial trees allowing seven outcomes for $X_{t+\Delta t}$ over the subsequent time step Δt. It is important to stipulate that there is no such thing as "the" binomial or trinomial tree. A newcomer in the world of tree models has a vast amount of possibilities from which an initial choice can be made. The difference between these numerous approaches resides in the convergence of the model to the analytical solution and the applicability of the tree model to a particular option type [51]. A lot of research has, for example, been done in the customization of tree models to handle barrier options or to accommodate the use of discrete dividends. In this section we will limit ourselves to a general introduction covering the topic of trinomial trees. Later, this introductory approach will be explored in more detail when covering the valuation of convertibles and other hybrids such as CoCo bonds.

Our starting point is the following Ito process. It represents the stochastic behavior of a financial variable X_t:

$$dX_t = A(X_t, t)dt + B(X_t, t)dW_t \tag{8.32}$$

The dynamics of the process above can be discretized by allowing the variable X_t to move forward in time while moving from node to node on a tree. The possible paths form the branches of an imaginary tree. When dealing with a binomial tree, the value of a modeled financial variable can move from X_t to $X_{t+\Delta t}$ in two particular ways: it can move up or down. The probability of an upward move is p_u, while the probability of a movement to a lower node is p_d. In the case of trinomial trees, there is also a middle node to which X_t can move. This node lies between the nodes corresponding to an upward or downward move. The corresponding probability of such an intermediate node is p_m.

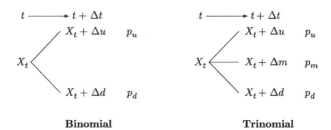

Binomial   **Trinomial**

Trinomial Tree

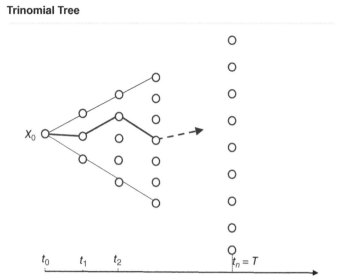

Figure 8.2   Trinomial tree-based simulation of a financial variable starting with an initial value X_0.

The scheme above represents the movement of X_t covering one single time step Δt. The complete tree is obtained by connecting these elementary trinomial movements together. In most tree models, the time step Δt is considered constant in the tree construction process. This facilitates the numerical implementation of the geometry of the tree into a computer algorithm. This is by no means a strict requirement, however. One can imagine that when building a pricing model for a convertible bond, there could be a need to have a finer grid around coupon or dividend dates. The movement of X from its current value X_0 to its final value X_T at a future time T is illustrated in Figure 8.2. The figure illustrates how the value of the variable X moves from its current value in the origin X_0 of the tree across all the different time slices $\{t_1, \ldots, t_n = T\}$ to a final value. The probability of X moving up and down in the tree depends on the parameters $A(X_t, t)$ and $B(X_t, t)$ specifying the Ito process.

8.3.2   Framework

The tree construction work in this chapter is going to be very generic. It is not tied to a particular instrument or asset class. As such, the method can be used to simulate share prices, interest rates, or even stochastic default risk. Its applicability is also independent of the process followed by these variables. A financial variable can, for example, follow a square-root or CEV process as described respectively in Equations (7.32) and (7.38). However, it is not because one's aim is to model a derivative security on an equity that the immediate goal should be the construction of a tree of share prices S directly. An intermediate trinomial tree is sometimes needed. The particular nature of a stochastic process could force us to construct a tree for an auxiliary stochastic variable $X = f(S)$ for which a tree construction is more straightforward. This auxiliary tree is then transformed back into a tree of share prices S. From the tree of share prices, the value P of the financial instrument can subsequently be derived.

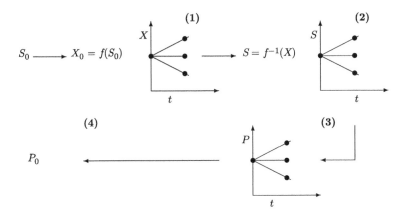

The picture above sketches the overall framework in order to calculate today's price P_0 for a derivative security on a share with current market price S_0:

1. Construct a tree for the auxiliary variable X starting at $X_0 = f(S_0)$.
2. Each of the nodes in the X-tree is transposed into a corresponding S-tree with node values $S = f^{-1}(X)$.
3. Starting from the S-tree, a tree for the financial derivative is constructed. Each node in the S-tree has a matching node in the P-tree.
4. Rolling back through the P-tree from the maturity date T till today's date ($t = 0$) culminates in the current price P_0.

Example: Instead of modeling the evolution of a share price S_t starting at the current price $S_0 = 100$, the value of $X_t = \log(S_t/S_0)$ will be modeled in a trinomial tree. In this process $X_0 = 0$ is going to be the initial node from where the stochastic variable X can move to three nodes in a subsequent time step: $X_{1,1}, X_{1,0}$, or $X_{1,-1}$. In this example the step size $\Delta u = -\Delta d = 5\%$ and $\Delta m = 0$. The distance between the nodes on the first time step is 5%. The nodes are said to be equidistant.

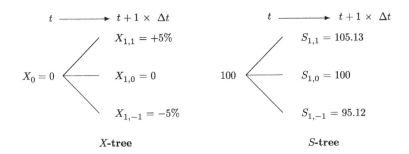

The jumps in the X-tree are additive and because $S_t = S_0 \exp(X_t)$, the nodes on the S-tree are no longer equidistant. The difference between two consecutive values of X is, for example,

$\Delta X = 5\%$. An up move in the S-tree is therefore equal to 5.13, whereas a down move is -4.88:

$$
\begin{aligned}
&\text{Up move}\\
&\Delta X && = +5\%\\
&S_{1,1} && = S_0 \exp(\Delta X)\\
&&& = 105.13
\end{aligned}
$$

$$
\begin{aligned}
&\text{Down move}\\
&\Delta X && = -5\%\\
&S_{1,-1} && = S_0 \exp(\Delta X)\\
&&& = 95.12
\end{aligned}
$$

(8.33)

A second time step now extends the X-tree, keeping, for example, the same step size of 5%. From node $X_{1,1}$, three possible node values are $X_{2,2} = 2 \times 5\% = 10\%$, $X_{2,1} = 1 \times 5\% = 5\%$, and $X_{2,0} = 0 \times 5\% = 0\%$. The corresponding S-nodes are: $S_{2,2} = 110.52$, $S_{2,1} = 105.13$, and $S_{2,0} = 100$.

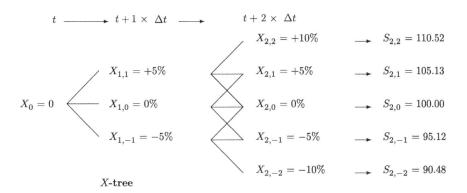

8.3.3 Geometry of the Trinomial Tree

The discretization obtained through a tree is two fold:

1. Time is no longer a continuous variable, it moves in multiples of Δt. All the nodes corresponding to a particular time step are said to belong to the same **time slice**.
2. A similar discretization takes place for the values of X. The value of $X_{t+\Delta t}$ is the result of an up move $\Delta u > 0$, a down move $\Delta d < 0$, or an intermediate move Δm, all originating from a node X_t at the previous time slice. The corresponding probabilities p_u, p_d, and p_m are the so-called **transition probabilities**.

The geometry of the tree is given in Figure 8.3; we adopted the notation and framework as specified in [44]. In this framework we assume that all the nodes on the same slice are equidistant from each other. Each time slice t_i can be associated with a corresponding interval ΔX_i. All the nodes on this particular time slice t_i are then integer multiples of the step size ΔX_i. In the figure above, $\Delta X_1 = \Delta X_2 = 5\%$.

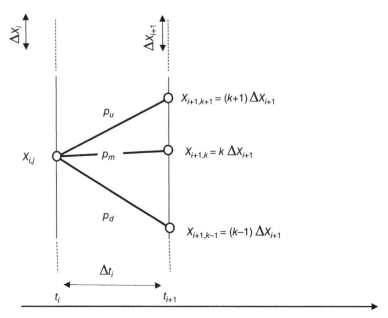

Figure 8.3 Schematic representation of the trinomial tree.

Starting from the initial node X_0 at t_0, the next node X_1 at time t_1 can take the following three values:

$$X_0 \to X_1 \begin{cases} X_{1,k+1} = (k+1) \times \Delta X_1 \\ X_{1,k} \phantom{{}+1} = k \times \Delta X_1 \\ X_{1,k-1} = (k-1) \times \Delta X_1 \end{cases} \quad \text{with integer } k \qquad (8.34)$$

It is important to stipulate that the step sizes can differ from time slice to time slice. At time t_{i+1}, for example, we can have that $\Delta X_{i+1} \neq \Delta X_i$. This approach was discussed in [44] and deviates from what is most often encountered in financial textbooks. It is indeed very common dealing with a constant jump size ΔX valid for all the time slices when constructing a trinomial or binomial tree. The generalized procedure will show its effectiveness when implementing stochastic processes for hybrid bonds where the underlying share price is far from being lognormally distributed.

We introduce the following notation in order to allow us to work out the algebra associated with this general tree-building procedure:

$$X_{i,j} \begin{cases} \text{Corresponds to time slice} = t_i \\ \text{Value of the node} = j \times \Delta X_i \text{ with integer } j \end{cases} \qquad (8.35)$$

The geometry of the tree is fully determined by the choice of the values for t_i and ΔX_i. With each time slice t_i we have a corresponding fixed step size ΔX_i. The probabilities p_u, p_m, and p_d of moving to the next node have to be calculated such that the geometry of the tree fits the chosen stochastic process. The first step in the construction of the tree is the choice of a particular stochastic process. After choosing a particular Ito process, to model the financial variable, the second step is the selection of the points t_i along which time slices are going to be created. In most cases the time slices will be spread evenly over the maturity of the derivative security that needs to be priced using the trinomial tree. Suppose we construct a tree with n steps, we will then have $\Delta t_i = t_{i+1} - t_i = T/n$. For certain hybrid instruments it will be of utmost importance to have a particular time slice present on the tree. This can, for example, be the case when dealing with a convertible bond with a reset mechanism for the conversion ratio. The reset date ideally corresponds to a time slice on the trinomial tree. Other dates of interest when a time slice can be considered are a put date, the end of the call protection, a coupon date, etc.

After having chosen, for every time slice t_i, a corresponding step size ΔX_i, we have to calculate the probabilities of our stochastic variable moving from its current node value to one of the following nodes. A node $X_{i,j}$ can move from time t_i to the next time slice t_{i+1} and end in one of the three following nodes: $X_{i+1,k+1}$, $X_{i+1,k}$, or $X_{i+1,k-1}$. These nodes are all integer multiples of the step size ΔX_{i+1}:

$$
\begin{aligned}
X_{i+1,k+1} &= (k+1)\Delta X_{i+1} \\
X_{i+1,k} &= k\Delta X_{i+1} \\
X_{i+1,k-1} &= (k-1)\Delta X_{i+1}
\end{aligned}
\tag{8.36}
$$

This has been represented graphically in Figure 8.3. The four-step process of the tree construction can be summarized as follows:

$$
\left\{
\begin{aligned}
&\text{1. Choosing the appropriate stochastic process} \\
&\quad dX_t = A(X_t, t)dt + B(X_t, t)dW_t \\
&\text{2. Selecting the time slices } t_i \\
&\text{3. Associating with a particular time slice a step size } \Delta X_i \\
&\text{4. Calculating the transition probabilities } p_u, p_m, \text{ and } p_d
\end{aligned}
\right.
\tag{8.37}
$$

The calculation of p_u, p_m, and p_d hence requires three equations. One of these is obvious: $p_u + p_m + p_d = 1$. The other two equations come respectively from fitting the variance and mean of the process simulated on the tree to the variance V and mean M corresponding to the underlying stochastic process of the variable X. Starting from an initial node $X_{i,j} = j\Delta X_i$ at time t_i, our stochastic variable can move to three different nodes at the next time slice t_{i+1}. The mean and variance of X_{i+1} at time t_{i+1} given its current starting value $X_{i,j}$ are respectively given by:

$$
\begin{aligned}
M_{i,j} &= \mathbb{E}[X_{i+1} \mid X_{i,j}] \\
&= p_u X_{i+1,k+1} + p_m X_{i+1,k} + p_d X_{i+1,k-1} \\
&= p_u(k+1)\Delta X_{i+1} + p_m k\Delta X_{i+1} + p_d(k-1)\Delta X_{i+1}
\end{aligned}
\tag{8.38}
$$

and

$$
\begin{aligned}
V_{i,j}^2 &= Var(X_{i+1} \mid X_{i,j}) \\
&= p_u(k+1)^2\Delta X_{i+1}^2 + p_m k^2\Delta X_{i+1}^2 + p_d(k-1)^2\Delta X_{i+1}^2 - M_{i,j}^2
\end{aligned}
$$

The equation above has to be combined with the fact that $p_u + p_m + p_d = 1$, which allows us to solve for the three transition probabilities:

$$\begin{cases} (p_u - p_d)\Delta X_{i+1} = M_{i,j} - k\Delta X_{i+1} \\ (p_u + p_d)\Delta X_{i+1}^2 = V_{i,j}^2 + (M_{i,j} - k\Delta X_{i+1})^2 \end{cases} \tag{8.39}$$

This results in:

$$\begin{cases} p_u = \dfrac{V_{i,j}^2}{2\Delta X_{i+1}^2} + \dfrac{(M_{i,j} - k\Delta X_{i+1})^2}{2\Delta X_{i+1}^2} + \dfrac{(M_{i,j} - k\Delta X_{i+1})}{2\Delta X_{i+1}} \\[3mm] p_m = 1 - \dfrac{V_{i,j}^2}{\Delta X_{i+1}^2} - \dfrac{(M_{i,j} - k\Delta X_{i+1})^2}{\Delta X_{i+1}^2} \\[3mm] p_d = \dfrac{V_{i,j}^2}{2\Delta X_{i+1}^2} + \dfrac{(M_{i,j} - k\Delta X_{i+1})^2}{2\Delta X_{i+1}^2} - \dfrac{(M_{i,j} - k\Delta X_{i+1})}{2\Delta X_{i+1}} \end{cases} \tag{8.40}$$

A common choice is also to let $V_{i,j}$ not depend on j. We hence denote $V_{i,j}$ as V_i. With this choice, the variance of X_{i+1} only depends on the time interval between t_i and t_{i+1}, not on the level of $X_{i,j}$. Imposing that $V_{i,j}$ does not depend on the value of $X_{i,j}$ automatically constrains the kind of Ito processes that can be modeled on our trinomial tree. Heteroskedastic processes, where the variance of a stochastic variable changes with the value of this variable, cannot be modeled. We indeed imposed the assumption to have $V_{i,j}$ the same for all values of X_i belonging to the same time slice t_i. The diffusion coefficient in Equation (8.32) is hence only permitted to be a function of time and therefore $B(t)$ is taken instead of $B(X_t, t)$:

$$dX_t = A(X_t, t)dt + B(t)dW_t \tag{8.41}$$

This assumption constrains the nature of the Ito processes that can be simulated through our lattice model. The constant elasticity of variance process, which we specified earlier in Equation (7.38), is one of those stochastic processes that cannot be modeled straight away if we impose the condition that $V_{i,j}$ does not depend on the level of $X_{i,j}$. We will later see how a transformation of variables can turn a heteroskedastic process into a homoskedastic process. The transformed variable can be modeled into a trinomial tree.

The value k is the only degree of freedom left and will be chosen such that none of the probabilities p_u, p_m, and p_d are negative. We therefore impose $\Delta X_{i+1} = V_i\sqrt{3}$ and choose k in such a way that $X_{i+1,k}$ is as close as possible to $M_{i,j}$. The node corresponding to the probability p_m has to be as close as possible to the mean $M_{i,j}$. As a consequence, we have:

$$k = \text{round}\left(\frac{M_{i,j}}{\Delta X_{i+1}}\right) \tag{8.42}$$

where round(x) is the closest integer to the real number x. Equation (8.40) can now be simplified:

$$
\begin{cases}
p_u = \dfrac{1}{6} + \dfrac{(M_{i,j}-k\Delta X_{i+1})^2}{6V_i^2} + \dfrac{(M_{i,j}-k\Delta X_{i+1})}{2\sqrt{3}V_i} \\[3mm]
p_m = \dfrac{2}{3} - \dfrac{(M_{i,j}-k\Delta X_{i+1})^2}{3V_i^2} \\[3mm]
p_d = \dfrac{1}{6} + \dfrac{(M_{i,j}-k\Delta X_{i+1})^2}{6V_i^2} - \dfrac{(M_{i,j}-k\Delta X_{i+1})}{2\sqrt{3}V_i}
\end{cases}
\tag{8.43}
$$

In the analysis above we followed strictly the notation developed in the work of Damiano Brigo and Fabio Mercurio [44]. So far along the road, we have not required the tree to be recombining at all. A recombining trinomial tree is one where an up move followed by a down move results in the original starting point. Such a tree can be achieved when imposing a constant step size ΔX for all the different time slices and when considering, for example, a constant time step Δt and a constant volatility σ. These are the kind of trinomial trees that are most often encountered in the literature.

8.3.4 Modeling Share Prices on a Trinomial Tree

Introduction

To calculate the nodes on the tree and all the corresponding transition probabilities, we follow the four-step process specified in Equation (8.37).

1. **Choosing the appropriate stochastic process**
   We start with the assumption that the share price S is following a geometric Brownian motion with, in this case, a constant interest rate r, dividend yield q, and volatility σ. The risk-neutral stochastic process for the share price S_t is given by the following equation:

$$
dS_t = (r - q)S_t dt + \sigma S_t dW_t
\tag{8.44}
$$

Using Ito's lemma, one can prove that the stochastic differential equation for the logarithm of the share price $X_t = \log(S_t)$ is:

$$
dX_t = \left(r - q - \frac{1}{2}\sigma^2\right) dt + \sigma dW_t
\tag{8.45}
$$

The increment dX_t is the log return of the share price S_t observed over the interval dt. With the current share price equal to S_0, the process for X_t has its origin at $X_0 = \log(S_0)$.

The values of the conditional mean and variance can be determined starting from the properties of the stochastic process chosen to model the variable X:

$$
\begin{cases}
M_{i,j} = X_{i,j} + \left(r - q - \frac{1}{2}\sigma^2\right)(t_{i+1} - t_i) = X_{i,j} + \left(r - q - \frac{1}{2}\sigma^2\right)\Delta t_i \\[3mm]
V_i^2 = \sigma^2(t_{i+1} - t_i) = \sigma^2 \Delta t_i
\end{cases}
\tag{8.46}
$$

The first branches of the tree all start from the same node $X_{0,0} = \log(S_0)$. For this point we have:

$$\begin{cases} M_{0,0} = \log(S_0) + \left(r - q - \frac{1}{2}\sigma^2\right) \Delta t_0 \\ V_0^2 = \sigma^2 \Delta t_0 \end{cases} \qquad (8.47)$$

where $\Delta t_0 = t_1 - t_0$. $M_{0,0}$ is the expected value of X for the slice t_1 when starting at node $X_{0,0}$.

2. **Selecting the time slices**

   To illustrate the construction of the trinomial tree, we will use equidistant time slices to start with. Across the different time steps there are no particular points of interest that need particular attention (coupon dates, reset dates, etc.). The choice to use n constant time steps $\Delta t = (T - t)/n$ is therefore justified. The parameter T stands for the maturity date of the option. The variance V^2 of X on all the nodes of the tree is a constant because both σ and Δt are constant:

   $$V^2 = \sigma^2 \Delta t \qquad (8.48)$$

3. **Associating with a particular time slice a step size**

   The step size ΔX which specifies the increments each time X moves to a different time slice is equal to:

   $$\Delta X = V\sqrt{3} = \sigma\sqrt{3\Delta t} \qquad (8.49)$$

   In the following picture the first step of this n-step trinomial tree starting at $X_0 = \log(S_0)$ has been represented. For each node in the X-tree of the log prices, there is a corresponding node S on the tree of the share prices. The nodes in the X-tree move up and down with increments $\Delta X = \sigma\sqrt{3\Delta t}$ where the values of nodes in the S-tree are multiplied by $\exp(\sigma\sqrt{3\Delta t})$, 1, or $\exp(-\sigma\sqrt{3\Delta t})$ when moving to the next time slice:

4. **Calculating the transition probabilities**

   The probabilities p_u, p_m, and p_d can be calculated for this first branch of the tree using Equation (8.43). In the first branch starting at $X_0 = \log(S_0)$, $M_{0,0} = \log(S_0) + (r - q - \frac{1}{2}\sigma^2)\Delta t$.

Suppose that we have $k = 0$ in this first time step:

$$\begin{cases} p_u = \frac{1}{6} + \frac{M^2}{6V^2} + \frac{M}{2\sqrt{3}V} \\ p_m = \frac{2}{3} - \frac{M^2}{3V^2} \\ p_d = \frac{1}{6} + \frac{M^2}{6V^2} - \frac{M}{2\sqrt{3}V} \end{cases} \qquad (8.50)$$

The three nodes in the first time slice at $t = \Delta t$ now become the starting points for branches from which X can move to the next time slice $t = 2\Delta t$:

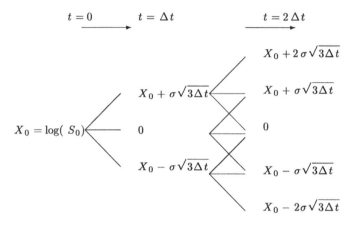

The corresponding equity tree is:

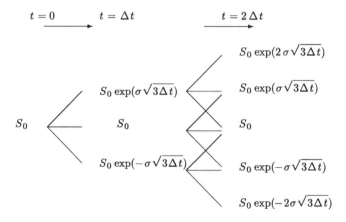

It is clear that we did not model the S-tree directly. The real construction work and the calculation of all the intermediate transition probabilities resided within the X-tree. The stochastic process X_t was obtained through a transformation and simplification of the share price process: $X_t = \log(S_t)$. A similar approach will be adopted when dealing with more sophisticated share price processes such as the CEV.

Numerical Example

The general four step procedure in the previous paragraphs, where a trinomial tree for a share price S was constructed from a tree of log prices $X = \log(S)$, will now be put into practice through a numerical example. The same step-by-step approach will be worked out.

1. **Choosing the appropriate stochastic process**
   The following pricing parameters for the geometric Brownian motion are chosen:
   - $T = 4$ years
   - $n = 2$ trinomial steps
   - $r = 3\%$
   - $q = 2\%$
   - $\sigma = 40\%$
   - $S_0 = 100$

2. **Selecting the time slices**
   The 4-year maturity will be covered in two steps only. The time step Δt is hence equal to 2. The variance V^2 of X from one slice to the other is constant given the fact that the equity volatility is constant as well:

$$V^2 = \sigma^2 \Delta t = 0.4 \times 0.4 \times 2 = 0.32 \qquad (8.51)$$

3. **Associating with a particular time slice a step size**
   The distance between two nodes belonging to the same time slice is going to be an integer multiple of ΔX:

$$\Delta X = V\sqrt{3} = 0.9798 \qquad (8.52)$$

4. **Calculating the transition probabilities**
   The step size ΔX is known and is constant for all the slices of the tree given our choice of the stochastic process, the constant time step, and the constant parameters. Hence, $\Delta X = \Delta X_1 = \Delta X_2$. We can now proceed with the calculation of the transition probabilities p_u, p_m, and p_d.
   (a) **First time slice $t = \Delta t$**
   The tree of the log prices X_t originates at $X_{0,0} = \log(100) = 4.6052$. The expected value of the three nodes originating from $X_{0,0}$ and ending at the first time slice is $M_{0,0}$ and is given by:

$$M_{0,0} = \log(S_0) + \left(r - q - \frac{1}{2}\sigma^2\right)\Delta t = 4.4652 \qquad (8.53)$$

The three nodes on the first slice are an integer multiple of ΔX_1. Using the notation introduced in Equation (8.36), the following picture illustrates the position of the three different nodes and their corresponding probabilities:

$t = 0$ $t = 2$

$(k + 1)\,\Delta X_1 = 0.9798\,(k + 1)$ p_u

$X_{0,0} = 4.6052$ $k\,\Delta X_1 = 0.9798k$ p_m

$(k - 1)\,\Delta X_1 = 0.9798(k - 1)$ p_d

From Equation (8.42) we can calculate the value of k for the nodes on the first time slice originating from $X_{0,0}$:

$$k = \text{round}\left(\frac{M_{0,0}}{\Delta X_1}\right) = \text{round}\left(\frac{4.4652}{0.9798}\right) = 5 \tag{8.54}$$

The position of the three X-nodes on $t = 2$ is hence fully determined. Only the transition probabilities need to be resolved:

$t = 0$ $t = 2$

$X_{1,6} = 6\Delta X_1 = 5.8788$ p_u

$X_{0,0} = 4.6052$ $X_{1,5} = 5\Delta X_1 = 4.8990$ p_m

$X_{1,4} = 4\Delta X_1 = 3.9192$ p_d

The transition probabilities are given by Equation (8.40). The solution of this is:

$$\begin{cases} p_u = \dfrac{V^2}{2\Delta X_1^2} + \dfrac{(M_{0,0} - k\Delta X_1)^2}{2\Delta X_1^2} + \dfrac{(M_{0,0} - k\Delta X_1)}{2\Delta X_1} = 0.0433 \\[2mm] p_m = 1 - \dfrac{V^2}{\Delta X_1^2} - \dfrac{(M_{0,0} - k\Delta X_1)^2}{\Delta X_1^2} = 0.4706 \\[2mm] p_d = \dfrac{V^2}{2\Delta X_1^2} + \dfrac{(M_{0,0} - k\Delta X_1)^2}{2\Delta X_1^2} - \dfrac{(M_{0,0} - k\Delta X_1)}{2\Delta X_1} = 0.4861 \end{cases} \tag{8.55}$$

(b) **Second and final time slice $t = 2\Delta t$**

The nodes $X_{1,6}$, $X_{1,5}$, and $X_{1,4}$ on the first slice are the starting nodes of nine other branches. These branches terminate in five different nodes positioned on the final slice of the trinomial tree:

Start node($t = 2$) $\rightarrow$ End nodes($t = 4$)

$X_{1,6}$ $\rightarrow \{X_{2,7}, X_{2,6}, X_{1,5}\}$

$X_{1,5}$ $\rightarrow \{X_{2,6}, X_{2,5}, X_{2,4}\}$

$X_{1,4}$ $\rightarrow \{X_{2,5}, X_{2,4}, X_{2,3}\}$

The numerical result of the calculations is summarized below:

Second Time Slice ($t = 4$)		
$X_{1,6}$	$X_{1,5}$	$X_{1,4}$
$X = 5.8788$	$X = 4.899$	$X = 3.9192$
$V^2 = 0.32$	$V^2 = 0.32$	$V^2 = 0.32$
$\Delta X_2 = 0.9798$	$\Delta X_2 = 0.9798$	$\Delta X_2 = 0.9798$
$M_{1,6} = 5.7388$	$M_{1,5} = 4.759$	$M_{1,4} = 3.7792$
$k = 6$	$k = 5$	$k = 4$
New Nodes	**New Nodes**	**New Nodes**
$X_{2,7} = 6.8586 \quad p_u = 0.1054$	$X_{2,6} = 5.8788 \quad p_u = 0.1054$	$X_{2,5} = 4.8990 \quad p_u = 0.1054$
$X_{2,6} = 5.8788 \quad p_m = 0.6462$	$X_{2,5} = 4.8990 \quad p_m = 0.6462$	$X_{2,4} = 3.9192 \quad p_m = 0.6462$
$X_{2,5} = 4.8990 \quad p_d = 0.2484$	$X_{2,4} = 3.9192 \quad p_d = 0.2484$	$X_{2,3} = 2.9394 \quad p_d = 0.2484$

There are in total five different final nodes in this two-step trinomial tree. Each of the nodes X has a corresponding share price. The node $X_{2,7}$ corresponds, for example, with $S_{2,7}$ where $S_{2,7} = \exp(X_{2,7})$.

Final Nodes ($t = 4$)			
	X	S	$Prob$
$X_{2,7}$	6.8586	$S_{2,7}$ 952.03	0.0046
$X_{2,6}$	5.8788	$S_{2,6}$ 357.38	0.0776
$X_{2,5}$	4.8990	$S_{2,5}$ 134.16	0.3661
$X_{2,4}$	3.9192	$S_{2,4}$ 50.36	0.4310
$X_{2,3}$	2.9394	$S_{2,3}$ 18.90	0.1207
		$\Sigma(Prob)=$	1.0000

The probabilities of arriving at a particular terminal node depend on the transition probabilities moving to the first and second time slice, respectively. The probability that the share price $S = 952.03$ at $t = 4$ is equal to the probability that the share price moves up twice in a row:

$$Prob(S_{t=4} = 952.03) = (p_u)_{\text{first time slice}} \times (p_u)_{\text{second time slice}}$$

$$= 0.0433 \times 0.1054 = 0.0046$$

$$= 0.46\%$$

Using the risk-neutral probabilities of the previous table, we can calculate the expected share price 4 years from now, $\mathbb{E}_Q(S_{t=4})$. This value is equal to 105.19, but does not correspond to the theoretical outcome given by Equation (8.56):

$$\mathbb{E}_Q[S_{t=4}] = S_0 \exp((r - q)T) = 100 \exp((r - q) \times 4) = 104.08 \qquad (8.56)$$

This difference results from the fact that we have approximated the full 4-year maturity with only two steps in a trinomial tree. Adding more steps will help $\mathbb{E}_Q[S_{t=4}]$, obtained from the tree, to converge to the correct theoretical result. The graphical representation of the tree can be found in Figure 8.4.

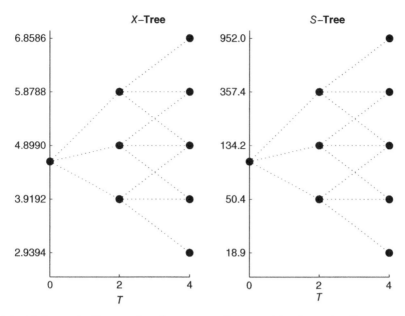

Figure 8.4 Nodes on the X-tree and on the corresponding tree of the share price S.

8.3.5 European Options on a Trinomial Tree

A buyer of a European option has the right to exercise this option at its maturity date. In case of a call option, the investor has the right to buy shares against the strike price K. For the holder of a put option, the exercise right is different. In case of a long position in a put, the investor has the right to sell the underlying share against the strike price. For European options the exercise can only be done at the maturity date. If the exercise right holds throughout the whole maturity of the call or put, we are dealing with American options. If the exercise possibility only prevails at a limited number of dates, the option is Bermudan.

The value of the share at the expiry date T of the option is S_T. The value of the call C_T and put P_T at maturity is given by their respective payoff formulas:

$$C_T = \max(S_T - K, 0)$$
$$P_T = \max(K - S_T, 0)$$
(8.57)

The current value at time t of the call or put option is denoted as C_t or P_t and is equal to the expected value of the discounted payoff. This result was worked out earlier in Equation (8.58). Using a constant continuous interest rate r, we have for the put option:

$$P_t = B_t \mathbb{E}_\mathbb{Q} \left[\frac{P_T}{B_T} \right] = \exp(-r(T-t)) \mathbb{E}_\mathbb{Q}[P_T]$$
(8.58)

The expectation of the final values of both calls and puts can be calculated using the payoff formulas in Equation (8.57) and the value of the share prices S_T simulated through the trinomial tree. The values for C_T and P_T for the two-step trinomial tree to price a 4-year at-the-money call option ($S = K = 100$) are given in the following table:

	X	S	Prob	C_T	P_T
	Final Nodes ($t = 4$)				
$X_{2,7}$	6.8586	952.03	0.0046	852.03	0
$X_{2,6}$	5.8788	357.38	0.0776	257.38	0
$X_{2,5}$	4.8990	134.16	0.3661	34.16	0
$X_{2,4}$	3.9192	50.36	0.4310	0	49.64
$X_{2,3}$	2.9394	18.90	0.1207	0	81.10

The value of the put at maturity T corresponding with, for example, the node $X_{2,3}$ is $P_{2,3}$. Its value is equal to $\max(100 - 18.90, 0) = 81.10$. Using a risk-neutral measure $\mathbb{Q}$, the probability of arriving at this final cash flow is equal to 12.07%. To calculate P_t we have to take all the possible final nodes for P_T and their corresponding probabilities into account. The current price of the put P_t is hence given by:

$$P_t = \exp(-r(T - t))\mathbb{E}_{\mathbb{Q}}[P_T]$$
$$= \exp(-r(T - t)) \sum_{i=3}^{7} Prob_{X_{2,i}} \times P_{2,i}$$
$$= 27.66$$

For the call price C_t we have:

$$C_t = \exp(-r(T - t))\mathbb{E}_{\mathbb{Q}}[C_T]$$
$$= \exp(-r(T - t)) \sum_{i=3}^{7} Prob_{X_{2,i}} \times C_{2,i}$$
$$= 32.28$$

The prices obtained for the European call and put are different from the options prices calculated using the Black–Scholes formula in Equation (8.28):

	Call	Put
Trinomial Tree	32.28	27.66
Black–Scholes Equation	29.98	26.36

The lack of convergence between the Black–Scholes option prices and the values obtained through the trinomial solution results from the limited number of steps taken in this particular numerical example. The 4-year maturity was simulated in only two time steps. Increasing the number of steps in the model improves the accuracy of the trinomial price. This is illustrated in Figure 8.5 for the call option where the steps in the tree were gradually increased from 2 to 50.

8.3.6 American Options

For European options, only the final payoff in the nodes of the last time slice intervenes in the calculation of the option price. This is no longer the case for American options, where the investor has the right to exercise the option throughout its full maturity. In every node of the trinomial tree, one has therefore to check whether it is optimal to exercise the option or

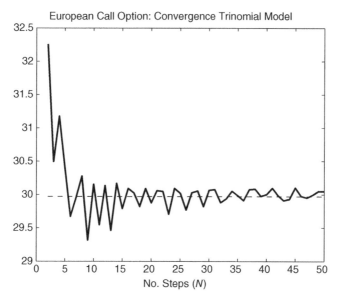

Figure 8.5 Convergence of the trinomial option price toward the closed-form Black–Scholes solution.

continue to hold on till the next time slice. This condition is checked while rolling back from the final nodes to the origin of the tree. The **continuation value** in each node is the value of the option in the node if one were not to exercise it and hold it at least till the following time slice. The **exercise value** corresponds to the cash flow generated through an early exercise at this particular point in the tree.

The trinomial trees for both the American call and put option are represented in Figure 8.6. A clear difference has been made between those nodes where the option will be exercised and those where the option will be kept "alive". On the first time slice ($t = 2$), the put will be exercised at node $S_{1,4}$. The call option will be exercised at node $S_{1,6}$. We now work out in detail the early exercise for the call at node $S_{1,6}$:

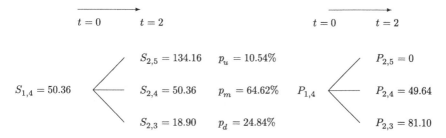

- **Continuation value $\overline{P}$**

$$\overline{P} = \exp(-0.03 \times \Delta t) \times (p_u P_{2,5} + p_m P_{2,4} + p_d P_{2,3})$$
$$= \exp(-0.03 \times 2) \times 52.22$$
$$= 49.18$$

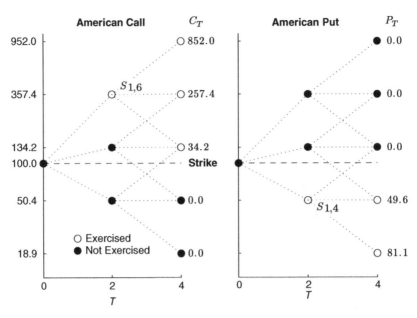

Figure 8.6 Trinomial trees to price a 4-year at-the-money American call and put option with strike 100 on a share S.

- **Exercise value P^***

$$P^* = \max(K - S_{1,4}, 0)$$
$$= \max(100 - 50.36, 0)$$
$$= 49.64$$

The put option is exercised because $\overline{P} < P^*$ and the investor will sell at this point in the tree the shares against the strike price K. In the case of American options the derivative's life is stopped at some time τ with $\tau \in [t, T]$. The time τ is the stopping time. After this point in time, the uncertainty in the financial instrument is gone since it is reduced to a known cash flow. This brings us to the concept of the exercise boundary or the free boundary $b(t)$. As soon as the share price S_t reaches this boundary level, the option will be exercised.

To illustrate the shape of $b(t)$, we revert to a numerical example. In Figure 8.7 we graph a trinomial tree that has been used to price a 4-year at-the-money American put option. There are four time steps in this trinomial tree. The other pricing parameters remain the same as in the previous example: $r = 3\%$, $q = 2\%$, and $\sigma = 40\%$. The boundary $b(t)$ below which the American put will be exercised has been graphed on top of the trinomial tree. As soon as $S_t < b(t)$, the investor will exercise the put and deliver shares against the strike price K to the counterparty of the transaction.

In the same figure we have added a second exercise boundary on top of the trinomial tree. This second boundary ($b_{q=10\%}(t)$) has been calculated for a much higher dividend yield $q = 10\%$ and is positioned below the boundary calculated for the 2% yield:

$$b_{q=10\%}(t) \leq b_{q=2\%}(t) \tag{8.59}$$

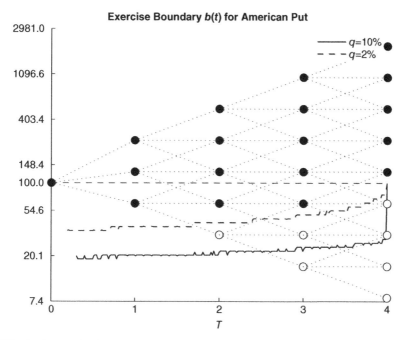

Figure 8.7 Early exercise boundary for an American put, using two dividend yields $q = 10\%$ and $q = 2\%$. The boundary $b(t)$ has been calculated using a 150-step trinomial tree.

This makes sense given the fact that for an investor it will be less advantageous to exercise the in-the-money put option when the dividend yield has increased. Exercising this put option delivers a cash amount K on which an interest rate of 3% is earned. When the dividend yield increases, the share price S needs to be lower to make an early exercise feasible. The exercise value has to be larger than the continuation value. To make an early exercise of the put worthwhile, the future interest renumeration received by investing the strike amount on the bank account will have to be larger than the dividends earned from holding on to the shares.

8.3.7 Bermudan Options: Imposing a Particular Time Slice

In this chapter the lattice approach has been introduced on a European option. After this we worked out a numerical example of an American option using the same trinomial tree and similar parameters. This allowed us to illustrate how to roll back through the nodes in the tree from the maturity date to the start date. The concept of the exercise boundary was also introduced. Let's move a step back and assume that the 4-year at-the-money put option can be exercised at the maturity date and also at one particular intermediate date only. This supplementary exercise date falls exactly 3 years and 3 weeks ($t = 3.06$) after the start date of the option. If the investor decides not to exercise the option at $t = 3.06$, he will have to wait till the maturity date at $t = 4$ for the last chance to exercise. This put option is an example of a Bermudan option because it offers a limited number of exercise possibilities. Bermudan options are not encountered very often in practice. The only merit of studying an example of a Bermudan option in this chapter is to illustrate how an extra time slice is easily added in the

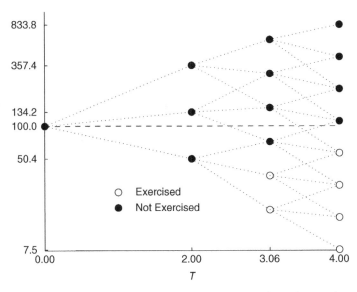

Figure 8.8 Trinomial tree constructed to price a Bermudan put option where early exercise is only allowed 3 years and 3 weeks after the issue date.

tree. Adding a particular time slice in a lattice model is going to be helpful when dealing with hybrids with particular scheduled points of interest in the life of the security. When dealing with hybrid bonds, we may consider the following points of interest:

- End of the call protection.
- Reset of the conversion ratio.
- Coupon payments.
- Dividend payments on the underlying share.
- Investor put on a particular date.

Figure 8.6 illustrated how at node $S_{1,4}$ it was optimal to exercise the American put option. Given the fact that early exercise is now only permitted 3 years and 3 weeks after the issue date, this node no longer allows an early exercise. In Figure 8.8 we illustrate how an extra time slice is added to have a perfect match with the early exercise date. This extra time slice fits the particular exercise date. This technique will prove to be more efficient than simply increasing the number of steps in order to add more granularity in the tree. Because of this change in the tree layout, Equation (8.40) will no longer be homogeneous across the different slices in the tree.

8.4 FINITE DIFFERENCE TECHNIQUE

Equation (8.61) can be solved numerically after replacing the continuous space (S, t) with a two-dimensional discrete grid. The discretization is different from what we covered earlier in the binomial or trinomial methods. The remaining maturity between the pricing date t and maturity T is broken up into k small time steps $\Delta t = (T - t)/k$. A similar discretization is applied on the domain of possible share prices $S: 0, \Delta S, 2\Delta S, \ldots, n\Delta S, \ldots$ The point $P_{i,j}$ on this pricing grid corresponds to the price of the hybrid security where $S = i\Delta S$ and the time equals $t + j\Delta t$. To find these prices, the derivatives in Equation (8.61) are replaced using finite differences:

$$\frac{\partial P}{\partial t} = \frac{P_{i,j} - P_{i,j-1}}{\Delta t} \tag{8.60}$$

$$\frac{\partial P}{\partial S} = \frac{P_{i+1,j} - P_{i,j}}{\Delta S}$$

$$\frac{\partial^2 P}{\partial S^2} = \frac{P_{i+1,j} - 2P_{i,j} + P_{i-1,j}}{\Delta S^2}$$

At Every point (i, j) of the grid the following equation needs to hold:

$$\frac{P_{i,j} - P_{i,j-1}}{\Delta t} + \frac{\sigma^2 S_{i,j}^2}{2} \frac{P_{i+1,j} - 2P_{i,j} + P_{i-1,j}}{\Delta S^2} + r S_{i,j} \frac{P_{i+1,j} - P_{i,j}}{\Delta S} - r P_{i,j} = 0 \tag{8.61}$$

In this large set of equations, the necessary boundary conditions have to be filled out. For example, at the maturity date $(j = k)$ and when dealing with a convertible bond where $S_{i,k} > C_P$, we have accordingly $P_{i,k} = C_r S_{i,k}$. The finite difference technique has been explained at length in [194]. In this reference work, a clear distinction is made between explicit and implicit finite difference schemes. There is a lot of similarity between tree models and finite difference schemes. This resemblance has its roots in the discretization of the (S, t)-space. The trinomial tree carves out a triangle, whereas the finite difference has a rectangular grid. While computationally more effective than tree models, finite difference techniques share with those tree models a common drawback. They might be effective while working in a single-factor setting where there is only one source of risk but when there are multiple sources of risk at work, the lattice and finite difference models become much harder to solve. In such a case of high dimensionality, the Monte Carlo or simulation method offers an elegant solution.

8.5 MONTE CARLO

8.5.1 Introduction

In Section 6.5.2 we had our first introduction to the Monte Carlo technique when performing a sensitivity analysis of pricing models for hybrid securities. Monte Carlo is a powerful technique, very well suited to price path-dependent securities with a complex payoff. On top of this, the technique does not suffer from the curse of dimensionality as is the case with models based on lattice or finite difference implementations. Moore's law[3] clearly reaches out a helping hand to Monte Carlo aficionados. Computer power is increasing and getting cheaper, a fact which will further lift the popularity of Monte Carlo in quantitative finance.

In order to price a hybrid security, a total of n paths for a financial variable X (interest rate, share price, credit spread, ...) are generated from the pricing date t till the final maturity date T for a particular set of k intermediate dates $\{t_1, \ldots, t_k\}$. Each of the simulated values of X on these particular dates intervenes in the final payoff of the security. The last date in this set most

---

[3] Moore's law is named after Intel co-founder Gordon Moore who claimed in 1965 that computer power was going to double approximately every 2 years. Up till now his prediction still holds.

often corresponds to the final maturity date: $t_k = T$. In the Monte Carlo method we therefore "travel forward" in time [44], working our way from the pricing date to the maturity date.

For each of the n runs, the simulation results in a set of k simulated values for the financial variable along each path i: $X_{i,1}, \ldots, X_{i,k}$ with $i \in \{1, 2, \ldots, n\}$. The final payoff of our security is given by a payoff function H that takes into account the simulated values $X_{i,1}, \ldots, X_{i,k}$ along every path i. The expected payoff of the security on the maturity date T is equal to:

$$P_T = \frac{1}{n} \sum_{i=1}^{n} H(X_{i,1}, \ldots, X_{i,k}) \tag{8.62}$$

Assuming, for example, a flat and deterministic interest rate curve, the current price of the hybrid is given by:

$$P_t = \exp(-r(T - t))P_T \tag{8.63}$$

Dealing with a high level of path dependency such as skipped coupon payments on a preferred share, a default on a corporate bond, or the stock price dropping below a predefined barrier level is very straight forward when it comes to using Monte Carlo. The only element that is changed is the final payoff function H. There is a situation in derivatives pricing, however, where the Monte Carlo method is struggling. This occurs when there is a possibility of early exercise. The paths are indeed propagated forward in time without any clue whether it is beneficial to exercise or not. The big push forward came after the publication of a paper written by Longstaff and Schwartz in 2001 where they applied the Monte Carlo technique to American options [140]. The Longstaff and Schwartz (LS) method allows us to work with Monte Carlo while dealing with the probability of an early exercise. This approach has now found wide acceptance in practice. Other Monte Carlo methods were developed later on. The work of Andersen [7] resulted in a method to derive an upper and lower boundary for the price of an American option priced through simulation. The LS approach provides only a lower bound to this price. Through some recent academic work [6, 134, 142], the Monte Carlo technique is gaining importance in the convertible bond community. The main reason for its popularity is the flexibility with which different underlying stochastic multi-factor processes can be used in the valuation of hybrids such as convertible bonds. The number of factors is not prohibitive, as would be the case in tree models.

8.5.2   Generating Random Numbers

Suppose that we are valuing a path-dependent derivative security where the underlying asset X follows a geometric Brownian motion:

$$dX_t = \mu X_t dt + \sigma X_t dW_t \tag{8.64}$$

Each path for the financial variable X originates from its current known value X_0 and will be simulated at future times $t_1, \ldots, t_n$ resulting in the path $X_1, \ldots, X_n$. Equation (8.64) is rewritten using discrete increments:

$$X_k = X_{k-1} + \mu X_{k-1}(t_k - t_{k-1}) + \sigma X_{k-1}\sqrt{t_k - t_{k-1}}Z, k = 1, \ldots, n \tag{8.65}$$

The random variable Z in the equation above is taken from a standard normal distribution:

$$Z \sim N(0, 1) \tag{8.66}$$

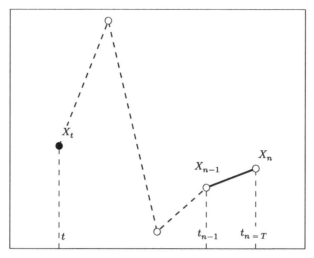

Figure 8.9   Simulation of a random variable X starting from an initial value X_t at time t to a final value X_n at $t = T$.

The discretization described in Equation (8.65) is simulated in Figure 8.9. This approach is easily implemented given the availability of random number generators for normal distributions in multiple software programs. Generating Z is going to be very straightforward. Another random number generator which is also frequently present in several widely used software packages deals with variables U following a uniform distribution on the interval $[0, 1]$.

It could get more complicated when dealing with a random variable X for which the distribution is different from a normal or uniform distribution. Suppose, for example, we want to simulate the arrival time of a particular event according to an exponential distribution. How could we simulate this and generate exponentially distributed random variables? In such a case we will sometimes have to produce these specific random variables X ourselves since standard software packages will fail to do the job. Fortunately, there is an easy work-around for this particular problem.

Suppose we want to generate a series of outcomes $X_i, \ldots, X_n$ for a random variable for which we know the cumulative distribution function $F(x)$. In such a case, we proceed step by step to generate the different outcomes X_i:

1. Generate a random variable U_i according to a uniform distribution on the interval $[0, 1]$.
2. Calculate $X_i = F^{-1}(U_i)$.
3. Repeat n times the two steps above, which results in a set of random variables X_i all according to the distribution function $F(x)$.

Proof: U_i follows a uniform distribution on the domain $[0, 1]$:

$$Prob(U_i \leq u) = u \tag{8.67}$$

F is a monotonically increasing function of x and its inverse function F^{-1} hence exists.

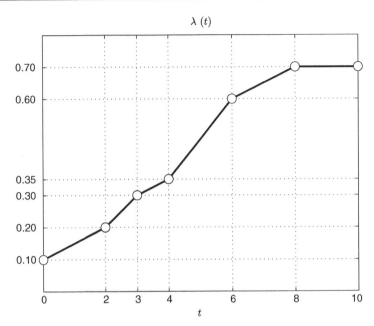

Figure 8.10   Intensity of a Poisson process modeling the announcement that the coupon will be skipped.

We have that $F(x) = u$ and $F^{-1}(u) = x$. Then:

$$\begin{aligned}
Prob(X_i \leq x) &= Prob(F^{-1}(U_i) \leq F^{-1}(u)) \\
&= Prob(U_i \leq u) \\
&= u = F(x)
\end{aligned} \tag{8.68}$$

The generated random number X_i has $F(x)$ as its cumulative distribution function.

Case Study

A portfolio manager is developing a key interest to invest in a hybrid bond where the coupon distribution can be stopped if a particular covenant linked to this bond fails to hold. Non-payment of a coupon would by no means imply a default event. The portfolio manager might model a skipped coupon payment as an exogenous event: a Poisson process with a time-in-homogenous intensity $\lambda(t)$. The assumed intensity of this process is, for example, a piecewise linear function as represented graphically in Figure 8.10. The probability of having to deal with such an event given the piecewise linearity of $\lambda(t)$ can be calculated using Equation (7.60). This cumulative distribution function $Prob(\tau < t)$ is illustrated in Figure 8.11.

If the Poisson process was time homogeneous, the intensity would be constant. Accordingly, the expected arrival time of having to deal with a breach of the bond covenant and the subsequent loss of the coupon is in this case equal to $1/\lambda$. In order to calculate the expected arrival time given a non-constant intensity function $\lambda(t)$, we can make use of the three-step Monte Carlo approach discussed above. Drawing two random numbers $U_1 = 0.4$ and $U_2 = 0.8$ from a uniform distribution on the interval $[0, 1]$ corresponds in this numerical example to the simulated arrival times $\tau_1 = 2.87$ years and $\tau_2 = 5.63$ years (Figure 8.12).

$Prob\,(\tau < t)$

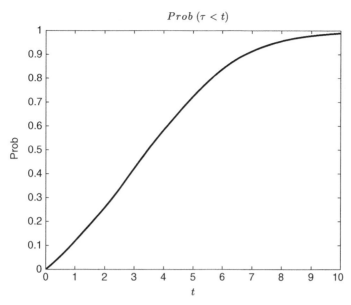

Figure 8.11   Probability of meeting a skipped coupon on the interval $[0, t]$.

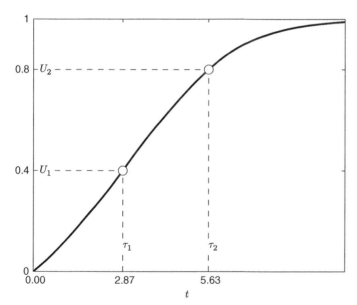

Figure 8.12   Generating two random event times τ from two random numbers U. The random variable U follows a uniform distribution on the interval $[0, 1]$.

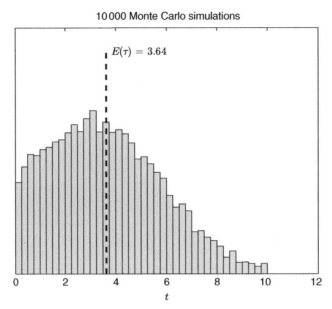

Figure 8.13 Histogram for a Monte Carlo generation of 10 000 runs. Each run generates a particular event time representing the arrival time of the announcement to stop paying coupons.

What is illustrated in Figure 8.12 can be extended to 10 000 Monte Carlo runs. Each run is thereby generating a random time τ corresponding to the event of the company declaring to stop paying coupons. The default times are generated according to the intensity function $\lambda(t)$. The histogram grouping the different results together is illustrated in Figure 8.13. In this example, $\mathbb{E}(\tau) = 3.64$ years. This is the expected arrival time of being confronted with the event that the issuer stops distributing coupons on this particular bond.

Modeling Hybrids: Advanced Issues

9.1 TAIL RISK IN HYBRIDS

So far we have been putting the emphasis on Brownian motion as the main engine governing the random walk of financial assets. This is a Gaussian setting because the increments of a Brownian motion W is normally distributed: $W_t - W_s \sim N(0, t - s)$. This assumption forces us indeed to accept that the log return of share prices between t and s is normally distributed according to the following equation:

$$\log(S_t) - \log(S_s) \sim N\left(\left(\mu - \frac{\sigma^2}{2}\right)(t - s), \sigma^2(t - s)\right), \quad t \geq s \qquad (9.1)$$

This idea has suited us for a lot of purposes. It allowed us to develop closed-form solutions for a lot of derivative securities. Accepting the normal density function also simplified the risk management of a trading desk. The concept of Value-at-Risk, for example, initially had the normal distribution as its backbone. This led, in the beginning, to a situation where the modeled asset prices and risk factors were very distant from the financial reality. As early as 1963, Mandelbrot already recognized in [145] the heavy-tailed nature of financial time series. This was elaborated further in [146]. A 3-sigma event is much more likely to be encountered in reality than suggested by the perfect bell-shaped Gaussian distribution. The market meltdown that took place when the subprime bubble burst in 2007 led to extreme movements in asset-backed portfolios. Or as one CFO of a major investment bank told a journalist of the *Financial Times* in August 2007: "... We were seeing things that were 25-standard deviation moves, several days in a row..."

How likely would such a 25-sigma event actually be? According to a study from the Centre for Risk & Insurance Studies[1] [79], this matches the likelihood of winning the UK National Lottery 21 times in a row. Each time harvesting a prize of 2.5 mn GBP for a ticket costing 1 GBP. The CFO did not only witness one single 25-sigma event, but experienced several of these outcomes in a row... Something clearly had to be wrong with respect to the way risk was traditionally quantified.

To illustrate tail risk in convertible bonds, we take the example of a manager of a convertible bond fund who decided to participate in the offering of a new convertible bond issued by Renewable Energy (Table 2.4). This bond was issued on October 13, 2009. At this particular date the share price of the underlying shares was equal to 31.92 NOK. The manager expected an annualized volatility σ equal to 40%. For a 3-year holding period, a loss matching a 1-sigma event corresponds to a log return of -69% ($\sqrt{3} \times 0.4 = -0.69$). Three years after the launch of the convertible, the stock price had collapsed to 1.45 NOK. The price of the convertible bond was also pulled into this descent to chaos. The log return of this movement is -3.09 ($= \log(1.45) - \log(31.92) = -3.09$).

---

[1] Nottingham University Business School.

The corresponding log return of this move is a 4.5-sigma event. This is a 3-year price drop that is theoretically only to occur with a probability equal to 1 out of 294 000 times or once every 800 years. The fat-tail risk of a financial asset corresponds to the existence of such extraordinary price movements; price movements whose appearance is far beyond what is suggested by a normal distribution. There are, in contrast, also a lot of "dull" days when the stock price does not move at all. The empirical density function is hence going to have a higher peak than what is suggested by a normal density function. This "heavy tail/high peak" observation illustrates the leptokurtotic behavior of financial assets. A leptokurtotic density function gives a high peak which declines more quickly than in the case of a normal distribution.

The property of a random variable X with mean μ having a high peak and heavy tails is measured through its kurtosis. For a variable following a normal distribution we have a kurtosis equal to 3. The calculation of the kurtosis is given by [104]:

$$\text{kurtosis} = \frac{\mathbb{E}[(X - \mu)^4]}{(\mathbb{E}[(X - \mu)^2])^2} \tag{9.2}$$

The kurtosis of the daily log returns of the share price of Renewable Energy in the 3-year period following October 13, 2009 was 7.79. This number reveals that this share price distribution was leptokurtotic.

The previous example was constructed around a case study of an equity. Fat-tail risk is also omnipresent in the hybrid space. Consider, for example, the loss-absorption mechanism that is triggered when the CET1 ratio of a bank falls below a well-defined level. Such an event will force one or more contingent convertibles issued by this financial institution to convert into shares. This might be an unlikely event but it has nevertheless a high negative outcome for the investor. An instrument with such a payoff has a lot of embedded tail risk and forces us to think differently when modeling the distribution of the underlying share price.

9.2 JUMP DIFFUSION

9.2.1 Introduction

Stock price returns are asymmetrical, their distribution function is skewed. The probability of obtaining an important negative price return is indeed larger than the probability of a similar upward swing in the share price. The parameter measuring this asymmetry is the skewness. Its calculation is given by:

$$\text{skewness} = \frac{\mathbb{E}[(X - \mu)^3]}{(\mathbb{E}[(X - \mu)^3])^{3/2}} \tag{9.3}$$

Applying the equation above to the daily share price returns of Renewable Energy in the 3-year period following the issuance of the convertible bond, we obtain a negative skewness of -0.43. This is an outspoken asymmetry to the left in the historical returns. These returns have negative bias; a perfect symmetrical density function, however, corresponds to a skewness which is equal to zero. Figure 9.1 illustrates this.

Allowing a normal-distributed variable to drop from time to time out of the expected range of outcomes will also create negative skewness. This is exactly what is achieved with a jump-diffusion process. A stochastic variable X_t follows a generalized Wiener process as described in Equation (7.19) and exhibits, on top of this, jumps at random times when it drops to a lower value. From these post-jump values it can proceed with the original diffusion process till the

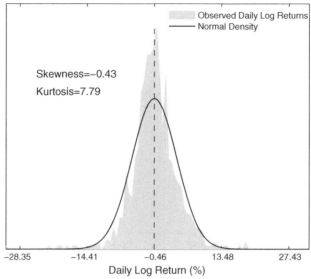

Source: Bloomberg.

Figure 9.1 Daily log returns of the stock price of Renewable Energy in the period 2009–2012.

next jump event occurs, and so on. This is summarized in the following stochastic differential equation:

$$dX_t = A(X_t, t)dt + B(X_t, t)dW_t - J(X_t, t)dN_t \tag{9.4}$$

The size of the jumps that occur at time t is given by $J(X_t, t)$. The occurrence of the jump is modeled using a Poisson process N_t with intensity λ:

$$dN_t = \begin{cases} 1 & \text{with probability } \lambda dt \\ 0 & \text{otherwise} \end{cases}$$

In the case of a geometric Brownian motion with constant parameters, we have $A(X_t, t) = \mu X_t$ and $B(X_t, t) = \sigma X_t$. If we consider in addition that the asset value X_t drops to zero when a jump event occurs, Equation (9.4) is simplified:

$$dX_t = \mu X_t dt + \sigma X_t dW_t - X_t dN_t \tag{9.5}$$

Through this equation, the random variable X_t drops to zero when a jump event takes place, and stays there. For all the subsequent price changes we then have that $dX_t = 0$. One of the first jump-diffusion models was proposed by Merton [149], a model for which a closed-form solution for a European call option was developed. Jump-diffusion models allow us to add skewness into the distribution of a financial asset. Allowing the stock price to drop out of the range confined by a normal distribution will remove the symmetry from the diffusion process. Adding the possibility of jumps brings the stochastic process closer to reality.

Example Imagine a stock price process where the drift μ is equal to zero and the volatility σ equals 8%. For this particular stock we can simulate over a 5-year horizon a jump-diffusion

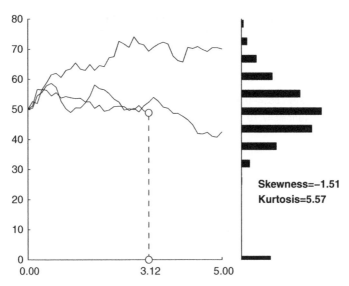

Figure 9.2   Monte Carlo simulation of a jump-diffusion process.

process with intensity $\lambda = 5\%$. The probability that a jump occurs is equal to 22.12% ($=1 - \exp(-5\lambda)$). This parameter can be derived from credit default swap data. Using credit default swaps, investors can protect themselves from a financial loss suffered when the issuer of a bond "jumps" to default. This will be covered in Chapter 10.

In Figure 9.2, three different paths out of a total of 10 000 simulations have been plotted onto a graph. Only one of these sample paths suffers from a jump taking place at time $t = 3.12$ years. The share price drops in this case to zero and keeps this price level for the remaining time of the Monte Carlo run. Combing a normal distribution for share price returns with a jump process creates flat tails and a negative skew. This is very well illustrated in Figure 9.2, where the histogram of the share prices obtained after this 5-year simulation is graphed as well. The kurtosis equals 5.57 and the skewness equals -1.51. Jump diffusion is hence going to be an important building block when constructing valuation and risk models for hybrid securities.

The jump diffusion introduced in Equation (9.5) only introduces one extra source of risk. This is the appearance of a jump controlled by the parameter λ. The jump size itself is assumed to be known and fixed beforehand. Jump-diffusion models with a random jump size are discussed at length in [102].

9.2.2   Share Price Process with Jump to Default

The stock-generating process when dealing with a geometric Brownian motion never generates a share price equal to zero. A zero value for S will never be reached in such a diffusion process. In some very particular diffusion processes, one can sometimes generate a share price equal to zero. This will be explained later when covering the constant elasticity of a variance model. However, it is important to be able to simulate a stock price attaining a value of zero. Such a stock price corresponds to a bankruptcy event. And modeling such a default situation with a worthless share price needs to be an integral part of the valuation of hybrid securities. To allow a state of default to be reached in the trinomial process, an extra step has to be introduced. This is a step where the stock price is allowed to jump to a default layer corresponding to $S = 0$. Once this state is reached, the stock price can never go up again; the stock price remains equal to zero and the value of the hybrid is equal to its recovery value π_{Hybrid}:

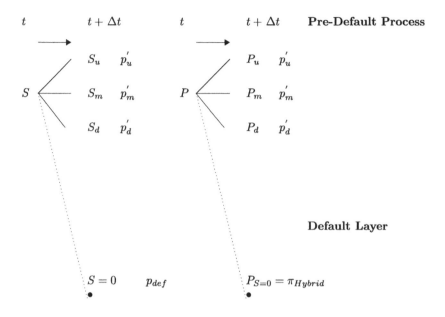

The previous picture illustrates how S can jump to a default layer and drags the valuation of the hybrid lower as well. In case of a default, the bond holders have a claim toward the issuer of the debt they invested in. Some fraction of the claim will eventually be paid back. This is the recovery rate and is expressed as a percentage of face value. The company might sell some of its assets to meet these claims. This recovery rate is highly dependent on the ranking of the bond in the capital structure of the issuer, and hence the recovery rate π_{Hybrid} depends on the subordination of the bond. For a deeply subordinated corporate hybrid it is therefore often assumed that $\pi_{Hybrid} = 0$. In Table 9.1 a comparison of the corporate recovery rates estimated by Moody's for the different seniorities can be found.

Table 9.1   Recovery rates for bonds as a percentage of face value in the period 1982–2008

Bond Seniority	Recovery Rate (%)
Senior Secured	52.30
Senior Unsecured	36.40
Senior Subordinated	31.70
Subordinated	31.00
Junior Subordinated	24.00
Preferreds	11.70

Source: www.moodys.com [152].

On default, the share holders will walk away and leave the bond holders facing the issuer who still has an outstanding debt toward them. This post-default value $P_{S=0}$ is in practice modeled in three different ways:

- **Par recovery**
  The bond holder recovers a certain percentage (π_{Hybrid}) of the face value N of the hybrid bond. The recovery value can be written as:

$$P_{S=0} = \pi_{Hybrid} \times N \tag{9.6}$$

  In this book, we will apply this particular definition of recovery rates in our numerical examples.
- **Par recovery + accrued**
  The recovery value takes into account that a fraction of the accrued interest can also be recovered after the default took place:

$$P_{S=0} = \pi_{Hybrid} \times (N + Acc_t) \tag{9.7}$$

- **Present value recovery**
  In this approach the time to maturity is taken into account. The face value of the bond is discounted with respect to the remaining maturity $T - t$:

$$P_{S=0} = \pi_{Hybrid} \times (N \exp(-r(T - t))) \tag{9.8}$$

  This is also called the T-bill recovery, as it is the recovery applied on an equivalent risk-free zero-coupon bond.
- **Market value recovery**
  The recovery value is a percentage of the pre-default market value of the convertible bond price.

The probabilities of default p_{def} and survival p_{surv} over the next time step Δt can be calculated using Equation (7.54) and are respectively given by:

$$p_{def} = 1 - \exp(-\lambda \Delta t)$$
$$p_{surv} = \exp(-\lambda \Delta t) \tag{9.9}$$

The parameter λ is the default intensity and represents the instantaneous default risk. This quantity can be derived from the credit default swap rates. The probability that default occurs over an infinitesimal interval dt is λdt. The transition probabilities in the jump diffusion model p'_u, p'_m, and p'_d are obtained through multiplication of the survival probability p_{surv} by the probabilities p_u, p_m, and p_d. These latter probabilities govern the pre-default part of the tree and have been explained in detail earlier (Equation (8.43)):

$$\begin{cases} p'_u = p_u \times p_{surv} \\ p'_m = p_m \times p_{surv} \\ p'_d = p_d \times p_{surv} \end{cases} \tag{9.10}$$

The stochastic differential equation describing the geometric Brownian motion of a stock price S needs to be adjusted when the stock is allowed to drop to zero in case of a bankruptcy. The pre-default share price process in a risk-neutral world is written as:

$$dS_t = (r + g)S_t dt + \sigma S_t dW_t \tag{9.11}$$

There is an extra parameter g that increases the drift in the equation above. This is compensation for the negative share price impact when a jump to default occurs [134]. The value of g is linked to the probability of default. Using an intensity-based model, we know that over a discrete time step Δt the default probability $p_{def} = 1 - \exp(-\lambda \Delta t)$. Using the risk-neutral measure and taking constant interest rates, we know that the current value of the share S_0 is equal to the discounted expected value of S at a future time T:

$$S_0 = \exp(-r(T - t))\mathbb{E}_\mathbb{Q}[S_T]$$
$$= \exp(-r(T - t)) \left(\mathbb{E}_\mathbb{Q}[S_T \mid \text{survival}] \times p_{surv} + \mathbb{E}_\mathbb{Q}[S_T \mid \text{default}] \times p_{def} \right) \qquad (9.12)$$
$$= \exp(-r(T - t)) \left(\mathbb{E}_\mathbb{Q}[S_T \mid \text{survival}] \times p_{surv} \right)$$

Assuming constant interest rates, we can write:

$$S_0 = \exp(-(r + \lambda)(T - t)) \, \mathbb{E}_\mathbb{Q}[S_T \mid \text{survival}]$$
$$= \exp(-(r + \lambda)(T - t)) \, \exp((r + g)(T - t))S_0$$

From the equation above we learn that $g = \lambda$. Hence:

$$dS_t = (r + \lambda)S_t dt + \sigma S_t dW_t \qquad (9.13)$$

When the stock distributes a dividend yield $q > 0$:

$$dS_t = (r - q + \lambda)S_t dt + \sigma S_t dW_t \qquad (9.14)$$

The pre-default process of a jump-diffusion model is the same as the diffusion model where no jumps are allowed but with an increase g in the drift term.

If one would like to deviate from the assumption that default is characterized by a stock price equal to 0, Equation (9.14) will need to be modified. The stock price no longer drops to 0 and we have to consider that some fraction of the pre-default share price π_S will be recovered. This approach was covered in [11] and the stochastic differential equation for the pre-default share price process now becomes:

$$dS_t = (r - q + (1 - \pi_S)\lambda)S_t dt + \sigma S_t dW_t \qquad (9.15)$$

9.2.3   Trinomial Trees with Jump to Default

We will work out a numerical example for a trinomial tree similar to the tree developed in Section 8.3.4. The tree will cover a period of 4 years in two steps only. Instead of a Black–Scholes environment where the stock tree approximates a geometric Brownian motion, we now introduce jumps. The parameters of the pre-default process are kept the same. A default intensity $\lambda = 5\%$ has been incorporated to accommodate for the possibility of a jump. The general tree-building procedure hardly changes when adding a default layer to the tree. In what follows we construct the tree while following the four-step procedure of Section 8.3.4.

1. **Choosing the appropriate stochastic process**
   The following pricing parameters for the jump-diffusion process are chosen:
   - $T = 4$ years
   - $n = 2$ trinomial steps
   - $r = 3\%$
   - $q = 2\%$
   - $\sigma = 40\%$
   - $S_0 = 100$
   - $\lambda = 5\%$

2. Selecting the time slices

The variance V^2 of X on the default-free part of the tree is constant and equal to:

$$V^2 = \sigma^2 \Delta t = 0.4 \times 0.4 \times 2 = 0.32 \tag{9.16}$$

3. Associating with a particular time slice a step size

The distance between two nodes on the pre-default part of the tree is an integer multiple of ΔX with:

$$\Delta X = V\sqrt{3} = 0.9798 \tag{9.17}$$

4. Calculating the transition probabilities

On each node of the tree there is a probability that default occurs during the next time step Δt:

$$\begin{aligned} p_{def} &= \exp(-\lambda \Delta t) \\ &= \exp(-0.05 \times 2) \\ &= 0.0952 \end{aligned}$$

Hence:

$$p_{surv} = 1 - p_{def} = 0.9048$$
$$= p'_u + p'_m + p'_d$$

(a) First time slice $t = \Delta t$

The tree of the log prices X_t originates at $X_{0,0} = \log(100) = 4.6052$. The expected value of the three nodes originating from $X_{0,0}$ and ending in the first time slice is $M_{0,0}$ and is given by:

$$M_{0,0} = \log(S_0) + \left(r - q + \lambda - \frac{1}{2}\sigma^2\right)\Delta t = 4.5652 \tag{9.18}$$

The nodes on the first time slice ($t = 2$) are laid out as specified in the picture below:

$t = 0$ $\qquad\qquad$ $t = 2$

$X_{0,0} = 4.6052$

$(k+1)\Delta X_1 = 0.9798(k+1)$ $\qquad$ p'_u

$k\Delta X_1 = 0.9798k$ $\qquad$ p'_m

$(k-1)\Delta X_1 = 0.9798(k-1)$ $\qquad$ p'_d

Default $\qquad$ p_{pdef}

Using Equation (8.42) we can calculate the value of k:

$$k = \text{round}\left(\frac{M_{0,0}}{\Delta X_1}\right) = \text{round}\left(\frac{4.5652}{0.9798}\right) = 5 \tag{9.19}$$

The positions of the three X-nodes at $t = 2$ are hence fully determined. Only the transition probabilities need to be resolved:

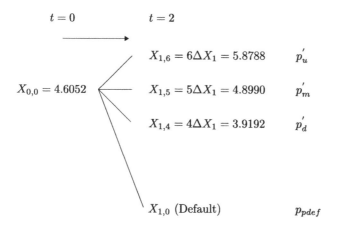

$t = 0$ $t = 2$

$X_{0,0} = 4.6052$

$X_{1,6} = 6\Delta X_1 = 5.8788$ p'_u

$X_{1,5} = 5\Delta X_1 = 4.8990$ p'_m

$X_{1,4} = 4\Delta X_1 = 3.9192$ p'_d

$X_{1,0}$ (Default) p_{pdef}

The transition probabilities are based on Equation (8.40) while taking into account the survival probability p_{surv}. The solution is:

$$\begin{cases} p'_u = \left(\dfrac{V^2}{2\Delta X_1^2} + \dfrac{(M_{0,0}-k\Delta X_1)^2}{2\Delta X_1^2} + \dfrac{(M_{0,0}-k\Delta X_1)}{2\Delta X_1} \right) \times p_{surv} = 0.0492 \\[2ex] p'_m = \left(1 - \dfrac{V^2}{\Delta X_1^2} - \dfrac{(M_{0,0}-k\Delta X_1)^2}{\Delta X_1^2} \right) \times p_{surv} = 0.4982 \\[2ex] p'_d = \left(\dfrac{V^2}{2\Delta X_1^2} + \dfrac{(M_{0,0}-k\Delta X_1)^2}{2\Delta X_1^2} - \dfrac{(M_{0,0}-k\Delta X_1)}{2\Delta X_1} \right) \times p_{surv} = 0.3574 \end{cases} \qquad (9.20)$$

(b) **Second and final time slice** $(t = 2\Delta t)$

The nodes $X_{1,6}$, $X_{1,5}$, $X_{1,4}$, and $X_{1,0}$ on the first slice are the starting nodes of a total of 13 other branches. The nodes $X_{1,6}$, $X_{1,5}$, and $X_{1,4}$ belong to that part of the first slice that has not encountered any default at all. For these pre-default nodes, there are four branches that connect to nodes on the second slice. One of these four branches connects the node $X_{2,0}$ on the default layer of the second slice, while the other three branches remain in the default-free part of the tree. The node $X_{1,0}$ represents a state of default in the first slice and is only allowed to move to $X_{2,0}$. Once defaulted, the share remains in a default state. The probability of going from $X_{1,0}$ to $X_{2,0}$ equals 1:

$$\text{Pre-Default Process} \begin{cases} X_{1,6} \rightarrow \{X_{2,7}, X_{2,6}, X_{2,5}, X_{2,0}\} \\ X_{1,5} \rightarrow \{X_{2,6}, X_{2,5}, X_{2,4}, X_{2,0}\} \\ X_{1,4} \rightarrow \{X_{2,5}, X_{2,4}, X_{2,3}, X_{2,0}\} \end{cases}$$

$$\text{Default Layer: } X_{1,0} \rightarrow \{X_{2,0}\} \qquad (9.21)$$

The numerical result of the calculations involving the nodes in the pre-default layer is summarized below:

Second Time Slice ($t = 4$)		
$X_{1,6}$	$X_{1,5}$	$X_{1,4}$
$X = 5.8788$	$X = 4.899$	$X = 3.9192$
$V^2 = 0.32$	$V^2 = 0.32$	$V^2 = 0.32$
$\Delta X_2 = 0.9798$	$\Delta X_2 = 0.9798$	$\Delta X_2 = 0.9798$
$M_{1,6} = 5.8388$	$M_{1,5} = 4.8590$	$M_{1,4} = 3.8792$
$k = 6$	$k = 5$	$k = 4$
New Nodes	**New Nodes**	**New Nodes**
$X_{2,7} = 6.8586 \quad p'_u = 0.1331$	$X_{2,6} = 5.8788 \quad p'_u = 0.1331$	$X_{2,5} = 4.8990 \quad p'_u = 0.1331$
$X_{2,6} = 5.8788 \quad p'_m = 0.6017$	$X_{2,5} = 4.8990 \quad p'_m = 0.6017$	$X_{2,4} = 3.9192 \quad p'_m = 0.6017$
$X_{2,5} = 4.8990 \quad p'_d = 0.1700$	$X_{2,4} = 3.9192 \quad p'_d = 0.1700$	$X_{2,3} = 2.9394 \quad p'_d = 0.1700$
$X_{2,0} = \text{Default} \quad p_{def} = 0.0952$	$X_{2,0} = \text{Default} \quad p_{def} = 0.0952$	$X_{2,0} = \text{Default} \quad p_{def} = 0.0952$

There are in total six different final nodes in this two-step trinomial tree. One node is on the default layer while the others are in the default-free part of the tree.

Final Nodes ($t = 4$)				
		X	**S**	**Prob**
Pre-Default	$X_{2,7}$	6.8586	$S_{2,7}$ 952.03	0.0065
	$X_{2,6}$	5.8788	$S_{2,6}$ 357.38	0.0959
	$X_{2,5}$	4.8990	$S_{2,5}$ 134.16	0.3557
	$X_{2,4}$	3.9192	$S_{2,4}$ 50.36	0.2998
	$X_{2,3}$	2.9394	$S_{2,3}$ 18.90	0.0608
Default Layer	$X_{2,0}$	Default	$S_{2,0}$ 0	0.1813
			$\Sigma(Prob)=$	1.0000

The probability of arriving at a default during the 4-year period modeled by the trinomial tree is equal to 18.13%. This result can be derived analytically:

$$1 - \exp(-\lambda(T - t)) = 1 - \exp(-0.05 \times 4) = 0.1813 \qquad (9.22)$$

The same result can also be derived when walking through the nodes on the tree. There are two ways to arrive at $X_{2,0}$, the node corresponding to $S = 0$ at the maturity date. The stock can reach default in the first time step or can jump to zero in the second time step after having survived the first time step:

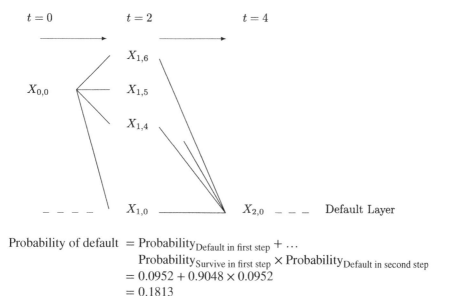

$$\text{Probability of default} = \text{Probability}_{\text{Default in first step}} + \cdots$$
$$\text{Probability}_{\text{Survive in first step}} \times \text{Probability}_{\text{Default in second step}}$$
$$= 0.0952 + 0.9048 \times 0.0952$$
$$= 0.1813$$

The complete two-step trinomial tree for displaying the nodes and branches covered in this numerical example can be found in Figure 9.3.

9.2.4   Pricing Convertible Bonds with Jump Diffusion

Currently, jump diffusion is the model of choice of many convertible bond practitioners. It is incorporated into most commercial software packages dealing with the valuation of derivative

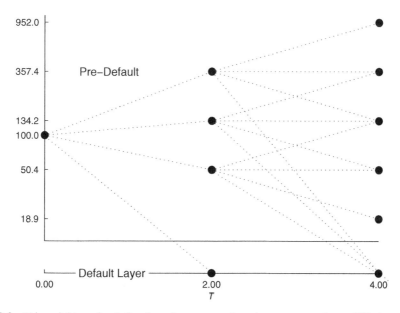

Figure 9.3   Trinomial tree simulation for a 4-year maturity using a two-step jump-diffusion process.

securities. Needless to say, there are material differences between these implementations. The use of a jump-diffusion model at one bank will lead to a different output at a different trading desk using a similar approach. These valuation differences result from the assumptions regarding dividend models, recovery mechanics, numerical approaches, etc.

Rolling Back in the Tree

The choice to use a lattice model in this book to deal with the valuation of hybrid bonds is based on its educational merits. In Section 8.3.6, American options were valued on a tree model. At every node S of the share price tree, the price of the option was calculated. This led to the construction of the option tree where every node P represents the corresponding derivatives' price of the node S.

Such a P-tree is constructed starting from the maturity date toward the pricing date. This ultimately terminates in the current price of the derivative security. The early exercise feature of American options has to be imposed and verified in every node of the tree, whether the exercise value exceeds the continuation value or not. In other words, is the bond worth more keeping it alive till the next node or should one opt for an immediate exercise?

Final Values

Once the geometry of the share price tree is worked out, all of its node values S and the corresponding probability of arriving at every single one of these nodes are known. The nodes S_T corresponding with the maturity date $t = T$ are called the final nodes. For a bond with face value N and a coupon C, the value P_T of the convertible bond at these nodes is:

$$P_T = \max(N + C, C_r \times S_T) \tag{9.23}$$

Continuation Values

From the final nodes P_T, the roll-back procedure starts. Moving one time slice back in time toward the origin of the tree brings us, for example, to node P corresponding to a share price level S. From this node, three different nodes originate: P_u, P_m, and P_d. All of these values are known since they are all on the final time slice. The probabilities of arriving at these latter values from node P are respectively p_u, p_m, and p_d. In the context of jump diffusion, there is also a probability ($p_{def} \neq 0$) of observing a default during the next time step Δt. In this case the value of the bond will drop to its recovery value π. The continuation value P_c in the current node is equal to the discounted expected value of the nodes in the next time slice:

$$P_c = \exp(-r\Delta t)\left(p_u \times P_u + p_m \times P_u + p_d \times P_d + p_{def} \times \pi\right) \tag{9.24}$$

Conversion Values

The conversion value or parity (P_a) is the cash value of the number of shares received by the bond holder on conversion. In the current node with share price S, the conversion amount is hence equal to $C_r \times S$. The bond holder will convert if parity exceeds the continuation value.

This is called an optional conversion since this decision is left at the discretion of the bond holder. If conversion is allowed, the convertible bond can take two values in the node:

$$P_a > P_c \Rightarrow P = P_a \text{ (optional conversion)}$$
$$P_a \leq P_c \Rightarrow P = P_c \text{ (no conversion)}$$

(9.25)

Rolling Backward

The picture below sketches a summary of the five steps involved in the roll-back process. All of this is very similar to the pricing of American options since these also have an early exercise possibility. Interventions in the nodes are not limited to the verification of the optional conversion, however. There can, for example, be an issuer call, an investor put, a refixing of the conversion price, etc.

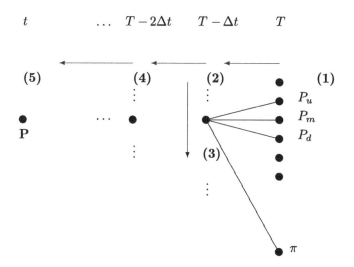

The five steps of the process are:

1. Calculation of the final node values.
2. Move to the preceding layer $T - \Delta t$.
3. Calculate at each of the nodes on this time slice the continuation value (P_c) using Equation (9.24) and determine the conversion value (P_a) of the convertible. The value of the convertible is set equal to P_a if optional conversion is advantageous to the investor. Otherwise, set P equal to P_c:

$$P = \max\{P_a, P_c\}$$

(9.26)

4. Roll backward to the preceding time slice $T - 2\Delta t$, after which step (3) is repeated again.
5. The node value obtained in the origin of the P-tree is the current value of the convertible bond.

Dealing with Calls and Puts

Through the existence of a call in the terms and conditions of the bond, the issuer can buy back the convertible against a price K. This is the early redemption amount. The investor, in contrast, always has the option to convert the bond into shares if such an issuer call takes place. This latter situation is called a forced conversion.

While a call option is interesting from the perspective of the issuer, an embedded put option favors the investor of the bond. Through the put option, the investor has the right to redeem the bond against the put amount P_v on the put date. This leaves us with four important combinations going from the inclusion of both a call and put feature to a convertible bond where none of these features are part of the anatomy of the bond:

P	No Call	Call
No Put	$\max\left(P_a, P_c\right)$	$\max\left(P_a, \min(K, P_c)\right)$
Put	$\max\left(P_a, P_v, P_c\right)$	$\max\left(P_a, P_v, \min(K, P_c)\right)$

The set of equations above only holds when there are no coupon payments in the convertible structure. If this is the case, the investor can possibly be entitled or not to the accrued interest Acc on an optional conversion, a forced conversion, a call, or a put. Unfortunately, the modalities in the prospectus regarding the attribution of accrued interest differ a lot. There is no one-size-fits-all convertible bond set-up.

Suppose that a convertible bond grants accrued interest in the case of an optional but not a forced conversion. In such a case the value in each of the nodes of the tree is controlled by the following set of equations:

Forced Conversion

$$\min(K, P_c) = K \Rightarrow P = \max(P_a, K)$$

(9.27)

Optional Conversion

$$\min(K, P_c) = P_c \Rightarrow P = \max(P_a + Acc, P_c)$$

Numerical Example

As a numerical example, we consider a 5-year convertible bond distributing an annual coupon of 2% with a face value N equal to 100. The bond is puttable exactly 3 years after the issue date against par ($P_v = 100$).

The share price S is 100 and the conversion price is 130. On conversion, the investor will therefore receive $C_r = \frac{100}{130} = 0.7692$ shares. The convertible can only be optionally converted after 2 years. From year 4 onwards, the issuer has the right to call back the bond against an early redemption amount K equal to 100. There is a call trigger $K_\%$ of 120% attached to this early buyback possibility for the issuer. The share price needs to be higher that 120% of the conversion price C_p. This corresponds to a share price level of 156. As long as this share price level is not breached, the convertible cannot be called and the holder of the bond cannot be forced into conversion.

The convertible bond will be priced using a jump-diffusion model with a default intensity λ of 3%. In case of default, the expected recovery value of the convertible π is 20%. The

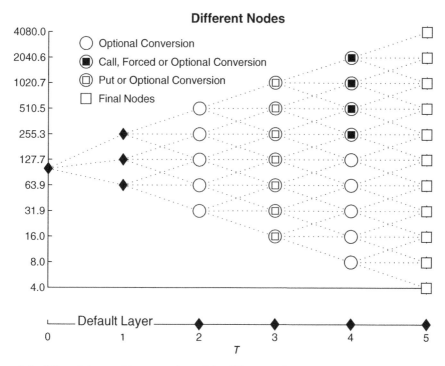

Figure 9.4   Trinomial tree with an overview of the different nodes in the tree.

volatility σ equals 40%, while the interest r and dividend yield q correspond respectively to 5% and 2%.

In this particular example, the tree is priced using five steps. The coupon payments coincide each time with a node. We assume that the coupons are always paid out in the pre-default part of the tree. An overview of the nodes is given in Figure 9.4. The figure points out the location of those nodes where the bond is optionally convertible, or where the bond is eligible for a put or an early redemption.

Starting from the trinomial tree in Figure 9.4, we start the roll-back procedure. The price of the convertible bond obtained in this five-step tree is 105.22.[2] The different node values generated by the roll-back procedure can be found in Figure 9.5. There are three nodes where the convertible is actually going to be put back by the investor ($\square$) and sold for the put amount $P_v = 100$. The node value at the corresponding nodes is still 102 given our assumption that this convertible always pays out the coupon even on call or put dates.

There are four nodes where the investor will be forced to convert given the issuer call ($\blacksquare$). There are in total three nodes where an optional conversion will take place ($\bigcirc$). One node in the second year and two in the third year after the issue date. The probability of arriving at each of these nodes depends on the transition probabilities p_u, p_m, p_d, and p_{def} starting from the current share price $S = 100$ at time $t = 0$.

---

[2] Increasing the number of steps n to 100 improves the accuracy and results in a price of 104.98.

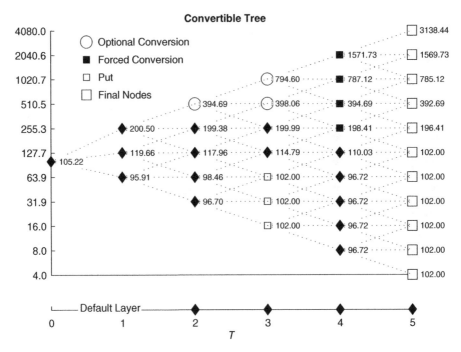

Figure 9.5 Trinomial tree with the values of the convertible bond in the different nodes.

This allows us to derive the following probability table from the tree:

	Probability (%)
Optional Conversion	2.21
Forced Conversion	14.99
Call	0.00
Redemption	24.58
Final Conversion	3.46
Default	10.78
Put	43.98
	$\Sigma = 100.00$

The probability of achieving a situation where an optional conversion occurs is very limited given its probability of 2.21%. The possibility of putting the bond at the third year is going to be the most likely outcome, and the expected life of the bond is therefore 3.65 years. This is shorter than the full maturity of 5 years.

9.2.5 Lost in Translation

At this stage we have introduced two popular models when it comes to price financial instruments whose payoff is dependent on the price of the underlying equity. Both models were implemented using a trinomial tree. The first model used a geometric Brownian motion as underlying stochastic process for the share price. This is the backbone of the Black–Scholes approach. The second model was a jump-diffusion model which allowed the share price to jump to a state of default. In practice, these models are very often used next to each other and get mixed up easily. This is because both approaches share a volatility number as one of the input parameters. The volatility for the Black–Scholes model and the jump-diffusion model are respectively denoted σ_{BS} and σ_{JD}. Yet both volatility numbers have a different meaning. In Black–Scholes σ_{BS} controls the random behavior of the process, while in a jump-diffusion model σ_{JD} corresponds to the volatility of the pre-default process only. It defines the random walk of the share price up till the moment a jump occurs. Given the fact that a fixed jump size equal to $-S_t$ was chosen, the share price collapses to zero and sticks to this price level once a jump occurs. The corresponding stochastic differential equations in a risk-neutral setting are:

Black–Scholes
$$dS_t \qquad = (r - q)S_t dt + \sigma_{BS}S_t dW_t$$

Jump-Diffusion
$$dS_t \qquad = (r + \lambda - q)S_t dt + \sigma_{JD}S_t dW_t - S_t dN_t$$

It is very likely to see a convertible bond trader revert to a jump-diffusion model, or a variant of this, in the day-to-day management of a portfolio of convertible bonds. After all, this model blends the bankruptcy risk of the underlying shares with a traditional geometric Brownian motion when the shares have not defaulted yet. This is exactly what appeals to a convertible bond practitioner. Very often both the Black–Scholes and the jump-diffusion model are used next to each other. Hence, there is a non-negligible risk that the convertible trader starts mixing up the Black–Scholes approach with the jump-diffusion model. Mixing σ_{BS} with σ_{JD} or vice versa can happen.

A convertible bond analyst may, for example, consult with a colleague on the equity derivatives desk. When asking his colleague for a reasonable volatility assumption to price and hedge a particular convertible security, he will presumably obtain an estimate for the value of σ_{BS}. The equity derivatives trader most probably uses Black–Scholes to deal with vanilla options. This is where an estimate for σ_{BS} gets plugged into σ_{JD} and confusion mounts.

To illustrate the consequences of this translation error, we consider a practical example of a 1-year option on a stock $S = 100$ with a strike $K = 110$. The other pricing parameters are a dividend yield $q = 0\%$, an interest rate $r = 3\%$, and $\sigma_{BS} = 40\%$. The price of this 1-year out-of-the-money call option is 13.16. For different ranges of λ, the implied volatility σ_{JD} was calculated and compared with σ_{BS}. Imagine that the credit spread for corporate debt of the issuer is, for example, equal to 200 bps. Using a recovery rate $\pi = 30\%$, this corresponds to $\lambda = 0.02/(1 - 0.3) = 286$ bps. The difference between σ_{JD} and σ_{BS} for this particular default intensity is equal to 2.9% (Figure 9.6).

9.3 CORRELATION

9.3.1 Correlation Risk in Hybrids

The correlation between two sets of data X and Y describes their statistical (linear) interdependence. Correlation is omnipresent in finance. Correlation estimates between equity prices and exchange rates are, for example, very often needed as a mandatory input factor when modeling convertible bonds or contingent convertibles. In the case of cross-currency convertible bonds

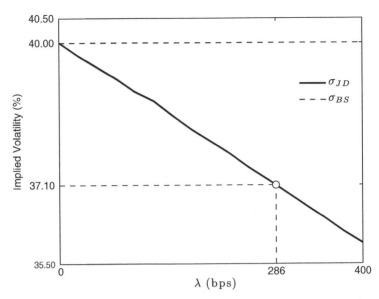

Figure 9.6   Calculation of the implied volatility σ_{JD} for a 1-year out-of-the-money option for different values of λ.

(Section 2.6.3), the exchange rate FX_{SB} between the currency of the underlying share and the currency in which the bond is denominated drives the parity of the convertible bond. A negative correlation between FX_{SB} and S corresponds to a situation where the positive effect of a price appreciation in the value S of the underlying share is eroded by a depreciation of the exchange rate. The same cross-currency effects sometimes prevail in contingent convertibles where the loss-absorption mechanism transforms a holding of a bond into an equity position denominated in a different currency.

Correlation will also appear in the world of hybrids when portfolio managers open up their valuation models toward more factors. Working out the valuation and risk of a contingent convertible through a stochastic volatility model, for example, demands an estimate for the expected correlation between share price and volatility movements. These changes are not independent of each other. It is a widely accepted paradigm that volatility will move higher when the share price weakens. The constant elasticity of a variance model explained in Equation (7.38) was constructed around this idea. Along the same line of thought, the improvement of a pricing model where interest rates are no longer considered to be deterministic demands a correlation estimate between the diffusion process of the share price and the stochastic process driving interest rates.

9.3.2   Definition

A correlation coefficient is a number in the range $[-1, 1]$ quantifying the extent of statistical dependence between observations for two random variables. We can start by making a distinction between the Spearman correlation coefficient and the Pearson correlation coefficient. In order to avoid Babylonian confusion, we prefer to label these correlation coefficients respectively as rank and linear correlation. Unless otherwise specified, we will always use the linear correlation coefficients in this work and represent this coefficient using the symbol ρ.

Suppose we have a d-dimensional random variable X. Such a variable has d components $X_1, \ldots, X_d$. Each of these components X_i has its own mean μ_i and variance σ_i^2:

$$\mu_i = \mathbb{E}[X_i] \tag{9.28}$$
$$\sigma_i^2 = \mathbb{E}[(X_i - \mu)^2]$$

Note further that $\rho_{ij} = \rho_{ji}$ and one can show that $-1 \leq \rho_{ij} \leq 1$.

The covariance Σ_{ij} specifies how the two variables X_i and X_j move together around their respective means μ_i and μ_j:

$$\Sigma_{ij} = \mathbb{E}[(X_i - \mu_i)(X_j - \mu_j)] \tag{9.29}$$

Normalizing this covariance Σ_{ij} with the volatilities σ_i and σ_j of the two random variables results in ρ_{ij}, the linear correlation coefficient between X_i and X_j:

$$\rho_{ij} = \frac{\Sigma_{ij}}{\sigma_i \sigma_j} \tag{9.30}$$

The correlation matrix of our d-dimensional random variable is a symmetrical $(\rho_{ij} = \rho_{ji})$ $d \times d$ matrix with ones on the diagonal $(\rho_{ii} = 1)$. In matrix form we can derive the covariance matrix Σ from the correlation matrix and a diagonal matrix containing the volatilities $\sigma_1, \ldots, \sigma_d$:

$$\Sigma = \begin{bmatrix} \sigma_1 & 0 & 0 \\ & \ddots & \\ 0 & \sigma_i & 0 \\ & & \ddots \\ 0 & 0 & \sigma_d \end{bmatrix} \times \begin{bmatrix} 1 & \cdots & \rho_{1i} & \cdots & \rho_{1d} \\ \vdots & \ddots & \vdots & & \vdots \\ \rho_{i1} & \cdots & 1 & \cdots & \rho_{id} \\ \vdots & & \vdots & \ddots & \vdots \\ \rho_{d1} & \cdots & \rho_{di} & \cdots & 1 \end{bmatrix} \times \begin{bmatrix} \sigma_1 & 0 & 0 \\ & \ddots & \\ 0 & \sigma_i & 0 \\ & & \ddots \\ 0 & 0 & \sigma_d \end{bmatrix}$$

The covariance matrix Σ is positive definite if, for all $x \in \mathbb{R}^d$: $x^T \Sigma x > 0$.

9.3.3   Correlating Wiener Processes

Starting from Equation (7.19) we can specify the stochastic process of d financial variables using a Wiener process for every single one of these processes:

$$dX_t = \begin{cases} dX_{1,t} = A_1(X_1, \ldots, X_d, t)dt + B_1(X_1, \ldots, X_d, t)dW_{1,t} \\ \vdots \\ dX_{d,t} = A_d(X_1, \ldots, X_d, t)dt + B_d(X_1, \ldots, X_d, t)dW_{d,t} \end{cases} \tag{9.31}$$

The variables $dX_{i,t}$ in the set of d equations above can be grouped into a vector process $X = \{X_t = (X_{1,t}, \ldots, X_{d,t}), t \geq 0\}$ representing the values of d financial variables such as share prices, interest rates, credit default swap spreads, etc. The engine driving this stochastic vector process X is the Brownian motion $W = \{W_t = (W_{1,t}, \ldots, W_{d,t}), t \geq 0\}$. The vector dW_t contains the increments of these d Brownian motions observed at time t over a small time step dt: $dW_{1,t}, \ldots, dW_{d,t}$.

One of the key properties of a Brownian motion was the fact that the increments dW_t observed over this time interval dt are normally distributed with zero mean and variance dt. In the one-dimensional Brownian motion this means that increments over a time step dt follow a $N(0, dt)$ distribution. Extending this to d correlated Brownian motions: $dW_t \sim N(0, \Sigma)$. The covariance matrix Σ represents in this equation the variance of each of the d Brownian motions and their interdependence. This is where a linear correlation coefficient ρ is introduced:

$$\Sigma_{ii} = dt$$
$$\Sigma_{ij} = \rho_{ij}dt, \quad i \neq j$$

(9.32)

In other words:

$$\mathbb{E}[dW_i dW_i] = dt$$
$$\mathbb{E}[dW_i dW_j] = \rho_{ij}dt, \quad i \neq j$$

(9.33)

Standard mathematical tools available in, for example, spreadsheet applications seldom allow a direct approach to simulate a set of correlated Brownian motions. The only tool one usually has at hand is a random number generator to produce d independent standard normal variables $Z_i \sim N(0, 1), i = 1, \ldots, d$. In matrix form:

$$Z \sim N(0, I_d)$$

(9.34)

where I_d is the $[d \times d]$ identity matrix.[3] We can generate $dW \sim N(0, \Sigma)$ from Z after applying a linear transformation to this standard normal variable:

$$dW = bZ$$

(9.35)

The transformation matrix b is a $[d \times d]$ matrix projecting each of the standard normal vectors Z into a new variable dW. Because of the linear transformation property of the normal distribution defined in Equation (7.8), we know:

$$dW \sim N(0, bI_d b^T)$$

(9.36)

or

$$dW \sim N(0, bb^T)$$

(9.37)

If we can determine the matrix b such that $\Sigma = bb^T$, we can then transform d independent standard normal variables Z_i into a vector containing d correlated normal variables dW_i such that the obtained covariance matches Σ. Deriving the matrix b from the covariance matrix Σ is done through a technique called Cholesky factorization. This is possible under the condition that Σ is positive definite.

9.3.4   Cholesky Factorization

A convenient choice for b is a matrix where all the entries above the diagonal are equal to zero. Opting for such a lower-triangular matrix makes the algebra relatively light. This is covered in the following example where we limit ourselves to three financial assets ($d = 3$). Each asset price is modeled through a geometric Brownian motion. In order to keep our example as

---

[3] Each element on the diagonal is equal to 1. The other elements are equal to 0.

educational as possible, we consider a constant drift and volatility for each of the three assets X_1, X_2, and X_3:

$$dX_1 = \mu_1 X_1 dt + \sigma_1 X_1 dW_1$$
$$dX_2 = \mu_2 X_2 dt + \sigma_2 X_2 dW_2 \tag{9.38}$$
$$dX_3 = \mu_3 X_3 dt + \sigma_3 X_3 dW_3$$

Assume that the three asset price changes share the same linear correlation ρ:
$\mathbb{E}[dW_1 dW_2] = \mathbb{E}[dW_2 dW_3] = \mathbb{E}[dW_1 dW_3] = \rho dt$. This means that:

$$dW = \begin{bmatrix} dW_1 \\ dW_2 \\ dW_3 \end{bmatrix} \sim N(0, \Sigma) \text{ with } \Sigma = dt \times \begin{bmatrix} 1 & \rho & \rho \\ \rho & 1 & \rho \\ \rho & \rho & 1 \end{bmatrix} \tag{9.39}$$

This uniform correlation matrix is not valid for just any choice of ρ. Imagine, for example, an outspoken negative correlation between W_1 and W_2. Such a choice would not allow us to have at the same time a negative correlation between W_1 and W_3 and W_2 and W_3.

Starting from three standard normal variables Z_1, Z_2, and Z_3, we can generate a random vector dW using a transformation matrix b:

$$dW = \begin{bmatrix} dW_1 \\ dW_2 \\ dW_3 \end{bmatrix} = \begin{bmatrix} b_{12} & 0 & 0 \\ b_{21} & b_{22} & 0 \\ b_{31} & b_{32} & b_{33} \end{bmatrix} \times \begin{bmatrix} Z_1 \\ Z_2 \\ Z_3 \end{bmatrix} \tag{9.40}$$

To impose a particular covariance matrix Σ, we need $bb^T = \Sigma$:

$$\begin{bmatrix} b_{11} & 0 & 0 \\ b_{21} & b_{22} & 0 \\ b_{31} & b_{32} & b_{33} \end{bmatrix} \times \begin{bmatrix} b_{11} & b_{21} & b_{31} \\ 0 & b_{22} & b_{32} \\ 0 & 0 & b_{33} \end{bmatrix} = dt \times \begin{bmatrix} 1 & \rho & \rho \\ \rho & 1 & \rho \\ \rho & \rho & 1 \end{bmatrix} \tag{9.41}$$

This leads to the following set of six equations allowing us to solve for each of the unknown elements of the transformation matrix b:

$$\begin{cases} b_{11}^2 & = dt \\ b_{21} b_{11} & = \rho dt \\ b_{31} b_{11} & = \rho dt \\ b_{21}^2 + b_{22}^2 & = dt \\ b_{31} b_{21} + b_{32} b_{22} & = \rho dt \\ b_{31}^2 + b_{32}^2 + b_{33}^2 & = dt \end{cases} \tag{9.42}$$

After some algebra we find the expression for the transformation matrix b:

$$
b = \begin{bmatrix} \sqrt{dt} & 0 & 0 \\ \rho\sqrt{dt} & \sqrt{dt(1-\rho^2)} & 0 \\ \rho\sqrt{dt} & \rho\sqrt{\frac{dt(1-\rho)}{(1+\rho)}} & \sqrt{\frac{dt(1-2\rho^2+\rho)}{1+\rho}} \end{bmatrix} = \sqrt{dt} \times \begin{bmatrix} 1 & 0 & 0 \\ \rho & \sqrt{1-\rho^2} & 0 \\ \rho & \rho\sqrt{\frac{1-\rho}{(1+\rho)}} & \sqrt{\frac{1-2\rho^2+\rho}{1+\rho}} \end{bmatrix} \tag{9.43}
$$

The matrix above helps us transform a set of three independent standard normal variables Z_1, Z_2, and Z_3 to a set of three normal variables dW_1, dW_2, and dW_3:

$$
\begin{aligned}
dW_1 &= \sqrt{dt}\, Z_1 \\
dW_2 &= \rho\sqrt{dt}\, Z_1 + \sqrt{dt}\sqrt{1-\rho^2}\, Z_2 \\
dW_3 &= \rho\sqrt{dt}\, Z_1 + \sqrt{dt}\rho\sqrt{\tfrac{1-\rho}{(1+\rho)}}\, Z_2 + \sqrt{dt}\sqrt{\tfrac{1-2\rho^2+\rho}{1+\rho}}\, Z_3
\end{aligned} \tag{9.44}
$$

All of the components of the vector dW obtained from the linear transformation of the $[d \times 1]$ vector Z share the same variance dt and have a covariance equal to ρdt. Combining Equations (9.38) and (9.44) hence allows us to generate the three asset price movements dX_1, dX_2, and dX_3 over the time interval dt:

$$
X_{i,t+dt} = X_{i,t} \exp\left(\left(\mu_i - \frac{\sigma_i^2}{2} \right) dt + \sigma_i dW_i \right) \text{ with } i \in \{1, 2, 3\} \tag{9.45}
$$

In Figure 9.7 there is an illustration of the transformation of a set of three standard normal uncorrelated variables Z into a set of correlated normal variables dW.

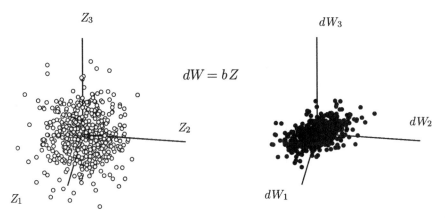

Figure 9.7 Transforming $Z \sim N(0, I)$ into $dW \sim N(0, \Sigma)$ using a lower-triangular transformation matrix b.

9.3.5 Cholesky Example

A manager considers picking one name from a short list of three selected preferred shares. For each of the shares the portfolio manager has come up with an estimate for the expected drift μ and volatility σ. The share price process is assumed to follow a geometric Brownian motion:

$$
\begin{array}{cccc}
\text{Preferred} & \mu & \sigma\ (\%) \\
X_1 & 0.01 & 10 \\
X_2 & 0.03 & 20 \\
X_3 & 0.05 & 30
\end{array}
\tag{9.46}
$$

Based on historical share prices, a correlation matrix for the three assets is constructed. In this case the correlation matrix is no longer uniform:

$$
\begin{bmatrix}
1.0 & 0.8 & 0.0 \\
0.8 & 1.0 & 0.1 \\
0.0 & 0.1 & 1.0
\end{bmatrix}
\tag{9.47}
$$

The manager wants to know what are the odds that the third preferred security X_3 is going to outperform the other two assets after an investment horizon of 6 months ($\Delta T = 0.5$). Using a Monte Carlo simulation and starting from the initial assumptions regarding drift, volatility, and correlation, the manager wants to calculate:

$$
Prob\left(\frac{X_{3,t+\Delta T}}{X_{3,t}} > \frac{X_{1,t+\Delta T}}{X_{1,t}} \text{ and } \frac{X_{3,t+\Delta T}}{X_{3,t}} > \frac{X_{2,t+\Delta T}}{X_{2,t}}\right)
\tag{9.48}
$$

The outcome can be obtained by running through the following four-step process:

1. **Generate standard normal variables**
   Using a random number generator, a total of $n = 5000$ variables Z_1, Z_2, and Z_3 are generated. This results in a [3×5000] matrix.
2. **Calculate the Cholesky matrix**
   The covariance between dW_1, dW_2, and dW_3 is contained in the following covariance matrix Σ:

$$
\Sigma = \Delta T \times \begin{bmatrix}
1.0 & 0.8 & 0.0 \\
0.8 & 1.0 & 0.1 \\
0.0 & 0.1 & 1.0
\end{bmatrix}
\tag{9.49}
$$

The transformation matrix b is therefore:

$$
b = \sqrt{\Delta T} \times \begin{bmatrix}
1.0000 & 0.0000 & 0.0000 \\
0.8000 & 0.6000 & 0.0000 \\
0.0000 & 0.1667 & 0.9860
\end{bmatrix}
\tag{9.50}
$$

3. **Calculate the increments of the three Brownian motions**
   $dW = bZ$.

4. **Calculate for each of the 5000 Monte Carlo runs**
   For $i \in \{1, 2, 3\}$:

$$\frac{X_{i,t+\Delta T}}{X_{i,t}} = \exp\left(\left(\mu_i - \frac{\sigma_i^2}{2}\right)\Delta T + \sigma_i dW_i\right) \tag{9.51}$$

Running through each of the four steps specified above allows us to calculate the probability that after 6 months, X_3 is the best-performing asset:

$$Prob\left(\frac{X_{3,t+\Delta T}}{X_{3,t}} > \frac{X_{1,t+\Delta T}}{X_{1,t}} \text{ and } \frac{X_{3,t+\Delta T}}{X_{3,t}} > \frac{X_{2,t+\Delta T}}{X_{2,t}}\right) = \mathbf{43.26\%} \tag{9.52}$$

9.3.6 Correlating Events

Introduction

In the previous section we modeled the interdependence between a set of d financial variables $X = \{X_1, \ldots, X_d\}$ and introduced for this purpose the linear correlation coefficient. The coefficient ρ_{ij} specifies the interdependence between the different Brownian motions whose increments dW_i and dW_j drive respectively the random changes in the price level of financial assets X_i and X_j. There is definitively a need to go beyond the modeling of correlations between price returns and to study diligently the joint occurrence of events such as, for example, missed coupon payments. Other events that impact the value of the portfolio are a rating change of one of the bonds in the portfolio or the default of one of the issuers. Since there is a probability that the event of one obligor defaulting on its debt is going to affect the likelihood of another company in the portfolio defaulting as well, we need to incorporate this correlation into our financial models.

In Section 7.5 we touched briefly upon this problem while examining a case study of three preferred securities; a study during which we wanted to understand what the odds were that we were going to encounter at least one cancelation on the coupon payments during the next 6 months. The result of this case study was straightforward because we started from the assumption that these events were independent of each other. If one of the companies of which we are holding a preferred share has a financial problem and has to skip a coupon payment on this preferred security, then this event is assumed not to have an impact on the likelihood that the other preferreds are going to impose a similar coupon cancelation.

Correlated Defaults

Imagine that all the bonds in our portfolio have been issued by corporations belonging to one and the same industry group. If this is the case, a negative headwind for the industry will be felt across all the issuers. It should not come as a surprise that a default event for one obligor will be followed by others. The assumption of complete independence or zero default correlation does not hold any more. But even if the issuers belong to different industry groups, their financial condition depends very much on the overall health of the economy. Any downturn in the economy will be felt across a wide range of companies. This is obvious when one studies the yearly default rates in the United States. The high concentration of defaults around 1933, 1991, 2001, and 2008 illustrates the correlation between such events. The phenomena of companies tending to default together or not default at all is indicative of a positive default correlation [141].

Suppose that the default of a company A is represented by an indicator variable X_A. Default corresponds to $X_A = 1$. The probability of default p_A over a time horizon T is given by $p_A = 1 - \exp(-\lambda_A T)$. Defaulting is the outcome of a Bernoulli experiment. There are two outcomes possible:

$$\begin{cases} \text{Probability of defaulting} = p_A & \text{with} \quad X_A = 1 \\ \text{Probability of surviving} = 1 - p_A & \text{with} \quad X_A = 0 \end{cases} \tag{9.53}$$

Introducing another state variable X_B allows us to define the default correlation ρ_D between the two companies A and B:

$$\begin{aligned} \rho_D &= \frac{\mathbb{E}[X_A X_B] - \mathbb{E}[X_A]\mathbb{E}[X_B]}{\sigma_A \sigma_B} \\ &= \frac{p_{AB} - p_A p_B}{\sqrt{p_A(1 - p_A)p_B(1 - p_B)}} \end{aligned} \tag{9.54}$$

with p_{AB} the probability that both A and B default over the same horizon.

The equation above assists in the calculation of the expected probability p_{AB} that the two obligors in our portfolio move together to a state of bankruptcy during a particular time frame. From CDS curves, one can derive the market-implied expected default probabilities p_A and p_B. The pairwise default correlation ρ_D allows us to calculate this joint default probability:

$$p_{AB} = p_A p_B + \rho_D \sqrt{p_A(1 - p_A)p_B(1 - p_B)} \tag{9.55}$$

The probability that A defaults knowing B encountered a default event $p_{A|B}$ is given by:

$$p_{A|B} = \frac{p_{AB}}{p_B} = p_A + \rho_D \sqrt{\frac{p_A}{p_B}(1 - p_A)(1 - p_B)} \tag{9.56}$$

The importance of default correlation can best be illustrated by taking a very small value for both p_A and p_B [173]. In this particular case, where $p_A = p_B = p \ll 1$, we find that:

$$p_{AB} \approx \rho_D p \tag{9.57}$$

$$p_{A|B} \approx \rho_D$$

The result above stresses the importance of the default correlation ρ_D when calculating conditional default probabilities such as $p_{A|B}$. Indeed, if $p_A = p_B = 1\%$ and $\rho_D = 0.8$, we have that $p_{AB} = 0.8\%$ and $p_{A|B} \approx 80\%$.

9.3.7 Using Equity Correlation

A real-world portfolio has more than two obligors and this immediately waters down the applicability of Equation (9.55). Suppose that we are dealing with d different obligors in the portfolio. How can one model the correlation of defaults? We could introduce correlation by allowing an interdependence between the different intensities $\lambda_1, \ldots, \lambda_d$. An alternative route is the Monte Carlo simulation of the different (correlated) default times $\tau_1, \ldots, \tau_d$. Assume, for example, a time homogeneous default process for each of the credits in the portfolio. Since τ_i is exponentially distributed with mean $\frac{1}{\lambda_i}$, the random variable $\omega_i = \tau_i \lambda_i$ is then an exponential variable with mean 1. There is a joint default during the next time interval T of two of the obligors i and j when we encounter a situation where both $\tau_i \leq T$ and $\tau_j \leq T$.

Simulating each of the exponential variables ω_i can be done, as explained in Section 8.5.2, by drawing a number U_i from a uniform distribution on the interval $[0, 1]$. For each of the d obligors we can generate n random numbers. Sampling these random numbers $U_1, \ldots, U_n$ generates a corresponding set of n default times τ_i for each asset in the portfolio:

$$\tau_i = -\frac{\log(1 - U_i)}{\lambda_i} \tag{9.58}$$

Generating a time series of correlated default times boils down to generating a correlated multivariate uniform distribution. Each vector $(U_i, \ldots, U_d)$ corresponds to a set of d correlated default times $(\tau_1, \ldots, \tau_d)$.

The vector $(U_i, \ldots, U_d)$ can be derived from a corresponding vector $(X_i, \ldots, X_d)$ of correlated standard normal variables $X_i \sim N(0, 1)$ using:

$$U_i = \Phi(X_i) \tag{9.59}$$

Imposing a correlation structure in the multivariate standard normal distribution can be done using the Cholesky factorization of the covariance matrix. This is explained in Section 9.3.3. The technique to deal with default correlation starting from a set of correlated Gaussian variables is called a **normal copula**. This is a popular approach and the problem of dealing with a correlation between exponential variables τ_i is achieved using auxiliary standard normal variables X_i. The transformation from X_i to U_i does not preserve correlation as such. In [83] and [100], other copula techniques are covered in more detail. As we will demonstrate in a practical example, there is a clear difference between the correlation ρ governing the interdependence between standard normal variables X_i and X_j and the obtained default correlation ρ_D which is the outcome of the Monte Carlo simulation. The simplified scheme of generating a single run out of the n simulations is carried out as follows:

(1) Generate d standard normal variables: $\quad\quad\quad\quad Z_i \sim N(0, 1)$
$\quad\quad\quad\quad\quad\quad\quad\quad\quad\quad\quad\quad\quad\quad\quad\quad\quad\quad\quad\quad\quad i \in \{1, \ldots, d\}$
$\quad\quad\quad\quad\quad\quad\quad\quad\quad\quad\quad\quad\quad\quad\quad\quad\quad\quad\quad\quad\quad\quad \downarrow$

(2) Introduce correlation using Cholesky: $\quad\quad\quad\quad X = bZ$
$\quad\quad\quad\quad\quad\quad\quad\quad\quad\quad\quad\quad\quad\quad\quad\quad\quad\quad\quad\quad \text{with } \Sigma = bb^T$
$\quad\quad\quad\quad\quad\quad\quad\quad\quad\quad\quad\quad\quad\quad\quad\quad\quad\quad\quad\quad\quad\quad \downarrow$

(3) Calculate the correlated uniformly distributed variables: $\quad U_i = \Phi(X_i) \quad (9.60)$
$\quad\quad\quad\quad\quad\quad\quad\quad\quad\quad\quad\quad\quad\quad\quad\quad\quad\quad\quad\quad\quad\quad \downarrow$

(4) Calculate the exponential variables: $\quad\quad\quad\quad\quad\quad \omega_i$
$\quad\quad\quad\quad\quad\quad\quad\quad\quad\quad\quad\quad\quad\quad\quad\quad\quad\quad\quad\quad\quad\quad \downarrow$

(5) Calculate the default times: $\quad\quad\quad\quad\quad\quad\quad\quad \tau_i = \frac{\omega_i}{\lambda_i}$
$\quad\quad\quad\quad\quad\quad\quad\quad\quad\quad\quad\quad\quad\quad\quad\quad\quad\quad\quad\quad\quad\quad \downarrow$
$\quad\quad\quad\quad\quad\quad\quad\quad\quad\quad\quad\quad\quad\quad\quad\quad\quad\quad \text{Back to step 1}$

Each of the five steps is repeated n times, generating a set of n vectors containing a simulated default time for each of the d obligors $(\tau_1, \ldots, \tau_d)$.

9.3.8 Case Study: Correlated Defaults

A portfolio manager has invested in three different long-dated high-yield fixed-income securities. The bonds have been issued by corporations active in the same sector and the assumption of default-independence no longer holds. The manager is interested in quantifying the default risk on this small portfolio and wants to calculate the expected number of bonds that will move into default over a time horizon of 5 years. A Poisson process is applied to model the default events. For each of the three companies, the intensity of the Poisson process is:

$$\lambda = [0.15 \quad 0.15 \quad 0.15]$$

In this example a uniform correlation matrix is used. This matrix is based on a single linear correlation coefficient $\rho = 0.7$. All the pairwise asset correlations are hence identical. The covariance matrix Σ is such that $X_i \sim N(0, 1)$:

$$\Sigma = \begin{bmatrix} 1.0 & 0.7 & 0.7 \\ 0.7 & 1.0 & 0.7 \\ 0.7 & 0.7 & 1.0 \end{bmatrix}$$

To keep the example straightforward, we limit ourselves to four Monte Carlo runs only. The 3×4 matrix Z has four columns, where each column deals with one single run for the three obligors in the portfolio:

$$Z = \begin{bmatrix} 0.5377 & 0.8622 & -0.4336 & 2.7694 \\ 1.8339 & 0.3188 & 0.3426 & -1.3499 \\ -2.2588 & -1.3077 & 3.5784 & 3.0349 \end{bmatrix}$$

From the covariance matrix Σ, we can determine the lower-triangular matrix b such that $\Sigma = bb^T$:

$$b = \begin{bmatrix} 1.0000 & 0 & 0 \\ 0.7000 & 0.7141 & 0 \\ 0.7000 & 0.2941 & 0.6508 \end{bmatrix}$$

From the different independent standard normal variables Z, we generate correlated standard normal variables $X = bZ$:

$$X = \begin{bmatrix} 0.5377 & 0.8622 & -0.4336 & 2.7694 \\ 1.6860 & 0.8312 & -0.0588 & 0.9746 \\ -0.5544 & -0.1538 & 2.1260 & 3.5168 \end{bmatrix}$$

This ultimately leads to correlated variables U distributed on the interval [0,1], from which we can derive the default times τ:

$$U = \Phi(X)$$

$$U = \begin{bmatrix} 0.7046 & 0.8057 & 0.3323 & 0.9972 \\ 0.9541 & 0.7971 & 0.4765 & 0.8351 \\ 0.2897 & 0.4389 & 0.9832 & 0.9998 \end{bmatrix}$$

Generating the default times $\tau = -\frac{\log(1-U)}{\lambda}$:

$$\tau = \begin{bmatrix} 8.13 & 10.92 & \mathbf{2.69} & 39.17 \\ 20.54 & 10.63 & \mathbf{4.32} & 12.02 \\ \mathbf{2.28} & \mathbf{3.85} & 27.26 & 56.19 \end{bmatrix} \qquad (9.61)$$

$$\text{Number of defaults before 5 years} = [1.00 \quad 1.00 \quad 2.00 \quad 0.00] \qquad (9.62)$$

Out of the limited number of Monte Carlo runs, we encountered one situation where two issuers defaulted on their debt in the 5-year period ($\tau < 5$) and two cases where there was only one default. In one run only we encountered no default at all during the time horizon. This corresponds to a survival probability equal to 25%. Driving up the number of Monte Carlo runs from 4 to 500 000 gives a more accurate result:

No. Defaults	Correlation ρ		
	0%	70%	Loss
0	10.54%	28.51%	—
1	35.31%	18.48%	100.00
2	39.51%	19.39%	200.00
3	14.64%	33.62%	300.00
Expected Loss ($)	158.25	158.12	
Standard Deviation ($)	86.42	121.90	

The zero-correlation case has a survival probability (0 defaults) over the 5-year horizon equal to 10.54%. This corresponds to the product of the individual survival probabilities. The impact of the correlation is at first sight very obvious. It increases the survival probability because the survival of one company is expected to have a positive effect on the financial health of the other names in the portfolios. This positive effect of an increasing default correlation is offset by a similar observation when all three names in the portfolio meet their fate. The probability of having to deal with a default in every single name in the portfolio also increases with correlation.

Assume that the loss on default is $100 for each of the securities. The expected loss is in both cases equal to $158.25.[4] The standard deviation of these losses is a lot bigger when the correlation is positive. An increase of the default correlation within a credit portfolio has a clear negative impact on the market risk of the portfolio. This is illustrated in Figure 9.8 for a wider range of correlations.

9.3.9   Case Study: Asset Correlation vs. Default Correlation

Using the same data as in the exercise above, we can derive for a particular linear correlation number the actual default correlation observed between the simulated default times. This is illustrated in Figure 9.9, and the result shows how the default correlation is lower than the linear

---

[4] The small difference when $\rho = 70\%$ is driven by the fact that a Monte Carlo simulation was used to estimate the result.

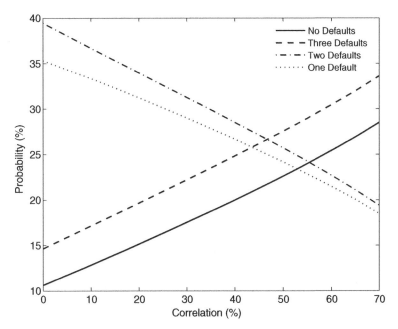

Figure 9.8   Impact of the correlation on the default risk of a portfolio of three bonds.

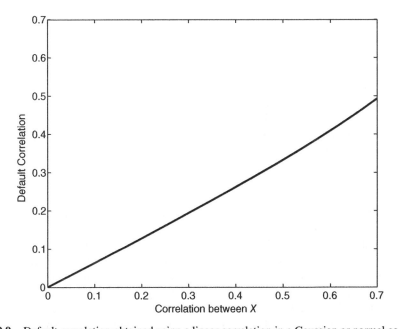

Figure 9.9   Default correlation obtained using a linear correlation in a Gaussian or normal copula.

correlation the Monte Carlo simulation originated from. The correlation between $X_1, \ldots, X_d$ was not preserved when constructing $\tau_1, \ldots, \tau_d$. This is an important remark and one of the reasons practitioners steer away from using Gaussian copulas.

9.4 STRUCTURAL MODELS

Valuation models which are based on observable market prices of corporate bonds, credit default swaps, interest rate swaps, share prices, etc. try to tie the value of a hybrid security to the value of these "vanilla" instruments. Structural or firm-value models step away from this and only model the value of the firm. The hybrid's theoretical value is then derived from its ranking compared with other capital instruments. The value of the firm V_t can be modeled starting from the same geometric Brownian motion given earlier in Equation (7.41):

$$dV_t = \mu V_t dt + \sigma_V V_t dW_t \qquad (9.63)$$

The firm value V_t is also called the asset value of the firm. The equation above assumes we can model the balance sheet of a company through its expected growth rate μ and volatility σ_V. Starting from a model for V, all the other capital instruments can theoretically be derived. In absence of any hybrid securities, the value of a company is equal to the sum of the value of its debt D_t and the book value of its equity E_t:

$$V_t = D_t + E_t \qquad (9.64)$$

In 1974, Robert Merton laid a solid foundation for structural modeling of debt and equity [150]. This early work is based on a company that has issued one single bond expiring at time T and finances the rest of its operations with equity. In this case the value of equity can be seen as the price of a European call option on the assets of this firm. Indeed, at the expiry date of the debt we have the following valuation for the book value:

$$E_T = \max(V_T - DT, 0) \qquad (9.65)$$

The equity holders clearly have economical ownership of the complete pool of assets of the firm after paying back the bond holders. If the asset pool is not large enough ($V_T < D_T$), the equity investors can walk away and leave the firm in the hands of the creditors. If this were to be the case, the equity investors will not exercise the call option which has a strike equal to the face value of the debt D_T. The bond holders are therefore facing a loss L if this happens:

$$L = 1 - \frac{V_T}{D_T} \qquad (9.66)$$

The book value of the equity, the senior bonds, deposits, and contingent convertibles of a financial institution should all add up to V_t. If one could model the stochastic process driving V_t, all these capital instruments building the balance sheet could be derived from it. A structural model takes the interaction between each of these components into account. If, one way or another, the value of the assets suffers a write-down, some of the components of the capital structure will be hit first. Equity investors are, for example, first in line followed by hybrid and subordinated debt. Modeling V_t as a stochastic process is a sophisticated task, since the assets of a company such as a bank are a mixed portfolio of bonds, loans, shares, and many off-balance-sheet components. Some of these instruments might be illiquid, hard to price, or carry extreme tail risk. The firm value V_t is a variable with an unobserved market price and hence the driving parameters of any model are hard to calibrate.

One of the first approaches to valuing convertible bonds after the introduction of the Black–Scholes formula came in 1977 and started from a structural approach. The paper, written by Jonathan Ingersoll [124], was the first application of the Black–Scholes formula on convertible bond pricing. Using a structural model, the theoretical value of callable and non-callable convertible debt has been priced. The same year, Brennan and Schwartz [42] priced a convertible bond P through a similar structural approach. The assets of the underlying company have a market price V_t. The liability side of the balance sheet consists solely of common equity and one convertible bond issue. The face value of the convertible bond is N, there are n_S outstanding shares with market price S, and n_C convertible bonds making up this capital structure. The firm value V_t at time t is therefore equal to:

$$V_t = n_S S_t + n_C P_t \qquad (9.67)$$

Each convertible bond can be converted into C_r shares and therefore will own, after conversion, a fraction χ of the firm:

$$\chi = \frac{C_r}{n_S + C_r n_C} \qquad (9.68)$$

The volatility of the market price of the firm is σ_V. This is the asset volatility and should not be confused with the equity volatility σ_S. The final payoff specifies the value of the convertible P_T at the maturity date $t = T$:

$$P_T = \begin{cases} \chi V_T & V_T > \dfrac{N}{\chi} & [a] \\[2mm] N & n_C N \leq V_T \leq \dfrac{N}{\chi} & [b] \\[2mm] \dfrac{V}{n_C} & V_T < N n_C & [c] \end{cases} \qquad (9.69)$$

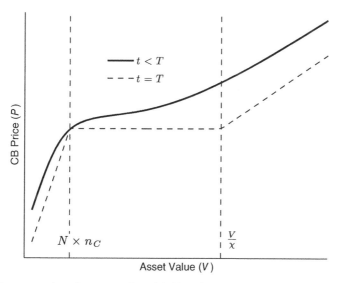

Figure 9.10 Representation of a structural model. The price P_t of a convertible bond for different firm values V is given at the expiration date T and before $(t < T)$.

Equation (9.69) splits up the value of the firm at the expiration date into three different price buckets. In each of these buckets, the bond will expire in a different way: there might be a conversion in shares [a], the investor might receive the face value of the bond [b], or there might be a default situation [c]. This default situation will occur when the value of the firm is smaller than the total face value of the convertible bond, $V_T < N n_C$. With these boundary conditions, the price of the convertible was solved using finite differences. The price graph for the convertible bond using this structural model is given in Figure 9.10. The figure clearly illustrates how the convertible bond price does not converge at all to the bond floor when the company is in distress. One could argue that this brings the structural models closer to reality. For low asset values V, the negative convexity of the convertible bond price is also elegantly captured and confirms what we discussed earlier in Section 2.2.6.

9.5 CONCLUSION

This chapter has provided the main building blocks to move deeper into hybrid territory. We have only covered the elementary stochastic processes and elaborated on the basic numerical techniques one can put to work in solving for the value of a particular hybrid security. This chapter constitutes the beginning of a journey that will take us deeper into the world of hybrid bonds.

Modeling Hybrids: Handling Credit

10.1 CREDIT SPREAD

10.1.1 Definition

A credit spread cs is an add-on to an existing risk-free rate r in order to discount risky cash flows. As such, this spread reflects the market's view on the credit quality of a particular bond. In absence of liquidity risk, the theoretical value at time t of a zero-coupon bond with face value N expiring at time T and using a continuously compounding risk-free interest rate r is:

$$P_t = N \exp(-(r + cs)(T - t)) \tag{10.1}$$

The same bond can have different credit spread definitions. This all depends on the choice of the risk-free reference curve. A corporate bond could yield 100 bps more than the yield offered on Treasury bonds. Using the Libor curve as reference, the spread could, for example, be only 50 bps. In this latter case the risk-free curve is the Libor curve. This spread is then called the Z-spread.[1] The Z-spread of the bond is the difference between the yield to maturity of the bond and the yield interpolated on the swap curve for the same maturity of the bond. The credit spread is an example of how a metric used in fixed-income mathematics fails to be reliable in the space of hybrid bonds.

Hybrid bonds have an embedded optionality, the existence of which questions the applicability of the credit spread to discount the cash flows. In the case of a convertible bond, it is the investor who has the option to convert the bond into shares. For contingent debt, the same investor can be forced to accept delivery of shares. Corporate hybrids, on the contrary, have a maturity that can be extended at the discretion of the issuer. Using a Z-spread in any investment decision involving hybrid bonds is therefore questionable. The Z-spread not only contains the credit risk but also embraces the value of the option. The discrepancies between the Z-spread of corporate bonds and fixed-income instruments with an embedded optionality are laid out in Table 10.1. In the case of a long embedded option, such as in convertible bonds, the Z-spread is lower than the Z-spread of corporate debt from the same issuer with a similar maturity. For short embedded optionality, the Z-spreads are higher. Using the example of the convertible bond issued by Nexans, a French electrical components company, we illustrate how the Z-spread difference is linked to the level of the share price. We define:

$$\Delta Z\text{-spread} = Z\text{-spread}_{\text{Corporate bond}} - Z\text{-spread}_{\text{Convertible bond}} \tag{10.2}$$

The value of the Z-spread depends on the value of the embedded optionality in the convertible bond. For increasing values of the parity of the convertible, the ΔZ-spread picks up in value as well. This is illustrated in Figure 10.1 for the period December 14, 2012 to May 24, 2013. The instrument-specific details of this convertible bond are given in Table 10.2.

---

[1] The Z-spread is often called the "zero volatility" spread, a name which makes perfect sense given the fact that this metric ignores the existence of any embedded option.

Table 10.1   Credit spreads (pricing date: May 24, 2013)

	Z-Spreads					
	Nexans		EDF		Credit Suisse	
	bps	Name	bps	Name	bps	Name
Corporate Bond	**269**	4.25% 2018	**107**	4.6% 2020	**85**	4.375% 2020
Convertible Bond	**174**	2.25% 2019				
Corporate Hybrid			**268**	5.25% Perp.		
CoCo					**482**	7.875% 2041

Source: Bloomberg.

10.1.2   Working with Credit Spreads

It is impossible to eradicate the concept of a credit spread from the calculus of hybrid securities. Market practitioners, while being fully aware of the caveats involved, will rely on a credit spread to discount cash flows from a hybrid bond. From Equation (6.5) we recall that under the risk-neutral measure, the value of a derivative security is the expected value of the discounted payoff. In case of a constant risk-free continuous interest rate r, the value of this security expiring at time T and ignoring any early exercise is:

$$P_t = \exp(-r(T - t))\mathbb{E}_\mathbb{Q}[P_T|\mathcal{F}_t] \tag{10.3}$$

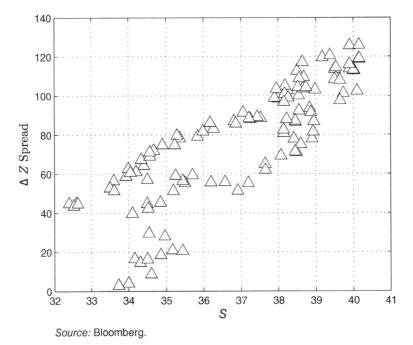

Source: Bloomberg.

Figure 10.1   Difference in the Z-spread between corporate and convertible debt for Nexans.

Table 10.2   Characteristics of the convertible bond issued by NEXANS

NEXANS 2.5% January 1, 2019			
ISIN	FR0011208115	SEDOL	B79TB81
ISSUE DATE	February 2, 2012	ISSUE PRICE	100 EUR
ISSUE SIZE	275 mn	FACE VALUE	72.74
STOCK	NEXANS	MATURITY	January 1, 2019
CONVERSION RATIO	1	CURRENCY	EUR
PUT PRICE	100%	PUT DATE	June 1, 2018
SOFT CALL FROM	January 1, 2016	SOFT CALL TRIGGER	130% (20 out of 40 days)
CALL PRICE (K)	100%		
COUPON	2.5%	COUPON FREQUENCY	ANNUAL

Source: Prospectus.

In a risk-neutral world and using a geometric Brownian motion, the share price process is governed by the following equation:

$$dS_t = (r - q)S_t dt + S_t \sigma_S dW_t \tag{10.4}$$

The credit spread cs is completely absent from the equation above. The share price is therefore said to **grow risk free**. To value the cash flows contingent on this share price process, the credit spread appears. In practice, Equation (10.3) is often modified to facilitate the use of this credit spread cs to calculate P_t:

$$P_t = \exp(-(r + cs)(T - t))\mathbb{E}_\mathbb{Q}[P_T | \mathcal{F}_t] \tag{10.5}$$

This equation is applied when rolling back through the different nodes on the trinomial tree. Different alternatives for the discount rate r_d are possible:

- **Discount risky:** $cs > 0$
  All the cash flows are discounted at the risky rate: $r_d = r + cs$.
- **Discount risk free:** $cs = 0$
  One could argue that the expected cash flows of a deep-in-the-money convertible bond need to be discounted at the risk-free rate r. The probability of converting the bond is high and the investor will likely receive shares. Shares can be hedged through a short position. This delta hedge turns the expected cash flow into a riskless asset which can be discounted at the risk-free rate. Hence the logical choice to impose is that cs is set equal to zero when rolling back through the nodes of the trinomial tree. In this case, $r_d = r$.
- **Discount blended:** $cs = f(\Delta)$
  Some of the nodes in the trinomial tree correspond to a situation where the convertible is almost like a corporate bond. There is no chance at all that there will be a forced or optional conversion. The convertible is close to being a corporate bond. Since in this case a convertible is a pure debt instrument, its value can be discounted using the credit spread cs which is added at the risk-free rate r. The other extreme situation corresponds to those nodes where a conversion is almost certain. In this particular case $\Delta_\% \approx 100\%$ and these cash flows can be discounted at the risk-free rate r. In [15] the authors propose adjusting the discount factor dynamically within the lattice structure. In this method, a distinction is made between the different nodes on the convertible tree using the conversion probability

(p_{conv}). With the same line of thought, we can define the discount rate r_d at each node of the tree as:

$$r_d = \Delta_\% \times r + (1 - \Delta_\%) \times (r + cs)$$
$$\Delta_\% \in [0, 1]$$

(10.6)

10.1.3 Option-Adjusted Spread

The calculation of the Z-spread is straightforward, since it does not involve any model for the embedded option. From the perspective of an investor relying on the concept of a Z-spread, the hybrid security is reduced to a stream of cash flows. Any optionality – such as a maturity extension, mandatory conversion, resets, etc. – is totally ignored.

A widely used alternative credit spread metric is the option-adjusted spread (OAS). This is the spread that has to be added to the interest rate r such that the theoretical price of the hybrid P_t matches its market price. The instrument is priced using a derivative model which properly captures the risk of the instrument. As an example, we cover the convertible bond issued by Nexans early 2012 (Table 10.2). The market price of the bond on May 24, 2013 is equal to €72.70.[2] Plugging a volatility equal to 30% into the model, assuming no dividends, and using a risk-free interest rate r equal to 0.45%, the OAS is equal to 263 bps. The impact of the OAS on the theoretical price of the convertible bond is illustrated in Figure 10.2. The fact that the OAS takes any embedded optionality into account makes it a better credit risk metric than, for example, the Z-spread.

10.2 DEFAULT INTENSITY

10.2.1 Introduction

The discount rate r_d that has to be plugged into a pricing model is sourced from the market prices of corporate bonds. As shown in [82], there is from a theoretical point of view a clear link between default risk and the level of those credit spreads. This relationship is somewhat obscured because the discount rate r_d derived from corporate bond data incorporates more than just credit risk. In [83], the authors propose the following definition of the discount rate:

$$r_d = r + cs + l$$

(10.7)

Here, l stands for the liquidity premium and covers the liquidity risk. There is no unique satisfactory measure to quantify liquidity risk [151] in order to come up with a proper estimate for l. Market practitioners will most often refer to tightness as a proper liquidity metric. This is measured by the bid–offer spreads in the quotation of the bonds. Other measures such as depth[3] and breadth[4] are alternative metrics used to justify a liquidity premium l when discounting cash flows generated by fixed-income securities.

In Section 7.2.5 we have already offered an introduction to Poisson processes. These stochastic processes are very much suited to deal with events such as default. The intensity

---

[2] The bond is quoted in cash terms and includes the accrued interest (dirty).
[3] The depth of a market refers to the existence of a large set of orders both on the buy and the sell side. It indicates the existence of market participants to take one of the sides of the transaction.
[4] The breadth of a market is related to the volume available on both the bid and the ask side. A corporate bond with a sufficient breadth can absorb large buy or sell orders without having an impact on the price of this bond.

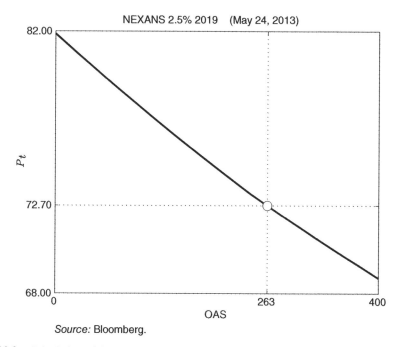

Source: Bloomberg.

Figure 10.2   Calculation of the OAS for the Nexans 2019 convertible bond on May 24, 2013.

λ is a parameter that governs this process and is, in this context, often referred to as default intensity. As such, λ measures the default risk in its purest form. This is an important difference compared with the credit spreads derived from bond data. The values of λ are also derived from market data, most often from credit default swap levels.

Default Intensity Model		Survival Probability
Time Homogeneous	λ constant	$\exp(-\lambda(t-s))$
Time Inhomogeneous	$\lambda(t)$	$\exp(-\int_s^t \lambda(u)du)$
Doubly Stochastic	λ stochastic	$\mathbb{E}_Q[\exp(-\int_s^t \lambda(u)du)]$

In the table above, the calculation of the survival probability p_{surv} for three different default intensity regimes is illustrated. The survival probability is the probability of the bond avoiding default between time s and t $(s < t)$ conditional on the fact that the bond survived up till time s. From the table above it is clear that there is an outspoken analogy between the default intensity λ and the interest rate r. The survival probabilities have a lot in common with discount factors. For the time-homogeneous version of the default process, we have:

$$
\begin{array}{ll}
\text{Survival between } s \text{ and } t & \exp(-\lambda(t-s)) \\
\text{Discounting from } t \text{ to } s & \exp(-r(t-s))
\end{array}
\tag{10.8}
$$

The relationship above illustrates the seeming interchangeability of the interest rate r with the default intensity λ [44]. This also holds for doubly stochastic processes. When λ is stochastic, the probability of survival between now ($t = 0$) and t is given by:

$$p_{surv} = \mathbb{E}_{\mathbb{Q}} \left[\exp \left(- \int_0^t \lambda(u) du \right) \right] \tag{10.9}$$

In practice, both interest rates and default risk are combined together when discounting cash flows distributed by fixed-income securities. These cash flows are considered risky because the issuer can default. When the short interest rate r is stochastic, the risk-free discount factor $D(0, t)$, which gives us the current price of \$1 paid at time t in absence of any default, is:

$$D(0, t) = \mathbb{E}_{\mathbb{Q}} \left(\exp \left(- \int_0^t r(u) du \right) \right) \tag{10.10}$$

The risky discount factor $\overline{D}(0, t)$ is different since there is a chance that default occurs. If a default were to occur which leaves no recovery value for the bond holder, we have that $\pi_{Bond} = 0$. With such a recovery rate, the risky discount factor is given by:

$$\overline{D}(0, t) = \mathbb{E}_{\mathbb{Q}} \left[\exp \left(- \int_0^t (r(u) + \lambda(u)) du \right) \right] \tag{10.11}$$

The formula above is very general and it takes the stochastic process of both r and λ into account. Any correlation between the interest rate and the default intensity will impact the value of $\overline{D}(0, t)$. In practice, one often assumes independence between the two parameters, which simplifies Equation (10.11):

$$\begin{aligned}
\overline{D}(0, t) &= \mathbb{E}_{\mathbb{Q}} \left[\exp \left(- \int_0^t (r(u) + \lambda(u)) du \right) \right] \\
&= \mathbb{E}_{\mathbb{Q}} \left[\exp \left(- \int_0^t r(u) du \right) \right] \mathbb{E}_{\mathbb{Q}} \left[\exp \left(- \int_0^t \lambda(u) du \right) \right] \\
&= D(0, t) \times p_{surv}
\end{aligned} \tag{10.12}$$

The calculation of the theoretical value of a defaultable cash flow is straightforward when assuming that default risk is uncorrelated with changes in the interest rates. The value of a defaultable cash flow is equal to its risk-free value multiplied by the survival probability.

10.3   CREDIT DEFAULT SWAPS

10.3.1   Definition

A hybrid security contains multiple components of risk. Using a theoretical model, it is possible to calculate the sensitivity of such a security toward changes in exchange rates, interest rates, equity prices, etc. The calculation of these "greeks" facilitates an investor hedging the unwanted components away. Credit risk is also eligible to be hedged away. This can be done by making use of the credit default swap market. A CDS trade is the purest form of credit trading. Through the execution of the credit default swap contract, two counterparties trade default risk. One of the counterparties protects the other if the underlying bond or issuer were to default before the maturity of the CDS contract. In this over-the-counter transaction, one of the counterparties is the buyer of protection while the other is the seller.

The buyer of protection pays on a regular (usually quarterly) basis a coupon to the seller. The coupon amount CF depends on the face value N of the contract, the coupon frequency, and the credit default swap rate. We will denote this rate as cr going forward.

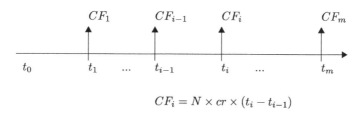

$$CF_i = N \times cr \times (t_i - t_{i-1})$$

The seller, who receives the coupon stream during the life of the contract, is offering insurance. The seller stands by ready to indemnify the buyer if a default event occurs. As soon as the underlying corporate bond, referenced by the CDS, defaults, the buyer will receive a payment from the seller. This payment is based on the loss given default (LGD) and depends on the recovery rate π:

$$LGD = N \times (1 - \pi) \tag{10.13}$$

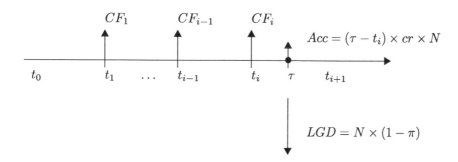

When default occurs at time τ, the scheduled coupon payments are halted immediately. The only residual payment that is still carried out by the buyer of protection to the seller is an accrued amount Acc. This accrued amount is earned by the default seller, because this seller carried default risk from the previous coupon date up till the time of default τ. The accrued amount when default takes place between t_{i-1} and t_i is:

$$Acc_i = (\tau - t_{i-1}) \times cr \times N \tag{10.14}$$

The difference between t_{i-1} and τ is most often measured with a day-count convention of 360 days.[5] The start date t_0 of the credit default swap is called the effective date. From this date onward till the maturity date t_m, the credit protection seller is liable for a default on the underlying bond.

---

[5] A/360 or 30/360.

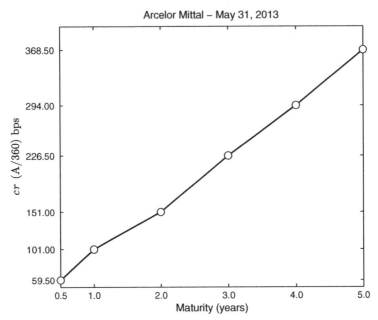

Source: Bloomberg, different market makers.

Figure 10.3   CDS term structure for Arcelor Mittal. Date: March 31, 2013.

10.3.2   Example of a CDS Curve

The credit default swap spreads quoted by the different investment banks for a particular reference bond depend on the maturity of the contract. This brings us to the concept of a CDS term structure when connecting the different quotes of the spreads for the different maturities together. This exercise was carried out on May 31, 2013 for the credit default swaps referencing the senior debt of Arcelor Mittal, an international steel producer. The term structure of this credit default swap curve is represented in Figure 10.3.

10.3.3   Availability of CDS Data

The credit default swap's valuation will depend on the default probability of the issuer referenced by the contract. From the value of the CDS it is therefore possible to calculate the implied default probability for a range of different maturities. Starting from these probabilities, it is possible to derive the value of the default intensity λ or even create a piece wise linear term structure of λ. This calibration exercise forms the perfect scenario to construct a jump-diffusion model where the probability of the jumps is implied from CDS data.

This is a first stumbling block when pricing hybrid securities. It is indeed a disappointing fact that not every hybrid bond comes with an associated CDS curve. More often, there is no credit default data available. Especially when dealing with companies with a small market cap, it will be almost impossible to find a dealer willing to make a market in credit default swaps. One will have to resort to corporate debt data from bonds issued by the same issuer. Credit spreads will be used as intermediary to calculate the implied default probability. This will be explained in Section 10.4.

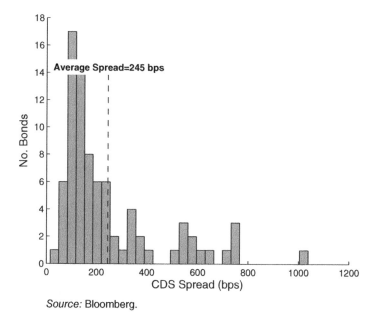

Source: Bloomberg.

Figure 10.4   Average CDS spread of 81 convertible bonds issued in the first quarter of 2013. Date: March 29, 2013.

Figure 10.4 illustrates the distribution of the 5-year CDS spreads (*cr*) for those convertible bonds issued in the first quarter of 2013 where a CDS curve was available. The values of *cr* were taken as of March 29, 2013.

10.3.4   Premium and Credit Leg

The credit default contract is a swap, it involves an exchange of two legs from the buyer to the seller and vice versa. The premium leg involves the regular coupon payments executed by the buyer of the contract. The second leg is the credit leg. The credit leg will only be paid out if default occurs. The two legs are represented in Figure 10.5. From this figure it is clear that the

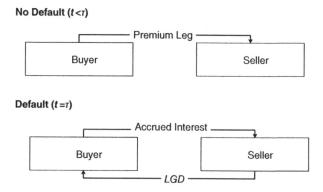

Figure 10.5   Payments involved in a CDS contract before default ($t < \tau$) and at the moment default occurs ($t = \tau$).

value of the credit default swap on the pricing date t depends on the value of the credit and the premium leg:

$$P_{cds,t} = \text{Value of CDS contract}_t = \text{Credit Leg}_t - \text{Premium Leg}_t \qquad (10.15)$$

From the statement above it is clear that after the start of the contract, the value of the CDS will depend very much on changes in the default probability. The more that a default is considered imminent, the higher the value of the contract from the perspective of the protection buyer. The likelihood of the payment of the LGD amount increases, as well as the probability that the coupon stream will be stopped. A long position in a credit default swap is considered a short credit position since it is equivalent to a short position in the underlying bond.

10.3.5 Valuation

Introduction

The structure of a vanilla credit default swap is specified by a set of parameters. A default swap starting at the effective date t_0, expiring at a maturity date t_m, distributing a quarterly coupon CF based on a CDS rate cr and a face value N is denoted CDS (t_0, t_m, cr, N). Its value $P_{cds,t}$ is driven by the structure of the default swap. Moreover, it also depends on the recovery rate π of the reference bond, the default intensity λ, the interest rate r, and the pricing date t. This can be summarized as:

$$P_{cds,t} = f_{cds}(t_0, t_m, cr, N, t, \lambda, \pi, r) \qquad (10.16)$$

Two different valuation models $f_{cds}(\ldots)$ for credit default swaps will be worked out. We start with a closed-form formula approach but also model a default swap on a trinomial tree. At the inception of the CDS, both premium and credit legs are equal in value. The value of the coupons paid by the protection buyer matches the value of the credit leg. When valuing the CDS at its inception, the pricing date is equal to the effective date $(t = t_0)$:

$$P_{cds,t_0} = 0 \quad \Longleftrightarrow \quad \text{Credit Leg}_{t_0} = \text{Premium Leg}_{t_0} \qquad (10.17)$$

Once the terms and conditions of the contract between both parties to the credit default swap have been agreed, its value $P_{cds,t}$ is driven by the random variable λ and the passage of time. Both the premium and the credit leg are impacted by these parameters. As the remaining maturity $|\,t_m - t\,|$ shrinks, the value of the premium leg decreases. The credit leg also becomes less valuable since the default probability erodes with the passage of time. Using a constant default intensity λ, we have indeed:

$$Prob(t < \tau \leq t_m) = 1 - \exp(-\lambda(t_m - t)) \qquad (10.18)$$

With a fixed recovery rate, the default intensity is the only random element in $P_{cds,t}$. An increase in λ makes the credit leg more valuable and decreases the value of the premium leg. The buyer of protection makes a profit and will receive a cash payment when closing out the transaction because $P_{cds,t} > 0$.

Having a valuation model $f_{cds}(\ldots)$ for credit default swaps will allow us to determine the value of λ. From the quoted credit default swap spreads cr, the valuation model will allow us to find λ such that $P_{cds,t_0} = 0$.

There is a lot of similarity with, for example, equity options. From the market prices of options, traders will calculate for each strike and maturity the corresponding implied volatility. This eventually results in a volatility surface. When quoting a price for an equity option, a market maker is implicitly making a two-way price in volatility. The same holds for a trader on a credit derivatives desk. While quoting a spread cr for a default swap for a particular underlying reference bond, a trader is actually giving a view on the default intensity λ.

Closed-Form Formula

The value of the CDS at time t can be calculated as the difference in value of the two sides of the swap. The calculation takes place from the viewpoint of the buyer: the premium leg is a cash outflow while the credit leg represents a cash inflow:

$$P_{cds,t} = \text{Credit Leg}_t - \text{Premium Leg}_t \tag{10.19}$$

In the following equations – in order to keep the algebra short – we opted for a constant value of λ and a pricing date t equal to the effective date t_0 of the contract.

Premium Leg

$$\text{Premium Leg}_t = \sum_{i=1}^{m} CF_i \times p_{surv,i} \times DF_i$$

with

$$\begin{aligned}
p_{surv,i} &= \exp(-\lambda(t_i - t)) \\
DF_i &= \exp(-r(t_i - t)) \\
CF_i &= N \times cr \times (t_i - t_{i-1}) \\
\Delta t_i &= (t_i - t_{i-1})
\end{aligned} \tag{10.20}$$

We obtain the following expression for the theoretical value of the premium leg:

$$\textbf{Premium Leg}_t = cr \times N \sum_{i=1}^{m} \Delta t_i \exp(-(r + \lambda)(t_i - t)) \tag{10.21}$$

Credit Leg

The value of the premium leg was priced in Equation (10.21) as the present value of a stream of risky cash flows. For the credit leg the approach will be different. Suppose default takes place between coupon dates t_{i-1} and t_i. We then have for the default time τ:

$$t_{i-1} < \tau \leq t_i \tag{10.22}$$

In this case there are two different cash flows. One cash flow is received by the buyer of the credit default swap. The second cash flow is paid by the protection buyer and stands for the accrued interest between the previous coupon date t_{i-1} and τ:

$$t_{i-1} < \tau \le t_i \begin{cases} \text{Buyer Receives } LGD \\ LGD = N(1 - \pi) \\[6pt] \text{Buyer Pays Accrued} \\ Acc = (\tau - t_{i-1}) \times cr \times N \\[6pt] \Rightarrow \text{Net Cash Flow Credit Leg} \\ = N(1 - \pi) - (\tau - t_{i-1}) \times cr \times N \end{cases} \qquad (10.23)$$

At this point we have to introduce two simplifications to get to a closed-form formula:

- We assume that the payout of the credit leg always takes place at a coupon date. So, if $\tau \in [t_{i-1}, t_i]$, the credit leg will be paid at t_i.
- We assume that if default takes place in the interval $[t_{i-1}, t_i]$, this will occur exactly halfway between the two coupon dates. Hence, we can write the net cash flow of the CDS if default occurs between t_{i-1} and t_i as:

$$\text{Net Cash Flow Credit Leg} = N(1 - \pi) - \frac{t_i - t_{i-1}}{2} \times cr \times N \qquad (10.24)$$

The probability that default takes place between t_{i-1} and t_i equals $p_{surv,i-1} - p_{surv,i}$. Hence, we have:

$$Prob(t_{i-1} < \tau \le t_i) = \exp(-\lambda t_{i-1}) - \exp(-\lambda t_i) \qquad (10.25)$$

The cash flows and their respective probabilities are summarized in the following table:

Default Time	Probability	Loss Given Default	Accrued Interest
$t = t_0 < \tau \le t_1$	$\exp(-\lambda t_0) - \exp(-\lambda t_1)$	$N(1 - \pi)$	$cr \frac{t_1 - t_0}{2} N$
$\vdots$		$\vdots$	
$t_{i-1} < \tau \le t_i$	$\exp(-\lambda t_{i-1}) - \exp(-\lambda t_i)$	$N(1 - \pi)$	$cr \frac{t_i - t_{i-1}}{2} N$
$\vdots$		$\vdots$	
$t_{m-1} < \tau \le t_m$	$\exp(-\lambda t_{m-1}) - \exp(-\lambda t_m)$	$N(1 - \pi)$	$cr \frac{t_m - t_{m-1}}{2} N$

$$(10.26)$$

Taking the different probabilities with which each of these cash flows can occur, we calculate the present value:

$$\textbf{Credit Leg}_t = N \sum_{i=1}^{m} \left(\exp(-\lambda t_{i-1}) - \exp(-\lambda t_i) \right) \left((1 - \pi) - cr \frac{t_i - t_{i-1}}{2} \right) \exp(-r(t_i - t))$$

$$(10.27)$$

The value of a credit default swap CDS (t_0, t_m, cr, N) is now fully determined:

$$P_{cds,t} = f_{cds}(t_0, t_m, cr, N, t, \lambda, \pi, r) = \text{Equation (10.27)} - \text{Equation (10.21)}$$

Credit Tree

An alternative to the closed-form solution is a lattice model representing the state of the underlying issuer. The life of the underlying bond of the credit default swap contract is cut up into different time steps. Each time step j corresponds to a node where the value of the CDS is $P_{cds,j}$. The difference (in years) between node j and the subsequent node $j + 1$ is Δt.

The node jumps to a default layer in the next time slice with probability $p_{def,j} = 1 - \exp(-\lambda\Delta t)$ and survives with probability $p_{surv,j} = \exp(-\lambda\Delta t)$.

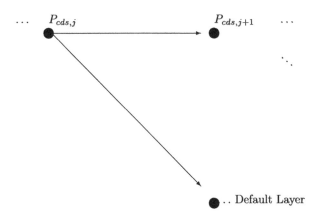

Contrary to the closed-form solution, we do not need to make any assumption at all as to where in between two coupon dates the bond can go into default. In the lattice model, the issuer is allowed to go bankrupt at any point in time between the effective date t_0 and the maturity date t_m of the credit default swap contract. In case of a default, the buyer of protection will receive a cash flow equal to $(1 - \pi) \times N$ from which the accrued interest Acc_j needs to be subtracted. The value of the CDS at node j is hence:

$$P_{cds,j} = \exp(-r\Delta t)\left(p_{surv,j} \times P_{cds,j+1} + p_{def,j} \times ((1 - \pi)N - Acc_j)\right)$$
$$= \exp(-r\Delta t)\left(\exp(-\lambda\Delta t)P_{cds,j+1} + (1 - \exp(-\lambda\Delta t))((1 - \pi)N - Acc_j)\right) \tag{10.28}$$

While rolling back from node j to node $j - 1$, the node values $P_{cds,j}$ need to be adjusted for coupon payments on the default swap. Eventually, after moving back across the n steps of the tree, we arrive at the value of the default swap on the pricing date $p_{cds,t}$.

10.3.6   Rule of Thumb

When imposing two extra assumptions, it is possible to develop a straightforward rule of thumb to derive λ from cr and π or vice versa. This back-of-the-envelope calculation is founded on the assumption that we can ignore the accrued interest payments Acc that are due when default takes place. In addition, one also considers the length of time between two coupon payments (Δt) to be constant. Doing so, both the premium and the credit leg are simplified:

$$\text{Premium Leg}_t \approx cr \times N \sum_{i=1}^{m} \Delta t \exp(-(r+\lambda)(t_i - t))$$

$$\text{Credit Leg}_t \approx N \sum_{i=1}^{m} \left(\exp(-\lambda t_{i-1}) - \exp(-\lambda t_i)\right)(1-\pi)\exp(-r(t_i - t)) \tag{10.29}$$

At inception, both legs of the default swap are equal in value. Hence, we can calculate the value of cr as a function of the default intensity λ and the recovery rate π:

$$cr \approx \frac{\sum_{i=1}^{m} \left(\exp(-\lambda t_{i-1}) - \exp(-\lambda t_i)\right)(1-\pi)\exp(-r(t_i - t))}{\sum_{i=1}^{m} \Delta t \exp(-(r+\lambda)(t_i - t))} \tag{10.30}$$

At the inception date $t = 0$ we can use the following simplification:

$$\exp(-\lambda t_{i-1}) - \exp(-\lambda t_i) \approx \lambda \Delta t \exp(-\lambda t_i) \tag{10.31}$$

Hence:

$$cr \approx (1-\pi)\lambda \tag{10.32}$$

Equation (10.32) offers the possibility to move directly from a CDS curve to a default probability. Imagine, for example, a credit default swap spread of 400 bps for a 5-year bond with an associated recovery value of 30%. We will have in this case that:

$$\lambda = \frac{cr}{1-\pi} = 0.04/0.7 = 5.71\% \tag{10.33}$$

The implied 5-year default probability p_{def} from this market quote is:

$$p_{def} = 1 - \exp(-\lambda \times 5) = 24.87\% \tag{10.34}$$

10.3.7 Market Convention

A purchaser of protection has bought from counterparty A a credit default swap on a reference bond with a spread cr_A. At inception of this deal the value of the CDS is zero given the fact that the premium leg is equal to the credit leg. Imagine that the credit quality of the underlying bonds weakens. This could tempt the holder of the CDS to close out the transaction and take a profit. The holder of the CDS can go to the counterparty A and ask to unwind the swap and cash out the profit on the deal. In practice, the investor will search for that counterparty bidding the most to buy protection. Doing so, the investor ends up selling protection to counterparty B while still holding on to the original protection purchased from counterparty A. The CDS with counterparty B immunizes the original deal with A:

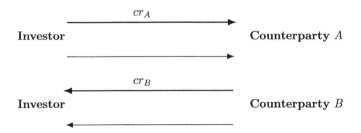

Both credit legs cancel each other out, which leaves the investor with a profit equal to a risky cash flow that depends on the difference between the level where the protection was sold and bought: $cr_B - cr_A$. This profit is far from being realized since it is subject to counterparty risk. The only way for the investor to generate a proper unwinding of the transaction is when both counterparties A and B decide to face each other in a new transaction where A is selling protection to B on the same reference bond. The investor can walk away and realize the profit.

The CDS market has experienced phenomenal growth, which has attracted the interest of many investors. As of December 31, 2011, the gross notional amount of all CDS contracts outstanding was \$25.9 tn [126]. The net amount is much less and was equal to \$2.7 tn. The mechanics behind a credit default swap were such that the closing out of a transaction was prone to operational risk and left a web of counterparty risk in the financial system. In 2009 the ISDA[6] imposed some important changes in the way default swaps are traded. Contracts now trade with fixed standardized spreads. For a CDS on a North American corporate bond, for example, the coupon is now 100 or 500 bps. The recovery rate is 40% and 20% for, respectively, senior and subordinated debt. The effective dates have also been fixed: March 20, June 20, September 20, and December 20 for any given year. These dates now correspond to the coupon dates. As such, this does not change the valuation of the CDS worked out above. The only consequence is that at the trade date, $P_{cds,t} \neq 0$. Logically, there is now a cash flow between the buyer and the seller. This cash flow is called the upfront amount.[7]

10.3.8   Case Study: Implied Default Probability

On December 20, 2013 (t_0) a portfolio manager enters into a default swap transaction with an investment bank. The investor buys protection from the effective date till the maturity date of March 20, 2015 (t_m). The CDS quotes a premium (cr) equal to 500 bps (30/360). The bond is very subordinated and has an expected recovery rate of only 20%. The continuous interest rate r is equal to 1%. **What is the implied default intensity** (λ)? Using Equation (10.32), we find that a good approximation for λ is given by:

$$\lambda = \frac{cr}{1 - \pi} = 0.05/0.8 = 6.25\% \tag{10.35}$$

Closed-Form Solution

If we have to find the exact value, we need an iterative process with a certain start value. Next we take, for example, $\lambda = 5\%$ as the starting value in the iterative calibration to find the value

---

[6] International Swaps and Derivatives Association.
[7] The ISDA offers on its website a set of tools to calculate these upfront premiums starting from a sample CDS curve.

of λ. The correct value of λ is such that $P_{cds,t_0} = 0$. The value P_{cds,t_0} will be calculated using the closed-form solution.

The following table illustrates the different cash flows (CF_i) of the premium leg on the dates t_i at which these coupons are being paid out. The nominal value of the CDS, N, is set equal to 100. For each of the coupon dates the survival probability $p_{surv,i}$ and the discount factor DF_i have been calculated as well. The premium leg is the sum of the discounted cash flows CF_i taking the respective survival probabilities into account, as worked out in Equation (10.21).

	Date	CF	p_{surv}	DF_i	Present Value
$t_0 = t$	20-Dec-13		1.0000		
t_1	20-Mar-14	1.25	0.9877	0.9975	1.2315
t_2	20-Jun-14	1.25	0.9754	0.9950	1.2132
t_3	20-Sep-14	1.25	0.9632	0.9925	1.1950
t_4	20-Dec-14	1.25	0.9512	0.9900	1.1771
t_5	20-Mar-15	1.25	0.9396	0.9876	1.1599
				Premium Leg	**5.9767**

The credit leg contains the amount (LGD) paid by the protection seller if a default has taken place. This is given by:

$$LGD = N \times (1 - \pi) = 100 \times (1 - 0.2) = 80 \tag{10.36}$$

The buyer of protection still owes the seller an accrued interest Acc_i when default takes place between t_{i-1} and t_i. The closed-form formula is based on the assumption that default takes place right in the middle of two consecutive coupon dates. We hence obtain:

$$Acc_i = \frac{CF_i}{2} = 0.625 \tag{10.37}$$

The credit leg is equal to 4.7587:

	Date	Acc_i	LGD	p_{def}	DF_i	Present Value
$t_0 = t$	20-Dec-13					
t_1	20-Mar-14	0.625	80	0.0123	0.9975	0.9739
t_2	20-Jun-14	0.625	80	0.0123	0.9950	0.9714
t_3	20-Sep-14	0.625	80	0.0122	0.9925	0.9611
t_4	20-Dec-14	0.625	80	0.0120	0.9900	0.9430
t_5	20-Mar-15	0.625	80	0.0116	0.9876	0.9093
					Credit Leg	**4.7587**

Since each of the legs of the swap is now known, we can calculate the value of the CDS:

$$P_{cds,t} = \text{Credit Leg}_t - \text{Premium Leg}_t$$
$$= 4.7587 - 5.9767 \tag{10.38}$$
$$= -1.2180$$

Since $P_{cds,t} < 0$, the theoretical value of the credit leg is too low given a coupon cr equal to 500 bps. The correct implied value of λ therefore has to be higher. The interpolation to find λ

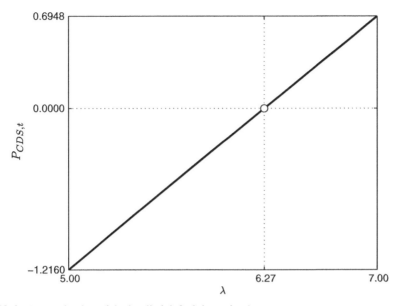

Figure 10.6   Determination of the implied default intensity λ.

is given in Figure 10.6. The correct value for λ is 6.27%, a result which is very close compared with the value obtained using the rule of thumb.

Solution on Credit Tree

The same numerical example is now worked out on a credit tree. In Figure 10.7 the convergence of the theoretical price $P_{cds,t}$ is illustrated. The same graph compares the closed-form solution with the value obtained through the lattice model. Both methods generate results that are very close. The value difference in the upfront premium for the CDS when λ is equal to 5% is 1 cent.

10.4   CREDIT TRIANGLE

10.4.1   Definition

The credit default swap market is our main source of values for the default intensity λ to plug into a jump-diffusion model. Accordingly, the corporate bond market can also be a reliable source to understand the credit risk of a particular issuer. As long as the corporate bond is liquid and does not contain any embedded option, the value of its credit spread is an adequate measure of the level of default risk.

Starting from the value of a credit spread cs, the theoretical value P_t of a zero-coupon bond paying out \$1 at time T is:

$$P_t = \exp(-(r + cs)\Delta t) \tag{10.39}$$

with $\Delta t = T - t$.

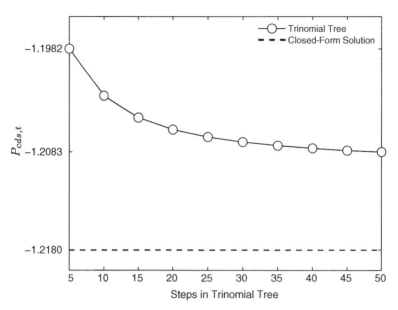

Figure 10.7   Value $P_{cds,t}$ for the default swap calculated for a different number of steps on a credit tree ($\lambda = 5\%$).

Starting from the default intensity λ of the issuer of the bond and its recovery rate π_{Bond}, we know that its theoretical value is equal to:

$$P_t = \left(\text{Probability Default} \times \pi_{Bond} + \text{Probability Survival}\right)\exp(-r\Delta t)$$
$$= \left((1 - \exp(\lambda\Delta t))\pi_{Bond} + \exp(-\lambda\Delta t)\right)\exp(-r\Delta t) \tag{10.40}$$

Substituting Equation (10.39) into Equation (10.40) and considering sufficiently small values for λ, Δt, and r such that $1 - r\Delta t \approx \exp(-r\Delta t)$, we obtain that:

$$cs = \lambda(1 - \pi_{Bond}) \tag{10.41}$$

This latter equation is better known as the credit triangle. This equation is a popular rule of thumb to move from the credit spread cs and recovery rate π_{Bond} of a bond to a value for λ. It is the equivalent in the corporate bond world of the rule of thumb for credit default swaps explained in Equation (10.32).

10.4.2   Case Study

Starting from the market price of a real-world corporate bond, we will derive the necessary data to calculate the default probability of the issuing company. For this purpose, a corporate bond issued in 2011 by Renault, the French car manufacturer, was taken. The market price of the bond on May 29, 2013 is equal to 106.75. On this date we calculate the default probability of the bond over the next year. The assumed recovery rate π_{Bond} is equal to 40%. A summary of the characteristics of the bond is given in Table 10.3.

Table 10.3   Characteristics of the corporate bond issued by Renault

RENAULT 4.625% May 25, 2016			
ISIN	FR001052117	CURRENCY	EUR
ISSUE DATE	May 25, 2011	ISSUE PRICE	100
ISSUE SIZE	750 mn	FACE VALUE	1000
ISSUER	RENAULT	MATURITY	May 25, 2016
COUPON	4.625%	COUPON FREQUENCY	ANNUAL

Source: Prospectus.

Z-spread and the Coupon Stream

As credit spread *cs* we take the Z-spread, which we consider on the pricing date equal to 150 bps. The cash flows generated by the bond are given in the table below, together with the matching payment dates. Using the corresponding (continuous) interest rate *r* for each of the coupon dates and a Z-spread of 150 bps, the sum of the discounted values corresponds to a theoretical price of 107.25:

cs	150 bps					
Pricing Date	May 29, 2013					
Date	**Coupon**	**Face Value**	*r*	**Discount Factor**		**Present Value**
May 25, 2014	46.25		0.30%	0.9824		45.43
May 25, 2015	46.25		0.41%	0.9627		44.53
May 25, 2016	46.25	1000.00	0.56%	0.9402		983.73
				Dirty Price		1073.69
				Accrued		9 (days)
				Accrued Interest		1.14
				Clean Price		1072.55
				Theoretical Price		**107.25**

Determining the Credit Spread

Starting from a credit spread equal to 150 bps, the corresponding theoretical price of the bond is equal to 107.25. Since the bond trades at a lower price, the credit spread will have to be higher than 150 bps. In Figure 10.8 the theoretical price of the corporate bond P_t has been calculated for a wide range of credit spreads: $cs \in [50, 300]$. Through interpolation we find that a credit spread of 168 bps corresponds to a match between P_t and the market price of the corporate bond. This implied credit spread is now our starting point to calculate the 1-year default probability.

Default Probability

To move from the level of the credit spread toward a default intensity, the credit triangle of Equation (10.41) will be applied:

$$\lambda = \frac{cs}{1 - \pi_{Bond}} = \frac{168 \text{ bps}}{1 - 0.4} = 2.8\% \qquad (10.42)$$

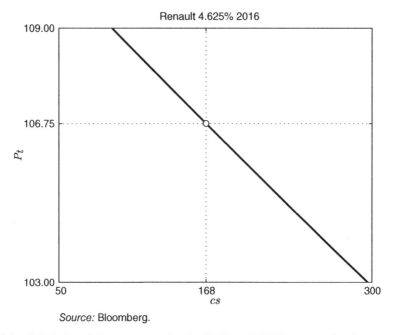

Source: Bloomberg.

Figure 10.8   Calculation of the credit spread cs for the Renault 2016 corporate bond corresponding to a market price equal to 106.75. Date: May 29, 2013.

The market-implied default probability that the corporate bond defaults during the next year can be calculated:

$$p_{def} = 1 - \exp(-\lambda \Delta T) = 1 - \exp(-0.028) = 2.76\% \qquad (10.43)$$

CDS Bond Basis

Starting from the market price of a corporate bond and going through a sequence of calculations, the default intensity can be deducted from this particular price level. A shorter route is, however, offered by the credit default swap market. Here the CDS spread offers a straightforward possibility to calculate default risk. The 3-year CDS rate to buy insurance on this corporate bond issued by Renault was, on May 29, 2013, equal to 127 bps. At first sight a trader could interpret the difference between the CDS rate ($cr = 127$ bps) and the Z-spread (168 bps) as an arbitrage opportunity. In this particular case, the bond is said to trade on a negative basis:

$$\text{CDS Bond Basis} = \text{CDS Spread} - Z\text{-spread} = -41 \text{ bps} < 0 \qquad (10.44)$$

Insuring an investment in the corporate bond and hedging this investment through the purchase of a credit default swap on this security turns the Renault bond into a risk-free security. This leaves the investor with a 41 bps annual coupon on top of the risk-free interest rate. This theoretical arbitrage contains a number of flaws. An obvious caveat in this reasoning is, for example, the fact that the Z-spread of the bond contains both credit risk and liquidity risk. The credit default swap may have hedged the credit risk of the bond, but any liquidity problem

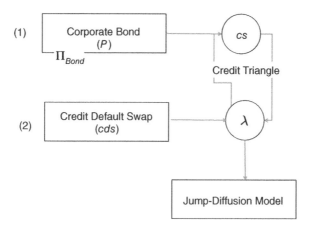

Figure 10.9 Two different ways to calibrate the jump component of a jump-diffusion process to market data.

remains unsolved. Moreover, the hedged position is not risk free since the investor now runs counterparty risk on the purchased credit default swap.

There are fundamental and sometimes instrument-specific reasons to explain the existence of such a negative basis. The structuring desk of an investment bank could, for example, be involved in the launch of a new synthetic CDO on a basket of corporate debt. This would drive down the spreads on credit default swaps of all the components of this basket. The basis could become positive when all the market participants seek to hedge the credit risk of a particular issuer. In this case the CDS spread moves up fast and the basis becomes positive. We refer the reader to [74] for an extensive analysis on the factors driving this CDS bond basis.

10.4.3 The Big Picture

A jump-diffusion model to price, for example, convertible or contingent debt has two input parameters: λ and σ_{JD}. The first parameter models the jumps while the latter parameter stands for the volatility of the share price. As seen before in this chapter, there are two different ways to determine the first input parameter: either through the price of a corporate bond or alternatively using credit default swap data. Figure 10.9 is a schematic overview of the two different approaches and how they interact with each other.

1. Starting from the value of a corporate bond, the value of the credit spread cs is obtained. Subsequently, and after applying the credit triangle, a value for λ can be plugged into the jump-diffusion model. This is the approach followed in the case study of Section 10.4.2.
2. Plugging the credit default swap spread cr into a valuation model for credit default swaps, one can find the implied value for the default intensity such that the credit leg equals the premium leg of the credit default swap.

10.5 STOCHASTIC CREDIT

Stochastic intensity is often modeled as a Cox process. Again this illustrates how concepts of interest rate dynamics are copied into the world of default risk [62]. The Cox process,

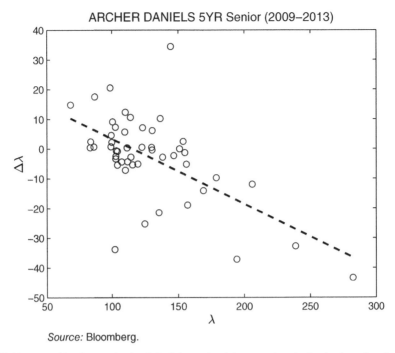

Source: Bloomberg.

Figure 10.10   Monthly changes in the default intensity $\Delta\lambda$ versus λ at the beginning of each month for Archer Daniels. Period: 2009–2012.

with original roots in interest rate modeling, was adapted to a stochastic process for default intensity:

$$d\lambda_t = \kappa(\eta - \lambda_t)dt + \zeta_\lambda\sqrt{\lambda_t}dW_t \qquad (10.45)$$

The stochastic differential equation above models the default intensity as a mean-reverting process. This means that the values of λ fluctuate around a long-term average η. The default intensity will converge back in the direction of η with a positive drift when $\lambda_t < \eta$ and a negative drift in the opposite case. The size of the random shocks is controlled by the parameter ζ_λ.

The variance of λ observed over a time interval $[s, t]$, starting at time s, is not proportional to the length of this interval. This is the most obvious difference compared with, for example, a geometric Brownian motion where the variance increases with time. The change in λ over the interval $|t - s|$ can be linked to the initial value λ_s:

$$\Delta\lambda = \lambda_t - \lambda_s = a + b\lambda_s + \epsilon_t \qquad (10.46)$$

where ϵ_t stands for the error term.

The parameters a and b are estimated using ordinary least squares. A regression coefficient $b < 0$ points to a mean-reverting property.[8] In Figure 10.10 the mean-reverting property of the monthly changes in the default intensity of Archer Daniels, a company with outstanding convertible debt, has been studied. The values of λ were obtained from 5-year credit default

---

[8] In econometrics, the hypothesis of mean reversion is verified through the augmented Dickey–Fuller test [103].

swaps on senior bonds. The monthly changes in λ were then regressed against the value of λ_s at the beginning of each month. The obtained results illustrate the mean-reverting property of the default intensity of this particular issuer.

When dealing with options on credit default swaps, the Black–Scholes method is often applied. In this case the Cox process of Equation (10.45) makes room for a geometric Brownian motion:

$$d\lambda = \lambda \sigma_\lambda dW_t \tag{10.47}$$

The mean-reversion property is lost when assuming, through the acceptance of Equation (10.47), that λ is now lognormally distributed. Starting from this equation, we easily arrive at an elegant closed-form solution to price European options on credit default swaps. In Chapter 12 a similar non-mean-reverting process for λ will be applied when dealing with contingent debt.

Constant Elasticity of Variance

11.1 FROM BLACK–SCHOLES TO CEV

11.1.1 Introduction

In Section 9.2 we left the Black–Scholes trail when introducing the jump-diffusion model. The equity prices became defaultable since a jump to zero was allowed. The probability of such a jump taking place was based on the reduced-form approach such as in [81]. The probability of "jumping" to default is now determined through the default intensity parameter λ. The share price process turns from a geometric Brownian motion into a jump-diffusion process:

$$dS_t = \mu S_t dt + \sigma_{JD} S_t dW_t - S_t dN_t \qquad (11.1)$$

with

$$dN_t = \begin{cases} 1 & \text{with probability } \lambda dt \\ 0 & \text{otherwise} \end{cases}$$

The volatility of the diffusion component of the process described in Equation (11.1) is σ_{JD} and is different from σ_S. The use of this latter volatility is constrained to the geometric Brownian motion.

The jump-diffusion process allows, in sharp contrast with the geometric Brownian motion, the share price level S to collapse. Here, we work with the setting that in case of default, $S_t = 0$. Such a jump to default takes place as soon as $dN_t = 1$ and hence $dS_t = -S_t$.

There are different alternatives allowing us to step away from the Black–Scholes framework. Jump-diffusion is only one of the many possible choices. The most accepted extensions to Black–Scholes are those solutions which allow for a closed-form or semi-closed-form formula for vanilla options. This explains the enthusiasm with which market practitioners embraced the Heston model when trying to incorporate stochastic volatility [118].

Next we will detail a model that is also very useful in the world of hybrid instruments: the constant elasticity of variance model. In Equation (7.38) we already introduced the CEV when studying in detail some Ito processes. The application of CEV-processes in finance was introduced by Cox and Ross [61, 63]. There has been quite some empirical support for the CEV model, for example, in [31] and [162]. The stochastic differential equation describing the share price movements in a risk-neutral world using CEV is:

$$dS_t = (r - q)S_t dt + \sigma_{CEV} S_t^{p_{CEV}} dW_t \qquad (11.2)$$

An obvious difference between CEV and geometric Brownian motion is the presence of two parameters instead of one: σ_{CEV} and p_{CEV}. The latter parameter is the so-called elasticity parameter.[1] In the CEV approach, the variance of the share price is linked to the share price

---

[1] Some alternative CEV representations use an elasticity coefficient $\beta + 1$ instead of p_{CEV}.

level as shown in the equation above. With the elasticity parameter $0 < p_{CEV} < 1$, the volatility will pick up as S decreases. This elasticity of the variance with respect to share price changes is controlled by p_{CEV}. Some special cases are as follows:

- Geometric Brownian motion: $p_{CEV} = 1$
- Square root process: $p_{CEV} = \frac{1}{2}$

In [65], the authors integrated a CEV-based equity process into a model to value hybrid securities. Their implementation also captured the interest rate, credit, and equity risk. The credit events were modeled as jump processes with intensity depending on the level of both equity and interest rates. Constant elasticity of variance was used to model the equity component of the hybrid security. The interest rate dynamics were captured making use of a one-factor HJM[2] model.

In this chapter we introduce the CEV-process and present its applicability to hybrid debt such as contingent convertibles and convertible bonds. In a final step, the calibration process of the CEV model to an existing volatility surface is analyzed in detail using a numerical example. The impact of a CEV-based valuation tool on convertible bonds is illustrated with a mandatory convertible and a convertible bond with a conversion price refix as example. The implementation of the CEV model is restricted here to single-factor processes only. Default intensity and interest rates are considered constant throughout this chapter. Linking the level of default risk to the share price level will be handled subsequently when dealing with contingent debt. An extended multi-factor framework, where both interest rates and default risk are genuine stochastic inputs, is presented in Chapter 13.

11.1.2 Leverage Effect

The business risk of a company is influenced by its financial leverage or the ratio of debt D over equity E.[3] The financial leverage points to the amount of debt a firm has to carry compared with the value of the equity of the firm. From an empirical point of view, the influence of large debt-to-equity ratios on the volatility was revealed in [53] where the stock price variance of a sample of 379 firms was studied. In this research, out of a set of several explanatory variables, the influence of financial leverage on equity volatility stood out. This leverage effect translates into an equity volatility that steps up when the equity value of the firm decreases and impacts the debt-to-equity ratio negatively.

From a theoretical angle, support for the existence of the leverage effect can be found in the structural valuation models. The structural approach to derivatives modeling was covered in Section 9.4. This method has its roots planted in the work of, for example, Robert Merton [150]. Rating agencies and many practitioners construct their view regarding solvency and the likelihood of a possible default using a structural model. In such a model the value of the firm V_t is generally described as a geometric Brownian motion with its own drift μ_V and volatility σ_V:

$$dV_t = \mu_V V_t + \sigma_V V_t dW_t \tag{11.3}$$

---

[2] Heath–Jarrow–Morton.
[3] We deliberately use the symbol E as a notation for the value of equity. This value is the book value while S stands for the market value or the market price of the equity.

Starting from the value D_t of the outstanding amount of debt, the value of the equity E_t can be derived from V_t since $V_t = E_t + D_t$. In a structural model, it can be shown that equity is actually a call on the assets of the firm. This was worked out before in Equation (9.65). The equity volatility σ_E can be derived from the unobservable asset volatility σ_V [97]. To achieve this result, just imagine that the value of the debt D remains unchanged so that $dD = 0$. The only random component left on the balance sheet is the value of the equity E. For the sake of simplicity, we consider the following driftless stochastic process for E driven by a Brownian motion dW_t:

$$dE_t = E_t \sigma_E dW_t \tag{11.4}$$

Hence we can write for the value of the firm:

$$dV_t = V_t \sigma_V dW_t \tag{11.5}$$

Both processes are characterized by their own appropriate volatility but share the same Brownian motion dW_t. The equity volatility σ_E can be considered as an observable parameter, whereas the asset volatility σ_V is unobservable. The asset volatility is the volatility of the company's balance sheet as a whole. A steel company's asset consists, for example, of inventory, machinery, and receivables. Suppose it were technically possible to receive a value for all the constituents of this complex and extended asset pool. Then, under this hypothetical case, it would be possible to calculate σ_V. Indeed, since $V = E + D$, we can write:

$$\frac{dV}{V} = \frac{dE}{E + D} \tag{11.6}$$

Hence:

$$\sigma_V = \sigma_E \frac{1}{1 + D/E}$$

or

$$\sigma_E = \sigma_V(1 + D/E) \tag{11.7}$$

This latter equation gives theoretical support to the fact that the financial leverage $\frac{D}{E}$ drives up the level of the equity volatility σ_E given a constant asset volatility. Further, if E decreases, its volatility σ_E will increase. This property is a valuable argument to start exploring the benefits of introducing the constant elasticity of variance when valuing hybrids.

11.1.3 Link with Black–Scholes

There is a connection between the initial share price variance obtained from both a geometric Brownian motion and a CEV process:

$$\text{Geometric Brownian Motion:} \quad dS_t = S_t(r - q)dt + S_t \sigma_S dW_t$$
$$\text{Constant Elasticity of Variance:} \quad dS_t = S_t(r - q)dt + S_t^{p_{CEV}} \sigma_{CEV} dW_t \tag{11.8}$$

From the two equations above, the Black–Scholes volatility σ_S can be linked to the parameter σ_{CEV}:

$$\sigma_S = \sigma_{CEV} S^{p_{CEV} - 1} \tag{11.9}$$

Hence we can write:

$$\frac{\partial \sigma_S}{\partial S} = (p_{CEV} - 1)\sigma_{CEV} S^{p_{CEV}-2}$$

$$= \frac{p_{CEV} - 1}{S}\sigma_{CEV} S^{p_{CEV}-1} \qquad (11.10)$$

$$= \frac{p_{CEV} - 1}{S}\sigma_S$$

To first order, the relationship between changes in the Black–Scholes volatility $\Delta\sigma_S$ and the share price ΔS when S is modeled as a CEV process is:

$$\frac{\Delta\sigma_S}{\sigma_S} \approx (p_{CEV} - 1)\frac{\Delta S}{S} \qquad (11.11)$$

This equation points out that the elasticity of the variance to share price changes is fully determined by the parameter p_{CEV}:

$$\text{Elasticity} = p_{CEV} - 1 \qquad (11.12)$$

This elasticity ties the changes in the Black–Scholes volatility to share price changes. This relationship is important when modeling skew. The skew obtained when calculating the implied Black–Scholes volatility σ_S from a set of option prices sharing the same maturity but with different strike prices K is:

$$\text{Skew} = \left(\frac{\partial \sigma_{BS}}{\partial K}\right) \qquad (11.13)$$

With $p_{CEV} < 1$, the Black–Scholes volatility increases for decreasing share prices when the underlying follows a CEV process instead of the geometric Brownian motion [41]. This intuitive result is important and will be supported by some numerical examples in Section 11.5.2.

Equation (11.9) is represented graphically in Figure 11.1. Starting from a volatility $\sigma_S = 20\%$ and $\sigma_{CEV} = 3$ for a share price $S = 100$, we can determine the value for the elasticity parameter p_{CEV}:

$$p_{CEV} = \frac{\log\left(\frac{\sigma_S}{\sigma_{CEV}}\right)}{\log(S)} + 1 = 0.4120 \qquad (11.14)$$

Doing so, the initial share price variances for both the geometric Brownian motion and the CEV process starting at the current share price level are identical. The same figure illustrates how the values for the parameter p_{CEV} increase for higher volatility levels σ_S.[4]

11.2 HISTORICAL PARAMETER ESTIMATION

Before one can even consider designing a valuation model to price options, convertible bonds, contingent convertibles, or other hybrid securities based on a CEV approach, one has to address the problem of parameter estimation. There are two parameters at work in any CEV process: σ_{CEV} and p_{CEV}. Both need to be adequately chosen such that the modeled share price corresponds to what has been observed in the past. This is a historical parameter estimation. Starting from a time series of the share price, one determines appropriate estimates for σ_{CEV}

---

[4] Note that σ_{CEV} should not be interpreted as a volatility. Only $\sigma_{CEV} S^{p_{CEV}-1}$ refers to a volatility.

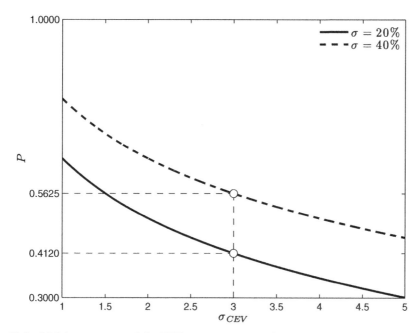

Figure 11.1   Link between σ_S and the CEV paramters σ_{CEV} and p_{CEV}.

and p_{CEV}. A similar approach is traditionally used when estimating values for σ_S to be plugged into a geometric Brownian motion. In this latter case only one parameter needs to be estimated. This is in contrast to the CEV case, where two estimates are involved.

If the share price has listed options, we could attempt a calibration such that the modeled option prices match the corresponding market prices. This is then a risk-neutral calibration. The Black–Scholes volatility surface is then replaced by the two parameters driving the CEV model. Parameters obtained through such a risk-neutral calibration are used to derive derivative prices. With a calibration, one tries to guarantee that the value of a hybrid security priced through, for example, a CEV model is consistent with the market prices for listed options on the same underlying share. The value of a hybrid bond is, as such, implied from options and credit default swap data.

In a first step, we start from the assumption that there is no option data available and that we can only do a historical calibration. The fact that the underlying share has no options outstanding is a situation that a convertible bond analyst will more than often encounter when pricing a new convertible bond. Fortunately there are different methods allowing us to estimate the CEV parameters from historical share price observations.

Historical Parameter Estimation (Beckers)

In [162] an overview was given regarding different estimation techniques for the CEV parameters based on historical share price levels. We start with a method that was worked out by Stan Beckers in [31].

One starts by rewriting Equation (11.9) as:

$$\log(\sigma_S) = \log(\sigma_{CEV}) + (p_{CEV} - 1)\log(S_t) \tag{11.15}$$

For now, our main interest is to estimate the parameter p_{CEV}. This estimation can be obtained when applying ordinary least squares to the following regression:

$$\log(\hat{\sigma}_S) = a + b\log(S_t) \tag{11.16}$$

with $b = p_{CEV} - 1$.

In this regression σ_S has been replaced by its historical estimate $\hat{\sigma}_{S_t}$. Starting from a time series $\{(S_1, \hat{\sigma}_{S_1}), (S_2, \hat{\sigma}_{S_2}), \ldots, (S_t, \hat{\sigma}_{S_t}), \ldots\}$ and determining the coefficient b through, for example, least squares eventually leads to an estimated value for p_{CEV}. This is practically impossible since the corresponding estimated volatility $\hat{\sigma}_{S_t}$ cannot be quantified. Having today's share price value S_t and the value S_{t+1} for the following business day gives only one single log return $\log(S_{t+1}) - \log(S_t)$. This is not enough to calculate $\hat{\sigma}_{S_t}$.

Therefore, the variable $|\log(\frac{S_{t+1}}{S_t})|$ will be used instead of $\hat{\sigma}_{S_t}$. The reason for this switch is based on a property of the normally distributed variable $X \sim N(\mu, \sigma^2)$. For small values of μ, we have:

$$\mathbb{E}[|X|] \approx \sigma\sqrt{\frac{2}{\pi}} \tag{11.17}$$

If $\log(\frac{S_{t+1}}{S_t})$ is normally distributed, one can hence state that $|\log(\frac{S_{t+1}}{S_t})|$ has an expected value proportional to $\hat{\sigma}_{S_t}$:

$$\mathbb{E}\left[\left|\log\left(\frac{S_{t+1}}{S_t}\right)\right|\right] \approx \sigma_S\sqrt{\frac{2}{\pi}} \tag{11.18}$$

Given the previous analysis, the regression is therefore respecified and allows the estimation of the coefficient b:

$$\log\left(\left|\log\left(\frac{S_{t+1}}{S_t}\right)\right|\right) = a' + b\log(S_t) \tag{11.19}$$

Example   This analysis is worked out for a practical example using a time series of seven share price observations. The data set was kept short on purpose, in order to keep the illustrative exercise comprehensible:

T	S_t	$\log(S_t)$	$\log(\frac{S_{t+1}}{S_t})$	$\log(|\log(\frac{S_{t+1}}{S_t})|)$
24-May-13	50.52	3.9224	2.4828%	−3.6958
28-May-13	51.79	3.9472	0.9417%	−4.6653
29-May-13	52.28	3.9566	1.8759%	−3.9761
30-May-13	53.27	3.9754	−2.4322%	−3.7164
31-May-13	51.99	3.9511	−0.0577%	−7.4573
3-Jun-13	51.96	3.9505	−1.4149%	−4.2581
4-Jun-13	51.23	3.9363		

From a linear regression of the values of $\log(S_t)$ against $\log(|\log(\frac{S_{t+1}}{S_t})|)$, the slope b is determined. For the data set above, the corresponding value equals: $p_{CEV} = 0.2498$.

Historical Parameter Estimation (Randal)

This method was suggested by John Randal [163] and starts from a property of $\log(S)$ when S is modeled as a CEV process. With:

$$dS_t = \mu S_t dt + \sigma_{CEV} S_t^{P_{CEV}} dW_t \tag{11.20}$$

and

$$Y = \log(S)$$

Ito's lemma is applied:

$$\frac{\partial Y}{\partial S} = \frac{1}{S}$$

$$\frac{\partial Y}{\partial t} = 0$$

$$\frac{\partial^2 Y}{\partial S^2} = -\frac{1}{S^2}$$

Hence:

$$dY_t = \frac{\partial Y}{\partial S} dS_t + \frac{1}{2}\frac{\partial^2 Y}{\partial S^2} dS_t^2 + \frac{\partial Y}{\partial t} dt$$

$$dY_t = \frac{1}{S}\left(\mu S_t dt + \sigma_{CEV} S_t^{P_{CEV}} dW_t\right) - \frac{1}{2S_t^2}\sigma_{CEV}^2 S_t^{2P_{CEV}} dt \tag{11.21}$$

$$dY_t = \left(\mu - \frac{1}{2}\sigma_{CEV}^2 S_t^{2(P_{CEV}-1)}\right) dt + \sigma_{CEV} S_t^{P_{CEV}-1} dW_t$$

Denote the standard deviation of the log return Y by σ_Y. Over the interval Δt, it is equal to $\sigma_{CEV} S^{P_{CEV}-1} \sqrt{\Delta t}$. This can be rewritten as:

$$\log(\sigma_Y) = \log(\sigma_{CEV}) + (P_{CEV} - 1)\log(S) + \frac{1}{2}\log(\Delta t) \tag{11.22}$$

In this approach, σ_Y is estimated using the standard deviation of the daily returns over a particular time frame. Through regression, the values for P_{CEV} and σ_{CEV} can be determined.

Example The applicability of this second estimation technique is illustrated on the share price of Cliffs Natural Resources, an international mining company. From the regression between $\log(S)$ and $\log(\sigma_Y)$ proposed in Equation (11.22), those CEV parameters that have the best explanatory power can be derived. In this practical example σ_Y was estimated using a time frame of 20 daily closing prices[5] preceding the observation of each $\log(S)$. The regression obtained in the period 2012–2013 is illustrated in Figure 11.2. The values obtained for P_{CEV} and σ_{CEV} are respectively equal to 0.4404 and 3.2132. The share price on June 7, 213 was equal to \$17.94. Using Equation (11.9), the CEV parameter can be used to calculate an estimate for the lognormal volatility σ_S:

$$\sigma_S = \sigma_{CEV} S^{P_{CEV}-1} = 3.2132 \times 17.94^{0.4404-1} = 63.87\% \tag{11.23}$$

---

[5] Since it is common to assume 250 business days in a year, we consider $\Delta t = 1/250$.

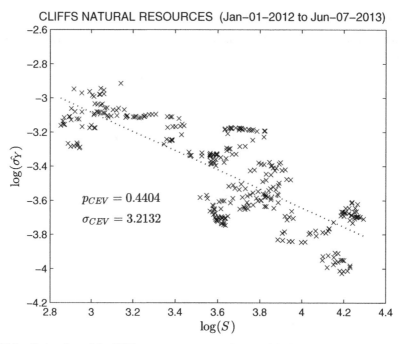

Figure 11.2   Estimation of the CEV parameters σ_{CEV} and p_{CEV} with the Randal method.

As shown in the table below, this lognormal volatility derived from the CEV estimates is very close to the historical volatility levels for the same stock observed on June 7, 2013:

Historical Volatility	
Horizon (days)	σ_S
10	59.82%
30	61.72%
90	72.49%

11.3   VALUATION: ANALYTICAL SOLUTION

11.3.1   Moving Away from Black–Scholes

Below, we repeat Equation (8.28) in order to illustrate the beauty and simplicity of the Black–Scholes formula allowing us to calculate the price of European call and put options. The results are denoted respectively as $P_{t,Call}$ and $P_{t,Put}$:

$$P_{t,Call} = S \exp(-q(T-t))\Phi(d1) - K \exp(-r(T-t))\Phi(d2)$$
$$P_{t,Put} = K \exp(-r(T-t))\Phi(-d2) - S \exp(-q(T-t))\Phi(-d1)$$

with

$$d1 = \frac{\log(S/K) + (r - q + \sigma_S^2/2)(T - t)}{\sigma_S \sqrt{T - t}} \qquad (11.24)$$

and

$$d2 = d1 - \sigma_S \sqrt{T - t}$$

The Black–Scholes model needs one single parameter σ_S to be estimated, while the other inputs $\{S, r, q\}$ are directly observable. The model is based on a set of assumptions. In Section 8.2, a detailed analysis of these assumptions was put forward. One of these assumptions, the fact that the share price is supposed to follow a geometric Brownian motion, is definitely the weakest element in the design of the formula. From a practical point of view, quantitative analysts have been quite productive creating work-arounds allowing their traders to keep using the above model even if the real world did not match the perfect and idealized Black–Scholes world. Therefore, adjustments have been introduced to account for discrete dividends, corrections to facilitate stock borrowing fees, or improvements to deal with transaction costs. Because of this, the Black–Scholes formula is still standing multiple decades after being conceived by Fisher Black, Myron Scholes, and Robert Merton. It is still the formula of choice for a practitioner kickstarting the analysis of a new derivative structure.

The most important correction, however, is the use of an implied volatility number. Traders are quoting European option prices not in terms of their dollar value, but in terms of the equivalent implied volatility. This is the value of σ_S such that the theoretical price of the option matches the market price. There will be a value of $\sigma_S(T, K)$ for every maturity date T and strike K. As a consequence, the volatility surface with a volatility term structure and skew was born. Nobody needed to rely on historical estimates $\hat{\sigma}_S$ and instead used implied volatility data even if this was considered as the wrong number to put in the wrong formula to obtain the right price of plain vanilla options [166].

Historical Estimation $S \underset{t}{\llcorner} \quad \longrightarrow \quad \hat{\sigma}_S$

$\longrightarrow$ Black–Scholes Formula

(European Options)

Volatility Surface $T \underset{K}{\boxplus} \quad \longrightarrow \quad \sigma_S(T, K)$

11.3.2 Semi-Closed-Form Formula

The existence of a closed-form solution puts any derivative pricing formula one step ahead compared with competing valuation models. A semi-closed-form solution fortunately exists for European options where the underlying share price is modeled as a CEV process. The first step in the direction of a closed-form solution to price derivatives with a CEV model can be found in [64]. This contribution involved an infinite summation to arrive at a value for $P_{t,Call}$ and $P_{t,Put}$. An important breakthrough was provided in [177] and involves two sets of equations. One set of equations offers a closed-form formula valid for $p_{CEV} > 1$ while the other deals with the more intuitive case where $0 < p_{CEV} < 1$. This latter situation matches an increasing volatility for decreasing share prices. Using the same notation as in [121]:

$$0 < p_{CEV} < 1$$
$$P_{t,Call} = S \exp(-q(T-t))\left(1 - \chi^2(a, b+2, c)\right) - K \exp(-r(T-t))\chi^2(c, b, a)$$
$$P_{t,Put} = K \exp(-r(T-t))\left(1 - \chi^2(c, b, a)\right) - S \exp(-q(T-t))\chi^2(a, b+2, c)$$

$$p_{CEV} > 1$$
$$P_{t,Call} = S \exp(-q(T-t))\left(1 - \chi^2(c, -b, a)\right) - K \exp(-r(T-t))\chi^2(a, 2-b, c)$$
$$P_{t,Put} = K \exp(-r(T-t))\left(1 - \chi^2(a, 2-b, c)\right) - S \exp(-q(T-t))\chi^2(c, -b, a)$$

$$(11.25)$$

where

$$a = \frac{[K \exp(-(r-q)(T-t))]^{2(1-p_{CEV})}}{v(1 - p_{CEV})^2} \tag{11.26}$$

$$b = \frac{1}{1 - p_{CEV}} \tag{11.27}$$

$$c = \frac{S^{2(1-p_{CEV})}}{v(1 - p_{CEV})^2} \tag{11.28}$$

$$v = \frac{\sigma_{CEV}^2}{2(r-q)(p_{CEV}-1)}\left[\exp\left(2(r-q)(p_{CEV}-1)(T-t)\right) - 1\right] \tag{11.29}$$

Equation (11.25) looks almost the same as the Black–Scholes formula. The main difference is the use of the non-central chi-squared function χ^2 instead of Φ. The value $\chi^2(x, k, v)$ is the probability that a variable with a non-central χ^2 distribution that has a non-centrality parameter v and k degrees of freedom is less than x. An algorithm to calculate $\chi^2(x, k, v)$ has been provided in [75]. Most commercial mathematical software packages offer an implementation of the non-central χ^2 distribution.

11.3.3 Numerical Example

The semi-closed-form formula is put to work in pricing a European call and put option with a 5-year maturity on a share price S equal to 100. The strike of the option is struck at 105. The other pricing parameters are:

- $r = 3\%$
- $q = 2\%$
- CEV parameters:

$$\sigma_{CEV} = 1.5$$
$$p_{CEV} = 0.6$$

Using a maturity of 5 years we can set $T - t = 5$ in the equations above and obtain the following intermediate results:

$$v = 11.0280$$
$$a = 22.5405$$
$$b = 2.5000$$
$$c = 22.5624$$

$$(11.30)$$

The calculations involving the probabilities for the non-central χ^2 variable are:

$$\begin{aligned}
\chi^2(a, b+2, c) &= 0.3544 \\
\chi^2(c, b, a) \quad &= 0.4377
\end{aligned} \tag{11.31}$$

The prices for the call and the put are respectively:

$$\begin{aligned}
P_{t,Call} &= 18.86 \\
P_{t,Put} &= 18.75
\end{aligned} \tag{11.32}$$

11.4 VALUATION: TRINOMIAL TREES FOR CEV

11.4.1 American Options

The closed-form solution of Equation (11.25) puts the CEV model at an advantage compared with other non-Black–Scholes models where an analytical solution is not available. Yet, there is a limit to its practical use. Hybrid instruments such as convertible bonds have an early exercise feature. The owner of the bond can request conversion into the underlying shares at any given date prior to the maturity date. This property cannot be captured in a closed-form formula. A similar constraint exists for American options. Exactly this American nature prohibits the use of Equation (11.25) in any calibration process to determine convenient values for σ_{CEV} and p_{CEV} for single stocks. Listed options on single stocks are indeed American, which rules out the use of Equation (11.25) and forces us to move in a different direction when developing pricing tools for a constant elasticity of variance framework.

11.4.2 Trinomial Trees for CEV

The CEV process for a share price S cannot be straightforwardly modeled into a trinomial tree. The generalized tree-building procedure is not applied on S but on a new variable X which is a function of this share price. A trinomial tree for this variable X is constructed instead.

In Section 8.3.2 we already saw how it is most often required to transform the financial variable into such an auxiliary variable. A trinomial tree will accordingly be constructed for this auxiliary variable. In Section 8.3.4 a trinomial tree for $\log(S)$ was, for example, assembled as a preliminary step from which the S-tree was derived in a second step. The same line of thought will be followed when constructing a trinomial tree to model the stochastic behavior of a share price S that is described using a constant elasticity of variance model. As laid out before, the share price behavior is in this case represented by the following stochastic differential equation:

$$dS_t = \mu S_t dt + \sigma_{CEV} S_t^{p_{CEV}} dW_t \tag{11.33}$$

We take $\mu = r - q$ considering a risk-neutral setting.

The share price is, in a first step, transformed into a variable $X = f(S)$ such that:

$$X_t = \frac{S_t^{1-p_{CEV}}}{1 - p_{CEV}} \tag{11.34}$$

This is called the X-transform. The opposite is the S-transform:

$$S_t = f^{-1}(X_t) \begin{cases} S_t = (X_t(1 - p_{CEV}))^{\frac{1}{1-p_{CEV}}} & \text{if } X > 0 \\ S_t = 0 & \text{otherwise} \end{cases} \quad (11.35)$$

This transform was proposed in [154] and using Ito's lemma we obtain:

$$dX_t = \left(\mu X_t(1 - p_{CEV}) - \frac{p_{CEV}\sigma_{CEV}^2}{2X_t(1 - p_{CEV})} \right) dt + \sigma_{CEV}dW_t \quad (11.36)$$

This turns the variable S_t into a homoskedastic variable X_t, where the variance is independent of the value of X_t itself. The graphical presentation below illustrates (1) the construction of a trinomial tree for X, which is subsequently (2) transformed back into a tree of share prices S. From the latter tree, the value P_0 of the hybrid security corresponding to the current share price S_0 can be derived (3).

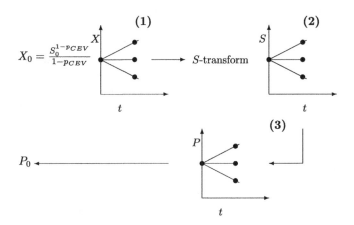

As such, there is no difference between the general framework described in Section 8.3.3 where $X = \log(S)$ was modeled when S itself followed a geometric Brownian motion. The four steps of the general trinomial tree construction in Equation (8.37) remain valid apart from two differences in the calculation of the conditional mean $M_{i,j}$ and variance $V_{i,j}$. Both $M_{i,j}$ and $V_{i,j}$ must be consistent with the chosen process for X.

1. Conditional mean:

$$M_{i,j} = \mathbb{E}[X_{i+1} \mid X_{i,j}]$$

$$= X_{i,j} + \left((r - q)X_{i,j}(1 - p_{CEV}) - \frac{p_{CEV}\sigma_{CEV}^2}{2X_{i,j}(1 - p_{CEV})} \right) \Delta t_i \quad (11.37)$$

with $\Delta t_i = t_{i+1} - t_i$.

2. Conditional variance:

$$V_{i,j}^2 = \sigma_{CEV}^2 \Delta t_i \quad (11.38)$$

11.4.3 Numerical Example

The same example as in Section 8.3.4 is worked out below. The share price S is again simulated in a two-step trinomial tree covering a total maturity of 4 years. The interest rate r is equal to 3% and the dividend yield q is 2%. The initial value of the share price S_0 from where the trinomial tree originates is 100. In what follows we will work out step by step the construction of this trinomial tree.

1. **Choosing the appropriate stochastic process**
   The CEV process is characterized by $\sigma_{CEV} = 4$ and $p_{CEV} = 0.5$. This corresponds at the start of the tree to a Black–Scholes volatility of 40%. At first the X-tree is simulated. Using Equation (11.34) we have that this tree originates at $X_{0,0} = 20$.
2. **Selecting the time slices**
   The 4-year maturity will be covered in two steps. The time step Δt is hence equal to 2. The variance V^2 of X from one slice to the other is constant:

$$V^2 = \sigma_{CEV}^2 \Delta t = 4 \times 4 \times 2 = 32 \tag{11.39}$$

3. **Associating with a particular time slice a step size**
   The distance between two nodes belonging to the same time slice is an integer multiple of ΔX:

$$\Delta X = V\sqrt{3} = 9.7980 \tag{11.40}$$

4. **Calculating the transition probabilities**
   The step size ΔX is known and is constant for all the slices of the tree because Δt is constant in this particular case.
   (a) **First time slice $t = \Delta t$**
   The tree for X_t originates at $X_{0,0} = 20$. The expected value of the three nodes originating from $X_{0,0}$ and terminating in the first time slice following $X_{0,0}$ is given by:

$$M_{0,0} = X_{0,0} + \left((r-q)X_{0,0}(1-p_{CEV}) - \frac{p_{CEV}\sigma_{CEV}^2}{2X_{0,0}(1-p_{CEV})} \right)\Delta t$$
$$= 19.4000 \tag{11.41}$$

The three nodes on the first slice are an integer multiple of ΔX: $(k+1)\Delta X, k\Delta X$, and $(k-1)\Delta X$.

Using the notation introduced in Equation (8.36), the following picture can be drawn:

$t = 0$ $t = 2$

$$X_{1,k+1} = (k+1)\Delta X = 9.7980(k+1) \qquad p_u$$

$X_{0,0} = 20$

$$X_{1,k} = k\Delta X = 9.7980k \qquad p_m$$

$$X_{1,k-1} = (k-1)\Delta X = 9.7980(k-1) \qquad p_d$$

Applying Equation (8.42) one can determine the value of k for the nodes on the first time slice originating at $X_{0,0}$:

$$k = \text{round}\left(\frac{M_{0,0}}{\Delta X}\right) = \text{round}\left(\frac{19.4000}{9.7980}\right) = 2 \qquad (11.42)$$

The position of the three X-nodes on $t = 2$ is hence:

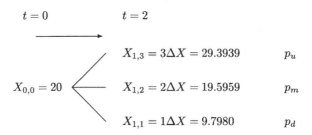

$t = 0$	$t = 2$	
	$X_{1,3} = 3\Delta X = 29.3939$	p_u
$X_{0,0} = 20$	$X_{1,2} = 2\Delta X = 19.5959$	p_m
	$X_{1,1} = 1\Delta X = 9.7980$	p_d

The transition probabilities can be calculated using Equation (8.40):

$$\begin{cases} p_u = 0.1569 \\ p_m = 0.6663 \\ p_d = 0.1768 \end{cases} \qquad (11.43)$$

(b) **Second and final time slice $t = 2\Delta t$**

The nodes $X_{1,3}$, $X_{1,2}$, and $X_{1,1}$ on the first slice are the starting nodes of nine other branches terminating in five different nodes on the final slice of the tree.

$$\begin{array}{ll} \text{Start Node}(t = 2) & \to \text{End Nodes}(t = 4) \\ X_{1,3} & \to \{X_{2,4}, X_{2,3}, X_{1,2}\} \\ X_{1,2} & \to \{X_{2,3}, X_{2,2}, X_{2,1}\} \\ X_{1,1} & \to \{X_{2,2}, X_{2,1}, X_{2,0}\} \end{array}$$

The numerical result of the calculations is summarized below:

Second Time Slice ($t = 4$)		
$X_{1,3}$	$X_{1,2}$	$X_{1,1}$
$X = 29.3939$	$X = 19.5959$	$X = 9.7980$
$V^2 = 32$	$V^2 = 32$	$V^2 = 32$
$\Delta X_2 = 9.7980$	$\Delta X_2 = 9.7980$	$\Delta X_2 = 9.7980$
$M_{1,3} = 29.1435$	$M_{1,2} = 18.9754$	$M_{1,1} = 8.2630$
$k = 3$	$k = 2$	$k = 1$
New Nodes	New Nodes	New Nodes
$X_{2,4} = 39.1918$ $\quad p_u = 0.1542$	$X_{2,3} = 29.3939$ $\quad p_u = 0.1370$	$X_{2,2} = 19.5959$ $\quad p_u = 0.1006$
$X_{2,3} = 29.3939$ $\quad p_m = 0.6660$	$X_{2,2} = 19.5959$ $\quad p_m = 0.6627$	$X_{2,1} = 9.7980$ $\quad p_m = 0.6421$
$X_{2,1} = 19.5959$ $\quad p_d = 0.1798$	$X_{2,1} = 9.7980$ $\quad p_d = 0.2003$	$X_{2,0} = 0.0000$ $\quad p_d = 0.2573$

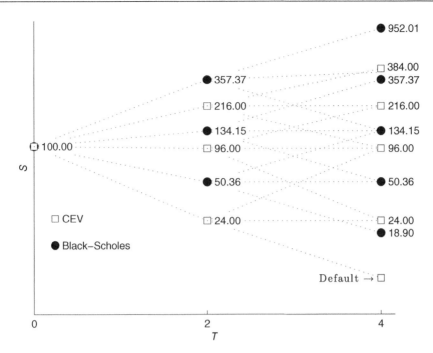

Figure 11.3   Trinomial tree for a CEV and Black–Scholes model for the same underlying share. CEV parameters: $\sigma_{CEV} = 4$, $p_{CEV} = 0.5$. Black–Scholes volatility: $\sigma_S = 40\%$.

The node $X_{2,0} = 0$ corresponds to a share price S equal to zero. One of the properties of a CEV process with $p_{CEV} < 1$ is the fact that the share price can reach zero. This corresponds to a default situation generated by a diffusion process, contrary to a default that takes place in a jump process. This is most obvious in Figure 11.3, where the trinomial tree from the CEV model was overlaid with the Black–Scholes tree.

Black–Scholes vs. CEV

Geometric Brownian motion is the backbone of the Black–Scholes model. In this context, $\log(S)$ follows a normal distribution. Accordingly, the share price S is lognormally distributed. The contrast with a share price governed by a constant elasticity of variance is illustrated in Figure 11.4. The density function for the share price S used in the previous exercise was obtained from a trinomial tree with $n = 80$ steps covering the 4-year maturity. Given our choice of the CEV parameter $p_{CEV} < 1$, the fat-tail property from the density function to the right for the CEV process is obvious.

Default through Diffusion

The fat-tail property embedded within CEV also has the additional probability that the share price can reach zero depending on the value of p_{CEV}. This can be explained when taking Equation (11.9) into consideration. It is obvious how the instantaneous "lognormal" volatility σ_S becomes explosive for small values of S when $p_{CEV} < 1$ [139]. Figure 11.5 illustrates this

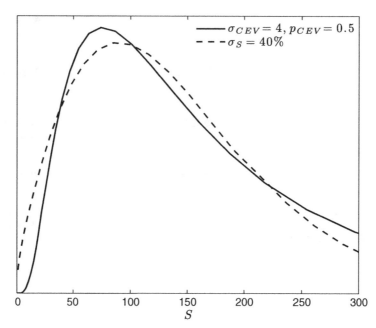

Figure 11.4 Density function for the share price S at $t = 4$ years, obtained from a trinomial tree for both a CEV and a Black–Scholes model.

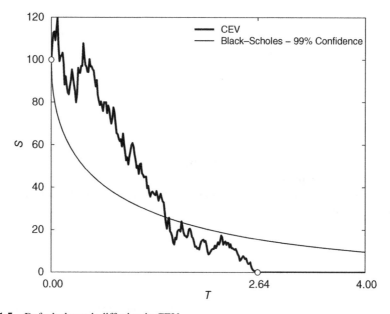

Figure 11.5 Default through diffusion in CEV.

clearly, while considering the same parameters as in the previous numerical example. Starting from a normal distribution of the logarithmic returns of S, a low threshold for the share price was calculated for a confidence interval of 99% and illustrated in Figure 11.5. This lower threshold is only valid in a Black–Scholes world. In the next step, a Monte Carlo simulation modeling the CEV process of the same share was carried out. The Monte Carlo technique is covered in detail in Section 12.8. For the moment, consider a Monte Carlo method as a computational algorithm to simulate repeatedly a random process. In this case the process is a share price modeled as a CEV process with parameters σ_{CEV} and p_{CEV}, as stipulated in Equation (11.2). The continuous process of S_t is turned into a discrete set of simulated values starting with the current share price S_0: $\{S_0, S_1, \ldots, S_i, S_{i+1}, \ldots\}$. As such, Equation (11.2) is rewritten as:

$$S_{i+1} = S_i + S_i \left((r - q)\Delta t_i + \sigma_{CEV} S_i^{p_{CEV}-1} \sqrt{\Delta t_i} Z_i \right) \tag{11.44}$$

with $\Delta t_i = t_{i+1} - t_i$.

The random component in the equation above is the variable $Z \sim N(0, 1)$. Starting at S_0, a random walk of the share price can be simulated. The equation above is only valid for $S_i > 0$, however. As soon as S falls through the zero level and takes negative values, we take the generally accepted view that the stock has defaulted and has to be kept at this level [41, 72]. In this case, the share price has reached a default at a stopping time τ:

$$\tau = \inf\{t > 0 : S_t = 0\} \tag{11.45}$$

We will treat this bankruptcy event as one where the share price S stays at this level and is not allowed to go up any more:

$$S_t = 0 \quad \text{for} \quad t \geq \tau \tag{11.46}$$

The stock price process is absorbed at this state and the level $S = 0$ is called an absorbing barrier. As an example, it is shown in Figure 11.5 how one of the paths drops below the lognormal or Black–Scholes boundary and reaches default at time $\tau = 2.64$ years. What is impossible in Black–Scholes is feasible in CEV: the stock price can reach zero through diffusion.

11.5 JUMP-EXTENDED CEV PROCESS

11.5.1 Introduction

The continuous CEV process carries a default probability with a CEV parameter $p_{CEV} < 1$. This is a situation where a state of bankruptcy is reached through diffusion. A share price $S = 0$ can now be obtained even in the complete absence of a jump component. In [49], the authors argue that the default probability obtained using CEV is too low to model bankruptcy in real-world cases. Hence they added to the CEV model of Equation (11.2) a jump process. This is the so-called jump-to-default extended constant elasticity of variance (JDCEV) process:

$$dS_t = (r - q + \lambda)S_t dt + \sigma_{CEV} S_t^{p_{CEV}} dW_t - S_t dN_t$$
$$dN_t = 1 \text{ with probability } \lambda dt \tag{11.47}$$
$$= 0 \text{ otherwise}$$

The JDCEV process can be seen as the CEV equivalent of the standard jump-diffusion process we discussed before in Section 9.2.

11.5.2 JDCEV-Generated Skew

The elasticity parameter p_{CEV} in the CEV process specifies the changes of the share price variance when this share price level moves to a different value. As discussed before, a value $p_{CEV} < 1$ will increase the variance for lower share prices. This observation goes hand in hand with the existence of a volatility skew. Turning the CEV model into a JDCEV model after the incorporation of the default intensity parameter λ will increase the skew as the share price is allowed to jump to a bankruptcy level. A numerical example will be worked out according to the framework specified below:

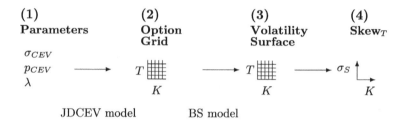

(1) From a set of JDCEV parameters, a grid of option prices (2) is generated for a range of maturities T and strikes K using the JDCEV model. From this option grid a volatility surface (3) of implied Black–Scholes volatilities is calculated. This set of implied volatility data allows us to determine the skew (4) for a particular maturity T. The observed skew is the logical consequence of looking at a JDCEV process through a pair of Black–Scholes glasses.

In this example we use a similar set of market data that served the Section 11.4.3 case study, where the construction of a trinomial tree was worked out in extensive detail. The interest rate r is equal to 3%, the dividend yield q is 2%. The share's market price is 100 and the JDCEV process is based on the following values:

- $\sigma_{CEV} = 4$
- $p_{CEV} = 0.5$
- $\lambda = 0.05$

For two different maturities, $T = 1$ and $T = 0.25$, the skew has been calculated. As can be seen in Figure 11.6, the skew generated by the JDCEV process increases with shorter maturities. This behavior corresponds to what is observed with real market data.

11.5.3 Convertible Bonds Priced under JDCEV

In Section 9.2.4 we worked out from scratch the pricing of a convertible bond in a jump-diffusion context. The jump-diffusion model blended the Black–Scholes world together with the intensity-based credit models. Option prices and credit default swap levels can serve as inputs in a jump-diffusion model. The jump component is parameterized by the parameters λ

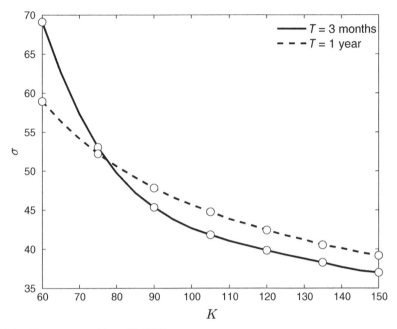

Figure 11.6   Skew generated by a JDCEV process.

and π, which stand respectively for the default intensity and the recovery rate. The diffusion component is quantified by one single parameter: the volatility σ_{JD}. As an introduction to jump-extended constant elasticity of variance models, the same bond as in the jump-diffusion example is considered. The characteristics of the bond are repeated below:

Sample Convertible Bond (%)			
Maturity	5 years	**Conversion Ratio** (C_r)	0.7692
Callable from	Year 4	**Conversion Price** (C_P)	130
Call Price (K)	100	**Put Date**	Year 3
Call Trigger $(K_\%)$	120%	**Put Amount** (P_v)	100
Face Value (N)	100	**Annual Coupon**	2%

The bond is priced using $\sigma_{CEV} = 4$ and $p_{CEV} = 0.5$. The share price S was kept equal to 100. The interest rate r and dividend yield q are respectively 5% and 2%. The recovery rate π equals 20% with a default intensity λ equal to 3%. Using the same number of steps $(n = 5)$, the price of the convertible moves from 105.22 to 102.18 using the JDCEV model. The impact of the put on the price of the convertible is reduced when comparing JDCEV with the jump-diffusion model. The different probabilities indicating how the convertible bond's existence is terminated are illustrated in the table below. The fact that a JDCEV model results in a lower probability for the bond being put at its third anniversary will increase its expected life or fugit. The fugit in the jump-diffusion model picks up from 3.65 years to 3.76 years when JDCEV is used.

	Probability (%)		
	JD	JDCEV	Impact
Optional Conversion	2.21	6.48	↑
Forced Conversion	14.99	23.82	↑
Call	0.00	0.00	
Redemption	24.58	25.27	↑
Final Conversion	3.46	4.58	↑
Default	10.78	11.96	↑
Put	43.98	27.89	↓↓

11.6 CASE STUDY: PRICING MANDATORIES WITH CEV

11.6.1 Mandatory Conversion

A redemption of a mandatory convertible bond always takes place in shares. This instrument has a double conversion ratio and contains therefore two embedded conversion prices. In the introductory chapter on convertible debt, this specific asset class was covered in Section 2.2.9. The number of shares received on conversion depends on the final share price level S_T observed at the maturity date of the mandatory:

$$\text{Number of Shares} = \begin{cases} C_{r,L} & \text{with } C_{r,L} = \dfrac{N}{C_{P,L}} \text{ if } S_T < C_{P,L} \\ C_r & \text{with } C_r = \dfrac{N}{S_T} \text{ if } S_T \geq C_{P,L} \text{ and } S \leq C_{P,H} \\ C_{r,H} & \text{with } C_{r,H} = \dfrac{N}{C_{P,H}} \text{ if } S_T > C_{P,H} \end{cases} \quad (11.48)$$

From the previous equation it is obvious that a lower final share price S_T will leave the investor with more shares than if the stock performed well. Because of this, the mandatory convertible contains both negative and positive convexity within one single structure. An illustration of this can be found in Figure 2.9. Because of the presence of a double-signed gamma, one can expect a more outspoken impact when moving from a Black–Scholes to a CEV model. The CEV model will attribute a lower volatility for share price levels around the higher strike ($S \approx C_{P,H}$) and a higher volatility when the share price trades in the vicinity of the lower strike ($S \approx C_{P,L}$) Because of this, the theoretical value produced by a CEV model will be more accurate than a constant volatility model. Some practitioners therefore already price a mandatory using two different volatilities, one corresponds to $C_{P,L}$ and the other to $C_{P,H}$. This double-volatility structure is a further illustration of how the Black–Scholes model is kept on the road through the inclusion of yet another fudge factor. These fudge factors do not solve the valuation problem, they simply avoid having to deal with the core of the issue. This is a choice one does not have to consider when selecting a CEV model to value mandatory convertible bonds with a payoff as described in Equation (11.48). The share price variance is now dependent on the share price level and there is no need to deal with an incorporation of two volatility numbers.

11.6.2 Numerical Example

A numerical example is used to demonstrate to what extent the flat volatility model overstates the true price of a mandatory convertible. The underlying share in this case study has a market price S equal to 100. The share has a dividend yield $q = 2\%$ and a flat Black–Scholes-style volatility $\sigma_S = 40\%$. This corresponds to the following set of CEV parameters: $\sigma_{CEV} = 15.9243$ and $p_{CEV} = 0.2$.

The mandatory distributes no coupons, has a lower conversion price $C_{P,L}$ equal to 80, and a higher conversion price $C_{P,L}$ equal to 120. Since the face value of the bond is 100, the two corresponding conversion prices are 1.20 and 0.83, respectively. For different share prices and for different maturities, the theoretical price of this particular mandatory has been calculated for both valuation models. The results are represented in Figure 11.7. From the calculation results for this particular numerical example, it is clear that the price obtained using the Black–Scholes model is higher than the theoretical value resulting from the CEV method.

In Figure 11.8, it is shown how this price difference decreases as the instrument approaches its maturity date. One year from the expiry date, the price difference is 223 bps for $S = 100$.

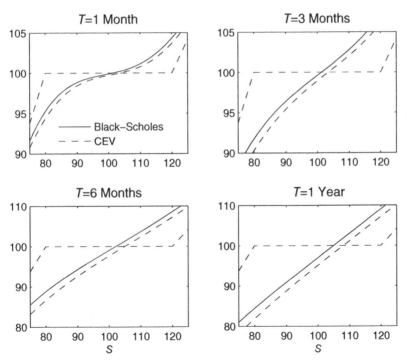

Figure 11.7 Theoretical price of a mandatory convertible using the Black–Scholes and CEV model for four different maturities.

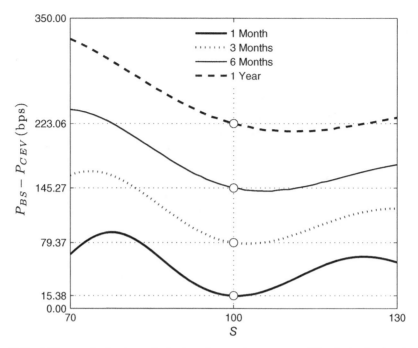

Figure 11.8 Difference in the theoretical price of a mandatory convertible obtained using the Black–Scholes and CEV model for four different maturities ($P_{BS} > P_{CEV}$).

Six months later, this price difference between the two models has decreased to 145 bps. Only at share price levels close enough to one of the two conversion prices will the overestimation of the Black–Scholes approach remain significant for dates close to the final maturity date of the mandatory bond.

11.7   CASE STUDY: PRICING CONVERTIBLES WITH A RESET

11.7.1   Refixing the Conversion Price

After the 1996 deregulation in the Japanese market a new kind of instrument feature [155] was added to the convertible universe. Convertibles were now equipped with "reset" or "refix" features. The conversion price could be revised downward on a reset date T_R from C_P to a new level C_P^* in the case of disappointing stock prices. An increase of the conversion price would take place in the opposite case. In the first case, the conversion ratio increases while in the second case, C_r gets adjusted downward. In practice, a cap α and floor β are applied in order to constrain the new conversion price within an acceptable range. Resetting C_P to C_P^* is based on the share price S_{T_R} observed on the reset date. In Chapter 2 this was specified in Equation (2.65), an equation which we repeat below:

$$C_P^* = \begin{cases} \alpha C_P & \text{if } S_{T_R} > \alpha C_P \\ S_{T_R} & \text{if } \beta C_P \leq S_{T_R} \leq \alpha C_P \\ \beta C_P & \text{if } S_{T_R} < \beta C_P \end{cases} \tag{11.49}$$

Lowering the conversion price lifts the conversion ratio to a higher level. Intuitively, this brings negative convexity into the portfolio since the lower the share price, the more shares the investor will eventually own after conversion. Close to the floor ($S \approx \beta C_P$), we have:

$$\Gamma = \left(\frac{\partial^2 P}{\partial S^2}\right) < 0$$

$$= \left(\frac{\partial \Delta}{\partial S}\right) < 0 \tag{11.50}$$

From the previous equation we learn that Δ increases when the share price S decreases close to the floor of the reset mechanism. This is a situation where an investor gets more exposed to share price movements as the share price itself falls to low levels. Inevitably this has an impact on the value of the convertible bond. The positive convexity resulting from the optional conversion into shares is somewhat blurred by this possibility of a negative gamma. Similar to mandatory convertibles, this is a practical illustration where a flat volatility model fails to stand the test of reality.

Without the reset feature and ignoring any possible default, a convertible security is a positive gamma product. Whatever the share price level, its equity convexity is positive. The behavior of this hybrid security is very similar to a combination of both a corporate bond and a call option on a certain amount of underlying shares. The inclusion of a reset in the term sheet changes all of this. This can be observed in Figure 11.9, where the price graph for a convertible bond expiring on $t = T$ has been plotted for the two extreme cases. First there is a situation where the reset has increased the conversion price to the cap ($C_P^* = \alpha C_P$) and second there is the opposite case where the refix took place at the floor ($C_P^* = \beta C_P$).

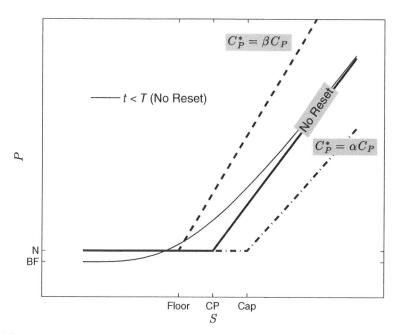

Figure 11.9   Price graph for a convertible bond in the case of a reset on the cap or on the floor.

Once the reset of the conversion ratio has taken place, one can observe from Figure 11.9 how the owner of the convertible bond is better off with a refix at the floor than with a refix at the higher level. For the same share price level, the parity of the bond will be higher in the first case. This has a consequence with respect to the equity sensitivity as well.

We have $\forall S_t$ with $t > T_R$:

$$(\Delta)_{C_P^* = \beta C_P} > (\Delta)_{C_P \text{unchanged}} > (\Delta)_{C_P^* = \alpha C_P} \tag{11.51}$$

At the reset date T_R, the owner of a convertible bond has the probability of either ending up with a high or a low conversion ratio. These are the two extreme cases. When the share price level is trading at depressed levels close to the floor and around the reset date, the likelihood of benefitting from an increase of the conversion ratio is high. In such a situation the possible reset of C_P to βC_P is the most likely outcome. The increase in C_r is almost certain to take place and will therefore have a prevailing impact on the theoretical value of the reset. This excludes the possibility of seeing the conversion price reset to the cap level αC_P.

On the contrary, if the share price S_{T_R} on the reset date is trading in between the cap and the floor, the conversion price is changed into the then prevailing share price level ($C_P^* = S_{T_R}$). The convertible bond's conversion price is reset and turns the bond into an at-the-money convertible. The value of the convertible does not change on the reset date for any value $S_{T_R} \in [\beta C_P, \alpha C_P]$. Between the two extreme cases, there is a continuum of feasible structures which the convertible bond may adopt on the reset date.

In Figure 11.10 the price graph for the convertible is represented for a date close to the reset date. A similar graph for a convertible without the inclusion of the reset feature has been

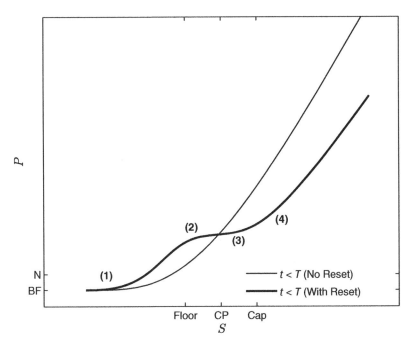

Figure 11.10 Price graph for a convertible bond with and without the reset.

illustrated as well. Going from left to right on the graph, in the direction of increasing share prices, we single out four points of interest that deserve our attention:

- **(1)** $\Delta = 0, \Gamma = 0$
  The share price has clearly fallen off a cliff and trades far below the floor βC_P. The conversion ratio's increase will not have any impact at all on the theoretical price of the convertible, which remains close to the bond floor (BF) in this particular situation. Small changes in the share price level have no immediate impact on the value of the convertible at this point on the graph.
- **(2)** $\Delta > 0, \Gamma < 0$
  Close to the floor where $S \approx \beta C_P$, the convertible bond has a positive delta. Its theoretical value responds positively to any increase in the share price level S. The fact that the delta itself does not increase with share price increases illustrates the negative convexity of the convertible at this particular share price level on the graph. This presence of a negative gamma may pull the share price into a proper death spiral following an increase in hedging activity from investors owning this particular instrument [120].
- **(3)** $\Delta \approx 0$
  In between the cap and the floor, the convertible's price is going to be relatively immune to share price changes. This is especially the case in the time frame immediately preceding the reset date. The parity P_a of the convertible is equal to its face value. The bond is kept at the same level of moneyness in this share price range. This finding results immediately from Equation (11.49).
- **(4)** $\Delta > 0, \Gamma > 0$
  As soon as the share price moves above the cap, the convexity of the convertible will pick up significantly, as can be seen in Figure 11.10. Given the change in the conversion price, the delta of the post-reset convertible will now be lower than before the conversion price reset.

11.7.2 Involvement of CEV

Taking the second derivative of the theoretical convertible price P on the graph in Figure 11.10 with respect to the share price S allows us to study the profile of the convertible's gamma in more detail. The results of this can be found in Figure 11.11. The four points of interest of Figure 11.10 have again been labeled on top of the graph. The influence of a reset on a convertible's convexity is more than outspoken. Going from low to high share prices, the gamma goes through different sign changes. The convertible has lost its status as a product which solely offers positive convexity to its investors. Owning an instrument with a double convexity needs to be handled with care. A positive gamma for a particular share price level can easily make room for a negative gamma at a different share price level. Whether this gamma is going to be problematic or not is going to depend on the realized volatility of the underlying share price on the moment Γ changes sign. This caveat emphasizes the dangers involved in relying too much on a flat volatility model to do the job.

In Chapter 2 we already elaborated on the value of a positive gamma for a portfolio with value Π:

$$\mathbb{E}[\delta \Pi] = \tfrac{1}{2} \Gamma \mathbb{E}[\delta S^2] > 0 \tag{11.52}$$

In the equation above, $\mathbb{E}[\delta \Pi]$ is the expected change in the value of a portfolio, whereas $\mathbb{E}[\delta S^2]$ stands for the expected squared share price changes. The latter is a measure of the variance of

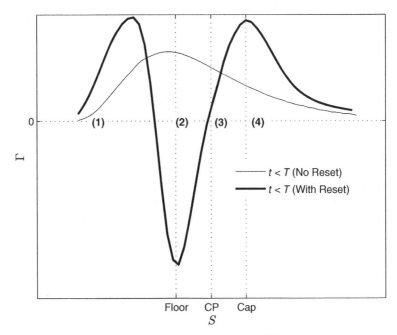

Figure 11.11 Gamma profile for a convertible bond with and without a reset.

the underlying equity of the instrument in the portfolio. A positive gamma pays off when the share price is volatile. The opposite is true when the gamma is negative. In this case, one has no interest at all in owning a volatile underlying stock.

The particular convexity profile of the convertible with a reset is a convincing enough argument to move away from a flat volatility as used by Black–Scholes or by the jump-diffusion approach. Models such as CEV or JDCEV, for example, that mechanically link the variance of a share to its price level S are now going to be more than appropriate. This is a merit that the constant elasticity of variance model has to share with other approaches such as the local volatility model [84], Heston [118], or variance gamma [143].

11.7.3 Numerical Example

In order to illustrate the use of a lattice technique such as trinomial trees to value convertible debt with a reset, we revert to a numerical example. The zero-coupon convertible bond used in this example has a reset after 2 years.

Convertible Bond with Reset			
Maturity	5 years	**Cap**	$\alpha = 1.3$
Reset Date	Year 2	**Floor**	$\beta = 0.8$
Face Value (N)	100	**Conversion Price**	100

The underlying share price S is equal to 100, which corresponds to the initial conversion price C_P. The interest rate r is equal to 5% and the underlying share of the convertible

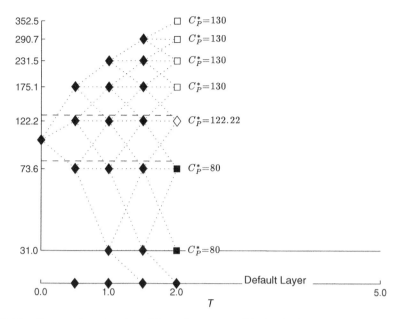

Figure 11.12   Construction of a trinomial tree for a convertible bond with a reset in year 2.

distributes a 2% dividend yield. The CEV parameters are $\sigma_{CEV} = 15.9243$ and $p_{CEV} = 0.2$. In this numerical example the default intensity is set equal to zero. As such, a jump to default is not going to occur. But since $p_{CEV} < 1$, a share price level $S = 0$ can still be attained through the CEV process. In such a case, the value of the convertible will be set to its recovery value $\pi = 20\%$.

In this exercise a trinomial tree is constructed for time slices up to the reset date in four trinomial steps. The nodes generated by this process are presented graphically in Figure 11.12. There are in total eight nodes on the time slice that corresponds to the trigger date $T_R = 2$:

- One of these nodes falls on the default layer ($S = 0$).
- The same figure points out how there are two nodes where the conversion price is reset to the lowest level ($C_P^* = 80$). This holds for the node values $S = 31$ and $S = 73.6$.
- Four of the nodes ($S \in \{175.1, 231.5, 290.7, 352.5\}$) are above the cap and here the conversion price is reset to 130.
- The remaining node ($S = 122.2$) that sits in between cap and floor is reset to the share price level on this particular node $C_P^* = 122.22$.

The value of the reset convertible in the node on the reset date is equal to the theoretical price of a convertible with a new conversion price C_P^* and with a remaining maturity of 3 years. These values can be calculated using a 3-year trinomial tree originating at each of the nodes on the time slice T_R. At the node where S is equal to 175.1, the value of the convertible bond is equal to 136.17. Rolling back from the nodes at the reset slice toward the origin of the tree leads to the theoretical price of this convertible bond. This price is equal to 106.65 (Figure 11.13). Note that the roll-back procedure needs to incorporate appropriately soft call triggers and put clauses. All of these features were omitted in this educational example, only the optional exercise possibility was kept as a potential early exercise.

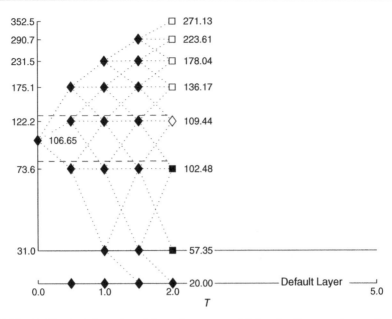

Figure 11.13 Rolling back in a trinomial tree for a convertible bond with a reset in year 2.

Building further on the same numerical example and using the same parameters, the impact of the cap and floor on the theoretical price of the convertible bond with a reset can be investigated. The only difference is the fact that the default intensity λ was set equal to 5%. The results of this analysis are summarized in Figure 11.14. In a first step, the cap level is fixed by imposing $\alpha = 1$. Using both a jump-diffusion and a JDCEV model, the impact ΔP on the theoretical price for increasing values of the floor β has been investigated. In analogy with the first simulation, a second simulation was carried out where the impact of increasing cap levels has been quantified after setting the floor $\beta = 1$.

The price difference for a particular combination of β and α is $\Delta P_{\beta,\alpha}$:

$$\Delta P_{\beta,\alpha} = P_{\beta,\alpha} - P_{\beta=1,\alpha=1} = P_{\beta,\alpha} - P \qquad (11.53)$$

The theoretical value P corresponds to the convertible stripped from a possible conversion price reset. This corresponds to a reset convertible where both β and α are equal to 1. Both jump-diffusion and JDCEV share a similar conclusion. Increasing caps and floors have a negative price impact. This makes absolute sense. In the case of increasing cap levels, for example, the investor will see a larger possible increase in the conversion price. A higher floor level will prevent the conversion price being fixed at lower levels. This will constrain a possible increase of the conversion ratio.

The price impact $\Delta P_{\beta,\alpha}$ is more moderate for the JDCEV model than if the jump-diffusion model was selected. In Figure 11.14, the difference between the two models is obvious when the cap is increased from 100% to 120%. The higher the cap, the more punitive a conversion price reset can be for the owner of the convertible. The investor sees the conversion ratio decrease and loses, as a consequence, convexity. Yet, this change in convexity is punished less hard in a CEV world than with a jump-diffusion model. The latter model attributes the same

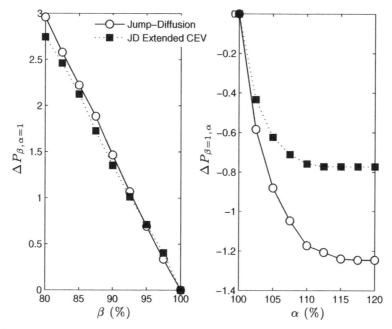

Figure 11.14 Price impact of changing the cap and floor levels in a reset structure.

volatility to a given convexity whatever the level of the share price. This is not the case when relying on a CEV approach.

11.8 CALIBRATION OF CEV

11.8.1 Introduction

Through a calibration process for a particular asset, the non-observable input parameters of a stochastic process describing this asset are determined such that the process fits the market. Under the concept of the market, we understand the collection of market prices for listed options, warrants, corporate bonds, and credit default swap spreads on this particular share. After a calibration, the discrepancy between the theoretical value of these instruments P^{theo} and their quoted market prices P^Q will be minimal. A successful calibration gives an immediate boost to the credibility of a chosen stochastic process. This explains without any doubt the worldwide popularity of stochastic volatility models, such as Heston, that allow in many situations for a successful calibration. One should not be fooled by the perfect calibration of the model. This conclusion was arrived at in [176]. Here, the authors calibrated seven different stochastic models to options on the Dow Jones Euro Stoxx 50 index. For the different approaches a perfect calibration was possible, leading to almost identical levels between both P^{theo} and P^Q. As such, all models result in identical marginal distributions. As soon as these calibration models were applied to non-vanilla instruments, the outcomes were very different however. The perfect fit to vanilla calls and puts did not evolve in similar theoretical prices for exotic options. For lookback call options a price range of more than 15% amongst the models was observed! This should bring any hybrid analyst dreaming of the one-size-fits-all stochastic model back to the ground with both feet.

11.8.2   Local or Global Calibration

In a CEV model there are two parameters that are the outcome of a possible calibration exercise: σ_{CEV} and p_{CEV}. The CEV model can be fit to a particular grid of option prices. In an advanced setting credit default swap spreads could be included as well. The difference between the theoretical and market prices is measured by a function F_t using a cross-section of M different options prices with different strikes K_i and maturities T_i on a particular date t:

$$F_t(\sigma_{CEV}, p_{CEV}) = \sqrt{\sum_{i=1}^{M} (P_{i,t}^{theo}(K_i, T_i, \sigma_{CEV}, p_{CEV}) - P_{i,t}^{Q}(K_i, T_i))^2} \qquad (11.54)$$

The optimal parameter set $[\sigma_{CEV}, p_{CEV}]$ is such that F_t reaches a minimum value using these two parameters:

$$[\sigma_{CEV}, p_{CEV}] = \underset{\sigma_{CEV}, p_{CEV}}{arg\,min} F_t(\sigma_{CEV}, p_{CEV}) \qquad (11.55)$$

This is a **local calibration** since the fitting is performed on data observed on one particular day only.

A **global calibration** applies the error function F_t to a wider data set since the option data for several dates $t_1, \ldots, t_i, \ldots$ is now incorporated into one error function.

11.8.3   Calibrating CEV: Step by Step

With a numerical example, we now illustrate the calibration of a CEV model where both σ_{CEV} and p_{CEV} are determined starting from an existing volatility surface. The call and put options from where the calibration starts are American and hence prohibit the use of a closed-form formula. Equation (11.25) is only valid for European options. The calculation of the estimated theoretical prices P^{theo} will take place through a lattice model instead.

Finding the minimum of the error function F_t starts with the choice of an initial estimate $\sigma_{CEV,0}$ and $p_{CEV,0}$. The search for the minimum of the function $F_t(\sigma_{CEV}, p_{CEV})$ is done using the Nelder–Mead simplex algorithm described in [153]. This technique is a heuristic search method different from, for example, the Levenberg–Marquardt algorithm [138]. The latter is a popular numerical solution applied in minimization problems of multidimensional non-linear functions. One can encounter numerical instability problems when trying to find the optimal values σ_{CEV} and p_{CEV} using Levenberg–Marquardt. In its search for the minimum of F_t, this algorithm uses two derivatives:

$$\frac{\partial P^{theo}}{\partial \sigma_{CEV}} \quad and \quad \frac{\partial P^{theo}}{\partial p_{CEV}} \qquad (11.56)$$

These represent the sensitivities of the theoretical price with respect to both CEV parameters. Since we use a lattice model when putting the CEV model to work, we suffer from a convergence issue. This has been illustrated before in Figure 8.5. As a result of this, the calculated sensitivities from Equation (11.56) lack the accuracy to reliably use the Levenberg–Marquardt routine. This justifies the use of the Nelder–Mead simplex algorithm.[6]

Before running through the different steps of this numerical exercise, it is important to emphasize that even this choice of minimization algorithm comes with a caveat, since there is no guarantee that the obtained result has actually converged to the real minimum. A local minimum may have been obtained instead. Hence the importance of the choice of the initial values $\sigma_{CEV,0}$ and $p_{CEV,0}$.

1. **Market data**
   The spot price S of the share for which we want to estimate the CEV parameters is equal to 10. The continuous interest rate is 3% and the share has a 1% dividend yield.

2. **Option date**
   In a second step one assembles a grid of (American) option prices. These are the market prices P^Q of a limited set of American call and put options on this underlying share. In this example, we only consider a very limited option grid. The strikes K are respectively, 9, 10, and 11 while there are only two maturities available: $T = 1$ year and $T = 3$ years.

		Option Prices (P^Q)				Implied Volatility (σ_{BS})		
			K				K	
	Call	9	10	11	Call	9	10	11
	1 year	2.15	1.65	1.24	1 year	40.68%	39.82%	39.07%
	3 years	3.28	2.84	2.45	3 years	40.70%	39.86%	39.09%
T	Put				Put			
	1 year	1.00	1.47	2.04	1 year	40.65%	39.78%	39.02%
	3 years	1.86	2.36	2.91	3 years	40.63%	39.75%	38.96%

For each of the American options in the table above, the implied Black–Scholes volatility σ_{BS} was calculated.

3. **Estimating $p_{CEV,0}$**
   The value of $p_{CEV,0}$ is estimated using historical prices of the share price S. This can be obtained using the regression technique specified in Equation (11.22). Assume that, in this educational example, the initial value for the elasticity parameter $p_{CEV,0}$ is equal to 0.52.

4. **Estimating $\sigma_{CEV,0}$**
   We repeat an earlier property of the CEV model that links the instantaneous variance of the share price to the Black–Scholes variance:

$$\sigma_{BS} = \sigma_{CEV}S^{p_{CEV}-1} \tag{11.57}$$

In our heuristic approach we propose taking the average at-the-money volatility $\overline{\sigma}_{BS}$ for both American call and put options covering both maturities. This value is equal to 39.80% and allows us, in combination with the earlier result for $p_{CEV,0}$, to calculate $\sigma_{CEV,0}$:

$$\sigma_{CEV,0} = \overline{\sigma}_{BS}S^{1-p_{CEV,0}}$$
$$= 0.398 \times S^{(1-0.52)} \tag{11.58}$$
$$= 1.20$$

---

[6] This algorithm is implemented in MatLab under the name fminsearch.

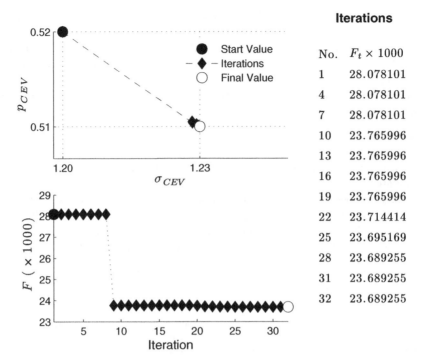

Iterations

No.	$F_t \times 1000$
1	28.078101
4	28.078101
7	28.078101
10	23.765996
13	23.765996
16	23.765996
19	23.765996
22	23.714414
25	23.695169
28	23.689255
31	23.689255
32	23.689255

Figure 11.15 Intermediate results of the Nelder–Mead simplex algorithm used to determine the optimal parameter set $[\sigma_{CEV}, p_{CEV}]$. The numerical results of F_t for a limited number of intermediate steps are provided.

5. **Minimizing F_t**

From the two initial values $\sigma_{CEV,0}$ and $p_{CEV,0}$, the calibration process starts. In Figure 11.15 the iterations of the search algorithm are illustrated step by step. The figure shows how the minimum value for F_t is obtained after 32 different iterations. The corresponding values for the CEV parameters are:

$$\sigma_{CEV} = 1.23$$
$$p_{CEV} = 0.51$$

(11.59)

The theoretical option prices P^{theo} are now close to the market prices P^Q of these options. These results are summarized in the table below:

	Option Prices (P^Q)				Option Prices (P^{theo})		
		K				K	
	Call	**9**	**10**	**11**	Call	**9**	**10**	**11**
	1 year	2.15	1.65	1.24	**1 year**	2.16	1.64	1.23
	3 years	3.28	2.84	2.45	**3 years**	3.28	2.84	2.43
T	Put				Put		
	1 year	1.00	1.47	2.04	**1 year**	1.00	1.47	2.03
	3 years	1.86	2.36	2.91	**3 years**	1.86	2.35	2.90

6. Results

The two CEV parameters can now be used to price derivative instruments based on the underlying stock S. One of the other possibilities is to extend the volatility surface from where the calibration originated to strikes and maturities beyond what is commonly available in the listed options market. The following implied volatility surface is constructed from CEV-generated option prices where σ_{CEV} and p_{CEV} were equal to 1.23 and 0.51, respectively:

	Call	5	9	10	11	15
				K		
T	1	46.75%	40.81%	39.76%	38.84%	35.93%
	3	46.69%	40.88%	39.83%	38.89%	36.03%
	8	46.28%	40.71%	39.72%	38.91%	36.10%

The table shows how the implied volatility for a call option with strike 15 and a maturity of 8 years is equal to 36.10%. The shaded area singles out those strikes and maturities for which the option prices were part of the calibration price. A calibrated CEV process hence helps to deliver long-dated and out-of-the-money volatilities. These volatility numbers are often not available given the fact that the listed options market for single names is short dated and does not offer liquid option prices for strikes that are too far out-of-the-money.

Pricing Contingent Debt

12.1 INTRODUCTION

In Chapter 3 we worked out an in-depth analysis of the anatomy of contingent convertibles (CoCos). These debt instruments convert into the equity of the issuing bank or suffer a write-down of the face value upon the appearance of a trigger event. This trigger mechanism provides an automatic strengthening of the capital structure of the bank. In this chapter the pricing of CoCos is handled from two different angles. Both methods can be considered practitioners' approaches and are directly applicable for a trading desk because they are based on observable market inputs. The first method has a credit derivatives background. The other approach puts CoCos in an equity derivatives framework. Both approaches were introduced in [69] and [70].

An equity derivatives specialist looks at this security as a potential long position in shares. A long position which is "knocked in" once a trigger event materializes. At the same moment the remaining coupon stream is wiped out. This is somehow different from a reverse convertible where a conversion into shares is only possible at maturity and not before.

A third alternative pricing model is a structural model. Under the structural philosophy based on, for example, the work of Robert Merton [149], one needs to model the assets on the balance sheet. This means that the development of a stochastic process for these assets is needed. Because the contingent convertible bonds have their conversion depending on an accounting ratio, a natural pricing framework is provided by structural models [192]. Structural models have the bank's balance sheet as the main driver of the CoCo's price. The big challenge for the structural model is the accurate estimation of the valuation parameters that drive the stochastic process of the assets. These input factors are most often unobservable variables. Structural models have been used in the calculation of default risk and have accordingly received much attention from rating agencies. An example of a structural model for the pricing of contingent capital can be found in [158]. Earlier, in Section 9.4, the possible application of structural models to price convertible bonds has already been covered. In this chapter on contingent debt, we do not follow the structural route but instead opt for two techniques based on observable market data such as share prices and volatility data.

The investor receives on conversion a predefined number of shares. This quantity is the conversion ratio (C_r). For a full write-down CoCo bond, one sets C_r equal to zero. The share price S^* at the moment the CoCo gets triggered will be low because all of this happens in a setting where the bank is going through a difficult period. However unlikely the probability of a trigger may be, the investor is going to deal with a large loss when ending up with a conversion into cheap shares. The risk profile of a CoCo corresponds clearly to an investment product with a low probability of a high loss and a high probability of a moderate gain. There has always been an appetite for this kind of risk in the markets. Particularly when investors are shopping for yield, CoCos likely catch their attention. Structured products such as auto-callables[1] carry

---

[1] Auto-callables are structured products with a performance linked to the price path followed by an underlying share price. This financial security may distribute a coupon when the share price is above the coupon barrier on the coupon date. The product is automatically called back by the issuer if the share price rises above the auto-call barrier. There are, of course, different varieties of

a risk profile that corresponds greatly to the risk embedded inside a CoCo bond. The popularity of auto-callables, which has spread globally to both Europe and the United States [10, 187], suggests that there will be an ongoing appetite for contingent debt.

12.2 CREDIT DERIVATIVES METHOD

12.2.1 Introduction

In a reduced-form approach, a default intensity parameter λ is used when modeling default. The probability that a financial institution, that issued a bond, defaults in the time interval $[t, t + dt]$ while surviving up to the time t is equal to λdt. Accordingly, one can show that the probability that the bond survives between time t and T is given by $\exp(-\lambda(T - t))$. This is the survival probability p_{surv}. The default probability p_{def} over the same horizon is hence $1 - \exp(-\lambda(T - t))$. This theory forms the basis of intensity-based credit modeling and has been covered extensively in Chapter 10. On default, the investor expects to recover a portion of the face value N of the bond. This is the recovery rate π. The loss for the investor is hence equal to $(1 - \pi) \times N$. To incorporate the default risk on corporate bonds, investors traditionally use a credit spread. When calculating the theoretical value of the bond, the credit spread will be added to the risk-free interest rate r. The relationship between the credit spread (cs), recovery rate, and default intensity is given by the well-known credit triangle explained in Section 10.4:

$$cs = (1 - \pi) \times \lambda \qquad (12.1)$$

The credit triangle is a rule of thumb linking the credit spread cs to the recovery rate π and default intensity λ. The credit spread is the product of the loss $(1 - \pi)$ and the instantaneous probability of this loss taking place (λ). This opens the door to model the trigger event where a CoCo is converted into shares as an extreme event similar to default in corporate debt or in credit default swaps. Hitting the CoCo trigger is modeled as such an extreme event. The default intensity λ is accordingly substituted with a trigger intensity $\lambda_{Trigger}$. From Equation (12.1), we can determine the value of the credit spread on contingent debt using the credit triangle:

$$cs_{CoCo} = (1 - \pi_{CoCo}) \times \lambda_{Trigger} \qquad (12.2)$$

12.2.2 Loss

The loss absorbed by the CoCo bond can be pre-specified as is the case for CoCos with a write-down mechanism. For a full write-down contingent convertible, $\pi_{CoCo} = 0$. In case of a CoCo with a conversion in shares, the losses will depend on the (unknown) level of the share price S^* when the trigger occurs. This is illustrated in Figure 12.1:

$$Loss_{CoCo} = N - C_r S^* = N \left(1 - \frac{S^*}{C_p} \right) = N(1 - \pi_{CoCo}) \qquad (12.3)$$

---

this structured product and many investment banks who issue these instruments have come up with a proprietary and attractive name for it. There is, however, always a probability for a substantial loss built into this security. There is a third barrier embedded into this structure. If the share price drops below this latter price level, the investor will have to take a haircut on the investment.

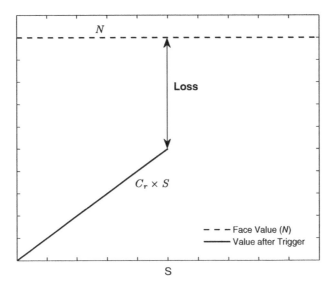

Figure 12.1   Loss on a contingent convertible when the trigger is hit and conversion in shares takes place.

The share price at the moment the bond is converted into shares is S^*. The recovery rate on the triggering of the convertible is hence given by the ratio of this share price and the conversion price C_P:

$$\pi_{CoCo} = \frac{S^*}{C_P} \qquad (12.4)$$

The latter equation illustrates the impact of the choice of the conversion price on the value of the CoCo. If the conversion price is set equal to the share price observed at the moment of the trigger, there is no loss on the investment for the investor. The investor receives shares immediately after the trigger at the market price of the shares on the trigger date. Because of the choice of $C_P = S^*$, the total value of these shares will be equal to the face value N. When the conversion price is set equal to the price of the shares on the issue date, a loss can be expected after conversion. The choice of C_P and the estimation of S^* allows us to calculate the loss or recovery component of Equation (12.1). The only missing link is the trigger intensity $\lambda_{Trigger}$.

12.2.3   Trigger Intensity ($\lambda_{Trigger}$)

A trigger could, for example, be defined as a regulator declaring the bank non-viable without further government support, a market parameter such as a stock price dropping below a predefined barrier, or the announcement by the bank that it has insufficient Common Equity Tier 1 capital. Modeling the act of a regulator to force the conversion of contingent debt is a difficult and even impossible task. Attaching a probability and timing to the failure of a bank to meet a particular accounting ratio is of similar complexity. Instead of directly modeling an accounting or a regulatory trigger, we turn the other way and consider the share price S as the only explanatory variable. Doing so, we associate with a trigger event a corresponding share price S^*. An accounting trigger where a Core Tier 1 ratio drops below a minimum level is

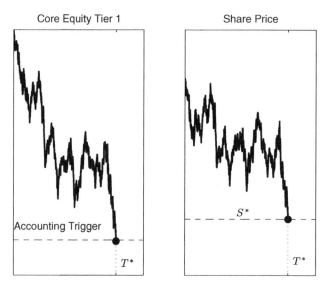

Figure 12.2   Linking an accounting trigger with a market trigger on the share price.

now replaced by an equivalent event where the stock price drops below a barrier S^*. Linking a market trigger S^* to an accounting trigger is illustrated in Figure 12.2.

The probability p^* that such a level is touched during the life of the contingent convertible is given by the following equation [181]:

$$p^* = \Phi\left(\frac{\log\left(\frac{S^*}{S}\right) - \mu\Delta T}{\sigma\sqrt{\Delta T}}\right) + \left(\frac{S^*}{S}\right)^{\frac{2\mu}{\sigma^2}} \Phi\left(\frac{\log\left(\frac{S^*}{S}\right) + \mu\Delta T}{\sigma\sqrt{\Delta T}}\right)$$

$$\mu = r - q - \frac{\sigma^2}{2}$$

q : Continuous dividend yield

r : Continuous interest rate   (12.5)

σ : Volatility

ΔT : Maturity of the contingent convertible $\Delta T = T - t$

S : Current share price

This is the first exit time equation used in barrier option pricing under Black–Scholes. It models the probability that a stock price S will touch the level S^* somewhere between time t and the expiration of the bond at time T. $\Phi(x)$ is the probability that a random variable X, which is following a standard normal distribution, takes a value smaller than x:

$$\Phi(x) = \text{Probability}(X \le x) \quad \text{with} \quad X \sim N(0, 1) \tag{12.6}$$

In this equation, p^* quantifies the probability that the trigger is going to take place. From p^* we can now determine λ_{Trigger}:

$$\lambda_{\text{Trigger}} = -\frac{\log(1 - p^*)}{T} \tag{12.7}$$

This subsequently gives the CoCo spread (cs_{CoCo}):[2]

$$cs_{CoCo} = -\frac{\log(1-p^*)}{T} \times \left(1 - \frac{S^*}{C_P}\right) \tag{12.8}$$

The probability of hitting the trigger is here modeled in a Black–Scholes setting. This choice allows us to obtain a closed-form solution which suits the comprehension of the loss absorption in a CoCo bond. Nothing prevents the logic and assumptions we have been using so far from being extended to other stochastic processes. The nature of the CoCo would indeed call for other approaches such as in [59], incorporating smile conform models.

The accounting trigger has been replaced by a share price trigger and through this replacement, we assume that there is a barrier level S^* that is equivalent to, for example, the Core Equity Tier 1 level dropping below the agreed minimum level. With our first pricing formula, we can now calculate the **implied trigger level** $\overline{S}^*$. This is the share price level embedded in the CoCo's price. It is the level where the market expects the underlying stock to trade at the very moment that the CoCo is converted into shares or written down. Using $\overline{S}^*$ is going to be useful when one has to compare several CoCo bonds that are trading in the market. The terms and conditions of these bonds may be very different, but this complexity can now be brought back to a single implied share price level $\overline{S}^*$.

12.2.4   CoCo Spread Calculation Example

Suppose we are dealing with a newly issued contingent convertible. The only trigger in this example is a regulatory trigger. The CoCo has a 10-year maturity. The underlying share price is set at $100, has a volatility ($\sigma$) equal to 30%, and is expected not to distribute any dividend at all ($q = 0$). The continuous interest rate (r) is 4%. We now assume that the occurrence of the trigger corresponds to a share price equal to half the current share price ($S^* = \$50$). The calculation of the credit spread under this assumption is given by the following three-step process:

1. Probability of hitting the trigger (Equation (12.5))
   $p^* = 48.30\%$
2. Trigger intensity (Equation (12.7))
   $\lambda_{Trigger} = -\frac{\log(1-0.4830)}{10} = 0.066 = 6.6\%$
3. Recovery (Equation (12.4))
   $\pi_{CoCo} = \frac{S^*}{C_P} = \frac{50}{100} = 50\%$

Hence: $cs_{CoCo} = 6.6\% \times 50\% = 330$ **bps**. Adding this spread to the continuous interest rate gives the total continuous yield on this CoCo: 7.30%.

12.2.5   Case Study: Lloyds Contingent Convertibles

As a case study we now consider one CoCo out of the series of CoCos issued by the Lloyds Banking Group in December 2009. A description of this CoCo bond has been provided in

---

[2] This spread is defined as a continuous interest rate and needs be scaled back to the yield and day count convention of the bond in particular.

Table 12.1   Data for one of the Lloyds convertible bonds (pricing date: May 3, 2013)

Lloyds 7.588% 2020			
Bond Data		Market Data	
PRICING DATE	May 5, 2013	S	54.05 (GBP)
ISIN	XS0459086582	r	1.29%
MATURITY	May 20, 2020	q	0
PRICE	108.37	σ	49.0%
ACCRUED	3.73		
DIRTY PRICE	112.10		
CURRENCY	GBP		
COUPON	7.588%		
FREQUENCY	Semi-Annual		
FACE VALUE	1000		

Table 3.1. This contingent convertible has a Tier 1 accounting trigger of 5%, at the occurrence of which the investor is forced to buy shares against a conversion price of 59 GBP (pence). Per bond, the investor will hence receive a predetermined number of shares (C_r):

$$C_r = \frac{100\,000}{59} = 1695 \text{ shares} \tag{12.9}$$

Starting from the price of the bond and using the credit derivatives method explained above, we will calculate in the following numerical example the implied trigger level $\overline{S}^*$. The data from which we start the calculation are given in Table 12.1.

On the pricing date of this particular case study, the clean price of the bond was equal to 108.37%. Given a face value of 1000 GBP and an accrued interest of 3.73%, the dirty cash amount for one bond is equal to 1000 GBP $\times$ (108.37% + 3.73%) = 1121 GBP. This investment generates a stream of future coupon payments that, given an initial outlay of 1121 GBP, corresponds to a credit spread of 501 bps (= cs_{CoCo}):

Coupon stream per bond			
Date	GBP	Date	GBP
12-May-13	37.942	12-May-17	37.942
12-Nov-13	37.942	12-Nov-17	37.942
12-May-14	37.942	12-May-18	37.942
12-Nov-14	37.942	12-Nov-18	37.942
12-May-15	37.942	12-May-19	37.942
12-Nov-15	37.942	12-Nov-19	37.942
12-May-16	37.942	12-May-20	37.942
12-Nov-16	37.942		

Through interpolation in Figure 12.3 we learn how the implied trigger level $\overline{S}^*$ corresponds to a share price equal to 9.2 pence. This is a lot lower than the forced conversion price (C_P),

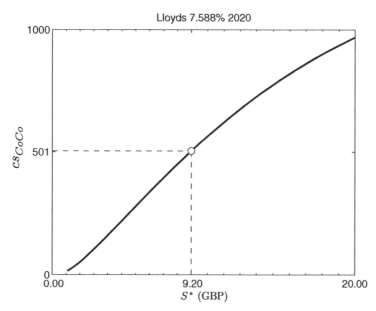

Figure 12.3   Calculation of the CoCo spread cs_{CoCo} for different trigger levels S^* (May 3, 2013).

equal to 59 pence. The embedded implied loss L_{CoCo} for the CoCo holder is therefore equal to:

$$L_{CoCo} = 1 - \frac{9.2}{59} = 84.41\% \tag{12.10}$$

The credit derivatives method is a straightforward approach; it is a mere rule of the thumb. The reason for this is the fact that the loss $(1 - \pi_{CoCo})$ is constrained to the write-down of the face value or the forced conversion in shares. No reference at all is made to the fact that the coupon stream also stops at the moment the trigger materializes.

The calculation of the implied trigger level has been repeated on a daily basis from January 2, 2013 to May 3, 2013 for this particular CoCo bond. The result of this calculation is summarized in Figure 12.4. The graph shows how, during this 5-month period, the expected losses were contained in the interval [84.25–88.15].

12.3 EQUITY DERIVATIVES METHOD

12.3.1 Introduction

Starting from the credit approach, which we prefer to label as a "rule of thumb," we can now construct an equity derivatives model to price CoCos and incorporate the fact that the coupon stream will also be knocked out. This second approach to CoCo pricing will be explained in detail in two steps. The first step starts with a CoCo without coupons, while the second part of the explanation incorporates coupons into the valuation. The equity derivatives model is constructed for the sake of exercise in a Black–Scholes assumption. Nothing holds us back from reaching out to smile conform models such as in [59].

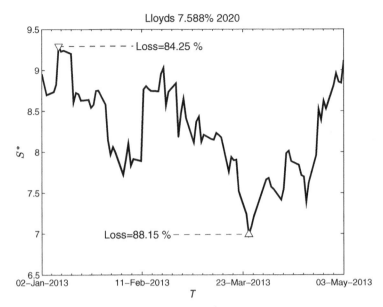

Figure 12.4   Calculation of the implied trigger level $\overline{S}^*$ for a Lloyds CoCo.

12.3.2   Step 1: Zero-Coupon CoCo

A zero-coupon contingent convertible has a face value N, which will be paid out at maturity T. The bond distributes no coupons and the conversion into shares will be forced upon the investors once the trigger is a fact. The final payoff of the CoCo is P_T and is given by the following equation:

$$\begin{cases} P_T = C_r S_T & \text{if triggered} \\ P_T = N & \text{if not triggered} \end{cases} \tag{12.11}$$

Next we define the trigger indicator $\mathbf{1}_{\{\text{Trigger}\}}$. This equals 1 when the CoCo is triggered and zero otherwise. After such a trigger, the bond holder is long C_r shares. When dealing with a market-based trigger where the share price has to fall below a predefined barrier S^*, this indicator is written as:

$$\mathbf{1}_{\{\min(S_t) \leq S^*\}} \tag{12.12}$$

Dealing with a contingent convertible where the Core Tier 1 ratio needs to be at any time t above 5% in order to avoid a conversion into shares, the indicator on this accounting trigger is defined as:

$$\mathbf{1}_{\{\min(CT1_t) \leq 5\%\}} \tag{12.13}$$

Equation (12.11) can be rewritten as:

$$P_T = N + C_r \times \left(S_T - \frac{N}{C_r} \right) \mathbf{1}_{\{\text{Trigger}\}} \tag{12.14}$$

$$= N + C_r \times (S_T - C_P) \mathbf{1}_{\{\text{Trigger}\}}$$

One can observe in Equation (12.14) how the final payoff of a CoCo can be broken down into two components. There is first of all the face value of the bond N next to a possible purchase of C_r shares. This second component only materializes if a trigger actually took place during the life of the bond. We approximate this by a knock-in forward on the underlying shares. This models a possible purchase of C_r shares. The purchase price of each share is the conversion price C_P. A zero-coupon CoCo is a combined position of a (zero-coupon) corporate bond and a knock-in forward (F) on C_r shares of the issuer:

Zero-Coupon CoCo = Zero-Coupon Corporate Bond + Knock-In Forward(s)

The knock-in forward is priced as a long position in a knock-in call and a short position in a knock-in put. Both options share the same strike C_P and the same barrier S^*. The decomposition of a CoCo into corporate debt and C_r knock-in forwards on shares allows us to price contingent convertibles using a closed-form formula. The elegance of the pricing model comes at a cost, however. The approach chosen introduces a flaw in the model. In reality, the investor receives shares and not forwards with a price F on the trigger event. The conversion value at any time t after the trigger moment is hence $C_r S_t$ and not $C_r F_t$. The difference is obvious if the trigger event takes place a long time before the final expiration date of the bond. Being long shares or a forward on those shares carries a consequence if dividends were to be paid out, for example. The investor holding shares obtained through a conversion of the CoCo is immediately entitled to dividends and voting rights. Under the acceptable assumption that the dividend payout after a trigger takes place is going to be close to zero, the barrier option technique is an acceptable model. A bank will indeed not start paying out large dividends to the holders of its common equity when it has just recapitalized its balance sheet. The value of the zero-coupon CoCo on the valuation date P_t is then:

$$P_t = N \exp(-r(T - t)) + \text{Knock-In Forward} \qquad (12.15)$$

The corporate bond part in Equation (12.15) is calculated using the risk-free rate. The loss on conversion – which is to some extent a default event – is embedded in the knock-in forward part of the pricing model.

12.3.3   Step 2: Adding Coupons

The coupons of the CoCo will only be received as long as the trigger event has not materialized. This reduces the value of a CoCo compared with a straight corporate bond of the same issuer. Suppose the bond pays out k coupons with value c_i at times t_i. When a conversion trigger occurs, the coupon payments after this trigger date are omitted. This claim impacts the price of the CoCo. It needs to be valued as a short position in a binary down-and-in option (BDI).[3] For each coupon c_i, there is indeed a corresponding short position in a binary option expiring at the coupon date t_i that is knocked in when the barrier is hit. Each of the k binary options BDI comes with a rebate of c_i paid out at its expiry date t_i. The activation of the short binary option offsets the coupon payment expected at time t_i. This will be the case whenever there

---

[3] The full-blown name for this option is down-and-in cash-at-expiry-or-nothing option, we prefer to abbreviate it as a binary down-and-in option.

is a trigger before the coupon date t_i. A short position in this knock-in option models the possibility of losing the coupon:

$$\textbf{CoCo} = \textbf{Corporate Bond} + \textbf{Knock-In Forward(s)} - \sum \textbf{Binary Down-In Options}$$

For every coupon c_i there is a matching BDI option with a maturity corresponding to the maturity date t_i of each of the coupons, and a trigger event which matches the overall conversion trigger of the CoCo. The sum of these BDI options lowers the price of the CoCo. Their combined value is given by the following equation:

$$-\sum_{i=1}^{k} c_i \exp(-r(t_i - t)) \mathbf{1}_{\{\text{Trigger Time} \le t_i\}} \tag{12.16}$$

The price P_t of the CoCo is equal to a corporate bond (**A** in Equation (12.17)) to which a knock-in forward is added (**B**). The third component is the sum of the BDI options which offset the coupons c_i upon the occurrence of a trigger (**C**):

$$\mathbf{P} = \mathbf{A} + \mathbf{B} + \mathbf{C}$$

$$\mathbf{A} = N \exp(-r(T - t)) + \sum_{i=1}^{k} c_i \exp(-r(t_i - t))$$

$$\mathbf{B} = C_r \times [S \exp(-q(T - t))(S^*/S)^{2\lambda} \Phi(y_1)$$
$$- K \exp(-r(T - t))(S^*/S)^{2\lambda-2} \Phi(y_1 - \sigma\sqrt{(T - t)})$$
$$- K \exp(-r(T - t))\Phi(-x_1 + \sigma\sqrt{(T - t)}) + S \exp(-q(T - t))\Phi(-x_1)]$$

$$\mathbf{C} = -\sum_{i=1}^{k} c_i \exp(-r(t_i - t))[\Phi(-x_{1i} + \sigma\sqrt{(t_i - t)}) + (S^*/S)^{2\lambda-2}\Phi(y_{1i} - \sigma\sqrt{(t_i - t)})]$$

with

$$K = C_P$$

$$C_r = \frac{N}{C_P}$$

$$x_1 = \frac{\log(S/S^*)}{\sigma\sqrt{(T - t)}} + \lambda\sigma\sqrt{(T - t)}$$

$$y_1 = \frac{\log(S^*/S)}{\sigma\sqrt{(T - t)}} + \lambda\sigma\sqrt{(T - t)}$$

$$x_{1i} = \frac{\log(S/S^*)}{\sigma\sqrt{(t_i - t)}} + \lambda\sigma\sqrt{(t_i - t)}$$

$$y_{1i} = \frac{\log(S^*/S)}{\sigma\sqrt{(t_i - t)}} + \lambda\sigma\sqrt{(t_i - t)}$$

$$\lambda = \frac{r - q + \sigma^2/2}{\sigma^2}$$

$$\tag{12.17}$$

The corporate bond is also priced in **A** using a risk-free rate. Equation **B** prices the knock-in forward as a knock-in call minus a knock-in put. Each of the equations in (12.17) can be found in the work of Reiner and Rubinstein [169].

12.3.4   Numerical Example

Question: What Coupon Rate can be Offered?

Starting from Equation (12.17) we can now price a 5-year contingent convertible with face value €1000 on a share with a current price of €100 and a volatility equal to 45%. The risk-free continuous interest rate is 3% and the share distributes no dividends. The conversion can be caused by an accounting trigger, a market trigger, or a regulatory trigger. We assume that the share price S^* corresponding to such a trigger moment is €25. The conversion price is equal to the price at the issue date. This sets $C_r = 10 = \frac{1000}{100}$. The bank wants to issue the contingent convertible at par. What coupon rate should be offered to the investors in order to have an initial price equal to par?

Answer

In Figure 12.5 the price of the CoCo is plotted for different coupon levels keeping all the other parameters the same. Using the knock-in forward model, a coupon of 7.62% results in a theoretical price equal to par.

Calculations

Taking the coupon of 7.62%, we can work out the calculation in detail. The value of the CoCo can be broken down into several components as set out in Equation (12.17):

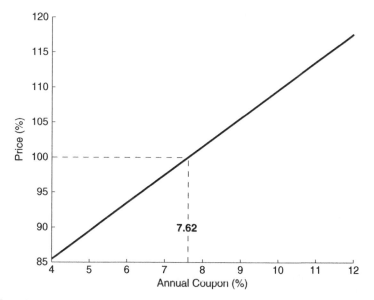

Figure 12.5   Price of a contingent convertible for different annual coupon levels.

- **Long corporate bond = 120.92%** (part A of Equation (12.17))
  The table below lists all the cash flows and the corresponding discount factors (DF) adding up to a total present value (PV) of 1209.23:

T	Coupon	N	DF	PV
1	76.2		0.9704	73.9479
2	76.2		0.9418	71.7625
3	76.2		0.9139	69.6416
4	76.2		0.8869	67.5833
5	76.2	1000	0.8607	926.2939
			Σ	**1209.23**

- **Long down-and-in forwards = −16.68%** (part B of Equation (12.17))
  There are 10 ($= N/C_p$) down-and-in forwards embedded in the structure. The pricing parameters are: $S = 100$, $r = 0.03$, $q = 0$, $\sigma = 0.45$, $S^* = 25$, $C_p = 100$. The theoretical value for one such knock-in is €−16.68. The total value of this option package in the contingent capital expressed as a percentage of the face value is:

$$-10 \times \frac{16.68}{1000} = -16.68\%$$

  The probability of possibly having to face a situation where a trigger materializes and converts the bond into shares obviously reduces the value of the bond.

- **Short binary down-and-in barrier options = −4.24%** (part C of Equation (12.17))
  There are in total five binary barrier options embedded in the structure, one maturing on every coupon date. Each of the annual coupons is worth €76.20 and can be knocked out if, before the coupon date, the trigger is breached. This can be replicated by combining each coupon with a corresponding short BDI. The rebate of each BDI is €76.20 and their corresponding values are given in the table below:

T	BDI
1	−0.2461
2	−3.3682
3	−8.3158
4	−13.1457
5	−17.2819
Σ	**−42.3577**

The short position in the BDI, with a rebate equal to the coupon, has a total value of €−42.3577.

Adding the value of the three components together results in a total theoretical value of the contingent convertible equal to 100%. The annual coupon of 7.62% provides a yield pick-up above the continuous risk-free interest rate. This is the compensation for the downside risk within the contingent convertible.

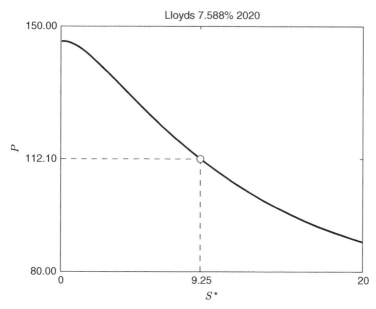

Figure 12.6   For different expected trigger levels S^*, the corresponding CoCo prices for Lloyds have been calculated. The implied trigger level is 9.25 pence.

12.3.5   Case Study: Lloyds Contingent Convertibles

Calculating the Implied Trigger Level $\overline{S}^*$

The derivatives approach can easily be applied to one of Lloyds' contingent convertibles. We limit ourselves to the example already priced before, where we used the credit derivatives approach. The data for this real-world example can be found in Table 12.1. Along the same lines of thought as in the credit derivatives method, we find through interpolation the value of S^* such that the theoretical CoCo price matches the (dirty) price equal to 112.10. The result of this exercise is represented in Figure 12.6 and reveals that the implied trigger level $\overline{S}^* = 9.25$. This result corresponds to an expected loss of 84.32%, which is very close to the credit derivatives solution.

The goal of building a model for a CoCo bond goes beyond the calculation of its theoretical price P. The applicability of the model stretches further than this fair value calculation and will allow us to calculate different price sensitivities. Given the fact that the only source of risk in this simple valuation tool is the share price S, a sensitivity measure such as $\Delta = \frac{\partial P}{\partial S}$ will prove useful. The calculation of Δ has been illustrated in Figure 12.7 and shows how the equity exposure increases when the share price S approaches the trigger level S^*. On May 3, 2013 and using the implied trigger level of 9.25, we obtain a theoretical delta of 670 shares per bond of this particular contingent convertible.

Comparing both Approaches

Using a limited selection out of the available CoCo bonds issued by Lloyds and using the two contingent convertibles of Credit Suisse, we can now put both valuation approaches to work.

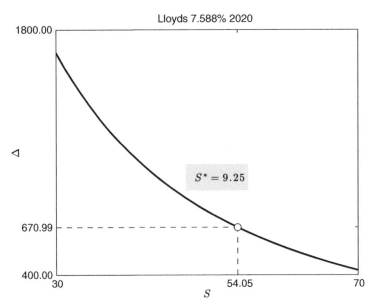

Figure 12.7   Calculation of the Δ for a Lloyds CoCo using a trigger level $S^* = 9.25$ GBp.

Starting from the market price of each of the CoCos, the implied volatility of the shares, the corresponding dividend yield, and the interest rate corresponding to the maturity of the CoCo, one can calculate the implied trigger level $\overline{S}^*$ for each of the bonds. The expected loss $Loss_{CoCo}$ can then be derived using Equation (12.3). This gives the possibility of comparing one CoCo against the other. One no longer has to compare yields or the distance from the accounting trigger. Calculating the embedded loss is a valid alternative when comparing CoCos. The outcome of this exercise has been provided in Table 12.2.

Table 12.2   Implied losses for contingent convertibles issued by Lloyds and Credit Suisse. Pricing date: May 3, 2013

			Lloyds		
				$Loss_{CoCo}$ (%)	
ISIN	Price	Coupon (%)	Maturity	Credit Derivatives	Equity Derivatives
XS0459086582	108.37	7.5884	12-May-20	84.41%	84.32%
XS0459087986	111.96	8.875	7-Feb-20	88.65%	87.94%
XS0459088109	114.13	9.334	7-Feb-20	88.74%	88.16%
			Credit Suisse		
				$Loss_{CoCo}$ (%)	
ISIN	Price	Coupon (%)	Maturity	Credit Derivatives	Equity Derivatives
XS0747231362	109.5	7.25	22-Feb-22	76.67%	76.84%
US90261AAB89	116.25	7.625	17-Aug-22	82.14%	82.15%

Source: Bloomberg.

Sensitivity to Volatility

Using the same Lloyds CoCo as in the previous example, we now investigate the sensitivity of the CoCo price with respect to changes in the volatility σ. The anatomy of the contingent convertible is such that an increase in σ has a negative impact on the price of the contingent convertible. A higher volatility increases the likelihood that the share price will hit the trigger level S^*. The investor in contingent debt is short vega:

$$\text{Vega}_{CoCo} = \frac{\partial P}{\partial \sigma} < 0 \qquad (12.18)$$

Earlier, in Section 6.5, we used an arbitrary CoCo bond as an example to illustrate the importance of the volatility as input in the valuation model. Figure 6.8 visualized the obvious importance of σ. Only for share prices S either very close to or very distant from the trigger level S^* was the influence of σ less important. At this stage we use the equity derivatives model to gain a better understanding of the vega of this particular contingent convertible issued by Lloyds. The results of this analysis can be found in Figure 12.8. For two price levels $S \in \{12, 40\}$, we studied for a wide range of volatilities $\sigma \in [20, 80]$ the vega profile. The main point of interest was to understand how the vega changes when σ changes in value. This greek is called the volga or "dVegadVol":

$$\text{Volga}_{CoCo} = \frac{\partial \text{Vega}_{CoCo}}{\partial \sigma} = \frac{\partial^2 P}{\partial \sigma^2} \qquad (12.19)$$

- $S = 12$

  In this situation, we deal with a share price which is very close to the trigger level $S^* = 9.25$. The vega is negative for all volatility levels, but appreciates when σ increases. The volga is hence positive. For high levels of σ, we have that Volga ≈ 0 and Vega ≈ 0. The CoCo is so

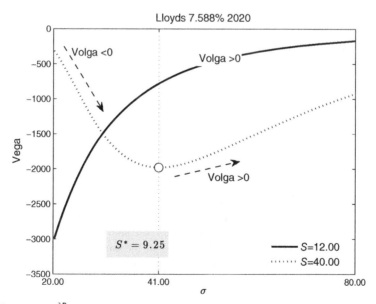

Figure 12.8 Vega $= \frac{\partial P}{\partial \sigma}$ for a Lloyds CoCo for two different share price levels. Pricing date: May 3, 2013.

close to being forced in conversion that a small change in the value of σ hardly impacts the value of the bond. From a theoretical perspective, the CoCo will have a profile very close to equity.

- $S = 40$

  This share price level is very distant from the implied trigger. The volga profile is different from the previous case where the bond was very close to being triggered. A visualization of this is given in Figure 12.8, and two different domains catch our attention:

  - Volga < 0 when $\sigma \in [20, 41]$

    In this range, a negative volatility convexity can be observed. The more σ appreciates in value, the more the vega of the CoCo turns negative.

  - Volga > 0 when $\sigma \in [41, 80]$

    From a certain volatility level onward ($\sigma = 41\%$), the convexity changes sign and becomes positive. In this case, an increase in the implied volatility actually reduces the negative vega of the bond.

The volga is the convexity of the price P of a financial security with respect to the volatility level σ. In case of a CoCo bond it informs us about the sensitivity of the theoretical price to the volatility of the volatility. Making abstraction of all the input parameters different from σ, the theoretical price change δP driven by the changes in σ is given by:

$$
\begin{aligned}
\delta P &= \cdots + \frac{\partial P}{\partial \sigma} \times \delta\sigma + \frac{1}{2}\frac{\partial^2 P}{\partial \sigma^2} \times (\delta\sigma)^2 + \cdots \\
&= \cdots + \text{Vega}_{CoCo} \times \delta\sigma + \frac{1}{2}\text{Volga}_{CoCo} \times (\delta\sigma)^2 + \cdots
\end{aligned}
\tag{12.20}
$$

From the equation above, we learn that the higher this volatility convexity, the more the value of the CoCo bond is driven by second-order changes in σ. This is the impact of the volatility of the volatility, which may motivate us to possibly use a stochastic volatility model.

12.3.6   Case Study: Tier 1 and Tier 2 CoCos

In Section 3.5.6 we explained how, in Basel III, CoCos have been confined to two possible categories when a bank wants to include them in its regulatory capital. CoCo bonds can be either Additional Tier 1 or Tier 2 bonds. One of the qualifications for a CoCo bond to qualify as a Tier 1 bond is the combination of the trigger level and the maturity date of the bond. To qualify as Additional Tier 1 capital, the trigger needs to be at least equal to 5.125%. In the same Basel III framework, these instruments also need to be perpetual in maturity. Using the equity derivatives method explained in Section 12.3, we can now investigate the difference in implied trigger level S^* between Tier 1 and Tier 2 CoCo bonds.

To illustrate this, we will refer to two contingent convertible issues by Credit Suisse. On September 17, 2013 this Swiss bank had in total five CoCo bonds outstanding. The corresponding face value was equal to $7.2 bn. In this case study we focus our attention more in particular on a Tier 1 and Tier 2 issue. Both bonds share the same loss-absorption mechanism and have a full write-down feature if the trigger level is hit. The instrument-specific details can be found in Table 12.3.

The Tier 2 bond issued by Credit Suisse categorizes as a private placement and was sold exclusively to Qatar Holding LLC and The Olayan Group [108]. In Figure 12.9 the implied trigger level for both CoCos has been calculated for the period August 27–September 17, 2013.

Table 12.3   Summarized description of the full write-down CoCos issued by Credit Suisse

	Tier 1	Tier 2
Issue Size	CHF 290 mn	$2.5 bn
Annoucement Date	August 1, 2013	August 20, 2013
Issue Date	September 4, 2013	August 8, 2013
Maturity	Perpetual	10 years
Callable	Callable after 5 years. On the call date the coupon is reset at the 5-year CHF swap rate + 520 bps	–
Coupon	6	6.5
Coupon Cancellation	Yes	No
Trigger Level (CET1)	5.125%	5.00%
Market	Domestic	Private placement

Source: Prospectus.

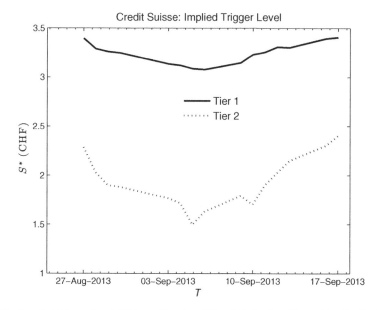

Figure 12.9   Implied trigger level S^* for a Tier 1 and Tier 2 CoCo bond issued by Credit Suisse.

Figure 12.9 clearly illustrates how the market perceives the Tier 1 bond as being more likely to be triggered than its Tier 2 equivalent. On September 17, 2013 we have, for example:[4]

$$S^*_{\text{Tier 1}} = 3.41 \text{ CHF} > S^*_{\text{Tier 2}} = 2.41 \text{ CHF} \tag{12.21}$$

12.4   COUPON DEFERRAL

The CoCo issued by the Spanish bank BBVA early May 2013 brought a novelty to the table through the introduction of coupons that are allowed to be deferred. A coupon deferral had already been accepted as a common feature in corporate or financial hybrids, but has now

---

[4] The maturity of the perpetual Tier 1 bond was in this exercise set equal to the first call date.

found its way to contingent capital as well. The investor in a BBVA contingent convertible can see an upcoming coupon payment canceled at the sole discretion of this bank or its regulator. The full anatomy of this bond has been given in Table 3.7 in Chapter 3. This non-cumulative cancelation increases the complexity of the model since the extra spread (cs_{CoCo}) earned as compensation for a possible loss absorption can now be wiped out as well.

To model a CoCo bond with a possible coupon deferral, we stick to the concept of the share price trigger S^*. This was introduced in the equity and credit derivatives approach we explained before. This share price level is associated with the triggering of an accounting ratio. Such a trigger level can be implied from the current market price of the CoCo. The result of this exercise is the implied trigger level $\overline{S}^*$ and can be interpreted as that particular share price that the market considers to prevail when the loss-absorption mechanism is put into action.

The existence of a coupon deferral changes the approach slightly because a coupon will now only be paid if two conditions are satisfied:

1. The trigger level S^* has not been breached.
2. The company is still a going concern and has the necessary cash available to distribute a coupon to the investors holding the contingent convertible bond.

It is not easy to quantify this latter condition. One can already argue that coupons are likely to be stopped when the issuer is not in a healthy financial condition. Such a precarious state will be reflected in a low share price. This is a starting point from where we introduce a strike S_q, which determines the minimal share price level below which coupon payments are not going to be made at all. The value of a CoCo bond with coupon deferral is now equal to the sum of three components:

$$\textbf{CoCo (with coupon deferral)} = \text{Zero-Coupon Bond} + \text{Knock-In Forward(s)}$$
$$+ \sum \text{Binary Down-and-Out Options}$$

The construction of a CoCo with coupon deferral relies on knock-out options. The model for a coupon deferral is based on coupons that can be knocked out if the share price trigger S^* is hit and that will only be paid as long as the share price level is, at the coupon payment date, trading above S_q.

Each binary down-and-out option (BDO)[5] generates at its expiry date t_i a coupon c_i if the share price S ends at this expiry date above the strike S_q and as long as the barrier level S^* has never been touched by the share price for $t < t_i$. The following set of two equations represents the conditions attached to a coupon payment on a coupon date t_i:

$$c_i \text{ is paid on } t_i \leftrightarrow \begin{cases} S_t > S^* \forall t < t_i \\ S_{t_i} > S_q \end{cases} \qquad (12.22)$$

Figure 12.10 provides an illustration of the four possible price paths for a share to illustrate how the parameter S_q controls the deferral mechanism. The CoCo bond expires at $t = T$ and has two intermediate coupon dates T_A and T_B. All the share price paths originate at $S = 100$. The first two paths are being triggered ($S < S^*$) respectively before and after the first coupon date. In order to be eligible for a coupon payout, we introduced the strike S_q. The third path is

---

[5] Full name: down-and-out binary-call options.

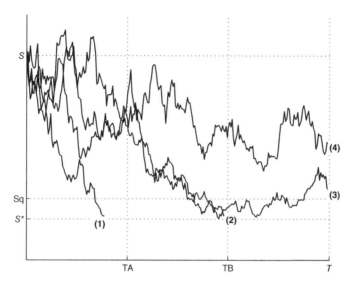

Figure 12.10   Simulation of four different share price paths to illustrate the coupon deferral. **Path 1**: CoCo is triggered before the first coupon date. **Path 2**: CoCo pays a first coupon and is then triggered. **Path 3**: CoCo pays the first but defers the second coupon. **Path 4**: None of the coupon payments are skipped.

at the first coupon date T_A above S_q, which allows the coupon payment. The same path fails to meet this price level at the next coupon payment date and the coupon is hence deferred.

The price P_t of the CoCo at time t is equal to a zero-coupon corporate bond (**D** in Equation (12.23)) to which a knock-in forward is added (**B** in Equation (12.17)). The third component is the sum of the BDO options that model the coupons c_i in absence of a trigger and coupon deferral (**E**):

$$\mathbf{P} = \mathbf{D} + \mathbf{B} + \mathbf{E}$$

$$\mathbf{D} = N \exp(-r(T - t))$$

$$\mathbf{E} = \sum_{i=1}^{k} c_i \exp(-r(t_i - t))[\Phi(x_i - \sigma\sqrt{(t_i - t)}) - (S^*/S)^{2\lambda-2}\Phi(y_i - \sigma\sqrt{(t_i - t)})]$$

with

$$x_i = \frac{\log(S/S_q)}{\sigma\sqrt{(t_i - t)}} + \lambda\sigma\sqrt{(t_i - t)}$$

$$y_i = \frac{\log((S^*)^2/(SS_q))}{\sigma\sqrt{(t_i - t)}} + \lambda\sigma\sqrt{(t_i - t)}$$

$$\lambda = \frac{r - q + \sigma^2/2}{\sigma^2}$$

$$(12.23)$$

Equations (12.23) can be put to work in studying the impact when allowing a coupon deferral. Logically, a contingent convertible with a possible coupon deferral has a higher coupon than a similar bond without this particular feature. This difference in coupon Δc compensates for the deferral risk. In Figure 12.11 we calculate Δc for a hypothetical 7-year

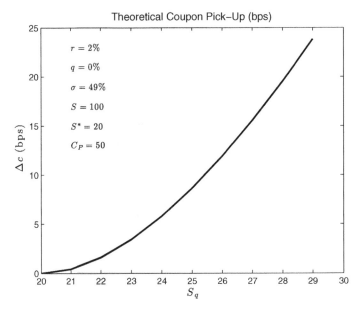

Figure 12.11   Increase in the coupon of 7-year CoCo bond when allowing a coupon deferral.

CoCo bond when imposing different levels for S_q. Both the deferral and non-deferral version share the same trigger level $S^* = 20$ and have the same price $P = 100$ at the issue date. The conversion price is $C_P = 50$. The difference between the coupons of these two bonds is equal to 24 bps when we take, for example, $S_q = 30$. The CoCo bonds were priced in the absence of dividends ($q = 0$) using the same continuous interest rate ($r = 2\%$) and the same volatility ($\sigma = 49\%$).

In another numerical example using a 7-year CoCo bond we no longer study the difference in coupon level but instead focus on the price difference ΔP between the two CoCo versions:

$$\Delta P = P_{\text{No Deferral}} - P_{\text{Deferral}} \qquad (12.24)$$

The current share price S equals 100 and both bonds trade at par $P = 100$. The levels of the annual coupons are 6.11% and 6.35% for, respectively, the CoCo without and with coupon deferral. The forced conversion in shares takes place at the same moment and both bonds hence share the same implied trigger level S^*, for which we assume $S^* = 20$. The price difference ΔP is plotted in Figure 12.12. Three points on this graph deserve our attention:

- **(1)**
  For this particular point on the graph, both CoCos share the same price $P = 100$ when $S = 100$. For a decreasing share price S, both bonds will decrease in value because S approaches the trigger level S^*. The CoCo bond with coupon deferral decreases at a faster pace, however, than the CoCo bond where coupons are not allowed to be deferred. There is indeed an additional risk component at work when deferral is allowed. A decrease in S not only brings the trigger level S^* closer but also the strike S_q of the BDO options.

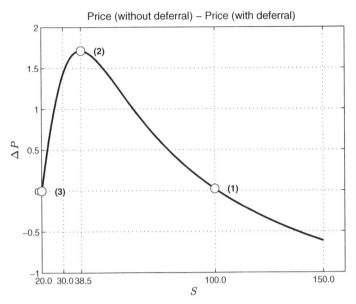

Figure 12.12 Price difference ΔP between a CoCo bond with no coupon deferral and a CoCo with possible deferral.

The inclusion of a coupon deferral changes the equity sensitivity of the bond. At this point ($S = 100$), we can hence state that:

$$\Delta P_{\text{No Deferral}} < \Delta P_{\text{Deferral}} \tag{12.25}$$

- **(2)**

  The price difference ΔP between the two varieties reaches a maximum when $S = 38.5$. At this point on the graph:

$$\Delta P_{\text{No Deferral}} = \Delta P_{\text{Deferral}} \tag{12.26}$$

  From here onwards ($20 < S < 38.5$), the CoCo without the deferral mechanism decreases at the fastest pace:

$$\Delta P_{\text{No Deferral}} > \Delta P_{\text{Deferral}} \tag{12.27}$$

- **(3)**

  When $S = 20$, the trigger level is reached for both contingent convertibles at the same time. At this distressed share price level, the coupon stream has stopped for both bonds and the forced conversion takes place. The investor will receive two shares for each bond, since $C_r = 100/C_P = 2$. At this point we have:

$$\Delta P_{\text{No Deferral}} = \Delta P_{\text{Deferral}} = 2 \tag{12.28}$$

12.5 USING LATTICE MODELS

Both the credit and equity derivatives methods were built on a Black–Scholes framework. This allowed us to rely on well-known formulas to model the loss of the coupons and the conversion of the face value in case of a trigger event. In that sense, a CoCo bond can be seen as a proper structured product since it is assembled from several building blocks:

- Digital barrier options to model the cancelation of the coupon stream.
- European knock-in calls and puts to quantify the possible forced ownership of shares.

For each of these building blocks a closed-form formula is available as long as one remains in the Black–Scholes world. This assumption facilitates the implementation of contingent debt models in traditional risk management software. One extra assumption that was taken on top of the known hypothesis surrounding Black–Scholes is the fact that the knock-in forward models the possible forced conversion in shares. The closed-form formula makes the investor the owner of shares at the expiry date T of the CoCo bond, not on the trigger date itself.

Valuation and risk models for contingent debt inevitably deal with tail risk. As such, these models value the unlikely event of a large loss taking place.

The existence of a volatility skew and smile will have a non-negligible impact on the way we look at contingent debt. We hence have to rely on a proper smile conform model such as, for example, in [59]. The existence of a volatility skew and smile is exactly the Achilles' heel of the closed-form solution we worked out before. CoCos are long dated and have strikes that are very distant from the share price at the issue date. This combination makes it difficult to find the appropriate volatility to plug into the valuation formulas we worked out before. The fact that the underlying share of the CoCo may have listed options trading on a regulated options exchange will often be of limited help. There is first of all an important maturity gap, since listed options on single stocks have short maturities compared with the long-dated contingent convertibles. The second issue is the quest for an estimate of an out-of-the-money volatility. It is unfortunately rather the exception than the rule to find market prices for options that are very distant from the at-the-money levels. There is more liquidity on single stock options for strike levels that are not too far away from the current share price.

A different numerical implementation has to be chosen if we want to take all of the remarks made above into account. This is where the equations of Sections 12.2 and 12.3 have to make room for different techniques. An obvious candidate is the Monte Carlo method. Another alternative is to rely on trinomial trees to accommodate for a different stochastic process. A generalized tree-building procedure for various diffusion processes with and without possible jumps has been worked out at length in Section 8.3.3.

A lattice model can now, for example, be used to quantify the difference from the closed-form formula. Trinomial trees model much closer the conversion risk of the CoCo. The node values in the tree that are located at or below the trigger level S^* are equal to the conversion value $C_r \times S$. At these points the investor becomes the immediate owner of shares. This is different from the closed-form formula, where the delivery was assumed to take place at the maturity date of the CoCo bond. In the equity derivatives method, this was indeed modeled through a down-and-in forward.

In a numerical example we consider a 5-year contingent convertible distributing an annual coupon of 5%. The current share price $S = 100$ and the interest rate $r = 1\%$. The conversion price $C_P = 100$ and the expected trigger level S^* is considered to be equal to 30. For a wide range of dividend yields $q \in [0\%, 10\%]$, the value of the CoCo P has been calculated using the two different models. The closed-form formula from the equity derivatives method is compared with the results obtained with a trinomial tree. Given the assumption underlying the closed-form formula, the discrepancy between both approaches increases for increasing dividend yields. This has been represented in Figure 12.13. The difference is small, however.

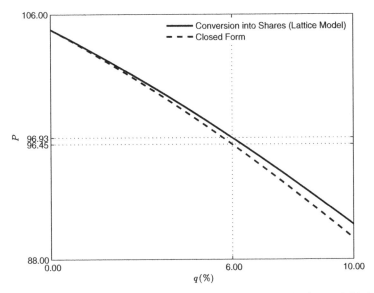

Figure 12.13   Price of a CoCo bond using a closed-form formula and the lattice model (trinomial tree).

For $q = 6\%$, there is a difference of 48 bps between the theoretical values resulting from both models.

12.6 LINKING CREDIT TO EQUITY

12.6.1   Introduction

Earlier, in Section 6.3.3, a map of financial models was provided. This educational overview pointed out that credit risk can be modeled as a standalone stochastic factor in a valuation model for hybrid bonds. Accordingly, the default intensity λ has its own volatility σ_λ and its own drift term μ_λ. These two components are combined together into a stochastic differential equation for λ. This attributes to λ its own stochastic process and moves the valuation problem from a single-factor to a two-factor model. Two stochastic variables are now involved: S and λ.

One notch lower in complexity are the "one-and-a-half" factor models. The value of λ here is parametrically linked to the level of the stock price. The relationship between credit (λ) and equity (S) is such that as the level of S goes down, λ goes up:

$$\frac{\partial \lambda(t, S)}{\partial S} \leq 0 \tag{12.29}$$

In the literature, the following parameterizations are often suggested:

Equity / Credit Link	Reference
$\lambda(t, S) = \lambda_0 \times (\frac{S_0}{S})^a$	[66, 183]
$\lambda(t, S) = b - c \log(S)$	[35]
$\lambda(t, S) = d + e \exp(-f S)$	[113]

The parameters $a, b, \ldots, f$ are constants. The first equation out of the limited list of functions for $\lambda(t, S)$ has the following natural limits:

$$\lim_{S \to 0} \lambda(t, S) = \infty$$
$$\lim_{S \to \infty} \lambda(t, S) = 0 \quad (12.30)$$

As long as default has not taken place, the changes in the share price S in a risk-neutral world are described using the following differential equation:

$$dS = (r - q + \lambda(t, S))Sdt + S\sigma_S dW_t \quad (12.31)$$

Using Ito's lemma one can obtain the stochastic differential equation for $\lambda(t, S)$ starting from the pre-default process in Equation (12.31). In this particular case, we apply Ito's lemma on the first of the three equations mentioned above:

$$\lambda(t, S) = \lambda_0 \times \left(\frac{S_0}{S} \right)^a \quad (12.32)$$

We label the parameter a as the **credit elasticity**. The credit elasticity determines the relationship between the share price S and the level of λ. For this purpose, we first determine:

$$\frac{\partial \lambda}{\partial S} = -a\lambda_0 \frac{S_0^a}{S^{(a+1)}}$$

$$\frac{\partial^2 \lambda}{\partial S^2} = a(a+1)\lambda_0 \frac{S_0^a}{S^{(a+2)}}$$

$$\frac{\partial \lambda}{\partial t} = 0$$

Combining these latter results with Equation (12.31), we obtain the differential equation for $\lambda(t, s)$:

$$\frac{d\lambda}{\lambda} = a\left(-(r - q + \lambda) + \frac{1}{2}(a+1)\sigma^2 \right) dt - a\sigma_S dWt \quad (12.33)$$

Or simplified:

$$d\lambda = \mu_\lambda \lambda dt + \sigma_\lambda \lambda dt \quad (12.34)$$

with

$$\mu_\lambda = a\left(-(r - q + \lambda) + \frac{1}{2}(a+1)\sigma^2 \right) \quad (12.35)$$

and

$$\sigma_\lambda = -a\sigma_S \quad (12.36)$$

Equation (12.34) shows how $d\lambda$ is a stochastic process with its own drift μ_λ and volatility σ_λ. The default intensity inherits its stochastic behavior from the stock price through the parametric function $\lambda(t, S)$. The volatility of the default intensity is σ_λ and equals the equity volatility σ_S scaled with the parameter $-a$ [8]. This means that any random change in S generates a change in λ of the opposite sign. Hence we obtain that $\frac{\partial \lambda}{\partial S} \leq 0$. If the share price goes down, default risk goes up. The drift term μ_λ has the property of being mean reverting. The speed of the reversion around the level $q - r + \frac{1}{2}(a+1)\sigma^2$ is given by the same parameter a.

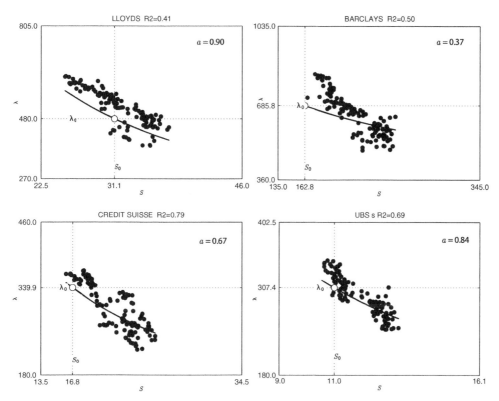

Figure 12.14   Estimation of the parameter a using historical data for Equation (12.32). Period: January 2012–June 2012.

The parameter a can be estimated from historical stock market and credit default swap data. A better alternative is a calibration exercise starting from a set of market prices of listed options. This has been outlined in [8] and guarantees a one-and-a-half factor model that is implied from market data. The calibration will be handled in Chapter 13.

As a first step, we will look at historical data to estimate the parameter a. In Figure 12.14, we calculated for four issuers of contingent convertibles (Lloyds, Barclays, Credit Suisse, and UBS) the value of a. The resulting estimates for a have been obtained through ordinary least squares using daily market levels for both the stock price and the corresponding 10-year default swap spread. The historical data set contains daily market data for the first 6 months of 2012. For each of the regressions, the coefficient of determination (R-squared) has been calculated as well and is provided in the table below together with the estimated values for a:

Issuer	a	R^2
LLOYDS	0.9	0.41
BARCLAYS	0.37	0.50
CREDIT SUISSE	0.67	0.79
UBS	0.84	0.69

12.6.2 Hedging Credit Through Equity

A small price change in the level of the convertible bond dP will result from a simultaneous change in the value of S and λ. To first order:

$$dP = \frac{\partial P}{\partial S} dS + \frac{\partial P}{\partial \lambda} d\lambda \tag{12.37}$$

Using the parametric relationship $\lambda(t, S)$:

$$dP = \left(\frac{\partial P}{\partial S} + \frac{\partial P}{\partial \lambda} \frac{\partial \lambda}{\partial S} \right) dS \tag{12.38}$$

The equity delta of the CoCo bond now has two components. The number of shares to be sold short as a delta hedge takes into account the equity as well as the credit risk:

$$\Delta = \frac{\partial P}{\partial S} + \frac{\partial P}{\partial \lambda} \frac{\partial \lambda}{\partial S}$$

$$= \text{Equity}_\Delta + \text{Credit}_\Delta$$

The equation above is the reason why such a model facilitates hedging the credit risk through equity. A trader who relies on this particular valuation and risk model has to be fully aware that the equity exposure Δ also contains a credit component: $\text{Credit}_\Delta > 0$. The number of shares that have to be sold short to offset the equity risk will therefore be higher than in a jump-diffusion model where λ is considered constant. The extra short in shares is a short equity position to hedge the credit risk. The supplementary amount of equity to be shorted against a long position in a contingent convertible depends on the chosen parametric link between S and λ.

Attention should be given to the fact that the introduction of $\lambda(t, S)$ carries an inherent trading risk. An uninformed trader is going to hedge the credit risk twice; once through the execution of a delta hedge while not realizing that this theoretical delta already contains a credit component and once using more obvious credit instruments such as credit default swaps. This is an example of an operational risk originating from an advanced model in the hands of a trader who is lagging behind on the learning curve.

12.6.3 Credit Elasticity

Impact on the Black–Scholes Volatility

This one-and-a-half factor model somehow changes the relationship between the Black–Scholes volatility σ_{BS} and the jump-diffusion volatility σ_{JD}. With $\lambda \neq 0$, we already knew that $\sigma_{BS} > \sigma_{JD}$. The implied Black–Scholes volatility is indeed an aggregate of both the jumps associated with a possible default and the diffusion process [8]. The impact of the credit elasticity parameter is such that an increase in a decreases the default risk for high share price levels $(S > S_0)$. A higher value of a makes a jump from a high share price S to zero less likely. Accordingly, one would expect the Black–Scholes volatility to be reduced when a increases:

$$a \uparrow \Rightarrow \sigma_{BS} \downarrow \tag{12.39}$$

To illustrate this we priced, for several values out of a limited domain for $a \in [0, 1]$, a 5-year European at-the-money put option. The interest rate r is 3%, the dividend yield q is zero, and the pre-default component of the jump-diffusion process has a volatility σ_{JD} equal to

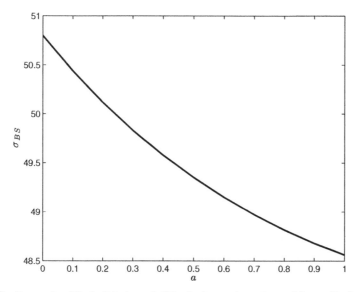

Figure 12.15   Decreasing Black–Scholes volatility for increasing values of the credit elasticity.

40%. Figure 12.15 illustrates how, for increasing values of the credit elasticity a, the implied Black–Scholes volatility σ_{BS} decreases.

Impact on the Skew

Allowing the stock price to jump to a default state has introduced a skewed distribution for the returns of the share price. In Section 9.2, we have already offered a brief introduction to this. The log returns are no longer symmetrically distributed. When jumps to $S = 0$ are allowed, the obtained result can no longer be modeled using a normal density function. Because of the default probability, the price of an out-of-the-money put option will increase. The opposite effect takes place for the theoretical price of an out-of-the-money call option. Defining skew for a particular expiry date as the slope of the implied Black–Scholes volatility σ_{BS} for European options with respect to the strike K, we have:

$$\text{Skew} = \left(\frac{\partial \sigma_{BS}}{\partial K}\right)_{\lambda \neq 0} < 0 \tag{12.40}$$

Practitioners will sometimes define skew as the difference between the implied volatility for European puts with a 90% strike minus the implied volatility of a call option struck at 110% of the spot level:

$$\text{Skew} = \frac{\partial \sigma_{BS}}{\partial K}$$
$$\approx \sigma_{BS90\% \text{ Put}} - \sigma_{BS110\% \text{ Call}}$$

Using the definition above, we now work out through a numerical example the impact of the credit elasticity. For this purpose we consider a 6-month maturity with $r = 3\%$, $q = 2\%$, and $\sigma_{JD} = 40\%$. The current default intensity λ_0 equals 5%. The spot price of the underlying shares is 100 ($= S_0$ in Equation (12.32)). When a is increased from 0 to 1, the skew for

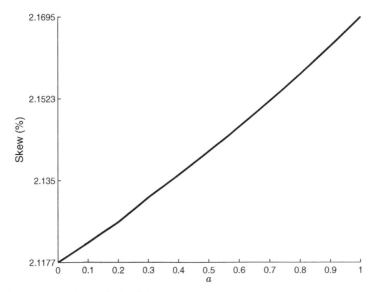

Figure 12.16   Impact of the credit elasticity on the skew.

this particular maturity only appreciates by 5 bps. Figure 12.16 witnesses the fact that the parameter a increases the skew moderately:

$$a \uparrow \Rightarrow \text{Skew} \uparrow \qquad (12.41)$$

Impact on the Valuation of CoCos

An increase of a lowers the volatility and steepens the skew moderately. Each of these two properties will have an opposite influence on the theoretical price P of a CoCo. The CoCo is a short vega product and its price will therefore appreciate when the volatility is lower. A higher skew through an increase of the parameter a has an opposite effect on the price. To see which of the two effects prevails, a numerical example will be worked out. For this purpose, a CoCo bond with a remaining maturity of 2 years and distributing an annual coupon of 10% has been chosen. The face value of this bond is 100 and it is equal to the conversion price C_P. In case of a forced conversion, each CoCo is converted into exactly one share. The current share price S is equal to 100 and the other market data is:

- $r = 3\%$
- $q = 2\%$
- $\sigma = 40\%$
- $\lambda_0 = 5\%$

The CoCo bond has been priced with a 15-step trinomial tree using the generalized tree-building procedure worked out in Section 8.3.4. In the appendix to this chapter, a detailed step-by-step explanation of the implementation of a jump-diffusion model with $\lambda(t, s)$ making use of trinomial trees has been provided.

Three different versions of the bond have been studied, each time with a different trigger price: $S^* \in \{20, 35, 50\}$. Figure 12.17 illustrates how a higher value for a has a positive effect

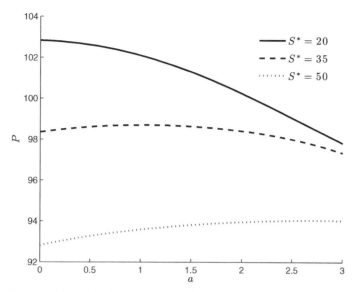

Figure 12.17   Impact of the credit elasticity on the price P of a CoCo bond.

on P when $S^* = 50$. When the trigger price is moved to lower levels $S^* \in \{20, 35\}$, the CoCo price is reduced for an increase in the credit elasticity a. This behavior illustrates that for a higher trigger level, the influence of a on the volatility prevails. When the volatility is lower, the CoCo's price is reduced. For values of S^* that are more distant from the current share price S, the influence of a on the skew prevails. This explains the fact that an increase in a has an opposite effect.

12.7   COCOS WITH UPSIDE: COCOCO

12.7.1   Downside Balanced with Upside

The loss-absorbing character of CoCos justifies the fact that these bonds distribute a larger coupon to their investors. The high coupon is a compensation for the risks run by the investor. Even if such a coupon is tax deductible, it could for some financial institutions be prohibitively expensive to issue contingent convertible debt. Through a combination of a forced with an optional conversion, the cost of issuing this instrument can be reduced however. Through the optional conversion, the investor has the discretion to convert the bond into shares. Such a conversion will take place when the value of the underlying shares (parity) is high. The optional conversion opens up the possibility for the investor to participate in the price appreciation of the underlying shares. This upside potential can compensate to some extent the downside that could arise from a conversion into shares or a haircut of the face value. This instrument blends a traditional convertible with contingent debt and has been named a "CoCoCo".

   This was exactly the approach chosen by Bank of Cyprus when it issued a similar instrument in May 2011 (Table 3.4). The market considered this issue a blueprint to open the CoCo market up to a new investor base, because the downside conversion risk can be balanced with upside potential [132]. In a CoCoCo the host instrument is no longer a standard corporate bond but a convertible bond. Next to a forced conversion, there is indeed also an optional conversion. The fact that the investor can elect to convert the bond into shares will reduce the coupon of the bond. The investor misses out on some of the yield but is offered instead a participation in a possible upside. The combination of both conversion types makes this instrument advantageous to the issuer from a cost of capital perspective.

A CoCoCo has two conversion ratios. The ratio $C_{r,CoCo}$ stands for the number of shares in case of a trigger event. The second conversion ratio C_r represents the number of shares in which the bond can be converted at the discretion of the investor.

12.7.2 Numerical Example

A numerical example allows us to compare the properties of both a 5-year CoCo and a 5-year CoCoCo. Both instruments are issued by the same company and share the same accounting and/or non-viability trigger. From this perspective they will share the same trigger price S^*, which we assume for the sake of the exercise to be equal to 10. The current share price S is equal to 100. The interest rate r is 3% and the share does not pay out any dividend, hence $q = 0$.

In case the trigger materializes, both bonds will absorb losses and because of this the investor will be forced to convert one bond into one share: $C_{r,CoCo} = 1$. In case of an optional conversion, only the CoCoCo investor can opt to convert each bond with a face value $N = 100$ into $\frac{1}{2}$ share: $C_r = 0.5$. The CoCo bond has an annual coupon of 3.55% while its CoCoCo equivalent earns a 2.88% coupon for its investors.

The instrument has a dual convexity and incorporates indeed positive and negative gamma. The negative convexity originates from the forced conversion and loss absorption, which becomes more likely when the share price trends lower. For higher share prices, the probability of a voluntary conversion by the investor increases, which attributes a positive convexity to this security. For lower share prices, the negative gamma will prevail while the opposite will be true for higher share price levels. This is the reason why it is impossible to model such an instrument in a Black–Scholes world where the volatility σ_{BS} is constant whatever the level of S. This is the reason that leads us to model a CoCoCo instrument using CEV rather than relying on a Black–Scholes approach which models share price changes as a geometric Brownian motion (GBM). The CEV model has been covered at length in Chapter 11.

$$\text{CEV:}\quad dS = (r-q)Sdt + S^{p_{CEV}}\sigma_{CEV}dW_t$$
$$\text{GBM:}\quad dS = (r-q)Sdt + S\sigma_{BS}dW_t \tag{12.42}$$

In this example we impose a volatility elasticity $p_{CEV} = 0.5$. This parameter choice corresponds indeed to a share price variance that increases for a decreasing share price. Starting from a Black–Scholes volatility σ_{BS} for a share price $S = 100$ equal to 30%, we can determine the corresponding CEV parameter σ_{CEV}:

$$\sigma_{CEV} = \frac{\sigma_{BS}}{S^{p_{CEV}-1}} = \frac{30\%}{100^{-0.5}} = 3 \tag{12.43}$$

For this particular parameter choice, the instantaneous variances at $S = 100$ in both the CEV and Black–Scholes world are equal. Both contingent convertibles have been priced with the CEV model and because of the particular coupon choice, the theoretical price P for both instruments is equal to par.

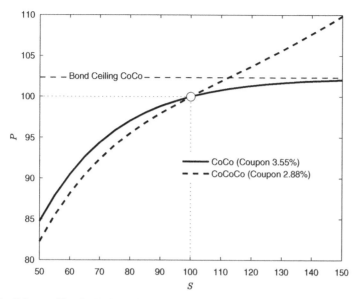

Figure 12.18   Price profile of a CoCo and a CoCoCo bond. Both instruments are issued at par but have different coupons.

The complete price profile for a wide range of possible share prices is provided in Figure 12.18. From this figure it is clear that the bond ceiling for the CoCo bond has vanished for its CoCoCo equivalent. The CoCo bond does not offer any upside potential at all. The maximum gain is given by the coupon stream and the repayment of the final redemption amount. This is where the CoCoCo steps in. Investors can participate in a share price increase, albeit it with a lower coupon remuneration. The lower coupon is compensated by the possible upside. A CoCo bond matures and meets its fate in two different ways: the trigger event takes place or the investor receives the face value at the maturity date. In case of a CoCoCo, there are two additional ways in which the bond can terminate: the investor converts the bond at the maturity date or goes for an optional conversion during the life of the bond. The following table calculates the probability of each of these events for our sample CoCoCo and CoCo:

	Probability (%)	
	CoCo	CoCoCo
Optional Conversion	0.00	12.05
Final Redemption at Par	97.36	83.37
Forced Conversion (CoCo is triggered)	2.64	2.64
Conversion at Maturity	0.00	1.94
$\Sigma =$	100.00	100.00

The two conversion probabilities are of opposite nature. The forced conversion imposes losses whereas the optional conversion allows the investor to participate in gains. The more the share

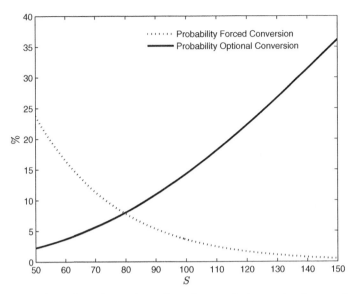

Figure 12.19 Probability of meeting a trigger (forced conversion) or optional conversion.

price S moves closer to S^*, the more the forced conversion prevails. For higher share price levels, the optional conversion will be much more likely. In Figure 12.19 both probabilities have been calculated for different values of S.

The forced conversion drives the negative equity convexity as an increase of the trigger probability, through a lower share price, and increases the delta of the contingent convertible.

For a CoCoCo bond, we are dealing with a double-signed convexity since the gamma turns positive for higher share prices (Figure 12.20). This change in sign results from the fact that

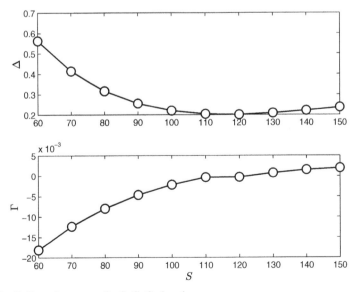

Figure 12.20 Delta and gamma of a CoCoCo bond.

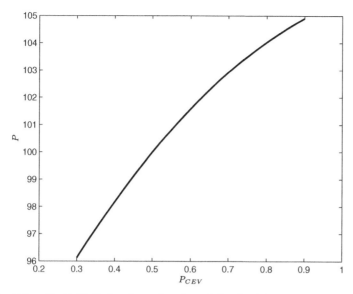

Figure 12.21   Price of a CoCoCo bond as a function of the elasticity parameter p_{CEV} when pricing using a CEV model.

the optional conversion prevails when S is very distant from S^*. At these share price levels, the CoCoCo is sharing most of its behavior with a traditional convertible bond. There is a presence of two different convexity behaviors in the same financial instrument: negative gamma for low share prices and positive gamma for higher share prices. This presence is a clear advocate for the implementation of, for example, a CEV model in contingent debt with an upside potential. These models have the advantage that they incorporate a higher share price variance for depressed share price levels and a lower variance when S is high. Ignoring this property when pricing CoCoCo using a constant volatility number will undermine the validity of its theoretical price.

One of the two volatility-related parameters in the CEV model is p_{CEV}. The lower the value for p_{CEV}, the more the variance of S increases when S drifts lower ($p_{CEV} < 1$). As expected, the price of a CoCoCo is sensitive to p_{CEV}. The downside gamma will be priced using a higher stock price variance than the nodes in the trinomial tree where the gamma is positive. The theoretical price will hence be lower when p_{CEV} decreases. A lower value for p_{CEV} creates a share price process where the equity volatility is higher when S has decreased. Decreasing the value of p_{CEV} will be punitive for the CoCoCo's theoretical value. This observation has been made in Figure 12.21, where the CoCoCo bond from our numerical example was repriced for different levels of P_{CEV} while keeping $S^{p-1}\sigma_{CEV}$ constant as specified in Equation (12.43).

12.8   ADDING STOCHASTIC CREDIT

12.8.1   Two-Factor Model

In Equation (12.36), we worked out a formula for the volatility of the default intensity λ. This was possible using Ito's lemma and only after having imposed a parametric link between the default intensity and the stock price. Through this link, the default intensity's stochastic behavior is inherited from the stochastic process describing the share price movements dS. The relationship between the share price and λ was modeled through a function $\lambda(t, S)$ which was implemented in a trinomial tree. From Equation (12.36) one can already conclude that the simplicity of a one-and-a-half factor model will not stand the test of reality. Moving ahead to a two-factor model is a logical next step. It is indeed obvious to consider default risk as a standalone stochastic process which is correlated, however, to equity. Using a jump-diffusion process, we propose the following two-factor model:

$$dS_t = (r - q + \lambda_t)S_t dt + \sigma_{JD} S_t dW_S - S_t dN_t$$
$$d\lambda_t = \sigma_\lambda \lambda_t dW_\lambda \qquad (12.44)$$
$$\mathbb{E}[dW_\lambda dW_S] = \rho dt$$

with

$$dN_t = \begin{cases} 1 & \text{with probability } \lambda_t dt \\ 0 & \text{otherwise} \end{cases}$$

There are three stochastic processes embedded in the proposed model of Equation (12.44), a Poisson process N_t and two Brownian motions: dW_S and dW_λ. Both S and λ have the respective volatilities σ_{JD} and σ_λ. The two factors of this model are tied together through the correlation parameter ρ. Using daily observations of share prices and credit default swap data during the period January 1, 2012 till July 1, 2012, the following table summarizes the estimates for σ_λ and ρ for some issuers of contingent debt. This is summarized in Figure 12.22 as well.

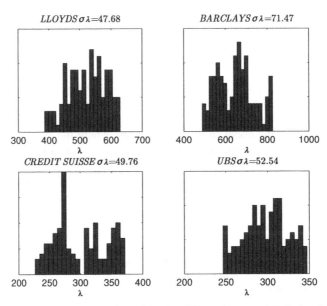

Figure 12.22   Histogram of the default intensities for different issuers of CoCo bonds. Period: January 2012–June 2012.

Issuer	σ_λ (%)	ρ
LLOYS	47.68	−0.62
BARCLAYS	71.47	−0.34
CREDIT SUISSE	49.76	−0.53
UBS	52.54	−0.61

12.8.2 Monte Carlo Method

In Section 6.3 it was explained that under the risk-neutral measure the price of a financial asset P_t expiring at time $T > t$ is given by:

$$P_t = B_t \mathbb{E}_\mathbb{Q}\left[\frac{P_T}{B_T}\middle| \mathcal{F}_t\right] \tag{12.45}$$

The value of the derivative security P_t at time t can be defined as a risk-neutral expectation of a discounted payoff. B_t was the value of the money market account at time t and P_T is the final payoff of the financial instrument. Dealing with a constant continuous interest rate r, we can write:

$$P_t = \exp(-r(T-t))\mathbb{E}_\mathbb{Q}[P_T|\mathcal{F}_t] \tag{12.46}$$

Assuming we know the risk-neutral density function $f(S_T)$ of the share price at maturity date T of the contract, the risk-neutral expectation to find the derivative price P_t can be expressed in an integral form as:

$$P_t = \exp(-r(T-t))\int_0^\infty f(S_T)P_T(S_T)dS_T \tag{12.47}$$

For a European call option with strike K, $P_T = (S_T - K)^+$. Working out the integral of Equation (12.47) while assuming a lognormal density function for S_T will result in the Black–Scholes solution. Adding more factors to a stochastic process, such as we did when creating the two-factor equity–credit model, increases the dimensionality of the problem. This introduces an additional complexity such that we have to rely on the Monte Carlo technique to work out the valuation. Monte Carlo means making use of random numbers as a tool to compute an integral such as the one in Equation (12.47). An early introduction to this technique was offered in Section 8.5. Additional hurdles in derivatives pricing are introduced through a possible path dependency. The value of the security depends not only on the value of the market data at the final maturity date. Instead, the path followed by, for example, the share price has to be taken into account. This is another hurdle that can easily be solved using Monte Carlo. For one-factor models of the likes of geometric Brownian motion, the Monte Carlo method generally does not offer any advantage at all compared with traditional methods such as closed-form formulas, finite differences, or trinomial trees [104].

For path-independent options based on a single factor such as, for example, the share price S, the valuation of a derivative security P_t through a Monte Carlo simulation is done in a four-step algorithm:

1. Generate n random prices $S_{i,T}$ with $i = 1, \ldots, n$ at maturity T.
2. Calculate for each $S_{i,T}$ the corresponding payoff $P_{i,T}$ using the appropriate payoff function. For path-dependent options the final payoff depends on a set of m share prices observed at intermediate dates t_k with $k = 1, \ldots, m$. Here a slightly different approach is needed. The final payoff $P_{i,T}$ is now calculated based on a payoff function $P_{t=T}(S_1, \ldots, S_m)$ where all the intermediate price observations intervene.
3. Discount each of the values $P_{i,T}$ using the risk-free rate r from T to the valuation date t of the option. This gives a discounted payoff $P_{i,0}$.
4. Take the average of these discounted values $P_{i,0}$ to obtain the Monte Carlo estimate.

The Monte Carlo estimate $\hat{P}_n$ for the derivative security P using n runs is:

$$\hat{P}_n = \frac{1}{n} \sum_{i=1}^{n} \exp(-r(T-t))P_{i,T} = \frac{1}{n} \sum_{i=1}^{n} P_{i,0} \tag{12.48}$$

The estimate $\hat{P}_n$ is unbiased, which means that:

$$E(\hat{P}_n) = P \tag{12.49}$$

The Monte Carlo estimate converges to P:

$$\lim_{n \to \infty} \hat{P}_n = P \tag{12.50}$$

The Monte Carlo price $\hat{P}_n$ is an estimate of the "true" price P. The error $\epsilon_n = \hat{P}_n - P$ is approximately normally distributed [104]:

$$\epsilon_n \sim N\left(0, \frac{\sigma_P^2}{n}\right) \tag{12.51}$$

where σ_P is estimated as:

$$\sigma_P = \sqrt{\frac{1}{n-1} \sum_{i=1}^{n} (\hat{P}_n - P_{i,0})^2} \tag{12.52}$$

This allows us to construct a confidence interval around the price estimate $\hat{P}_n$. Doubling the precision of the calculation result demands four times as many random paths. This additional workload increases the computational burden. The convergence rate of the Monte Carlo process is equal to $O(n^{-\frac{1}{2}})$ for large n. For a pricing problem with only one factor, the Monte Carlo method is therefore at a computational disadvantage compared with other numerical techniques such as lattice methods or finite differences. For options on multiple factors (as is the case for our CoCo bond), the convergence rate $O(n^{-\frac{1}{2}})$ of the Monte Carlo approach remains the same and will outperform traditional methods.

Lattice methods, on the other hand, suffer from the "curse of dimensionality." A two-factor model can be implemented in a trinomial tree. The tree is then transformed into a so-called trinomial pyramid since it has three-dimensions: time and the two stochastic factors [52]. The construction of this three dimensional lattice and rolling back through it to calculate the value of a derivative security is computationally expensive.

12.8.3   Pricing CoCos in a Two-Factor Model

In the two-factor model there are two sources of risk: λ and S. The continuous stochastic process described by Equation (12.44) is to be simulated in n Monte Carlo runs. For each of these runs, m different time steps t_j from the pricing date till the maturity date T need to be generated: $t_j \in \{t_1, \ldots, t_m = T\}$. The random generated values for λ and S for time t_j during the ith run are, respectively, $\lambda_{i,j}$ and $S_{i,j}$:

$$
\begin{aligned}
S_{i,j+1} &= S_{i,j} + S_{i,j}\left((r - q + \lambda_{i,j})\Delta t_j + \sigma_{JD}\sqrt{\Delta t_j}Z_{1,i,j}\right) \\
\lambda_{i,j+1} &= \lambda_{i,j} + \lambda_{i,j}\left(\sigma_\lambda\sqrt{\Delta t_j}Z_{2,i,j}\right)
\end{aligned}
\tag{12.53}
$$

with $\Delta t_j = t_{j+1} - t_j$.

For each time step t_j in every single run i, two correlated standard normally distributed numbers $Z_{1,i,j}$ and $Z_{2,i,j}$ are generated. Based on what was explained in detail in Section 9.3, one can obtain two correlated normally distributed random variables starting from a pair of two independent standard normal variables $X, Y \sim N(0, 1)$:

$$
\begin{aligned}
Z_1 &= X \\
Z_2 &= \rho X + \sqrt{1 - \rho^2}Y
\end{aligned}
\tag{12.54}
$$

The Poisson component dN_t of the two-factor jump-diffusion process was omitted from Equation (12.53). Doing so, the simulated share price will not drop to the default state where $S = 0$. The default risk will be handled differently and will be incorporated when discounting the cash flows along the generated paths for λ and S in each of the n runs.

Figure 12.23 represents one elementary step out of a set of Monte Carlo runs. The default intensity moves from λ_j to λ_{j+1}, while the share price changes from S_j to S_{j+1} during the interval Δt_j. During the life of the CoCo bond, several cash flows will appear. The investor can, for example, receive a coupon payment c. A different cash flow can consist of the value of the shares received on a forced conversion. The latter will happen when the simulated share price drops below the trigger level S^*. After the forced conversion, there are no remaining cash flows left since the bond became a share. The discounted value of these cash flows at point t_j for the ith run is denoted as $CF_{i,j}$. The value of $CF_{i,j}$ at t_i depends on the value of the cash flow $CF_{i,j+1}$ at t_{j+1} and is given by:

$$
\begin{aligned}
&t_j \text{ is a coupon date} \\
&CF_{i,j} \qquad\qquad\qquad = c + \exp(-(r + \lambda_j)\Delta t_j)CF_{i,j+1} \\
\\
&t_j \text{ is not a coupon date} \\
&CF_{i,j} \qquad\qquad\qquad = \exp(-(r + \lambda_j)\Delta t_j)CF_{i,j+1}
\end{aligned}
\tag{12.55}
$$

Discounting the cash flows through all the m time steps toward the pricing date delivers for every run the value $CF_{i,0}$. The Monte Carlo $\hat{P}_n$ estimate for the CoCo price is hence given by:

$$
\hat{P}_n = \frac{1}{n}\sum_{i=1}^{n}CF_{i,0}
\tag{12.56}
$$

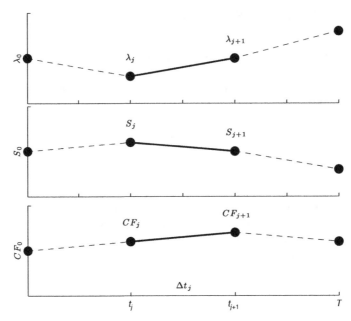

Figure 12.23   Simulation of two time steps t_j and t_{j+1} out of a Monte Carlo simulation for two variables λ and S.

12.8.4   Case Study

To illustrate the pricing of a CoCo bond in a two-factor model where both equity and credit are stochastic, a numerical example is considered. For this purpose a CoCo bond with a remaining maturity of 5 years and distributing an annual coupon of 10% has been chosen. The face value is 100 and is equal to the conversion price C_P. The current share price S is equal to 100 and the other market data is:

- $r = 3\%$
- $q = 2\%$
- $\sigma_{JD} = 40\%$
- $\lambda_0 = 5\%$
- $\rho = -0.1$

The bond has been priced for different values of $\sigma_\lambda \in [0, 0.8]$ and two trigger levels have been considered: $S^* = 5$ and $S^* = 50$. Both represent respectively a low and a high trigger CoCo. When $\sigma_\lambda = 0$, the values for the bonds are 106.47 and 83.14. This corresponds to the solution obtained through the jump-diffusion model with only S as stochastic factor.

From Figure 12.24 one can observe how, in this particular case, the low and the high trigger CoCo react differently when adding credit as an extra factor in the model. The price of the low trigger CoCo moves by 121 bps from 106.47 to a value of 107.68 when taking $\sigma_\lambda = 50\%$. Considering the bond with the higher trigger level, the price impact is only 13 bps.

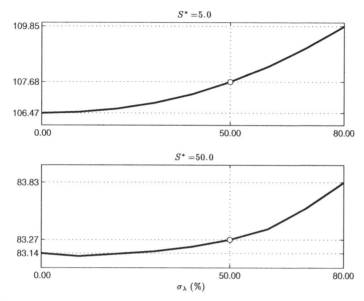

Figure 12.24 Price impact on the theoretical value of two different CoCo bonds when adding stochastic credit. Monte Carlo simulation: $n = 20\,000$ and $m = 500$.

12.9 AVOIDING DEATH SPIRALS

In Figure 3.11, we illustrated the increase of the equity exposure of a contingent convertible for falling share prices. The existence of such negative convexity could necessitate continuous selling from the investor. A decrease in the share price would indeed force this investor to sell more shares to set off against the increased equity sensitivity. The execution of this latter delta hedge drags the share price lower and another adjustment of the short equity exposure would be needed. This negative spiral is called a death spiral and will be very obvious if the shares of the issuer of the CoCo are characterized by poor liquidity [71].

To make matters worse, this negative gamma increases as the contingent convertible approaches maturity. This is illustrated in Figure 12.25 by adding the dimension of the remaining time to maturity to the theoretical price graph of a CoCo bond. For a share price level $S = A$, the deltas are respectively $\Delta_{A,T2}$ and $\Delta_{A,T1}$ for the maturities $T2 > T1$. Close to the trigger point S^*, the equity sensitivity is clearly higher when the CoCo is closer to the final expiration date: $\Delta_{A,T1} > \Delta_{A,T2}$.

These deltas obviously can get very large and out of control (Figure 12.26 (A)). Only a sufficient amount of shares trading in a liquid market can avoid a collapse in the share price. The size of the CoCo issue needs to be in line with the free float and the possibility of borrowing the underlying shares. Close to the trigger level, the delta of the contingent convertible can take extreme values as illustrated in Figure 12.26(A). This is even amplified when the trigger is about to be breached close to the final maturity date. There is indeed a lot at stake for an investor. In the Lloyds' case we have $14 bn that has its fate linked to one single trigger level. In the case of Credit Suisse, for example, a total amount of $2 bn is converted into equity when the 7% CT1 trigger is breached or when the Swiss regulator imposes the non-viability trigger.

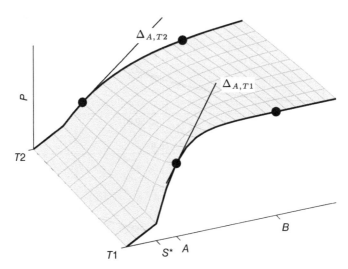

Figure 12.25 Theoretical contingent convertible bond price for different maturities and underlying share prices.

In both cases, the fate of a large amount of money is pegged to one single event. This creates a high equity sensitivity of the contingent convertible around the trigger level. According to the model, a small share price movement can set off a large loss for the CoCo holder. Hence, a large short exposure in shares will be needed to neutralize this risk. It is exactly this large short

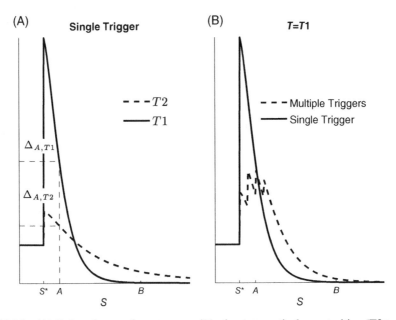

Figure 12.26 (A) Delta of a contingent convertible for two particular maturities ($T2 > T1$). (B) Decrease in Δ of a multiple versus single trigger CoCo.

exposure that will drive the stock price even further down. Instead of issuing one large CoCo with one single trigger, a financial institution could issue a contingent convertible containing multiple triggers. Each of the triggers has a different accounting trigger and only converts a fraction of the bond. This seriously lowers any death spiral risk, as shown in Figure 12.26(B) where four trigger levels are used. This clearly improves the feedback effect of the hedging on the share price.

12.10 APPENDIX: PRICING CONTINGENT DEBT ON A TRINOMIAL TREE

12.10.1 Generalized Procedure

We will work out a numerical example for a trinomial tree following step by step the general tree-building procedure developed in Section 8.3.4. The procedure is slightly modified to take into account the parametric link $\lambda(t, S)$ between the default intensity and the level of the share price. The data for the contingent convertible is:

- Trigger level (S^*): 35
- Annual Coupon: 10% (30/360)
- Face Value: 100
- Issue Date: January 1, 2014 (= Pricing Date)
- Expiry Date: January 1, 2016

1. **Choosing the appropriate stochastic process**
   The market data of the underlying share price is:
   - $r = 3\%$
   - $q = 2\%$
   - $\sigma = 40\%$
   - $S_0 = 100$
   - $\lambda_0 = 5\%$

   The share price is assumed to follow a jump-diffusion process with a link between the default intensity λ and the share price S. In this one-and-a-half factor model we have chosen a credit elasticity a equal to 2. Equation (12.32) modifies to:

$$\lambda(t, S) = 0.05 \times \left(\frac{100}{S} \right)^2 \tag{12.57}$$

   For the sake of the exercise, the tree will cover a period of 2 years in four steps only. In two of the time slices (January 2015 and 2016), a coupon equal to 10 will be paid out. There is no coupon deferral mechanism embedded in this CoCo.

2. **Selecting the time slices**
   The trinomial tree is a numerical representation of the logarithm of the share price: $X = \log(S)$. The variance V^2 of X on the default-free part of the tree is constant and is in the first slice equal to:

$$V^2 = \sigma^2 \Delta t = 0.4 \times 0.4 \times \frac{183}{365} = 0.08 \tag{12.58}$$

3. **Associating with a particular time slice a step size**

The distance between two nodes on the pre-default part of the tree and belonging to the same time slice is an integer multiple of ΔX:

$$\Delta X = V\sqrt{3} = 0.4905 \qquad (12.59)$$

4. **Calculating the transition probabilities**

The main difference from the trinomial trees constructed earlier in Section 8.3.4 is that the default probability p_{def} in each of the nodes now depends on the corresponding share price level.

For the node with value $X_{i,j}$ on time slice i, the corresponding share price level is $\exp(X_{i,j})$. The probability $p_{def_{i,j}}$ that the stock price $S_{i,j}$ will reach default when moving from slice i to $i+1$ is:

$$p_{def_{i,j}} = 1 - \exp(-\lambda_{i,j}\Delta t) \qquad (12.60)$$

with

$$\lambda_{i,j} = \lambda_0 \left(\frac{S_0}{S_{i,j}}\right)^2 \qquad (12.61)$$

The trinomial tree resulting from the procedure described above is represented in Figure 12.27. The default probability p_{def} of jumping to default in the next time step has been put as a label next to each of the nodes in the tree. In the layer corresponding to $t =$ January 1, 2015, we

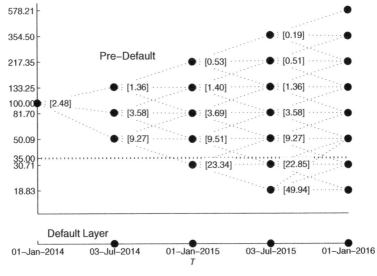

Figure 12.27 Four-step trinomial tree modeling a CoCo bond with $S^* = 35$. Each node has been labeled with the corresponding probability of reaching default in the next time step.

consider, for example, the node $S = 30.71$. For this particular node the default probability is calculated as follows:

$$\Delta t = \frac{183}{365} = 0.5014$$

$$\lambda = \lambda_0 \times \left(\frac{S_0}{S}\right)^2$$

$$= 0.05 \times \left(\frac{100.00}{30.71}\right)^2$$

$$= 0.5302$$

$$p_{def} = 1 - \exp(-\lambda \Delta T)$$

$$= 23.34\%$$

For all the nodes $S_{i,j}$ situated below S^*, the corresponding conversion value of the CoCo bond is $C_r \times S_{i,j}$ with $C_r = 1$. The position of the nodes with respect to the trigger level has an impact on the value of the CoCo bond. The four-step trinomial tree in this example offers a limited amount of granularity. There are five points of the pre-default part of the tree situated below the specified trigger level. None of these nodes is located on the **specified trigger** itself. This observation brings us to the definition of the **effective trigger**. The effective trigger level results from connecting the highest nodes satisfying the trigger condition $S \leq S^*$. Adding more nodes through an increase in the number of time steps will bring the effective trigger closer to the specified trigger and improve the accuracy of the obtained price. This convergence to the correct theoretical price does not always happen at a satisfying rate and is an illustration of the non-linearity error [67]. The non-linearity error exists because the characteristics of the financial security modeled through a lattice model do not coincide with a particular node on the tree. In Figure 12.28, it is shown how the nodes with values 30.71, 31.00, and 30.71 located on, respectively, time slices 2, 3, and 4 form the effective trigger.

12.10.2   Positioning Nodes on the Trigger

The lack of convergence of a lattice model has already been observed when pricing barrier options [39]. Only when the barrier passes through the nodes of the tree will the correct price be reached in a limited number of steps. In [1], the authors explain the use of a lattice method ("adaptive mesh method") where the density of the trinomial grid is increased at certain points on the tree. The resolution of the tree is increased around those nodes where the non-linearity occurs. The method is particularly useful for barrier options but could be applied in the area of contingent convertibles as well. In the nodes close to those points where the discrete barrier gets monitored, the previous time step is cut into two extra time steps. In [73], the authors presented an interpolation technique to obtain a satisfactory convergence.

Another possible intervention on the geometry of the tree is to stretch the tree such that important share price levels are positioned on nodes of the tree. Using a stretching parameter has been introduced in [16]. In the generalized tree-building procedure of Section 8.3.4, one can impose multiple important share price levels to be positioned on the nodes of the tree. This will have its use in instruments such as contingent convertibles where the conversion price C_p, the trigger level S^*, and the coupon deferral level S_q have a significant price impact. The nodes on the tree are therefore forced to pass through these crucial share price levels.

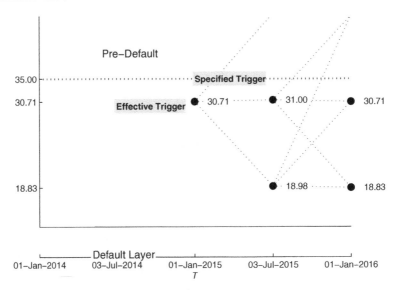

Figure 12.28   Two last steps of a four-step trinomial tree modeling a CoCo bond with $S^* = 35$. The tree only shows the nodes below the trigger level.

As an example, one can take node $S = 50.63$ on the first time slice after the pricing date (Figure 12.29). From this node the share price can jump in the tree to four possible node values when moving from $t =$ July 3, 2014 to $t =$ January 1, 2015. One of these nodes corresponds to default, where $S = 0$:

$$S = 50.63 \rightarrow \{81.70, 50.09, 30.71, 0.00\}$$

$$\text{with corresponding probabilities:} \qquad (12.62)$$
$$\{p_u, p_m, p_d, p_{def}\}$$
$$\{0.229, 0.584, 0.094, 0.093\}$$

Two nodes are located below $S^*(= 35)$ while two nodes are located above this trigger level. From Equation (12.59) we know that the distance between the node values $X = \log(S)$ was taken equal to $\Delta X = 0.4905$. Since this was an arbitrary choice, one can change ΔX such that $X = \log(35)$ for one of the nodes belonging to the next time slice. This is obtained when choosing $\Delta X' = 0.4444$. From node $S = 50.63$, the share price now jumps to different node values, one of which corresponds to the specified trigger:

$$S = 50.63 \rightarrow \{85.13, 54.59, 35.00, 0.00\}$$

$$\text{with corresponding probabilities:} \qquad (12.63)$$
$$\{p_u, p_m, p_d, p_{def}\}$$
$$\{0.171, 0.541, 0.195, 0.093\}$$

Figure 12.29 illustrates the first three time slices of the modified tree.

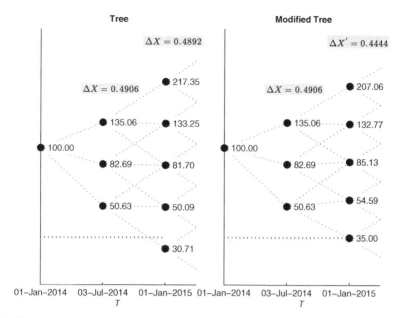

Figure 12.29 Changing the tree geometry in order for the specified trigger ($S^* = 35$) to pass through the nodes.

Modifying ΔX to $\Delta X'$ has to be repeated in all of the time slices where the trigger levels fall between two nodes of the pre-default tree. This modification to the tree-building procedure improves the convergence of the obtained solution.

12.10.3   Solving the CoCo Price

The complete geography of the trinomial tree, where as many nodes as possible have been positioned on the trigger level, is depicted in Figure 12.30. Special attention has been given to two types of nodes on the tree. On each of these nodes, the value of the CoCo bond is known. These points are the boundary values of the valuation problem:

- **Trigger nodes**
  These are nodes on the tree where $S \leq S^*$ and a trigger event materializes. For these particular points of interest, the value of the CoCo bond is equal to the conversion value $C_r \times S$. For the nodes on the default layer, the value of the CoCo bond is equal to zero, which corresponds to the assumed default state of the share price.
- **Redemption nodes**
  These nodes are positioned on the final maturity date ($t = T$), where a trigger has not taken place. The value of the bond P_T is equal to its face value increased by the final coupon. In this numerical example, $P_T = 110$.

In order to know the current value of the CoCo bond, one has to roll backwards in the tree. This process starts from the boundary values on the nodes where redemption takes place or the bond is triggered. Assume, for example, that we want to know the value of the CoCo bond

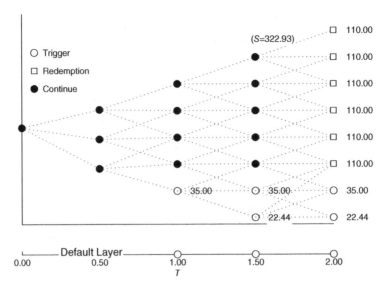

Figure 12.30 Solving for the price of the CoCo while rolling back through the tree.

in a node 6 months before the expiry date where $S = 322.93$. This point has been marked in Figure 12.27, to calculate the default probability:

$$\Delta t = \frac{182}{365} = 0.4986$$

$$\lambda = \lambda_0 \times \left(\frac{S_0}{S}\right)^2$$

$$= 0.05 \times \left(\frac{100.00}{322.9316}\right)^2$$

$$= 0.00479$$

$$p_{def} = 1 - \exp(-\lambda \Delta T)$$
$$= 0.239\%$$

The value P of the CoCo bond in this node is:

$$P = \exp(-r\Delta t)\left(p_u \times 110 + p_m \times 110 + p_d \times 110 + p_{def} \times 0\right)$$
$$= \exp(-r\Delta t)\left(p_u \times 110 + p_m \times 110 + p_d \times 110\right)$$
$$= \exp(-r\Delta t)\left((1 - p_{def}) \times 110\right)$$
$$= 108.11$$

Rolling further back from this node at the penultimate time slice toward the pricing date at the origin of the tree leads ultimately to a CoCo price equal to **97.52**.

Multi-Factor Models for Hybrids

13.1 INTRODUCTION

In Section 6.5 the sensitivity of both a convertible and a CoCo bond has been investigated with respect to share price, interest rate, and volatility movements. From this theoretical analysis we retain that there are multiple factors contributing to the theoretical price of a hybrid security. For each asset class we can single out specific situations where one factor stands out and is responsible for the price movements in the contingent convertible. A CoCo bond that is about to be triggered will be most sensitive to equity movements. In this extreme situation a CoCo demonstrates its equity behavior. On the other side of the spectrum, when the trigger is very distant, the CoCo can be considered equivalent to a senior corporate bond.

These theoretical findings were supported by the earlier outcome of a statistical experiment carried out in Section 2.3.1. For a sample security, we revealed how much of the day-to-day movements in the market price of the security can be explained by changes in interest rates, credit spreads, or equity prices. The same answer prevails: there is no single factor capable of explaining all of the day-to-day movements in the price of a convertible bond or a similar hybrid security such as a CoCo bond. Yet, in most of the valuation models we have been studying so far, the share price was the only stochastic component taken into consideration. Equity was the only source of risk and its stochastic process was the backbone of the valuation model. This choice seemed logical given the convertibility of these instruments into shares. The following table summarizes the different asset types that have been covered so far and the stochastic process for which the valuation was done.

Asset Type	Factor	Model	Section	Chapter
Reverse Convertible	Equity	Black–Scholes	8.2.4	8
Convertible Bond	Equity	Jump-Diffusion	9.2.4	9
Convertible Bond	Firm Value	Structural Model	9.4	9
Credit Default Swaps	Credit	Intensity-Based	10.3	10
Convertible Bond	Equity	CEV	11.4.4	11
Convertible Bond	Equity	Jumps & CEV	11.5	11
Mandatory	Equity	CEV	11.6	11
CoCo Bond	Equity	Black–Scholes	12.3	12
CoCo with Coupon Deferral	Equity	Black–Scholes	12.4	12
CoCo	Equity (Credit)	Jump-Diffusion	12.6	12
CoCo with Upside	Equity	CEV	12.7	12

The first time we moved away from a one-factor model was through a one-and-a-half factor model. This was explained through a case study using a CoCo bond as example in Section 12.6. In this approach, default risk was not considered to be constant any longer. This was a first difference from the earlier jump-diffusion models. The one-and-a-half factor model handles the default intensity (λ) as a deterministic function of the share price level. The function

$\lambda(S)$ can be estimated using historical data or – even better – through a proper risk-neutral calibration using the market prices of convertible bonds.

In Section 12.8 we introduced the first two-factor model when allowing the co-existence of two stochastic components in the valuation of contingent debt. In this two-factor model the equity prices and default intensity were each modeled as a geometric Brownian motion. The numerical solution was obtained using a Monte Carlo simulation. From this first application of a two-factor model it is straightforward to move on and add extra sources of risk, ultimately arriving at a proper multi-factor valuation tool. For each of the factors a stochastic process has to be chosen and discretized as in Equation (12.53). An additional challenge is now the specification of the relationship between the different stochastic processes. This is where correlation makes its first appearance.

Moving ahead in a multi-factor setting, one has to leave the trinomial tree behind since this technique is not suited to deal with the addition of supplementary state variables. The addition of an extra risk dimension in the model opens therefore the door for Monte Carlo simulation as the numerical technique of choice to value hybrid securities. A simulation-based technique such as Monte Carlo often outranks the traditional approaches based on finite differences or trinomial trees when several state variables are allowed to intervene.

13.2   EARLY EXERCISE

The introduction of the Monte Carlo technique gives more flexibility to a convertible bond analyst seeking to model exactly what is contained in the term sheet. An n out of m soft call condition[1] can, for example, be effortlessly included in a Monte Carlo-based valuation model. The same advantage is found when dealing with resets, dividend protection features, etc. There is one feature in a convertible bond, however, that forces us to think differently when applying a Monte Carlo simulation. The method described in Equation (12.55), where cash flows CF are discounted along the different Monte Carlo paths, now has to be handled with care. The reason for this is the possibility of early exercise. The bond holder can decide to convert the bond into a predetermined amount of shares (C_r) at his discretion. Issuer calls and investor puts also add a similar layer of complexity.

Through its early conversion feature, the convertible with maturity date T has a lot in common with American options where the derivative's life is stopped at some time τ with $\tau \in [0, T]$. The time τ is the exercise time, a stopping time. After this, the uncertainty in the convertible is gone since it is reduced to a known cash flow. The value of the convertible P_τ at this particular moment is equal to parity $P_a = C_r \times S_\tau$.[2] The price of the convertible is the maximized value of the discounted cash flows $C_r \times S_\tau$ across all of the possible stopping times τ. This supremum can be achieved for some optimal stopping time τ^* using the exercise or conversion boundary $b(t)$:

$$\tau^* = \inf\{t \geq 0 : S_t \geq b(t)\} \tag{13.1}$$

As soon as the share price S_t reaches the exercise boundary $b(t)$, the bond will be converted by a rational investor. At this point in time the convertible ceases to exist and is replaced by C_r

---

[1] The convertible bond is callable by the issuer if the share price closes n out of m consecutive business days above a specified trigger level.
[2] For reasons of clarity in the equations, coupons are not considered at all in this chapter. Incorporating coupon payments is straightforward, however, and can be done at no extra computational cost.

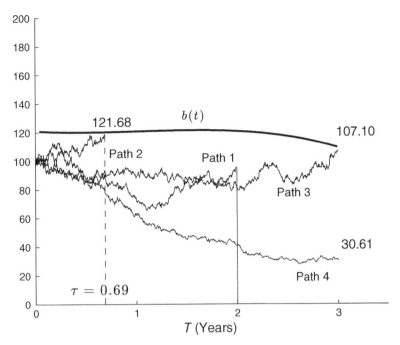

Figure 13.1   Three random walks simulated for a share price. One path crosses the exercise boundary at $t = 0.69$ years.

shares. It would be suboptimal not to convert and keep the convertible bond in the portfolio. It was long considered inappropriate to solve this stopping time problem using Monte Carlo. Some Monte Carlo techniques focus on the determination of a parametric expression for this exercise or conversion boundary. These methods belong to the so-called parametric approach. The parameters maximizing the value of the convertible bond determine the shape of the conversion boundary. An example of this is given in [101], where for American put options the exercise boundary $b(t)$ is approximated using a piecewise linear function. All the points S_t located below the curve $b(t)$ have the property of $P_{a,t}$ being higher than the continuation value $P_{c,t}$.

In Figure 13.1 three different paths for a share price S are plotted. All paths originate from the current share price $S_0 = 100$. The share is modeled through a jump-diffusion process with interest rate r equal to 3%, volatility σ_{JD} equal to 40%, and a dividend yield q of 5%. The default intensity λ is set equal to 5%. In the event of a default, the bond's value P drops to a recovery value equal to 20% of the face value N. Hence, π is equal to 20. Using these data, four sample random walks were simulated. We recall from Chapter 9 that the simulated jump-diffusion process (JD) is a blend of a geometric Brownian motion (GBM) and a pure jump process:

$$
\begin{array}{ccc}
\text{JD} & = \text{Pre-Default (GBM)} & + \text{Jump} \\
& \downarrow & \downarrow \\
dS_t & = (r + \lambda - q)S_t dt + \sigma_{JD} S_t dW_t & - S_t dN_t
\end{array}
\qquad (13.2)
$$

Starting from this very limited number of four Monte Carlo simulations and using our knowledge of the conversion boundary $b(t)$, we can in theory value a convertible bond. In this numerical example the conversion ratio C_r is set equal to 1. There are no call, no put features and to keep matters as simple as possible, the bond does not generate any coupon at all. The four paths considered each have a particular stopping value for the share price S and generate respectively cash flows CF_1, CF_2, CF_3, and CF_4. The theoretical value of the convertible at $t = 0$ is P_0 and is given by:

$$P_0 = \frac{1}{4}\left(CF_{1,0} + CF_{2,0} + CF_{3,0} + CF_{4,0}\right) \tag{13.3}$$

In this equation, the value $CF_{i,0}$ stands for the present value of the cash flow calculated at time $t = 0$ and generated along path i. Since this convertible bond does not distribute a coupon, a cash flow can occur on four different occasions only.

1. **Default:** The investor receives a cash flow equal to the recovery value.
2. **Optional conversion:** The investor receives C_r shares when converting the bond into shares.
3. **Final conversion:** The conversion takes place at the maturity date $t = T$.
4. **Redemption:** The investor receives back the face value N at the maturity date.

The three paths of the simulation are represented in Figure 13.1 and generate cash according to one of the possibilities in the list above.

- **Path 1**

  Along this path the issuer defaults in year 2. The value CF_0 is equal to a present value of 20, the recovery value of the bond received when default takes place:

  $$CF_1, 0 = \exp(-r \times \tau) \times \pi = 18.84 \tag{13.4}$$

- **Path 2**

  This is the path where the share price crosses, after 0.69 years from the pricing date, the exercise boundary. Because $C_r = 1$, the value of the convertible at this point is equal to $P_a = 121.68$. The cash flow generated by the first path CF_1 comes from the optional conversion at the stopping time $\tau = 0.69$. The value of the cash flow generated by the convertible for this particular path and point in time is $CF_{1,\tau} = 121.68$. Hence, we can write:

  $$\begin{aligned} CF_{2,0} &= \exp(-r \times \tau)C_r S_\tau \\ &= \exp(-0.03 \times 0.69) \times 121.68 \\ &= 119.19 \end{aligned} \tag{13.5}$$

- **Path 3**

  The convertible ends in-the-money at the maturity date ($t = T = 3$) and will be converted into shares. The value of this path at the maturity date is $CF_{3,3} = 107.10$. This price path never crosses the exercise boundary and the convertible will never be stopped through an optional conversion. The present value of the cash flow is therefore:

  $$\begin{aligned} CF_{3,0} &= \exp(-rT)C_r S_T \\ &= \exp(-0.03 \times 3) \times 107.10 \\ &= 97.88 \end{aligned} \tag{13.6}$$

- **Path 4**

  The share price never crosses the boundary $b(t)$ and ends below the conversion price at $t = T$. The convertible bond will be redeemed at par by the issuer. Hence, $CF_{4,3} = N = 100$. The present value of this final redemption is:

  $$\begin{aligned} CF_{4,0} &= \exp(-rT)N \\ &= \exp(-0.03 \times 3) \times 100 \\ &= 91.39 \end{aligned} \tag{13.7}$$

Relying on our knowledge of the conversion boundary $b(t)$ and four Monte Carlo runs, the price estimate for the convertible is **81.83**:

$$P_0 = \frac{1}{4} \times (18.84 + 119.19 + 97.88 + 91.39) = 81.83 \tag{13.8}$$

When there are multiple variables, the exercise boundary becomes much harder to estimate. This would be the case if one introduced stochastic credit in the pricing of a derivative security. The conversion boundary would then take the shape of a domain within the $[S, \lambda]$ space since both state variables λ and S intervene in the comparison of the continuation value P_c with the conversion value P_a.

At the outset of the valuation problem we do not have any knowledge regarding $b(t)$, however. This is a serious setback and the Monte Carlo technique has therefore to be applied differently. The conversion boundary is determined by those points where the continuation value P_c is equal to the conversion value P_a of the convertible. Verifying that $P_c > P_a$ needs to take place continuously throughout the life of the convertible bond. As long as this verification holds up, it is optimal for the investor not to convert the bond into shares. In practice, a limited number of m conversion dates $t_k \in \{t_1, \ldots, t_m\}$ is chosen. Only on these particular dates will the condition of optional conversion be checked. Going forward, we use the following notation for a Monte Carlo estimate of a convertible price P using n runs and m conversion dates: $\hat{P}_{n,m}$. Later we will see how to add call and put dates to the list of dates t_k and deal with these extra features as well.

We need to estimate a conditional expectation to calculate the continuation value. One has to quantify the expected value of the convertible bond on the next conversion date t_{k+1} given the current value of the share S_{t_k} and the other state variables. It is therefore appropriate to write that alongside the ith run of the n Monte Carlo paths, we have to estimate at all of the m points S_{i,t_k} the expectation $\mathbb{E}[P_{c,i,t_{k+1}} \mid S_{i,t_k}]$ with $i = 1, \ldots, n$ and $k = 1, \ldots, m$. This is a dynamic programming problem because a new Monte Carlo run would be needed, which in turn would require another Monte Carlo run, and so on... The continuation value is the price of the same derivative security priced at time t_k with an underlying share price S_{i,t_k}. This is illustrated in Figure 13.2, where in order to calculate the continuation value we have to start a new Monte Carlo simulation at each of the exercise points t_k and for each of the n runs. This is an impossible burden on the calculation time of the instrument.

In lattice methods the calculation of the continuation value is straightforward given the limited branching order of the tree. The continuation value is the probability weighted discounted value of the price in the following nodes. For the Monte Carlo method, the Longstaff and Schwartz approach, which is explained in the next section [140], estimates this conditional expectation using least squares and thereby avoids the pitfall of running a series of embedded Monte Carlo simulations as illustrated in Figure 13.2.

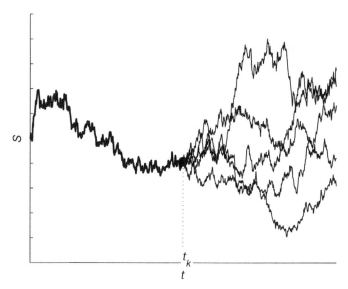

Figure 13.2 On each conversion date t_k and for each path, a new set of Monte Carlo simulations is needed to calculate the continuation value of the convertible P_c at t_k.

13.3   AMERICAN MONTE CARLO

In this section a detailed analysis will be provided to integrate the possibility of an early redemption of a convertible bond into a Monte Carlo simulation. The premature exit of the convertible bond can result from an optional conversion, an investor put, or an issuer call. To keep the algebra as clear as possible, the analysis starts with the application of American Monte Carlo using one single underlying factor only. The same approach can be rolled out to other instruments with an early exercise possibility, such as the notorious Bank of Cyprus CoCoCo bond [76].

13.3.1   Longstaff and Schwartz (LS) Technique

The pricing model in this section builds further on the least-squares regression approach proposed by Longstaff and Schwartz [140]. The integration of credit risk was done making use of default intensity as explained in [134]. The mechanics and principles behind the LS method can best be described by making use of Figure 13.3 illustrating n Monte Carlo paths simulating a particular share price process S. A total of m days has been considered where the bond can be converted into shares. These are the points t_k. This is a first approximation, since the convertible bond is in reality continuously convertible up till the maturity date. Selecting m conversion dates reduces the American nature of the convertible bond to a Bermudan derivative. The following notation is used:

- S_{i,t_k}: Share price level on path i observed at time t_k.
- t_m: Maturity date of the convertible bond ($t_m = T$).
- r_{i,t_k}: Continuous interest rate r observed on path i and at time t_k.
- $P_{surv,i,t_k,t_{k+1}}$: Survival probability between t_k and t_{k+1} on path i.

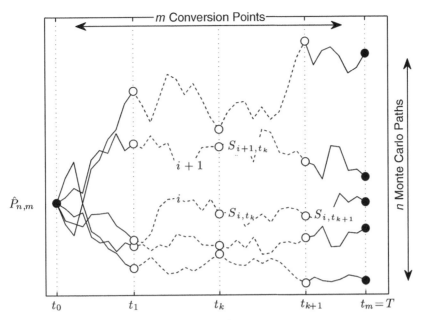

Figure 13.3 n Monte Carlo paths with m conversion dates t_k.

- $P_{def,i,t_k,t_{k+1}}$: Default probability between t_k and t_{k+1} on path i. Assuming that the default intensity is also stochastic, one has to consider the existence of a path i consisting of $\{\lambda_{i,t_1}, \ldots, \lambda_{i,t_k}, \lambda_{i,t_{k+1}}, \ldots, \lambda_{i,t_m}\}$ corresponding to every simulated path i for the share price S. If this were the case, the correlation $\rho_{\lambda S}$ has to be taken into account. The default probability between t_k and t_{k+1} is given by:

$$P_{def,i,t_k,t_{k+1}} = 1 - \exp(\lambda_{i,t_k}(t_{k+1} - t_k)) \tag{13.9}$$

- π: Recovery rate of the convertible bond (%).
- N: Face value of the convertible bond.
- P_a: Parity of the bond ($= C_r \times S$). In the absence of coupons, this is also called the conversion value since it is equal to the cash value of the underlying shares. For a convertible bond that distributes coupons, the accrued interest needs to be added to P_a depending on the specifications of the convertible bond.
- P_{a,i,t_k}: Parity of the convertible on path i at time t_k.
- P_{i,t_k}: Value of the convertible bond on path i at time t_k.
- P_{c,i,t_k}: Continuation value of the convertible bond on path i at time t_k. The continuation value P_c is the value of the convertible bond if one decided not to convert. The continuation value P_{c,i,t_k} depends on the expected value of the convertible in the next time slice t_{k+1} given the current value of the share price S_{i,t_k} or other state variables in time slice t_k on path i. Assuming a constant continuous interest rate r:

$$
\begin{aligned}
P_{c,i,t_k} &= \exp(-r(t_{k+1} - t_k))\mathbb{E}_Q[P_{i,t_{k+1}} \mid S_{i,t_k}] \\
&- \exp(-r(t_{k+1} - t_k))\mathbb{E}_Q[P_{surv,i,t_k,t_{k+1}} \times P_{i,t_{k+1}} + P_{def,i,t_k,t_{k+1}} \times \pi \times N \mid S_{i,t_k}]
\end{aligned}
$$
$$\tag{13.10}$$

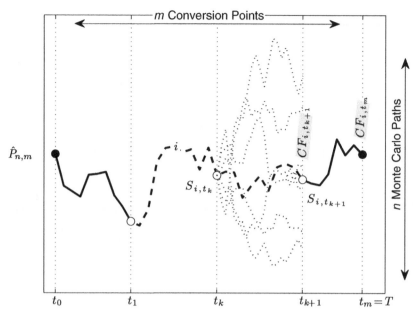

Figure 13.4   Path i with m conversion dates t_k.

- $\hat{P}_{n,m}$: Estimated convertible bond price using a Monte Carlo simulation with n paths and m conversion points. This price estimate is obtained at t_0 from the values of the convertible at time t_1 (assuming no coupons):

$$\hat{P}_{n,m} = \frac{1}{n} \sum_{i=1}^{n} \exp(-r(t_1 - t_0)) \left(P_{surv,i,t_0,t_1} \times P_{i,t_1} + P_{def,i,t_0,t_1} \times \pi \times N \right) \quad (13.11)$$

From Equation (13.10) it is obvious that arriving at an estimate for the continuation value P_{c,i,t_k} along the different dates t_k and paths i can only be done if one has at each of these nodes full knowledge regarding the value $\mathbb{E}_{\mathbb{Q}}[P_{i,t_{k+1}} \mid S_{i,t_k}]$. A logical next step would therefore be to generate at each of the nodes S_{i,t_k} a new set of Monte Carlo paths till the subsequent time slice t_{k+1}. From t_{k+1}, we would then have to produce another set of Monte Carlo simulations, etc. The number of price paths would literally explode, as shown in Figure 13.4.

In Figure 13.4, the final cash flow CF_{i,t_m} is pointed out. This cash flow is generated at the final maturity date ($t_m = T$) for a share on path i and if no optional conversion were to have taken place at any of the previous points $t_k < t_m$. The value CF_{i,t_m} depends on the final share price level S_{i,t_m} only. In the absence of coupons, we have:

$$CF_{i,t_m} = \max(N, C_r \times S_{i,t_m}) \quad (13.12)$$

Rolling back along path i from t_m to t_{k+1}, we arrive at the cash flow $CF_{i,t_{k+1}}$. This cash flow is by no means equal to $\mathbb{E}_{\mathbb{Q}}[P_{i,t_{k+1}} \mid S_{i,t_k}]$ since starting at the point S_{i,t_k}, the share price can leave path i to arrive at a value different from $S_{i,t+k}$. This is pointed out in Figure 13.4. We have yet to introduce the discounted value of the cash flow $CF_{i,t_{k+1}}$ calculated at time t_k, and denote this as Y_{i,t_k}:

$$Y_{i,t_k} = \exp(-r(t_{k+1} - t_k)) \left(P_{surv,i,t_k,t_{k+1}} \times CF_{i,t_{k+1}} + P_{def,i,t_k,t_{k+1}} \times \pi \times N \right) \quad (13.13)$$

For all points S_{i,t_k} on the time slice t_k, we can determine the corresponding value Y_{i,t_k}. The starting point of the procedure described by Longstaff and Schwartz is the collection $\{(S_{1,t_k} Y_{1,t_k}), \ldots, (S_{i,t_k} Y_{i,t_k}), \ldots, (S_{n,t_k} Y_{n,t_k})\}$. These points will help to determine an analytic expression $P_{c,t_k}(S)$ for the continuation value of the convertible bond on the time slice t_k. The LS procedure is built on the assumption that the continuation value can be calculated using a linear combination of basis functions $\psi_j(S)$:

$$P_{c,t_k}(S) = \sum_{j=1}^{\infty} a_{k,j} \psi_{k,j}(S) \quad (13.14)$$

Normally the same set of basis functions is chosen across the different exercise dates. This simplifies Equation (13.14) to:

$$P_{c,t_k}(S) = \sum_{j=1}^{\infty} a_{k,j} \psi_j(S) \quad (13.15)$$

Next we limit the number of basis functions to L, which results in a workable expression for the function $P_{c,t_k}(S)$:

$$P_{c,t_k}(S) = \sum_{j=1}^{L} a_{k,j} \psi_j(S) \quad (13.16)$$

The easiest possible choice for the basis functions ψ when dealing with only the share price S as state variable is a polynomial. Using $L = 4$, we have

$$\psi_1 = 1$$
$$\psi_2 = \left(\frac{S}{S_0} \right)$$
$$\psi_3 = \left(\frac{S}{S_0} \right)^2 \quad (13.17)$$
$$\psi_4 = \left(\frac{S}{S_0} \right)^3$$

This turns the continuation value P_{c,t_k} at time t_k into a polynomial of degree $L - 1$ in S. The fact that $\frac{S}{S_0}$ is used instead of S is driven by reasons of numerical stability. In the original Longstaff and Schwartz paper, the authors used Laguerre as well as Hermite polynomials for ψ. Their overall conclusion was that the LS approach was robust with respect to the choice of basis functions.

The values of the coefficients $a_{k,j}$ are obtained using a least-squares regression between the data from the data set $\{(S_{1,t_k} Y_{1,t_k}), \ldots, (S_{i,t_k} Y_{i,t_k}), \ldots, (S_{n,t_k} Y_{n,t_k})\}$ and the basis functions $\psi_{i,1,\ldots,L}$. This regression is repeated for every point t_k for which the continuation value P_c needs to be calculated. In a multi-factor model with, for example, two different state variables X and Y, the set of basis functions ψ is based on both factors. In addition, basis functions need to include the cross-product XY as argument as well. The function $\psi_j(XY)$ quantifies in such a case the impact of the interaction of both factors on the continuation value at a particular point in time.

The above procedure is repeated when rolling back from time t_k to the previous time slice t_{k-1}. In each of these following time slices, the following steps are executed one by one:

1. Determine the cash flow CF_{i,t_k} on the same path i occurring for the previous time slice t_k.
2. Calculate the discounted value of this cash flow at time t_{k-1}: $Y_{i,t_{k-1}}$.
3. Determine those points $S_{i,t_{k-1}}$ where optional conversion is possible. These are the points where the convertible bond is in-the-money: $S_{i,t_{k-1}} \times C_r > N$.
4. For these paths, determine the coefficients $a_{k-1,j}$ of the L basis functions $\psi_{1,...,L}$ based on the data set $\{(S_{1,t_{k-1}}Y_{1,t_{k-1}}), \ldots, (S_{i,t_{k-1}}Y_{i,t_{k-1}}), \ldots, (S_{n,t_{k-1}}Y_{n,t_{k-1}})\}$ using least squares. Only in-the-money points are to be included in this regression.
5. Calculate using the L basis functions ψ_j and the coefficients $a_{k-1,j}$ the continuation value $P_{c,i,t_{k-1}}$ for those paths i where optional conversion was possible on the time slice t_{k-1}.
6. The value of the convertible at time t_{k-1} for those paths where conversion is possible and assuming that no conversion took place before t_{k-1} is $P_{i,t_{k-1}}$:

$$P_{i,t_{k-1}} = \max(P_{c,i,t_{k-1}}, c_r \times S_{i,t_{k-1}}) \tag{13.18}$$

For the other paths we have $P_{i,t_{k-1}} = Y_{i,t_{k-1}}$.
7. Roll back to the previous time slice t_{k-2} and repeat the procedure. This roll-back procedure is repeated up till the current time t_0.

13.3.2 Convergence

The different steps regarding the application of the LS method are going to be illustrated with a numerical example. Going through all the different steps clarifies the enormous flexibility of this technique to address multi-asset problems with complex payoffs and a possibility for early exercise. The practical implementation of the LS method involves assumptions or shortcuts. Each of these assumptions impacts the convergence of the Monte Carlo price toward the correct solution:

1. **m conversion points**
   The possibility of a continuous conversion throughout the life of the bond is constrained by imposing a reduced set of m dates for which the conversion is verified. These are the points where the continuation value is checked against the conversion value of the bond. This leads to a suboptimal conversion behavior and explains why the LS method delivers a lower bound on the correct theoretical price.
2. **L basis functions**
   The infinite sum of basis functions in Equation (13.15) is reduced to a linear combination of L functions ψ_j.
3. **n Monte Carlo paths**
   The numbers of paths for each of the factors is constrained to n. The convergence toward the "true" price of the convertible bond improves when more paths are taken into account.

13.3.3 Example: Longstaff and Schwartz (LS) Step by Step

The convertible bond covered in this introductory example has a 3-year maturity and a conversion ratio C_r equal to 0.8. The bond with face value 100 has no coupons and contains neither call nor put features. The integration of both calls and puts will be done at a later stage. The underlying share price of this educational convertible bond is 100. The volatility σ is equal to 40%. The dividend yield q is equal to 5%, while the interest rate r is 3%. The default risk of the underlying share is modeled using a default intensity λ equal to 5%. In case of a default, the recovery rate π is equal to 40%.

Simulated Share Prices

The number of Monte Carlo paths is restricted to 10 for the sake of the example. The checks for optimal conversion will take place for four points t_k with $k \in \{0, 1, 2, 3\}$. The different share price paths are illustrated in the table below:

Path	0	1	2	3
		t_k		
1	100.000	117.947	66.497	36.863
2	100.000	198.091	158.426	507.378
3	100.000	38.537	42.043	53.455
4	100.000	134.295	534.536	495.802
5	100.000	108.059	311.205	393.999
6	100.000	76.715	123.122	200.966
7	100.000	45.678	51.679	14.601
8	100.000	234.794	194.739	138.587
9	100.000	67.377	15.317	14.942
10	100.000	83.736	26.308	18.803

Time Slice t_3

Path	S	P	Status
1	36.863	100.000	Redemption
2	507.378	405.903	Final Conversion
3	53.455	100.000	Redemption
4	495.802	396.641	Final Conversion
5	393.999	315.199	Final Conversion
6	200.966	160.772	Final Conversion
7	14.601	100.000	Redemption
8	138.587	110.870	Final Conversion
9	14.942	100.000	Redemption
10	18.803	100.000	Redemption

The algorithm starts in the final time slice at the maturity date of the convertible. At the maturity date $T = t_3$, the bond will be converted by an investor when $S_{t_3} > 125 \ (= N/C_r)$. Such a final conversion takes place in five paths $i \in \{2, 4, 5, 6, 8\}$. In the other paths, the bond will be redeemed at par by the issuer.

Time Slice $t_k = 2$

From the time slice t_3, we can roll back to t_2. The values of the share price S_{i,t_2} in the different paths for this particular time slice are given in the table below. The cash flow, CF_{i,t_3} in each of the paths that occur in the previous time slice t_3 can be found in the same table as well:

Path	Conversion	t_2				
		S_{i,t_2}	P_{i,t_2}	P_{c,i,t_2}	Y_{i,t_2}	CF_{i,t_3}
1		66.497				100.000
2		158.426				405.903
3		42.043				100.000
4		534.536				396.641
5		311.205				315.199
6		123.122				160.772
7		51.679				100.000
8		194.739				110.870
9		15.317				100.000
10		26.308				100.000

In a first step the discounted value Y_{i,t_2} of each of the cash flows CF_{i,t_3} can be calculated using Equation (13.13). For the first path, for example, the value Y_{1,t_2} is hence given by:

$$\begin{aligned} Y_{i,t_2} &= \exp(-r(t_3 - t_2))\left(100\exp(-\lambda(t_3 - t2)) + 40(1 - \exp(-\lambda(t_3 - t2)))\right) \\ &= \exp(-0.03)\left(100 \times 0.9512 + 40 \times 0.0488\right) \\ &= 94.205 \end{aligned} \quad (13.19)$$

Accordingly, the values of Y_{i,t_2} for the other paths of the Monte Carlo simulation are given in the following table:

Path	Conversion	t_2				
		S_{i,t_2}	P_{i,t_2}	P_{c,i,t_2}	Y_{i,t_2}	CF_{i,t_3}
1		66.497			94.205	100.000
2		158.426			376.588	405.903
3		42.043			94.205	100.000
4		534.536			368.039	396.641
5		311.205			292.859	315.199
6		123.122			150.305	160.772
7		51.679			94.205	100.000
8		194.739			104.239	110.870
9		15.317			94.205	100.000
10		26.308			94.205	100.000

There are four paths on this table where an optional conversion is possible. These are the paths $i \in \{2, 4, 5, 8\}$ because for each of these paths the share price at time t_2 is higher than the conversion price of the convertible bond: $S_{i,t_2} > C_p (= 125)$. The optional conversion will only materialize if $S_{i,t_2} \times C_r > P_{c,i,t_2}$. The next logical step in the LS approach is hence the determination of the continuation values P_{c,i,t_2} for share prices where an optional conversion is possible. The knowledge of the continuation value is a prerequisite to calculate the value of the convertible bond. The four basis functions ψ_j are the polynomials proposed in Equation (13.17). The analytical expression for the continuation value of the convertible in time slice t_2 is therefore given by:

$$P_{c,t_2}(S) = a_{0,2} + a_{1,2}\left(\frac{S}{S_0}\right) + a_{2,2}\left(\frac{S}{S_0}\right)^2 + a_{3,2}\left(\frac{S}{S_0}\right)^3 \qquad (13.20)$$

The different coefficients $a_{j,2}$ are obtained using a least-squares regression to fit the polynomial $P_{c,t_2}(S)$ to the values $(S, Y)_{i,t_2}$. The result of this regression is given below:

Path	S_{i,t_2}	$(\frac{S_{i,t_2}}{S_0})$	Y_{i,t_2}		Coefficient	
2	158.426	1.584	376.588		$a_{0,2}$	5026.557
4	534.536	5.345	368.039	$\Rightarrow$	$a_{1,2}$	−5233.358
5	311.205	3.112	292.859		$a_{2,2}$	1718.018
8	194.739	1.947	104.239		$a_{3,2}$	−168.747

In this educational example, we have 4 data points to estimate 4 coefficients which results in a perfect fit between P_c and Y. The analytical expression for the continuation value is:

$$P_{c,t_2}(S) = 5026.557 - 5233.358\left(\frac{S}{S_0}\right) + 1718.018\left(\frac{S}{S_0}\right)^2 - 168.747\left(\frac{S}{S_0}\right)^3$$

The continuation values have been calculated for the paths $i \in \{2,4,5,8\}$ and are shown in the following table. Comparing the continuation value with the conversion value shows that in two paths for the time t_2, an optional conversion will occur. This is the case for both path 4 and 8.

Path	Conversion	S_{i,t_2}	P_{i,t_2}	P_{c,i,t_2}	Y_{i,t_2}	CF_{i,t_3}
				t_2		
1	—	66.497	94.205	←	94.205	100.000
2	—	158.426	376.588	376.588	376.588	405.903
3	—	42.043	94.205	←	94.205	100.000
4	yes	534.536	427.628	368.039	368.039	396.641
5	—	311.205	292.859	292.859	292.859	315.199
6	—	123.122	150.305	←	150.305	160.772
7	—	51.679	94.205	←	94.205	100.000
8	yes	194.739	155.791	104.239	104.239	110.870
9	—	15.317	94.205	←	94.205	100.000
10	—	26.308	94.205	←	94.205	100.000

In those paths where under no circumstances is an optional conversion possible at time slice t_2 because the share price is lower than the conversion price or because $P_c > P_a$, the value of the convertible is set equal to Y_{i,t_2}. This is the case for $i \in \{1,2,3,5,6,7, 9,10\}$.

Time Slice $t_k = 1$

We can now repeat the process for the time slice t_1, similar to different calculation steps in the previous time slice. We start from the terminal values CF_{i,t_2} of the previous step, which are equal to P_{i,t_2}.

		t_1				
Path	Conversion	S_{i,t_1}	P_{i,t_1}	P_{c,i,t_1}	Y_{i,t_1}	CF_{i,t_2}
1		117.947				94.205
2		198.091				376.588
3		38.537				94.205
4		134.295				427.628
5		108.059				292.859
6		76.715				150.305
7		45.678				94.205
8		234.794				155.791
9		67.377				94.205
10		83.736				94.205

In a first step the discounted value Y_{i,t_1} of each of the cash flows CF_{i,t_2} is determined using Equation (13.13). The results are given in the table below:

		t_1				
Path	Conversion	S_{i,t_1}	P_{i,t_1}	P_{c,i,t_1}	Y_{i,t_1}	CF_{i,t_2}
1		117.947			88.855	94.205
2		198.091			349.528	376.588
3		38.537			88.855	94.205
4		134.295			396.644	427.628
5		108.059			272.236	292.859
6		76.715			140.642	150.305
7		45.678			88.855	94.205
8		234.794			145.706	155.791
9		67.377			88.855	94.205
10		83.736			88.855	94.205

From the table above it is clear that there are three possible paths where a conversion can occur. These are the paths $i \in \{2,4,8\}$. For these points the value of S_{i,t_1} is larger than the conversion price C_P. These are the points where the calculation of the continuation value P_{c,i,t_1}

is needed to subsequently judge if an optional conversion makes sense for a rational investor. The results of this least-squares regression are detailed below:

Path	S_{i,t_1}	$(\frac{S_{i,t_1}}{S_0})$	Y_{i,t_1}		Coefficient	
2	198.091	1.981	349.528		$a_{0,1}$	0.000
4	134.295	1.343	396.644	$\Rightarrow$	$a_{1,1}$	214.032
8	234.794	2.348	145.706		$a_{2,1}$	227.964
					$a_{3,1}$	−124.658

The value of the continuation value is obtained using the following expression:

$$P_{c,t_1}(S) = 214.032 \left(\frac{S}{S_0}\right) + 227.964 \left(\frac{S}{S_0}\right)^2 - 124.658 \left(\frac{S}{S_0}\right)^3$$

This ultimately leads to the fact that there is only one path ($i = 8$) where the optional conversion actually does take place. In this path only, the conversion value outranks the continuation value. The convertible bond value for the points where $S_{i,t_1} < C_P$ or $P_c > P_a$ is set equal to Y_{i,t_1}.

				t_1		
Path	Conversion	S_{i,t_1}	P_{i,t_1}	P_{c,i,t_1}	Y_{i,t_1}	CF_{i,t_2}
1	—	117.947	88.855	←	88.855	94.205
2	—	198.091	349.528	349.528	349.528	376.588
3	—	38.537	88.855	←	88.855	94.205
4	—	134.295	396.644	396.644	396.644	427.628
5	—	108.059	272.236	←	272.236	292.859
6	—	76.715	140.642	←	140.642	150.305
7	—	45.678	88.855	←	88.855	94.205
8	yes	234.794	187.835	145.706	145.706	155.791
9	—	67.377	88.855	←	88.855	94.205
10	—	83.736	88.855	←	88.855	94.205

Value of the Convertible

Taking the average discounted value of the P_{i,t_1} leads to the price of the convertible bond at time t_0:

$$\hat{P}_{n,m} = \sum_{i=1}^{n} \exp(-r(t_1 - t_0)) \left(P_{i,t_1} \times p_{surv,t_0,t_1} + \pi \times N \times p_{def,t_0,t_1} \right) \qquad (13.21)$$
$$= 167.238$$

The value $\hat{P}_{n,m}$ is larger than parity, which is equal to 80 at the pricing date of the bond. The value of the convertible bond P was estimated using only 10 runs and a handful of points where an optional conversion was allowed to take place. This price estimate is denoted as $\hat{P}_{10,4}$ and is equal to 167.238. This numerical result lacks a lot of accuracy. Its value is very distant from the correct theoretical price. This is witnessed in Figure 13.5, where the Monte Carlo estimate

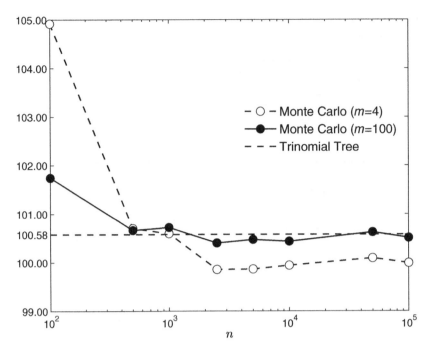

Figure 13.5 Theoretical price of the 3-year convertible bond obtained through a trinomial tree and Monte Carlo.

for an increasing number of simulations is compared with the price obtained using a trinomial tree. The same figure also illustrates to what extent the price estimate depends on the number of conversion points m. There is a notable improvement in price accuracy when imposing m equal to 100, for example. Figure 13.5 clearly points out that the convergence is driven by two parameters of the Monte Carlo technique: the number of points where a conversion is allowed to take place (m) and the number of paths (n).

13.3.4 Adding Calls and Puts

Incorporating call and put clauses in the LS technique has been covered in [67]. It is important to note that instead of using for every time slice t_k one single regression, multiple least-squares regressions are used. One set of basis functions will calculate the continuation value of the convertible in those points where a put is likely to be exercised. Another set concerns those share prices where a forced conversion can take place and, finally, there is a regression to calculate the continuation value in the points where an optional conversion is possible.

To illustrate this we consider the same convertible bond as in the previous example but introduce an investor put 1 year before the final maturity date. At time $t = 2$, the investor can now sell the bond back for the put amount p_v equal to 95.

In all the paths i belonging to a time slice t_k, we follow step by step the same approach as in the numerical example of Section 13.3.3. The exception is the time slice $t_k = 2$ where the

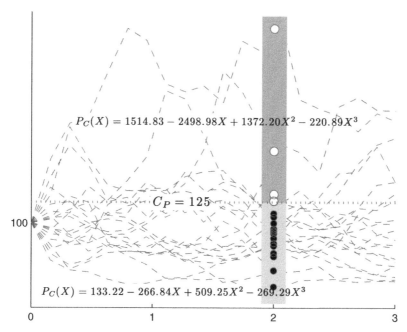

$$P_C(X) = 1514.83 - 2498.98X + 1372.20X^2 - 220.89X^3$$

$$C_P = 125$$

$$P_C(X) = 133.22 - 266.84X + 509.25X^2 - 269.29X^3$$

Figure 13.6   Continuation value calculated for points where the convertible can be called and where a put is possible ($X = \frac{S}{S_0}$).

investor has the right to sell back the bond at 95% of the face value N. The continuation value is calculated separately for two different regions:

- **Convertible can be put**
  A rational investor will put the bond if the continuation value of the convertible is smaller than the put amount ($P_c < P_v$). Since P_c is as yet unknown, we will consider the convertible bond eligible for a possible put when $S_{i,t_k} < P_v/C_r$. This corresponds to a share price level of 118.75 in this specific example. All the paths where this condition is fulfilled at $t_k = 2$ are grouped together. For these points the least-squares regression is performed separately in order to obtain an analytical solution for the continuation value for the points on these paths. This is clearly singled out in Figure 13.6.
- **Optional conversion is possible**
  The optional conversion is possible when $P_v/C_r < S_{i,t_k} > C_P$. Again the regression to obtain the coefficients for Equation (13.15) uses a limited set out of the n Monte Carlo paths.

Splitting up the least-squares regression across two different regions is called a **constrained** regression compared with an approach where all the points $(S, Y)_{i,t_k}$ contribute determine the coefficients of the basis functions. This latter method is an **unconstrained** regression.

Figure 13.7 illustrates the importance of making a difference between the different paths i in each of the conversion points t_k where the least-squares regression is performed. Using the same convertible bond in a Monte Carlo simulation where n is set equal to 50 000 points shows the lack of convergence of the unconstrained regression. The constrained regression, in

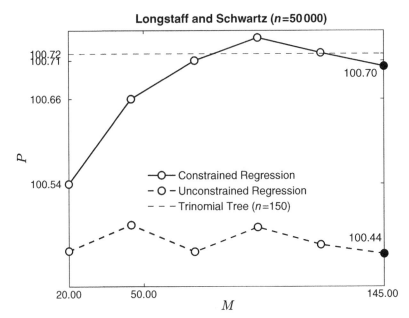

Figure 13.7 Convergence of the Monte Carlo price using both constrained and unconstrained regression.

contrast, results for $m = 145$ in a price estimate equal to 100.70. This is only 2 bps away from the price generated using a trinomial tree for the same convertible bond.

13.4 MULTI-FACTOR MODELS

In the chapter on contingent capital, stochastic credit was accepted as a second state variable next to the share price of the issuer. This led to the implementation of Monte Carlo simulations to deal with contingent debt in this particular two-factor setting. Now we incorporate two-factor models into the asset class of convertible bonds.

13.4.1 Adding Stochastic Interest Rates

A logical extension to the single-factor model based exclusively on equity prices is the inclusion of a stochastic interest rate. The stochastic differential equation describing the pre-default share price process was:

$$dS_t = (r - q + \lambda)S_t dt + S_t \sigma_{JD} dW_s \tag{13.22}$$

One now has to combine Equation (13.22) with a stochastic differential equation describing the interest rate movements. There is, however, no stochastic process that stands out when it comes to modeling interest rates. A wide range of interest rate models is available. We refer the reader to the work of Brigo and Mercurio [44] for an extensive analysis of the different possible interest rate models and their implementation.

We briefly mention one single model: the **Hull–White model** developed in 1990 by John Hull and Alan White [122] as an extension of the earlier Vasicek model released in 1977 [188].

The Hull–White model owes its popularity to the fact that it is a no-arbitrage model. It can be fitted to the current term structure of interest rates. This interest rate model is a one-factor model and its random behavior is determined by the Brownian motion W_r:

$$dr_t = \kappa(\theta(t) - r_t)dt + \sigma_{HW}dW_r \tag{13.23}$$

The short rate r_t of Equation (13.23) is the interest rate applied on a very short time interval. The Hull–White model is hence labeled as a short rate model. The mean-reverting property of interest rates is elegantly captured in Equation (13.23) through a long-term interest rate level $\theta(t)$ and the parameter κ controlling the speed of this reversion process. The parameter σ_{HW} is the volatility of the short rate. The function $\theta(t)$ can be derived from the term structure of the interest rates or, accordingly, zero-coupon bonds. Starting from the Hull–White model one can determine a closed-form solution for European interest rate options. This property gives the Hull–White model a competitive edge compared with some other interest rate models.

In this work, the incorporation of stochastic interest rates will take place in a simplified setting. The chosen methodology differs from Equation (13.23). The goal is to understand whether interest rate volatility matters or not when pricing convertible bonds. Is equity volatility the prevailing parameter? What about the correlation between equity and interest rates? Is there a difference between call and put features? These are all questions that are going to be addressed one by one.

In order to do this, we rely on a standard market model for European bond or interest rate options such as caps and floors. This model assumes that the interest rate r at a particular maturity date follows a lognormal distribution. Such a model is very often the model of choice to price interest rate derivatives such as caps, floors, or swaptions. This corresponds to the following description of the interest rate process:

$$dr = \sigma_r r dW_r \tag{13.24}$$

Similarly to the equity process, we have again a Brownian motion (dW_r) as the random component driving interest rates up and down. Both Brownian motions dW_S and dW_r are correlated:

$$\mathbb{E}(dW_S dW_r) = \rho dt$$

The geometric Brownian motion used in Equation (13.24) to describe stochastic interest rates misses the mean-reverting property of the Hull–White short rate model. Hence, the model laid out in Equation (13.24) does not adequately describe how the interest rate evolves over time and is therefore less suited to be used in path-dependent options which are often embedded in hybrid structures. For the sake of clarity, we will start nevertheless with this model to deal with an interest rate as a new state variable in the valuation of convertible bonds. The same geometric Brownian motion was chosen when introducing stochastic credit risk into a valuation model for contingent debt. Replacing, afterwards, Equation (13.24) with the more advanced Hull–White model of Equation (13.23) is straightforward.

13.4.2 Equity–Interest Rate Correlation

The two sources of risk are r and S. Their continuous stochastic process was described, respectively, by Equations (13.24) and (13.22). This is the staring point from which n Monte Carlo runs will be simulated. For each of the generated paths, different values at discrete times $t_0, t_1, \ldots, t_j, \ldots, t_m = T$ from the pricing date till the maturity date T need to be generated.

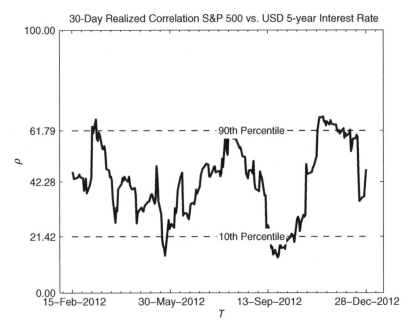

Figure 13.8   Correlation between US equity and 5-year interest rates.

The verification of the optional conversion, forced conversion, or investor put will be carried out at m of these generated points. The random generated values for r and S for time t_j and path i are denoted, respectively, as $r_{i,j}$ and $S_{i,j}$:

$$
\begin{aligned}
S_{i,j+1} &= S_{i,j} + S_{i,j}\left((r - q + \lambda_{i,j})\Delta t_j + \sigma_{JD}\sqrt{\Delta t_j}Z_{1,i,j}\right) \\
r_{i,j+1} &= r_{i,j} + r_{i,j}\left(\sigma_r\sqrt{\Delta t_j}Z_{2,i,j}\right)
\end{aligned}
\tag{13.25}
$$

with $\Delta t_j = t_{j+1} - t_j$.

The two correlated standard normally distributed numbers $Z_{1,i,j}$ and $Z_{2,i,j}$ are generated according to Equation (12.54). In Figure 13.8 we calculated the realized correlation between the daily log returns of the S&P 500 index and the 5-year USD interest rate for the year 2012. This graph gives us a broad idea about the correlation between rates and equity. The 90% and 10% percentiles are respectively 61.79% and 21.42%. The average realized correlation using a 30-day rolling window is 42.28%.

The same study was extended across a broader range of equity indices in Figure 13.9. The realized correlation between each of these indices and a corresponding 5-year interest rate was determined for different time windows. For each of these windows, the 90% and 10% percentiles were calculated and summarized into one figure.

13.4.3   Adapting Longstaff and Schwartz (LS)

The estimation of the continuation value at each of the m points t_j in order to verify an optional conversion or an investor put changes slightly in this multi-asset context. The basis functions

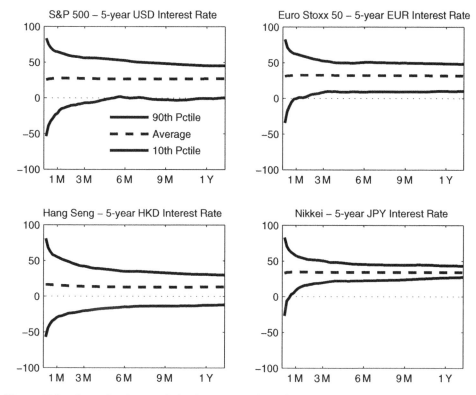

Figure 13.9   Cones for the correlation between equity and 5-year interest rates across the financial markets.

no longer depend solely on the share price S, but also on the interest rate level r. This leads to the following choice of basis functions for the continuation value $P_{c,t}(S, r)$:

$$P_{c,t}(S, r) = a_{0,t} + a_{1,t}(\frac{S}{S_0}) + a_{2,t}(\frac{S}{S_0})^2 + \ldots$$
$$a_{3,t}(\frac{r}{r_0}) + a_{4,t}(\frac{r}{r_0})^2 + \ldots \qquad (13.26)$$
$$a_{5,t}(\frac{r}{r_0})(\frac{S}{S_0})$$

The parameters S_0 and r_0 are, respectively, the initial share price and interest rate levels.

13.4.4   Convertible Bond under Stochastic Interest Rates

A numerical example will help us to understand the impact of stochastic interest rates on the theoretical price of a convertible bond. For this purpose we introduce a convertible bond with a 5-year maturity and a conversion price C_P equal to 125. The initial interest rate r is equal to 3%, the dividend yield q is 5%. The default risk is characterized by a default intensity (λ) of 5% and a recovery rate π of 40%. The current share price level S equals 100 and the equity volatility of the jump-diffusion process (σ_{JD}) is 40%.

An American Monte Carlo simulation with $n = 100.000$ and $m = 200$ was used to estimate the price of the convertible bond. The theoretical price of the convertible under different correlation and interest rate levels is summarized in the table below:

		$P_a = 80$		
		$\sigma_r(\%)$		
		0	25	50
	−50	97.84	97.43	97.27
$\rho(\%)$	0	97.84	97.95	98.27
	50	97.84	98.49	99.37

The table illustrates how the theoretical price of the convertible, in case of a zero correlation ($\rho = 0$) and an interest rate volatility (σ_r) of 50%, increases from 97.84 to 98.27. This increase of 43 bps corresponds approximately to half the bid-offer spread of a liquid convertible bond. The price difference between the two-factor model where $\sigma_r \neq 0$ and the zero-interest volatility model ($\sigma_r = 0$) is ΔP. These theoretical price changes ΔP obviously depend on the combined choice of ρ and σ_r:

ΔP bps		$P_a = 80$	
		$\sigma_r(\%)$	
		25	50
	−50	(42)	(58)
$\rho(\%)$	0	11	43
	50	65	152

$$\Delta P = P_{\sigma_r \neq 0} - P_{\sigma_r = 0}$$

A positive correlation parameter increases the value of the convertible bond as witnessed by the summary in the table above. The opposite is true when the correlation between S and r is negative. A higher correlation number makes the theoretical value of the convertible bond more sensitive to changes in interest rate volatility. The price of the convertible only increases by 32 bps when the interest rate volatility σ_r is increased from 25% to 50% if $\rho = 0$. The same change in σ_r increases the value of the convertible by 87 bps if $\rho = 50\%$. It is worthwhile trying to understand the intuition behind this result. For this purpose, we have to move beyond the outcome of the Monte Carlo simulation.

The two-factor model $P(S, r)$ specifies the theoretical price of a convertible bond as a function of both the share price S and the interest rate r. Using a limited Taylor series expansion of $P(S, r)$ allows us to write the following for the price changes δP of the theoretical value of the convertible in a two-factor model:

$$\delta P = \frac{\partial P}{\partial S} \delta S + \frac{\partial P}{\partial r} \delta r + \frac{1}{2} \frac{\partial^2 P}{\partial S^2} (\delta S)^2 + \frac{1}{2} \frac{\partial^2 P}{\partial r^2} (\delta r)^2 + \frac{\partial^2 P}{\partial S \partial r} (\delta r \delta S) + \dots \quad (13.27)$$

Taking the expected value from both sides of the previous equation:

$$\mathbb{E}[\delta P] \approx \frac{\partial P}{\partial S} \mathbb{E}[\delta S] + \frac{\partial P}{\partial r} \mathbb{E}[\delta r] + \frac{1}{2} \frac{\partial^2 P}{\partial S^2} \mathbb{E}[(\delta S)^2] + \frac{1}{2} \frac{\partial^2 P}{\partial r^2} \mathbb{E}[(\delta r)^2] + \frac{\partial^2 P}{\partial S \partial r} \mathbb{E}[(\delta r \delta S)]$$

$$(13.28)$$

Two components in the latter equation are of interest to us when trying to understand the sensitivity of the convertible bond to both correlation and interest rate volatility:

$$\text{Gamma Component} \quad \frac{1}{2}\frac{\partial^2 P}{\partial r^2}\mathbb{E}[(\delta r)^2]$$

and

(13.29)

$$\text{Cross-Gamma Component} \quad \frac{\partial^2 P}{\partial S \partial r}\mathbb{E}[(\delta r \delta S)]$$

These two terms help us to understand intuitively the expected price change $\mathbb{E}[\delta P]$ of the convertible in a pricing model with stochastic interest rates.

- **Gamma component**: Impact of σ_r

  This component combines the interest rate convexity $\frac{\partial^2 P}{\partial r^2}$ of the convertible bond with the expected randomness $\mathbb{E}[(\delta r)^2]$ of the interest rate r. Sensu strictu, however, the interest rate variance σ_r^2 is not really equal to $\mathbb{E}[(\delta r)^2]$. This gamma component of Equation (13.28) shows that the larger the interest rate convexity, the more the price of the convertible bond is sensitive to interest rate volatility. From this component one can already conclude that long-dated convertible bonds will be more sensitive to changes in σ_r given their larger interest rate convexity.
- **Cross-gamma component**: Impact of ρ

  The cross-gamma component is the product of $\frac{\partial^2 P}{\partial S \partial r}$ and $\mathbb{E}[(\delta r \delta S)]$.
  - $\mathbb{E}[(\delta r \delta S)]$ This term stands for the expected co-movements of both interest rates (δr) and share prices (δS) and hence introduces correlation (ρ) into the valuation framework:

$$\rho > 0 \rightarrow \mathbb{E}[(\delta r \delta S)] > 0$$
$$\rho < 0 \rightarrow \mathbb{E}[(\delta r \delta S)] < 0$$

(13.30)

  This term illustrates why the convertible bond's theoretical price increases with growing interest rate volatility in case of a positive correlation.
  - $\frac{\partial^2 P}{\partial S \partial r}$

    This is a so-called cross-greek since it measures at the same time how the interest rate sensitivity (*Rho*) changes with changes in the share price level, or how the equity sensitivity (Δ) is influenced by interest rate movements:

$$\frac{\partial^2 P}{\partial S \partial r} = \frac{\partial Rho}{\partial S} = \frac{\partial \Delta}{\partial r}$$

(13.31)

The two components above allow us to gather a better understanding as to where and when a convertible bond's theoretical price is most sensitive to stochastic interest rates or the correlation ρ. In the table below we calculate the price changes ΔP for different parity levels and different combinations of σ_r and ρ. Whatever the parity level, the impact of σ_r on the theoretical price of a convertible is limited as long as the correlation between S and r is close to zero. In this particular case, only the gamma component of Equation (13.28) is influenced by σ_r. The cross-gamma component is irrelevant since for small correlation values we will have that $\mathbb{E}[(\delta r \delta S)] \approx 0$.

ΔP (bps)	$P_a = 40$ σ_r (%)		$P_a = 80$ σ_r (%)		$P_a = 120$ σ_r (%)	
	25	50	25	50	25	50
ρ (%) −50	−13	3	−42	−58	−49	−80
0	10	47	11	43	10	29
50	36	104	65	152	65	139

$$\Delta P = P_{\sigma_r \neq 0} - P_{\sigma_r = 0}$$

From the same table we retain that the sensitivity to correlation changes is smaller when the parity is low. For a share price $S = 50$, the parity is equal to 40 ($P_a = C_r \times S$). Considering at this parity level an interest rate volatility $\sigma_r = 50\%$, the theoretical price of the convertible increases by 57 bps when ρ changes from 0% to 50%. Increasing the parity P_a to 80, the price of the convertible bond now increases by 109 bps when, using the same interest rate volatility of 50%, the correlation changes from 0% to 50%. This tells us that the cross-gamma component has to be dependent on the share price level. Otherwise, this result could not be explained.

This is illustrated in Figure 13.10 where, for different parity levels, the value of $\frac{\partial^2 P}{\partial S \partial r}$ was calculated. This figure reveals how the cross-gamma component increases along with the parity. For increasing parity levels, the theoretical price of the convertible hence reacts more to correlation changes.

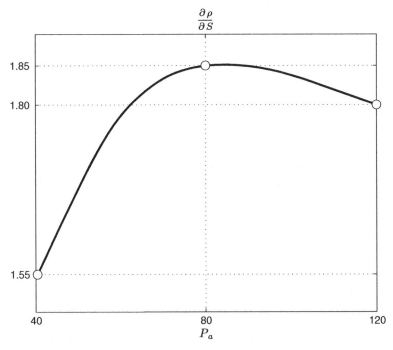

Figure 13.10   Cross-gamma component for different levels of parity.

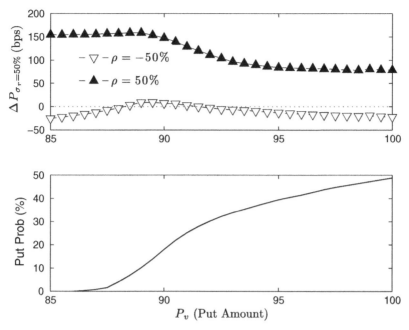

Figure 13.11   Impact of increasing levels of P_v on the sensitive of the price of a convertible bond toward a change in interest rate volatility.

13.4.5   Adding Investor Put

The sensitivity of the convertible's price to stochastic interest rates is also influenced by the structure of the convertible. To illustrate this, a put feature is included in the 5-year convertible bond we used in the previous example. The investor now has the right to sell back the bond 3 years after the issue date against the cash amount P_v. The higher the value P_v, the more likely the investor will exercise the put. Adding the put feature to the convertible bond reduces its effective maturity. There is now an even higher probability that the bond will expire before the final maturity date is reached. Without the put the only way for a bond to cease to exist before ever reaching the maturity date was either an optional conversion or a default. Adding a put hence reduces the expected life of the bond. This maturity reduces the interest rate convexity of the convertible and therefore its sensitivity to stochastic interest rate. Figure 13.11 illustrates to what extent higher values of P_v increase, for this particular bond, the probability of being put by the investor in year 3. The same figure illustrates how ΔP decreases for higher put amounts P_v.

13.5   CONCLUSION

This chapter has offered an introduction to the application of American Monte Carlo techniques such as the Longstaff and Schwartz (LS) approach. It has shown the effectiveness of this method when dealing with hybrid products with an early exercise probability in a multi-factor setting. The incorporation of several state variables brings the valuation model closer to the real world. The different examples in this chapter can be extended to corporate hybrids or contingent convertibles with an optional conversion.

References

[1] Ahn, D-H., Figlewski, S., and Gao, B. Pricing discrete barrier options with an adaptive mesh model. *The Journal of Derivatives*, summer: 33–43, 1999.

[2] Alloway, T. Contingent capital comes to pass, with a little help from the EC. Available at http://ftalphaville.ft.com.

[3] Alloway, T. Another Danish bank falls into a fjord of failure. *Financial Times*, June 2011.

[4] Alloway, T. Armageddon bank. *Financial Times*, February 2011.

[5] Ammann, M., Kind, A., and Wilde, C. Are convertible bonds underpriced? An analysis of the French market. *Journal of Banking & Finance*, 27: 635–653, 2003.

[6] Ammann, M., Kind, A., and Wilde, C. Simulation-based pricing of convertible bonds. *Journal of Empirical Finance*, 15: 310–331, 2008.

[7] Andersen, L. and Broadie, M. Primal–dual simulation algorithm for pricing multidimensional American options. *Management Science*, 50(9): 1222–1234, 2004.

[8] Andersen, L. and Buffum, D. Calibration and implementation of convertible bond models. Available at http://ssrn.com/abstract=355308, April 2002.

[9] Anderson, J. Subordinated bonds: Revisiting step-up Tier 1s and ECNs. Technical report, UBS, July 2013.

[10] Auto-callables begin to find a U.S. audience. *Derivatives Week*, XVI(1), January 2007.

[11] Ayache, E., Forsyth, P.A., and Vetzal, K.R. Next generation models for convertible bonds with credit risk. *Wilmott*, December 2002.

[12] Bail-in liabilities: Replacing public subsidy with private insurance. Technical report, KPMG, July 2012.

[13] Bank of International Settlements (press release). Group of central bank governors and heads of supervision reinforces Basel Committee reform package. Available at http://www.bis.org/press/p100111.htm, January 2010.

[14] Bank of International Settlements (press release). Basel Committee issues final elements of the reforms to raise the quality of regulatory capital, January 2011.

[15] Bardhan, I., Bergier, A., Derman, E., Dosembet, C., and Kani, I. Valuing convertible bonds as derivatives. Technical report, Goldman Sachs, November 1994.

[16] Bardia, K. A Multinomial Lattice Option Pricing Methodology for Valuing Risky Ventures. PhD thesis, Case Western University, July 1990.

[17] Basel Committee on Banking Supervision. International convergence of capital measurement and capital standards. Technical report, Bank of International Settlements, July 1988.

[18] Basel Committee on Banking Supervision. International convergence of capital measurement and capital standards. Technical report, Bank of International Settlements, June 2004.

[19] Basel Committee on Banking Supervision. Enhancements to the Basel II framework. Technical report, Bank of International Settlements, July 2009.

[20] Basel Committee on Banking Supervision. Strengthening the resilience of the banking sector. Consultative document, December 2009.

[21] Basel Committee on Banking Supervision. Countercyclical capital buffer proposal. Technical report, Bank of International Settlements, September 2010.

[22] Basel Committee on Banking Supervision (press release). Technical report, Bank of International Settlements, September 2010.

[23] Basel Committee on Banking Supervision. Global systemically important banks: Assessment methodology and the additional loss absorbency requirement. Technical report, Bank of International Settlements, July 2011.

[24] Basel Committee on Banking Supervision. Basel III definition of capital – Frequently asked questions. Technical report, Bank for International Settlements, December 2011.

[25] Basel Committee on Banking Supervision. Basel III: A global regulatory framework for more resilient banks and banking systems. Technical report, Bank for International Settlements, December 2010.

[26] Basel Committee on Banking Supervision. Proposal to ensure the loss absorbency of regulatory capital at the point of non-viability. Consultative document, August 2010.

[27] Basel Committee on Banking Supervision. Global systemically important banks: assessment methodology and the additional loss absorbency requirement. Technical report, Bank for International Settlements, November 2011.

[28] Basel III Handbook. Technical report, Accenture, 2011.

[29] Basel Committee on Banking Supervision. Report to G20 finance ministers and central bank governors on Basel III implementation. Technical report, Bank for International Settlements, October 2012.

[30] Basel Committee on Banking Supervision. Basel III: The liquidity coverage ratio and liquidity risk monitoring tools. Technical report, Bank for International Settlements, January 2013.

[31] Beckers, S. The constant elasticity of variance model and its implications for option pricing. *The Journal of Finance*, 35(3): 661–673, 1980.

[32] BIS quarterly review. Technical report, Bank for International Settlements, September 2013.

[33] Black, F. and Scholes, M. The pricing of options and corporate liabilities. *The Journal of Political Economy*, 81(3): 637–654, 1973.

[34] Blamont, M. SocGen CEO calls leverage ratio a crude measure. Reuters, July 11, 2013.

[35] Bloch, D. and Miralles, P. Credit treatment in convertible bond models. Technical report, Dresdner Kleinwort Wasserstein, 2002.

[36] Bortkiewicz, L.J. Das gesetz der kleinen zahlen. *Monatshefte für Mathematik*, 9, 1898.

[37] Bowman, L. Bank capital: CoCos could be tough nut to crack. Published at www.euromoney.com, December 2010.

[38] Bowman, L. Recapitalization: Spanish bondholders braced for bail-in. *Euromoney*, August 2012.

[39] Boyle, P. and Lau, S.K. Bumping up against the barrier with the binomial method. *Journal of Derivativs*, Summer: 6–14, 1994.

[40] Brady, N. We need simpler rules to rein in the banks. *Financial Times*, August 27, 2012.

[41] Brechner, D.R. and Lindsay, A.E. Results on the CEV process, past and present. Technical report, University of British Columbia, March 2010.

[42] Brennan, M. and Schwartz, E. Convertible bonds: Valuation and optimal strategies for call and conversion. *The Journal of Finance*, 32: 1699–1715, 1977.

[43] Brennan, M. and Schwartz, E. Analyzing convertible bonds. *Journal of Financial and Quantitative Analysis*, 15: 907–929, 1980.

[44] Brigo, D. and Mercurio, F. *Interest Rate Models – Theory and Practice*. Springer-Finance, Berlin, 2006.

[45] Bruni, F. and Llewellyn, D.T. (eds) *The Failure of Northern Rock: A Multi-dimensional Case Study*. The European Money and Finance Forum, 2009.

[46] Burghardt, G. and Lane, M. How to tell if options are cheap. *Journal of Portfolio Management*, 16(2): 72–78, 1990.

[47] Calello, P. and Ervin, W. From bail-out to bail-in. *The Economist*, January 2010.

[48] Cannata, F. and Quagliariello, M. The role of Basel II in the subprime financial crisis: guilty or not guilty? Technical report, University of Bocconi, January 2009.

[49] Carr, P. and Linetsky, V. A jump to default extended CEV model: An application of Bessel processes. *Finance and Stochastics*, 10(3): 303–330, 2006.

[50] Carver, L. No more heroes? *Risk Magazine*, July 2012.

[51] Chance, D.M. A synthesis of binomial option pricing models for lognormally distributed assets. Available at http://ssrn.com/abstract=969834, November 2007.

[52] Cheung, W. and Nelken, I. Over the rainbow. *Risk Magazine*, pages 313–317, April 1995.

[53] Christie, A. The stochastic behavior of common stock variance. *Journal of Financial Economics*, 10: 407–432, 1982.

[54] Claessens, S., Herring, R.J., Schoenmaker, D., and Summe, K.A. A safer world financial system: Improving the resolution of systemic institutions. Technical report, International Center for Monetary and Banking Studies (ICMB), 2010.

[55] Clark, J. Quick change. *Risk Magazine*, pages 30–32, October 2010.

[56] Clark, J. Where there's a will. *Risk Magazine*, pages 21–23, January 2010.

[57] Contingent convertible bonds in the European Union: Structuring considerations and current legal issues. Technical report, Latham & Watkins, July 2012.

[58] Commission of Experts. Final report of the Commission of Experts for limiting the economic risks posed by large companies. Technical report, Swiss National Bank, September 2010.

[59] Corcuera, J.M., De Spiegeleer, J., Ferreiro-Castilla, A., Kyprianou, A.E., Madan, D.B., and Schoutens, W. Efficient pricing of contingent convertibles under smile conform models. Available at SSRN: http://ssrn.com/abstract=1954671, November 2011.

[60] Corcuera, J.M., Fajardo, J., Jonsson, H., and Schoutens, W. Closed-form pricing formulas for CoCa CoCo. Available at SSRN: http://ssrn.com/abstract=2206493, January 2013.

[61] Cox, J. Notes on Option Pricing I: Constant Elasticity of Variance Diffusions. Working Paper, Stanford University, 1975.

[62] Cox, J., Ingersoll, J., and Ross, S. A theory of the term structure of interest rates. *Econometrica*, 53(2): 385–408, 1985.

[63] Cox, J. and Ross, S. The valuation of options for alternative stochastic processes. *Journal of Financial Economics*, 3: 145–166, 1976.

[64] Cox, J., Ross, S., and Rubinstein, M. Option pricing: A simplified approach. *Journal of Financial Economics*, 7: 229–264, 1979.

[65] Das, S.R. and Sundaram, R.K. An integrated model for hybrid securities. *Management Science*, 53(9): 1439–1451, 2007.

[66] Davis, M. and Lischka, F.R. Convertible bonds with market and credit risk. Technical report, Tokyo-Mitsubishi International plc, October 1999.

[67] De Spiegeleer, J. and Schoutens, W. *The Handbook of Convertible Bonds: Pricing, Strategies and Risk Management*. Wiley, Chichester, 2010.

[68] De Spiegeleer, J. and Schoutens, W. *Contingent Convertible (CoCo) Notes: Structuring & Pricing*. EuroMoney Books, London, 2011.

[69] De Spiegeleer, J. and Schoutens, W. Pricing contingent convertibles: A derivatives approach. Available at SSRN: http://ssrn.com/paper=1795092, March 2011.

[70] De Spiegeleer, J. and Schoutens, W. Pricing contingent convertibles: A derivatives approach. *Journal of Derivatives*, 20(2): 27–36, 2012.

[71] De Spiegeleer, J. and Schoutens, W. Multiple trigger CoCo: Contingent debt without death spiral risk. *Financial Markets, Institutions and Instruments*, 22(2), 2013.

[72] Delbaen, F. and Shirakawa, H. A note of option pricing for constant elasticity of variance model. Technical Report No. 96-03, Technische Hochschole Zurich and Tokyo Institute of Technology.

[73] Derman, E., Kani, I., Ergener, D., and Bardhan, I. Enhanced numerical methods for options with barriers. Technical report, Goldman Sachs, May 1995.

[74] De Wit, J. Exploring the CDS-bond basis. Technical report, National Bank of Belgium, November 2006.

[75] Ding, C. Algorithm AS275: Computing the non-central chi-squared distribution function. *Applied Statistics*, 41: 478–482, 1992.

[76] Di Girolamo, F. *Innovation in financial instruments: A challenge for the financial sector*. PhD thesis, KU Leuven, January 2013.

[77] Dombret, A. Reform of the global financial system. Technical report, Deutsche Bundesbank, June 2011.

[78] Donnellan, A. Trust fades in last bastion of bank funding. Reuters, July 2012.

[79] Dowd, K., Cotter, J., Humphrey, C., and Woods, M. How unlucky is 25-sigma? Technical report, Nottingham University Business School, March 2008.

[80] Duarte, J., Longstaff, F.A., and Yu, F. Risk and return in fixed income arbitrage: Nickels in front of a steamroller? *The Review of Financial Studies*, 20(3): 769–811, 2005.

[81] Duffie, D.J. Numerical analysis of jump diffusion models: A partial differential equation approach. Technical report.

[82] Duffie, D. and Singleton, K.J. Modeling term structures of defaultable bonds. *The Review of Financial Studies*, 12(4): 687–720, 1999.

[83] Duffie, D. and Singleton, K.J. *Credit Risk*. Princeton Series In Finance, Princeton, NJ, 2003.

[84] Dupire, B. Pricing with a smile. *Risk Magazine*, 7: 18–20, January 1994.

[85] EBA. Capital buffers for addressing market concerns over sovereign exposures. Technical report, European Banking Authority, October 2011.

[86] EBA consultation paper on draft regulatory technical standards on the concept of gain on sale associated with future margin income in a securitisation context. Technical report, European Banking Authority, July 2012.

[87] European Commission. Regulation of the European Parliament and of the Council on Prudential Requirements for Credit Institutions and Investment Firms. Technical report, European Commission, July 2011.

[88] European Commission. Proposal for a directive of the European Parliament and of the Council establishing a framework for the recovery and resolution of credit institutions and investment firms. Technical report, European Commission, June 2012.

[89] European Council. Presidency conclusions Corcuera, J.M., Fajardo, J., Jonsson, H., and Schoutens, W, October 15, 2008.

[90] Elton, E., Gruber, M., Brown, S., and Goetzmann, W. *Modern Portfolio Theory and Investment Analysis*. Wiley, New York, 2009.

[91] European Banking Authority. Buffer convertible capital securities. Technical report, EBA, December 2011.

[92] Ewing, A. Danish banks face funding relief as bail-in isolation ends. Bloomberg, November 2011.

[93] Exckmann, A., Lutz, D., and Sperl, U. The benefits of convertible bonds. Technical report, UBS, 2007.

[94] Financial Stability Board. Effective resolution of systemically important financial institutions. Technical report, July 2011.

[95] Financial Stability Board. Key attributes of effective resolution regimes for financial institutions. Technical report, November 2011.

[96] Financial Stability Board. Overview of progress in the implementation of the G20 recommendations for strengthening financial stability, November 2011.

[97] Finger, C., Tierney, J., Finkelstein, V., and Pan, G. Credit grades technical document. Technical report, Riskmetrics Group, 2002.

[98] Flannery, M.J. No pain, no gain? Effecting market discipline via "reverse convertibles debentures." Technical report, Graduate School of Business Administration, University of Florida, November 2002.

[99] Flannery, M.J. Stabilizing large financial institutions with contingent capital certificates. Technical report, Graduate School of Business Administration, University of Florida, October 2009.

[100] Fusai, G. and Roncoroni, A. *Implementing Models in Quantitative Finance: Methods and Cases*. Springer-Finance, Berlin, 2008.

[101] Garcia, D. Convergence and biases of Monte Carlo estimates of American option prices using a parametric exercise rule. *Journal of Economic Dynamics and Control*, 27: 1855–1879, 2003.

[102] Gatheral, J. *The Volatility Surface*. Wiley, New York, 2006.

[103] Geman, H. Mean reversion versus random walk in oil and natural gas prices. *Advances in Mathematical Finance*, Fu, M., Jarrow, R.A. and Yen, J.-Y. (eds), Birkhauser, pages 219–222, 2007.

[104] Glasserman, P. *Monte Carlo Methods in Financial Engineering*. Springer-Verlag, Berlin, 2003.

[105] Glasserman, P. and Nouri, B. Contingent capital with a capital-ratio trigger. Available at SSRN: http://ssrn.com/abstract=1669686, August 2010.

[106] Glionna, J. and Crivelli, M. Analysis of bank capital. Technical report, Barclays Capital, November 2009.

[107] Glionna, J., Crivelli, M., and Pigott, C. Basel III: A significant positive for bondholders. Technical report, Barclays Capital, September 2010.

[108] Glover, J. Credit Suisse sells its first public Tier 1 contingent bonds. Bloomberg, August 2013.

[109] Glover, J. and Moses, A. Bank senior bond risk rises amid reports ECB is backing bail-ins. Bloomberg, July 2012.

[110] Goldstein, M. and Veron, N. Too big to fail: The transatlantic debate. Working Paper Series, January 2011.

[111] Goodhart, C.A.E. and Persaud, A. How to avoid the next crisis. *Financial Times*, January 30, 2008.

[112] Grau, A.J., Forsyth, P.A., and Vetzal, K.R. Vetzal. Convertible bonds with call notice periods. Technical report, School of Computer Science, University of Waterloo, Canada, March 2003.

[113] Gregory, J. and Arvanitis, A. *The Complete Guide to Pricing, Hedging and Risk Management*. Risk Books, London, 2001.

[114] Haldane, A.G. Capital discipline. Speech given at the American Economic Association, Denver, January 2011.

[115] Hannoun, H. The Basel III capital framework: A decisive breakthrough. BoJ-BIS High Level Seminar on Financial Regulatory Reform: Implications for Asia and the Pacific. Hong Kong SAR, November 2010.

[116] Hendriks, J. A Monte Carlo code for particle transport: An algorithm for all seasons. *Los Alamos Science*, 22, 1994.

[117] Henriques, R., Bowe, A., Finsterbusch, A., and White, D. Coco relative value. Technical report, JP Morgan, March 2013.

[118] Heston, S. A closed-form solution for options with stochastic volatility with applications to bond and currency options. *The Review of Financial Studies*, 6(2): 327–343, 1993.

[119] Hildebrand, P.M. Is Basel II enough? The benefits of a leverage ratio. Technical report. Speech held at the London School of Economics, December 2008.

[120] Hillion, P. and Vermaelen, T. Death spiral convertibles. May 2001.

[121] Hull, J. *Options, Futures and other Derivatives*, 7th edn. Prentice-Hall, Englewood Cliffs, NJ, 1989.

[122] Hull, J. and White, A. Pricing interest rate derivative securities. *The Review of Financial Studies*, 3(3): 573–592, 1990.

[123] Independent Commission on Banking. Technical report, ICB, September 2011.

[124] Ingersoll, J.E. A contingent-claims valuation of convertible securities. *Journal of Financial Economics*, 4: 289–232, 1977.

[125] International framework for liquidity risk measurement, standards and monitoring. Consultative document, Basel Committee on Banking Supervision, December 2009.

[126] ISDA (International Swaps and Derivatives Association). http://www.isdacdsmarketplace.com.

[127] Jarrow, R. and Turnbull, S. Pricing derivatives on financial securities subject to credit risk. *The Journal of Finance*, 50: 53–86, 1995.

[128] Joint administrators' progress report for the period 15 September 2008 to 14 March 2009. Technical report, Lehman Brothers International (Europe). In Administration, April 2009.

[129] Joshi, M. *The Concepts and Practice of Mathematical Finance*. Cambridge University Press, Cambridge, 2003.

[130] Keenan, O. and Staszewski, R. European corporate hybrids: All you ever wanted to know about corporate hybrids. Technical report, JP Morgan, September 2013.

[131] Kennedy, F., O'Connor, M., and Muldoon, C. Convertible structures. Technical report, Deutsche Bank, March 2002.

[132] Khasawneh, R. and Agnew, H. Contingent convertibles go CoCoCo. *eFinancial News*, March 2011.

[133] Kim, Y.-J. Option pricing under stochastic interest rates: An empirical investigation. Technical report, Tokyo Metropolitan University, January 2011.

[134] Kind, A. and Wilde, C. Pricing convertible bonds with Monte Carlo simulation. Available at http://ssrn.com/abstract=676507, 2008.

[135] Larsen, T.P. and Magnussen, J. Corporate hybrid capital. Technical report, Danske Markets, August 2010.

[136] Leaders' statement, the Pittsburgh Summit. Available at http://www.g20.org, September 2009.

[137] Leland, H. Option pricing and replication with transaction costs. *The Journal of Finance*, 40(5): 1283–1301, 1985.

[138] Levenberg, K. A method for the solution of certain non-linear problems in least squares. *Quarterly Journal of Applied Mathematics*, 2: 164–168, 1944.

[139] Linetsky, V. and Mendoza, R. *Encyclopedia of Quantitative Finance*, Cont, R. (ed), pages 328–334. Wiley, Chichester, 2010.

[140] Longstaff, F.A. and Schwartz, E. Valuing American options by simulation: A simple least-squares approach. *The Review of Financial Studies*, 14(1): 113–147, 2001.

[141] Lucas, D. Default correlation: From definition to proposed solutions. Technical report, UBS, August 2004.

[142] Lvov, D., Yigitbasioglu, A.B. and El Bachir, N. Pricing convertible bonds by simulation. Technical report, ICMA Centre – University of Reading. Available at SSRN: http://ssrn.com/abstract=950213, December 2004.

[143] Madan, D.B., Carr, P., and Chang, E.C. Chang. The variance gamma process and option pricing. *European Finance Review*, 2: 79–105, 1998.

[144] Maes, S. and Schoutens, W. Contingent capital: An in-depth discussion. Technical report, KU Leuven, August 2010.

[145] Mandelbrot, B. The variation of certain speculative prices. *Journal of Business*, 36: 392–417, 1963.

[146] Mandelbrot, B. and Hudson, R.L. *The (Mis)behavior of Markets*. Basic Books, London, 2006.

[147] Mattila, R., Hassan, H., and MacFarlane, A. Hybrids: Back in the spotlight. Technical report, Mitsubishi UFJ Securities International plc, January 2013.

[148] Meli, J., Gupta, S., Gennis, A., and Preclaw, R. Retail markup. Technical report, Barclays Capital, April 2012.

[149] Merton, R.C. Theory of rational option pricing. *The Bell Journal of Economics and Management Science*, 4: 141–183, 1973.

[150] Merton, R.C. On the pricing of corporate debt: The risk structure of interest rates. *The Journal of Finance*, 29: 449–470, 1974.

[151] Mohanty, M.S. Improving liquidity in government bond markets. Technical report, Bank for International Settlements, May 2002.

[152] Moody's. Corporate default and recovery rates, 1920–2008. Technical report. Available at http://www.moodys.com, February 2009.

[153] Nelder, J. and Mead, R. A simplex method for function minimization. *Computer Journal*, 7:308–313, 1965.

[154] Nelson, D.B. and Ramaswamy, K. Simple binomial processes as diffusion approximations in financial models. *The Review of Financial Studies*, 3(3): 393–430, 1990.

[155] Ohtake, F., Oda, N., and Yoshiba, T. Market price analysis and risk management for convertible bonds. *Monetary and Economic Studies, Institute for Monetary and Economic Studies, Bank of Japan*, 17(2): 47–89, 1999.

[156] Olsen, L., Allison, A., Beattle, H., and Winnicki, D. Cococos – convertible contingent convertibles an alluring evolution. Technical report, Barclays Capital, July 2011.

[157] OSFI. Non-viability contingent capital. Technical report, Office of the Superintendent of Financial Institutions Canada, August 2011.

[158] Pennacchi, G. A structural model of contingent bank capital, April 2010.

[158a] Pennacchi, G., Vermaelen, T., and Wolff, C. Contingent capital: The case for COERCs. Working paper, INSEAD, 2010.

[159] Policy measures to address systemically important financial institutions. Available at www.fsb.org, November 2011.

[160] Portilla, A., Prenio, J., Schraa, D., and Sunstrum, D. A review of the 2012 Basel work program. Technical report, The Institute of International Finance, January 2012.

[161] Proctor, C. Ring-fences and firewalls: The future of the UK banking industry? Technical report, August 2011.

[162] Randal, J. The constant elasticity of variance option pricing model. Master's thesis, Victoria University of Wellington, April 1998.

[163] Randal, J. The constant elasticity of variance model: A useful alternative to Black–Scholes? Technical report, Victoria University of Wellington, August 2001.

[164] Rating symbols and definitions. Technical report, Moody's, April 2012.

[165] Raviv, A. Bank stability and market discipline: Debt-for- equity swap versus subordinated notes. Available at SSRN: http://ssrn.com/abstract=575862, 2004.

[166] Rebonato, R. *Volatility and Correlation: The Perfect Hedger and the Fox*. Wiley, Chichester, 2004.

[167] Report to congress on study of a contingent capital requirement for certain nonbank financial companies and bank holding companies, July 2012.

[168] Results of the Basel III monitoring exercise as of 30 June 2011. Technical report, European Banking Authority, April 2012.

[169] Rubinstein, M. and Reiner, E. Unscrambling the binary code. *Risk Magazine*, pages 75–83, October 1991.

[170] Saltelli, A. Sensitivity analysis for importance assessment. *Risk Analysis*, 22(3), 2002.

[171] Saltelli, A. Global sensitivity analysis. Technical report, European Commission, Joint Research Centre of Ispra, 2005.

[172] Schaffner, B. A valuation framework for pricing hybrid bonds. Technical report, University of St. Gallen, December 2010.

[173] Schönbucher, P.J. *Credit Derivatives Pricing Models*. Wiley, Chichester, 2003.

[174] Schoutens, W. *Levy Processes in Finance: Pricing Financial Derivatives*. Wiley, Chichester, 2003.

[175] Schoutens, W. and Cariboni, J. *Levy Processes in Credit Risk*. Wiley, Chichester, 2009.

[176] Schoutens, W., Tistaert, J., and Simons, E. A perfect calibration! Now what? *Wilmott Magazine*, March 2004.

[177] Schroder, M. Computing the constant elasticity of variance option pricing formula. *The Journal of Finance*, 44(1): 211–219, 1989.

[178] Sorkin, A.R. *Too Big too Fail*. Penguin Group, London, 2009.

[179] Squam Lake Working Group on Financial Regulation. An expedited resolution mechanism for distressed financial firms: Regulatory hybrid securities, April 2009.

[180] Stevis, M. Spain to cede bank control. *Wall Street Journal*, July 2012.

[181] Su, L. and Rieger, M.O. How likely is it to hit a barrier? Theoretical and empirical estimates. Technical Report Working Paper No. 594, National Centre of Competence in Research, Financial Valuation and Risk Management, October 2009.

[182] Szpiro, G.G. *Pricing the Future: Finance, Physics, and the 300-year Journey to the Black–Scholes Equation*. Basic Books, London, November 2011.

[183] Takahashi, A., Kobayasho, T., and Nakagawa, N. Pricing convertible bonds with defaultrisk: A Duffie singleton approach. *The Journal of Fixed Income*, 11(3): 20–29, 2001.

[184] Tang, S., Sheets, A., Naraparaju, P., Hjort, V., and Sood, N. Corporate hybrids – looking under the hood. Technical report, Morgan Stanley, January 2013.

[185] The cumulative impact on the global economy of changes in the financial regulatory framework. Technical report, Institute of International Finance, September 2011.

[186] Thomas, R., Julius, J., and Pisarek, M. Bail-in ball. Technical report, Bank of America Merrill Lynch, June 2013.

[187] Trincal, E. Volume stays strong at $410 million; two large autocallable notes top issuance. *Structured Product News*, April 2010.

[188] Vasicek, O. An equilibrium characterisation of the term structure. *Journal of Financial Economics*, 5(2): 177–188, 1977.

[189] Walsh, C. *Key Management Ratios*. Financial Times Series, London, 2008.

[190] Watt, M. Mending the RWA machine. *Risk Magazine*, pages 17–20, January 2013.

[191] Wellink, N. Basel III and beyond. Speech held at the FSI and EMEAP Working Group on Banking Supervision, Kula Lumpur, January 2011.

[192] Wilkens, S. and Bethke, N. Contingent convertible ("coco") bonds: A first empirical assessment of selected pricing models. Available at SSRN: http://ssrn.com/abstract=2126791, April 2013.

[193] Willemann, S., Davies, Z., Winnicki, D., Harar, D., Kallianiotis, I., and Simmonds, J. When everyone else is buying. Technical report, Barclays Capital, April 2013.

[194] Wilmott, P., Dewynne, J., and Howison, S. *Option Pricing, Mathematical Models and Computation.* Oxford Financial Press, Oxford, 1993.

[195] Wilmott, P. and Whalley, E. Counting the costs. *Risk Magazine*, 6(10), 1993.

[196] Yu, E. and Shaw, W. On the valuation of derivatives with snapshot reset features. *International Journal of Theoretical and Applied Finance*, 11(8): 905–941, August 2009.

[197] Zhao, Y. and Ziemba, W.T. On Leland's option hedging strategy with transaction costs. Technical report, Sauder School of Business Working Paper, July 2003.

Index

Index compiled by Terry Halliday

Printed and bound by CPI Group (UK) Ltd, Croydon, CR0 4YY

23/04/2025

14660949-0002